SRA Real Math

EXERCISE BOOK

Grade 5

Stephen S. Willoughby

•

Carl Bereiter

•

Peter Hilton

•

Joseph H. Rubinstein

•

Joan Moss

•

Jean Pedersen

SRA

Columbus, OH

The McGraw·Hill Companies

SRAonline.com

SRA

Printed in the United States of America.

Send all inquiries to:
SRA/McGraw-Hill
8787 Orion Place
Columbus, OH 43240-4027

ISBN 0-07-603724-X

1 2 3 4 5 6 7 8 9 BCH 12 11 10 09 08 07 06

The McGraw·Hill Companies

Table of Contents

Exercise Book

Table of Contents

Exercise Book

Table of Contents

Exercise Book

Table of Contents

Exercise Book

Name ______________________ Date ____________

Whole Numbers Refresher

Student Edition • page 3

The students in Ms. Johnson's class vote each week to pick the class secretary. This week, Alicia, Paco, and Carol ran for the position. Each student voted by listing the three candidates in order.

Carol Alicia Paco	Paco Carol Alicia	Alicia Carol Paco	Alicia Carol Paco

Ms. Johnson's class counted all the ballots and wrote the results in a table. Unfortunately, they lost the number of first-place votes that Carol received.

Candidate	1st Place Votes	2nd Place Votes	3rd Place Votes
Alicia	11	4	13
Paco	9	16	3
Carol		8	12

Answer the following questions.

1. How can you figure out how many first-place votes Carol received?

____

____

2. If only Alicia and Paco had run, who do you think would have won? Explain.

____

____

3. Based on the results, who do you think should be the class secretary this week? Why? ______________________

____

4. If there are three candidates next week, how should Ms. Johnson's class decide the winner? ______________________

____

LESSON 1.1

Estimating and Measuring

Student Edition • page 4

Latoya is doing a measuring activity. First, she estimates how tall a person is and writes it on her table. Next, she measures and records the actual height of that person. She finds the difference between the estimate and the measurement. Then she repeats the procedure with the next person.

Name	Estimate (centimeters)	Measurement (centimeters)	Difference
Joan	133	140	7
Aretha	137	139	2
Florence	135	136	1
Carlos	140	141	1

Complete this measuring activity in a small group. Estimate and then measure each person. Record the results in a table like the one above. Find the differences between your estimates and measurements. Then answer the questions below.

1. Extended Response Did Latoya's estimates get better after the first one?

____

2. Extended Response Did your estimates get better after the first one? Why?

____

____

3. Are any of the students you measured the same height?

____

LESSON 1.2

Name ______________________ Date ____________

Graphing Height

Student Edition • page 6

Everyone in Latoya's class did the measuring activity on page 2. Then they made a table of all the students and their heights. Here is part of that table.

Name	Height (cm)	Name	Height (cm)	Name	Height (cm)
Judy	133	Marco	141	Melvin	143
Chen	134	Carlos	141	Lance	143
Tami	135	Steve	142	Tiwa	144
Myra	135	Liz	142	Melba	146

Latoya decided to make a graph showing the number of students at each height. Her graph looked like this:

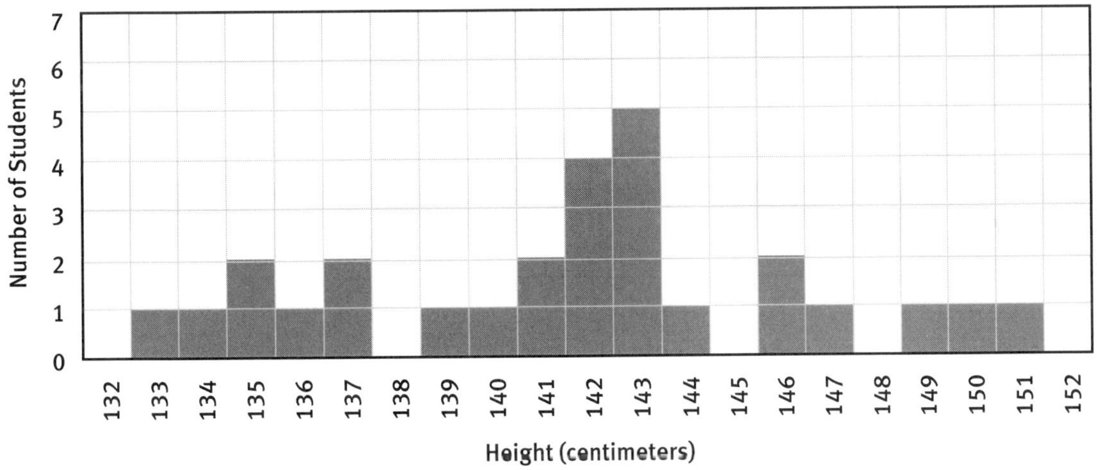

Answer these questions.

1. What grade do you think Latoya is in? ____________

2. **Extended Response** What can you predict about height measurements for a class one grade level before Latoya's? What about for a class that is one grade after Latoya's? Explain.

____

____

____

LESSON 1.2

Student Edition • page 7

3 **Extended Response** If you knew of a student in a different city who was in the same grade as Latoya, but you did not know what the student looked like, could you make a reasonable estimate about the height of that student? Would you be surprised if your estimate was wrong? Could you make a reasonable estimate about the distribution of heights of all the students in that person's class? Explain.

____

____

____

Complete the following activity. Then answer the question.

4 Using the information in the table from the measuring activity in Lesson 1.1, make your own bar graph like the one Latoya made.

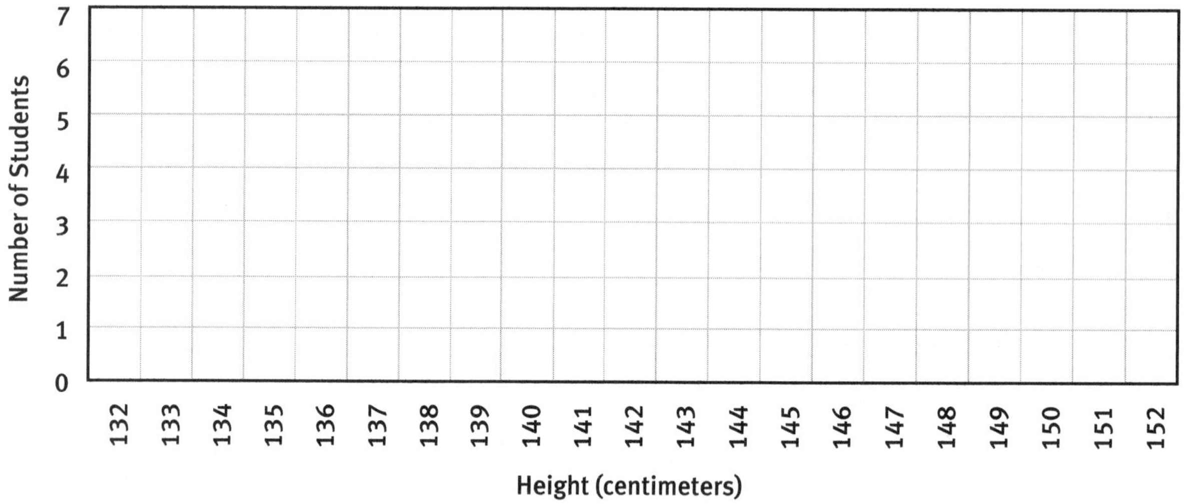

5 Can you predict what the graph would look like if you made it at the end of the school year?

____

____

Name ______________________ **Date** ____________

Student Edition • page 7

Count on or back. Write the missing numbers.

6. 78, 79, 80, ____________, 88

7. 107, 106, 105, ____________, 98

8. 396, 397, 398, ____________, 406

9. 5,996; 5,997; 5,998; ____________; 6,004

10. 5,003; 5,002; 5,001; ____________; 4,997

11. 76,097; 76,098; 76,099; ____________; 76,103

12. 842,003; 842,002; 842,001; ____________; 841,997

Answer the following questions.

13. **Extended Response** Suki's parents are planning a neighborhood picnic. They bought 4 packs of 8 hotdogs and 3 bags of 10 hotdog buns. If Suki eats 2 of the hotdogs without buns before the picnic, which will her parents have more of—hotdogs or buns? How many more? Explain your answer.

____

____

____

14. Early Roman soldiers were paid with salt. One year, they were paid 3 rations of salt for their service. A year later, they were given 5 rations. The following year they received 8 rations. After another year, the soldiers got 12 rations. If this pattern continued, how many rations could the soldiers expect to get the next year? Describe the pattern.

____

____

LESSON 1.3

Place Value

Student Edition • pages 8–9

Write these numbers in expanded form.

1. 917,563 = ____________________
2. 589,421 = ____________________
3. 900,060,728 = ____________________
4. 800,740,054 = ____________________
5. List the numbers above from greatest to least.

____

____

Write these numbers in standard form. Use the example as a guide.

Example: 7,000 + 20 + 6 = 7,026

6. 40,000 + 2,000 + 50 + 9 = __________
7. 800,000 + 60,000 + 7,000 + 600 + 40 + 2 = __________
8. 70,000 + 5,000 + 20 + 7 = __________
9. 8,000 + 600 + 40 + 1 = __________
10. List the numbers above in order from greatest to least.

____

____

LESSON 1.3

Name ______________________ Date ____________

Student Edition • page 9

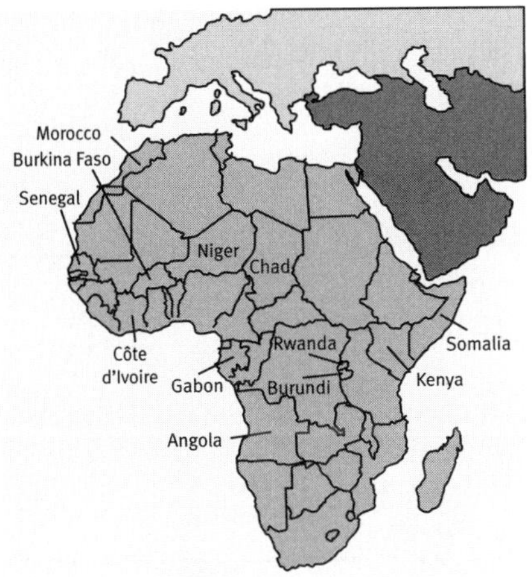

African Country	Area (sq. miles)
Burkina Faso	105,870
Burundi	10,747
Côte d'Ivoire	124,502
Gabon	103,346
Kenya	244,960
Niger	482,206
Rwanda	10,169
Somalia	246,199

Answer the following questions.

11. Which country has a greater area, Kenya or Somalia? ____________

12. Which country has a greater area, Burundi or Rwanda? ____________

13. Which country has a greater area, Niger or Côte d'Ivoire? ____________

14. Which country has a greater area, Gabon or Burkina Faso? ____________

15. Which country has a greater area, Gabon or Burundi? ____________

16. **Extended Response** Is Morocco's area more or less than 100,000 square miles? How can you tell?

____

____

17. List the countries in order from greatest to least area.

____

____

18. If the areas of the three largest countries listed in the table are added together and the areas of the other five are added together, which total is greater? How much greater?

____

____

LESSON 1.4

Applying Math

Student Edition • page 10

Answer each question.

1. Anne earns $9 a day. How much money does she earn in 5 days? ______

2. Kele bought 8 comic books for $16. Each cost the same amount. How much did each book cost? ______

3. Lu has saved $6. His friend Charles has saved $3. If they combine their money, can they buy a set of checkers that costs $7? ______

4. The Tigers football team scored 3 touchdowns (6 points each), 2 extra points (1 point each), and 2 field goals (3 points each). How many total points did the Tigers score? ______

5. **Extended Response** Mike said, "My next birthday is in 13 months." Is that possible? Explain.

______

______

6. Lakeesha and 3 friends bought 2 pizzas. Each pizza was cut into 6 equal slices. If they share the pizzas equally, how many slices should each person get?

______

7. Soccer balls cost $8 each. Brad has $20. What is the greatest number of soccer balls he can buy? ______

8. **Extended Response** Alma and her friends are working together to put on a show. They are setting up 45 chairs. Can they make 8 rows with the same number of chairs in each row, using all the chairs? Explain your answer.

______

______

9. Parking in Camargo's Garage costs $3 for the first hour and $2 for every hour after that. How much would it cost to park in Camargo's Garage for 5 hours?

______

Name ______________________ **Date** ____________

Student Edition • **pages 10–11**

10 Janice had $15. Then she earned $30 on her paper route this week. If used CDs cost $8 each, what is the greatest number she can buy? ____________

By thinking about the situations, you should be able to answer the following questions.

11 Think about a stack of cubes that looks like the one in the figure, with three cubes along each edge. How many cubes are in the entire stack? ____________

12 Suppose you painted the outside of this stack. How many of the little cubes would not be painted at all? How many would be painted on only one face? Two faces? Three faces? Four faces? Five faces? Six faces? Do the numbers add up to 27?

____

____

____

13 Think about a stack of cubes with only two cubes along each edge. How many cubes would there be in the entire stack? If you painted the outside of the stack, how many of the little cubes would not be painted at all? How many would be painted on only one face? How many would be painted on two faces? How many would be painted on three faces? How many would be painted on more than three faces?

____

____

____

14 Consider a stack of cubes with four cubes along each edge. If the outside of this stack were painted, how many of the little cubes would not be painted at all? How many would be painted on only one side? How many would be painted on just two sides? How many would be painted on three sides?

____

____

____

Student Edition • page 12

Amy and Beth ran for student council president at Red Oak School. These slips of paper show the results for each grade in the school. Who won the election? By how many votes did she win?

Grade 1	Grade 2	Grade 3	Grade 4	Grade 5
Amy 57	Amy 61	Beth 63	Amy 56	Amy 55
Beth 54	Beth 59	Amy 48	Beth 53	Beth 51

Ken decided to solve the problem this way:

I Made a Plan and Made a Table.

I put all the results in a table.

I added up all the votes for Amy.

I added up all the votes for Beth to see who had more votes. That person was the winner.

I subtracted the loser's votes from the winner's votes to find the difference.

Grade	Amy	Beth
1	57	54
2		
3		
4		
5		
Total		

Think **about Ken's strategy. Answer the following questions.**

1. How is the table helpful for solving the problem?

____

____

2. Will Ken's strategy work?

____

____

____

Name ______________________ Date ______________

Student Edition • page 13

Carrie solved the problem this way:

I also Made a Plan and Made a Table.

I used the table to show who won for each grade and by how much.

I used the differences to figure out who got more votes in all and how many more.

Grade	Who won?	By how many votes?
1	Amy	3
2		
3		
4		
5		
Total		

Think about Carrie's strategy. Answer the following questions.

3. How could you use mental math to figure out that, for first grade, Amy won by 3 votes?

____

____

4. Amy received more votes in four of the five grades. Does that mean that Amy won? Why or why not?

____

____

5. Can you use Carrie's method to get the correct answer?

____

____

6. Solve the problem of who won the election and by how many votes. Use Ken's, Carrie's, or a strategy of your own. Why did you choose the strategy you did?

____

____

____

CHAPTER 1

Cumulative Review

Student Edition • page 14

Missing Addends Grade 4 Lesson 1.7

Solve for *n*.

1. $n + 5 = 7$ ______
2. $15 + n = 10$ ______
3. $2 + n = 10$ ______
4. $2 + n = 7$ ______
5. $15 - n = 9$ ______
6. $15 - n = 8$ ______
7. $10 + n = 20$ ______
8. $10 + n = 4$ ______
9. $0 + n = 9$ ______
10. $n + 6 = 14$ ______

Using a Bar Graph Grade 4 Lesson 12.5

Interpret the graph.

Answer the questions that follow.

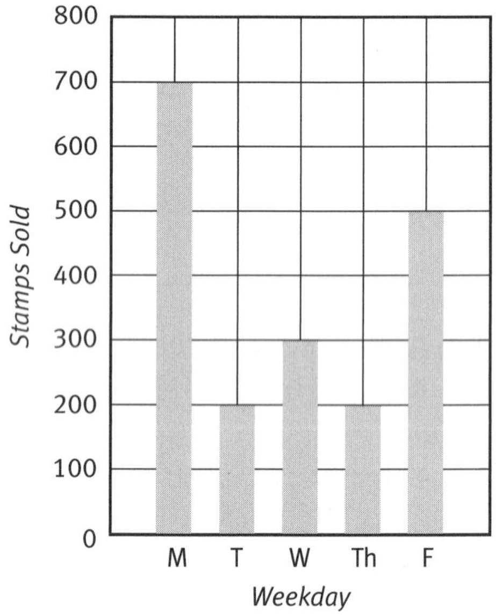

11. How many stamps were sold on Tuesday and Wednesday?

    a. 200 **b.** 400
    c. 500 **d.** 700

12. How many more stamps were sold on Friday than on Thursday?

    a. 200 **b.** 500
    c. 300 **d.** 100

13. On what day were the most stamps sold?

    a. Wednesday **b.** Thursday **c.** Friday **d.** Monday

14. How many stamps were sold during that week?

    a. 2,200 **b.** 1,900 **c.** 2,000 **d.** 1,500

15. On which two days were the same number of stamps sold?

    a. Tuesday and Thursday **b.** Wednesday and Friday
    c. Tuesday and Thursday **d.** Tuesday and Wednesday

Cumulative Review

Name ______________________ Date ______________

Student Edition • page 15

Perimeter **Grade 4 Lesson 10.14**

Solve.

16. A square has a side length of 7 meters. What is its perimeter? ______________

17. A rectangle has a length of 9 feet. What could its perimeter be?

    a. 15 feet **b.** 18 feet **c.** 10 feet **d.** 24 feet

18. A rectangle has a perimeter of 14 yards, and the lengths of the sides are whole numbers of yards. What could the length and width of the rectangle be?

    ____

    ____

19. Two squares have perimeters of 40 meters and 16 meters. What is the difference in the length of their sides? ______________

Place Value **Lesson 1.3**

Write the following numbers in standard form.

20. 5,000 + 700 + 70 + 8 = ______________

21. 400,000 + 6,000 + 30 + 7 = ______________

22. 1,000,000 + 50,000 + 600 + 20 = ______________

Write the following numbers in expanded form.

23. 767,405 = ______________________________

24. 3,702,061 = ______________________________

25. 800,660 = ______________________________

LESSON 1.5

Order and Parentheses

Student Edition • page 18

Solve for n.

1. $8 \times (3 + 1) = n$ ______
2. $(8 \times 3) + 1 = n$ ______
3. $12 \div (6 \div 2) = n$ ______
4. $(12 \div 6) \div 2 = n$ ______
5. $2 + (7 \times 2) = n$ ______
6. $(6 + 1) \times (3 - 1) = n$ ______
7. $12 \div (4 - 3 + 1) = n$ ______
8. $(2 + 4) \div (10 - 7) = n$ ______
9. $6 + (2 \times 3) = n$ ______
10. $(6 + 2) \times 3 = n$ ______

For each expression, see how many different answers you can get by putting parentheses in different places. The first two are done for you.

$3 + 5 + 7 = n$

$(3 + 5) + 7 = 15$

$3 + (5 + 7) = 15$

There is only one possible value.

$10 - 5 - 3 = n$

$(10 - 5) - 3 = 2$

$10 - (5 - 3) = 8$

There are two possible values.

11. $3 \times 4 \times 5 = n$ ______ ______
12. $24 \div 6 - 2 = n$ ______ ______
13. $24 \div 6 \div 2 = n$ ______ ______
14. $24 - 6 \div 2 = n$ ______ ______
15. $24 + 6 \times 2 = n$ ______ ______
16. $24 + 6 + 2 = n$ ______ ______

Name ________________________ Date ____________

Student Edition • page 18

Solve the following problems.

17. Sam can get his learning permit for his driver's license at the end of the calendar year. Today is April 30. How many days are there until the end of the year? Explain how you can find the answer without adding the number of days in each of the 8 months.

____

____

____

18. How can you tell when an expression will have only one value? Explain your answer.

____

____

____

LESSON 1.6

Arithmetic Laws

Student Edition • page 21

Use what you just learned to help you do these exercises quickly.

1. 73 + 64 = ______
2. 64 + 73 = ______
3. 3 × 8 = ______
4. 8 × 3 = ______
5. 8 + (92 + 47) = ______
6. (92 + 47) + 8 = ______
7. 193 + 0 = ______
8. 193 × 1 = ______
9. 2,538 × 0 = ______
10. 100 × 86 = ______
11. (73 × 86) + (27 × 86) = ______
12. 3 × 8 × 94 × 0 × 504 = ______
13. (57 × 85) + (43 × 85) = ______
14. 5 × 4 × 3 × 2 × 1 × 0 = ______
15. 6 × (200 + 8) = ______
16. (18 × 49) + (82 × 49) = ______
17. (65 × 86) + (65 × 14) = ______
18. 256 × 73 × 1 × 42 × 0 = ______
19. 0 + 1 + 2 + 3 + 4 + 5 + 6 + 7 + 8 = 36
20. 8 + 7 + 6 + 5 + 4 + 3 + 2 + 1 + 0 = 36

Solve the following problems.

21. Abigail's thirteenth birthday is on August 26. Tomorrow will be March 1. How many days are there until she will be thirteen? ______
22. **Extended Response** Explain how you can get the answer to Problem 21 without adding the number of days in each of the 6 months.

______

______

______

LESSON 1.7

Name ______________________ Date ____________

Adding Multidigit Numbers

Student Edition • pages 23–24

Find each sum. Use shortcuts when you can.

1. $24 + 37$
2. $42 + 65$
3. $123 + 78$
4. $327 + 123$
5. $7619 + 835$
6. $9723 + 64$
7. $879 + 1839$
8. $2376 + 6539$
9. $5225 + 2552$
10. $1025 + 1025$
11. $673 + 900$
12. $598 + 601$
13. $1940 + 60$
14. $2293 + 4815$
15. $562 + 4015$
16. $275347001 + 125893178$
17. $457091140 + 230708729$
18. $56 + 78 + 49$
19. $247 + 138 + 787$
20. $509 + 746 + 666$
21. $500 + 55 + 500$
22. $9000 + 700 + 2000$
23. $879 + 773 + 254 + 866$
24. $300 + 201 + 370 + 120$
25. $200 + 200 + 200 + 200$

In each exercise, two of the answers don't make sense, and one answer is correct. Choose the correct answers.

26. 694 + 426 = ______________
   a. 1,390
   b. 1,120
   c. 870

27. 463 + 217 = ______________
   a. 1,290
   b. 770
   c. 680

LESSON 1.7

Student Edition • page 24

(28) 7,200 + 320 = ____________
a. 7,520
b. 10,500
c. 450

(29) 2,738 + 575 = ____________
a. 2,023
b. 3,313
c. 7,215

(30) 5,525 + 5,735 = ____________
a. 1,260
b. 25,260
c. 11,260

(31) 4,783 + 9,790 = ____________
a. 14,573
b. 10,573
c. 14,570

(32) 9,762 + 1,003 = ____________
a. 10,765
b. 9,865
c. 8,559

(33) 6,840 + 2,203 = ____________
a. 9,043
b. 28,843
c. 2,883

(34) 6,123 + 1,098 = ____________
a. 11,832
b. 5,331
c. 7,221

Solve the following problems.

(35) An election was held to choose a mayor for Smallsville. There were 3 candidates in the election. The first candidate received 1,023 votes, the second received 2,017 votes, and the third received 1,477 votes. Smallsville has a voting-age population of nearly 5,000 people. About how many voters did *not* vote for one of the 3 candidates?

____

(36) **Extended Response** It is 328 miles from Smallsville to the state capital. A bus takes 43 people from Smallsville to the state capital for a tour. How many miles will the bus have traveled after it returns from the capital? How did you get your answer? Explain.

____

____

____

LESSON 1.8

Name ______________________ Date ____________

Subtracting Multidigit Numbers

Student Edition • page 27

Find the difference. Use shortcuts when you can.

1. 83 − 21 = ____________
2. 64 − 29 = ____________
3. 417 − 236 = ____________
4. 521 − 432 = ____________
5. 605 − 506 = ____________
6. 307 − 158 = ____________
7. 700 − 698 = ____________
8. 500 − 125 = ____________
9. 100 − 37 = ____________
10. 614 − 328 = ____________

Add or subtract. Watch the signs.

11. 655 + 345 = ____________
12. 1,000 − 345 = ____________
13. 1,000 − 655 = ____________
14. 2,001 − 1,980 = ____________
15. 247 + 68 = ____________
16. 921 + 79 = ____________
17. 1,000 − 6 = ____________
18. 5,005 + 1,234 = ____________

LESSON 1.8

Student Edition • page 28

Add or subtract. Watch the signs.

19. 3,000 − 256 = ______
20. 256 + 2,744 = ______
21. 3,000 − 2,744 = ______
22. 4,548 + 9,874 = ______
23. 6,719 + 32 = ______
24. 235 + 444 = ______
25. 637 − 555 = ______
26. 197 − 96 = ______
27. 5,729 − 1,990 = ______
28. 45 + 208 = ______
29. 908,278,331 − 645,125,986 = ______
30. 538,293,874 − 216,192,834 = ______

Solve these problems.

31. **Extended Response** The Coldsborough Town Hall was dedicated on December 20, 1895. Because of a blizzard, its 100th anniversary (centennial) celebration was postponed for two weeks. This resulted in the celebration not taking place until the next year. Why did this happen? Explain.

______

______

______

32. Last year, 226 students were in the fourth grade at Karen's school. Over the summer, 17 of them moved away. If 6 new students joined the class, how many fifth graders are there this year? ______

LESSON 1.9

Name ______________________ Date ____________

Applying Addition and Subtraction

Student Edition • page 30

Add or subtract. Watch the signs.

1. $\begin{array}{r} 470 \\ -\ 300 \\ \hline \end{array}$

2. $\begin{array}{r} 45 \\ -\ 29 \\ \hline \end{array}$

3. $\begin{array}{r} 243 \\ +\ 342 \\ \hline \end{array}$

4. $\begin{array}{r} 360 \\ -\ 180 \\ \hline \end{array}$

5. $\begin{array}{r} 2070 \\ -\ 199 \\ \hline \end{array}$

6. $\begin{array}{r} 847 \\ +\ 36 \\ \hline \end{array}$

7. $\begin{array}{r} 9000 \\ +\ 8927 \\ \hline \end{array}$

8. $\begin{array}{r} 1000 \\ +\ 525 \\ \hline \end{array}$

9. $\begin{array}{r} 5470 \\ +\ 129 \\ \hline \end{array}$

10. $\begin{array}{r} 601 \\ -\ 176 \\ \hline \end{array}$

11. $\begin{array}{r} 8010 \\ +\ 189 \\ \hline \end{array}$

12. $\begin{array}{r} 6006 \\ -\ 808 \\ \hline \end{array}$

Choose the best approximation.

13. In one day, the United States Bureau of Engraving and Printing printed 12,450,000 $5 bills. What was the approximate value of the $5 bills printed that day?

    a. about $12,000,000

    b. about $62,000,000

    c. about $100,000,000

14. The words to "The Star-Spangled Banner" were written by Francis Scott Key in 1814. About how many years ago was that?

    a. about 120

    b. about 200

    c. about 350

LESSON 1.9

Student Edition • page 31

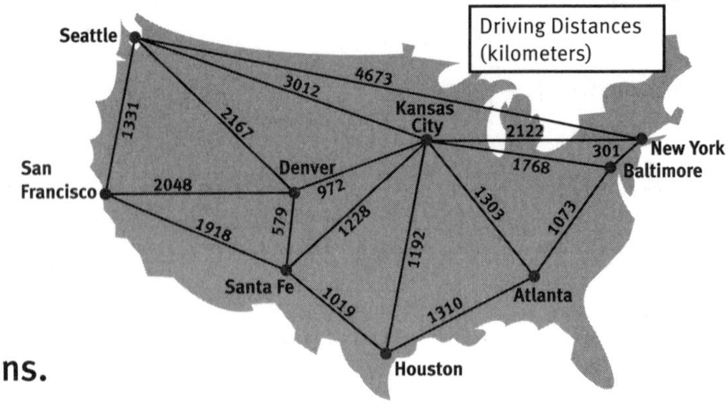

Use the map to answer these questions.

15. How many kilometers is it from San Francisco to Denver? ______

16. How many kilometers is it from San Francisco to Kansas City if you go through Denver? ______

17. If you were going from Santa Fe to Kansas City, how much farther would it be to go through Denver? ______

18. Suppose you were going from San Francisco to Kansas City, and you wanted to visit Santa Fe and Denver on the way.

    a. Would it be shorter to visit Santa Fe or Denver first? ______

    b. How many kilometers shorter? ______

19. **Extended Response** Suppose you were in Kansas City and you wanted to visit Baltimore and New York City. Which round trip would be shorter? Why?

    a. Kansas City to Baltimore to New York City and back to Kansas City

    b. Kansas City to New York City to Baltimore and back to Kansas City

______

______

20. **Extended Response** Plan a trip that begins and ends in Seattle and goes through every city on the map. Try to make the trip as short as you can. How many kilometers is the trip you planned? Compare your answer with other students' answers.

______

______

______

LESSON 1.10

Name ______________________ Date ____________

Roman Numerals

Student Edition • page 32

Try to figure out the value of each letter by examining the following list. Answer the questions below.

Arabic	Roman
25	XXV
35	XXXV
235	CCXXXV
137	CXXXVII
1237	MCCXXXVII
1737	MDCCXXXVII
1787	MDCCLXXXVII

1. What is the value of M? ____________
2. What is the value of D? ____________
3. What is the value of C? ____________
4. What is the value of I? ____________
5. What is the value of V? ____________
6. What is the value of X? ____________
7. What is the value of L? ____________

LESSON 1.10

Student Edition • page 33

Complete the exercises below. Remember what you just learned about the values of the different numerals.

8. MCCC + C = ____________

9. XXX − I = ____________

10. MMCCXXX + X = ____________

11. CLXV + IIII = ____________

Look it up. When did the following events occur? Use Roman numerals to write the years.

12. The Declaration of Independence was signed. ____________

13. The United States Civil War ended. ____________

14. Dr. Martin Luther King Jr. was awarded the Nobel Prize for peace. ____________

15. Christopher Columbus landed in America. ____________

16. Pilgrims landed on Plymouth Rock. ____________

Answer the following questions.

17. The pages of a book's preface are often numbered with Roman numerals. If there is information you need on page 13 of the preface, what Roman numeral would you look for? ____________

18. **Extended Response** If you were watching a movie and saw the Roman numeral MMIV at the end of the credits, what number do you think it might represent? Explain.

____

____

Name ______________________ **Date** ____________

Student Edition • page 34

To understand what happened in the election of 2000, you need to know the method that is used to elect the president of the United States.

Each state has a certain number of electoral votes based on its population. The table on page 26 shows how many of these electoral votes each state has. In general, if a majority of people in a state vote for a candidate, that candidate receives all the electoral votes for that state.

To win, a candidate needs at least 270 electoral votes, which is 1 more than half the total of 538.

Student Edition • page 35

Electoral Votes for Each State					
Alabama	9	Kentucky	8	North Dakota	3
Alaska	3	Louisiana	9	Ohio	21
Arizona	8	Maine	4	Oklahoma	8
Arkansas	6	Maryland	10	Oregon	7
California	54	Massachusetts	12	Pennsylvania	23
Colorado	8	Michigan	18	Rhode Island	4
Connecticut	8	Minnesota	10	South Carolina	8
Delaware	3	Mississippi	7	South Dakota	3
D.C.	3	Missouri	11	Tennessee	11
Florida	25	Montana	3	Texas	32
Georgia	13	Nebraska	5	Utah	5
Hawaii	4	Nevada	4	Vermont	3
Idaho	4	New Hampshire	4	Virginia	13
Illinois	22	New Jersey	15	Washington	11
Indiana	12	New Mexico	5	West Virginia	5
Iowa	7	New York	33	Wisconsin	11
Kansas	6	North Carolina	14	Wyoming	3

By 11 P.M. on election night, George W. Bush had 242 electoral votes and Al Gore had 237.

Solve the following problems. Use the information on pages 25–26 to help you.

1. Suppose Al Gore had won all the states that were still undecided at 11 P.M. Would he have won the election? Explain.

____

____

2. At 11 P.M., was it still possible for this election to end in a tie? Explain.

____

____

Name ______________________ Date ______________

Student Edition • page 36

Club	Members	Electoral Votes
Computer Club	15	3
Music Club	33	6
Soccer Club	51	10
Student Council	11	2

- Each group gets a certain number of electoral votes, depending on how many members it has.
- The members of each group will vote. If a majority of students in a group vote for the bake sale, then the bake sale gets *all* of the electoral votes for that club. If the majority votes for the raffle, then the raffle gets *all* of the electoral votes for that group.
- The winner is the fundraiser that gets more than half of the total electoral votes.

Solve **the following problems. Look for strategies that will make your work easier.**

3. Is it possible for the same number of students to vote for the bake sale and the raffle? How can you tell?

____

____

4. Could the bake sale and the raffle get the same number of electoral votes? How do you know?

____

____

5. What rule do you think the students used to decide how many electoral votes each group would have?

____

____

6. An odd thing happened. Even though more students voted for the bake sale than for the raffle, the raffle won. How could that be?

____

____

Cumulative Review

Student Edition • page 37

Order and Parentheses **Lesson 1.5**

Solve for *n*.

1. $6 \times (4 + 1) = n$ ______
2. $(5 \times 3) + 2 = n$ ______
3. $12 \div (12 \div 2) = n$ ______
4. $(36 \div 6)\ 4 - = n$ ______
5. $5 + (7 \times 8) = n$ ______
6. $(6 + 4) \times (6 - 4) = n$ ______

Arithmetic Properties **Lesson 1.6**

Use arithmetic properties to help complete these exercises quickly.

7. $18 + (82 + 35) =$ ______
8. $94 + 46 + 6 =$ ______
9. $3 \times 8 \times 54 \times 0 \times 123 =$ ______
10. $(77 \times 35) + (23 \times 35) =$ ______
11. $6 \times (100 + 7) =$ ______
12. $8 + 7 + 6 + 5 + 4 + 3 + 2 + 1 + 0 =$ ______

Space Figures **Grade 4 Lesson 10.10**

Identify the following shapes.

13. 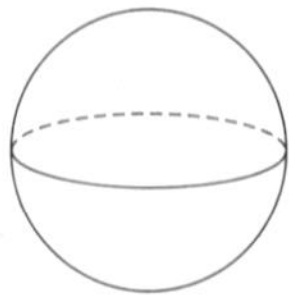

______

14. 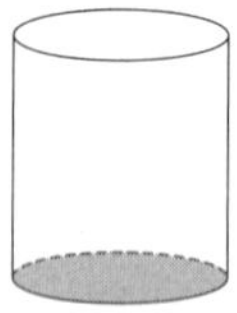

______

15. 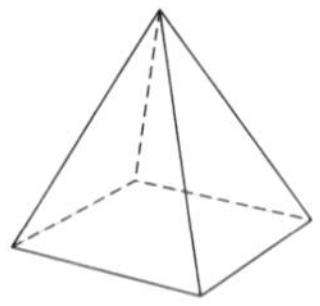

______

16. 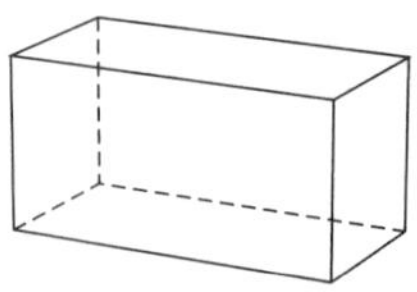

______

17. 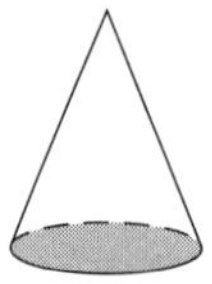

______

18. 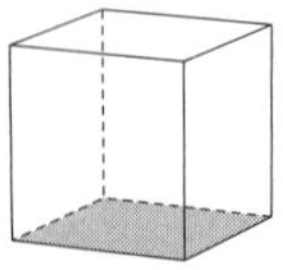

______

Cumulative Review

Name ______________________ **Date** ______________

Student Edition • page 38

Adding and Subtracting Multidigit Numbers Lessons 1.6–1.7

Add or subtract. Use shortcuts when you can.

19. $\begin{array}{r} 123 \\ +\ 78 \\ \hline \end{array}$

20. $\begin{array}{r} 327 \\ +\ 123 \\ \hline \end{array}$

21. $\begin{array}{r} 7619 \\ +\ 835 \\ \hline \end{array}$

22. $\begin{array}{r} 4066 \\ +\ 3883 \\ \hline \end{array}$

23. 64 − 29 = ______

24. 417 − 236 = ______

25. 521 − 432 = ______

26. 605 − 506 = ______

Applying Addition and Subtraction Lesson 1.9

Solve.

27. The McDaniels drove 567 miles on Friday and 478 miles on Saturday. How far did they drive altogether? ______

28. Timmy counted his baseball cards and said he had 352. Rico said he had 125 more than Timmy. How many cards did Rico have? ______

29. Two bowling teams were competing for the league championship. The Strikers had scores of 156, 178, and 193, while the Alley Cats had scores of 144, 180, and 199. Which team had the greatest team score and by how many points did they win? ______

30. Stephanie is 9 years old. She is 5 years younger than her older brother and 2 years older than her younger brother. How old is Stephanie's younger brother? ______

CHAPTER 1

Key Ideas Review

Student Edition • page 39

Write the following numbers in expanded form.

1. 6,259 ______________ ______________
2. 10,678 ______________ ______________
3. 6,205 ______________ ______________

Solve the following problems.

4. $3 \times (6 + 4) = n$ ______________
5. How can the Associative and Distributive Laws reduce work for a multiplication problem? Explain your answer and provide an example.

____

____

6. Why is the product not affected in the following expressions?

$(3 \times 6) \times 2$ $3 \times (6 \times 2)$

____

7. How do parentheses affect a problem?

____

Add or subtract.

8. Trisha wants to buy some of the items in the table using $36 she received for her birthday. List two different sets of items she could purchase.

____

____

sleeping bag	$24
book	$16
poster	$8
DVD	$19
volleyball	$12

9. $\begin{array}{r} 15374 \\ +\ 2791 \\ \hline \end{array}$

10. $\begin{array}{r} 10000 \\ -\ 6432 \\ \hline \end{array}$

CHAPTER 1 Chapter Review

Name ____________________ Date ____________

Student Edition • page 40

Write the following numbers in expanded form. **Lesson 1.3**

1. 52,054 = ____________________
2. 349,401 = ____________________
3. 600,060,708 = ____________________
4. 107,008,054 = ____________________

Solve for *n*. **Lesson 1.5**

5. $6 \times (2 + 3) = n$ ____________
6. $10 \div (7 - 2) = n$ ____________
7. $(36 \div 6) + 6 = n$ ____________
8. $15 \div (8 - 3) = n$ ____________

Add. **Lesson 1.7**

9. $\begin{array}{r} 345 \\ +\ 587 \\ \hline \end{array}$

10. $\begin{array}{r} 429 \\ 36 \\ +\ 141 \\ \hline \end{array}$

11. $\begin{array}{r} 5683 \\ +\ 2842 \\ \hline \end{array}$

12. $\begin{array}{r} 23845 \\ +\ 42658 \\ \hline \end{array}$

Subtract. **Lesson 1.8**

13. $\begin{array}{r} 517 \\ -\ 234 \\ \hline \end{array}$

14. $\begin{array}{r} 700 \\ -\ 318 \\ \hline \end{array}$

15. $\begin{array}{r} 4526 \\ -\ 1837 \\ \hline \end{array}$

16. $\begin{array}{r} 63400 \\ -\ 31734 \\ \hline \end{array}$

Chapter Review

Student Edition • page 41

This table shows the lengths of the ten longest rivers in the world. Use the table to answer the following questions. **Lesson 1.9**

River	Length (in miles)
Amazon	3,912
Huang He (Yellow)	2,900
Irtish	2,758
Mississippi-Missouri-Red Rock	3,880
Nile	4,180
Ob	3,459
Paraná	2,795
Yangtze Kiang	3,602
Yenisei	2,800
Zaire (Congo)	2,716

17. Which river is the longest? ______________

18. Which river is longer than the Zaire but not as long as the Paraná? ______________

19. How much longer than the Ob is the Nile? ______________

20. Suppose a person traveled from the source of the Amazon to the mouth and back again to the source. How many miles would he or she travel in all? ______________

21. Which is longer—the Nile or the combined lengths of the two shortest rivers listed? By how much? ______________

22. What is the difference between the length of the Nile and the length of the next longest river? ______________

Practice Test

Name ______________________ Date ____________

Student Edition • page 42

Count on or back.
Write the missing numbers.

1. 8,097; 8,098; 8,099;

   ______; ______;

   ______; ______;

   8,104

2. 51,013; 51,012; 51,011;

   ______; ______;

   ______; ______;

   51,006

Write the following numbers in standard form.

3. 400,000 + 50,000 + 2,000 + 3

   ____

4. 10,000 + 400 + 20

   ____

Write the following numbers in expanded form.

5. 700,802

   ____

6. 53,002,710

   ____

Solve for *n*.

7. $6 \times (8 + 1) = n$ ______

8. $(6 \times 8) + 1 = n$ ______

Answer the following questions.

9. According to a recent census, Arkansas has a population of 2,673,400, Iowa has a population of 2,926,324, and Mississippi has a population of 2,844,658. Which state has a greater population, Iowa or Mississippi?

   ____

10. Jorge drinks 8 ounces of water 2 times a day. How many ounces does he drink in 4 days?

    ____

11. A baseball stadium can seat 32,780 people. If 31,455 people attended last night's baseball game, how many seats were empty?

    ____

Practice Test

Student Edition • page 43

Choose the correct answer.

12. Which number has the greatest value?

Ⓐ 22,200 Ⓑ 22,002

Ⓒ 22,202 Ⓓ 22,022

13. Kevin invited 44 people to his birthday party. If he can fit 6 people to a table, how many tables will he need for his party?

Ⓐ 6 Ⓑ 7

Ⓒ 8 Ⓓ 9

14.

$$\begin{array}{r} 24058 \\ +\ \ 2580 \\ \hline \end{array}$$

Ⓐ 26,638 Ⓑ 26,538

Ⓒ 22,538 Ⓓ 21,478

15.

$$\begin{array}{r} 26057 \\ -\ \ \ 967 \\ \hline \end{array}$$

Ⓐ 25,010 Ⓑ 25,090

Ⓒ 26,910 Ⓓ 27,014

16. Dylan has saved \$16. His brother has saved \$12. If they combine their money to buy a game that costs \$25, how much money will they have left?

Ⓐ \$28 Ⓑ \$13

Ⓒ \$4 Ⓓ \$3

17. Which unit of measurement should be used to measure the length of a room?

Ⓐ centimeters Ⓑ miles

Ⓒ inches Ⓓ feet

18. Solve for *n*.

$20 - (4 \times 3) = n$

Ⓐ $n = 8$ Ⓑ $n = 13$

Ⓒ $n = 32$ Ⓓ $n = 48$

19.

$$\begin{array}{r} 199500079 \\ +\ \ \ \ 1890341 \\ \hline \end{array}$$

Ⓐ 197,609,739 Ⓑ 200,390,310

Ⓒ 201,390,420 Ⓓ 201,400,320

20.

$$\begin{array}{r} 500999 \\ -\ \ \ 45126 \\ \hline \end{array}$$

Ⓐ 546,125 Ⓑ 455,873

Ⓒ 445,873 Ⓓ 50,873

Practice Test

Name ______________________________ Date ____________

Student Edition • page 44

Choose the correct answer.

21. Which equation is an example of the identity element for addition?

Ⓐ $3 \times 2 = 2 \times 3$

Ⓑ $4 \times 1 = 4$

Ⓒ $(4 + 5) + 9 = 4 + (5 + 9)$

Ⓓ $5 + 0 = 5$

22. Which line is a line of symmetry?

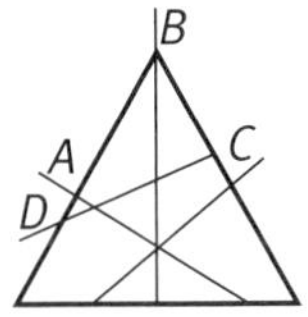

Ⓐ line *A*

Ⓑ line *B*

Ⓒ line *C*

Ⓓ line *D*

23. Round 2.07 to the nearest tenth.

Ⓐ 2.0 Ⓑ 2

Ⓒ 2.17 Ⓓ 2.1

24. Which of the following sets has the numbers in order from least to greatest?

Ⓐ 4.44, 4.08, 4.115, 4.002

Ⓑ 4.08, 4.115, 4.002, 4.44

Ⓒ 4.002, 4.08, 4.115, 4.44

Ⓓ 4.002, 4.08, 4.44, 4.115

25. What is 2,415.468 rounded to the nearest hundred?

Ⓐ 2,420 Ⓑ 2,415.5

Ⓒ 2,415.47 Ⓓ 2,400

26. $4\overline{)428}$

Ⓐ 107 Ⓑ 108

Ⓒ 112 Ⓓ 114

27. What is the measure of an obtuse angle?

Ⓐ less than 90°

Ⓑ 90°

Ⓒ greater than 90°

Ⓓ greater than 180°

28. How many inches are in 14 yards?

Ⓐ 36 Ⓑ 42

Ⓒ 140 Ⓓ 504

Practice Test

Student Edition • page 45

Extended Response **Solve** the following problems.

29. There are 12,058 people who take the bus to and from work each day in Ranthem. About 4,500 more people take the train to work than take the bus. If there are 45,000 people who commute to work each day, how many do *not* take the bus or train to work? Explain.

30. The fifth-grade class had a car wash to raise money for a field trip. They asked for donations of $3 per car. They collected $270 on Saturday and $180 on Sunday. If 20 people did *not* make a donation for their car, how many cars did the fifth graders wash in all? Explain.

Name ______________________ Date ______________

Multiplication and Division Refresher

Student Edition • page 47

Wow, was it loud! I bet there were 50,000 people there.

Tonight's attendance is 19,374!

About 10,000 fans watched as . . .

Use the seating charts below and the photo on *Student Edition* page 46 to answer the following questions.

1. Which of the three estimates do you think is closest to the actual number of people at the game?

   ____

2. How did you decide which figure is closest? Explain your answer.

   ____

   ____

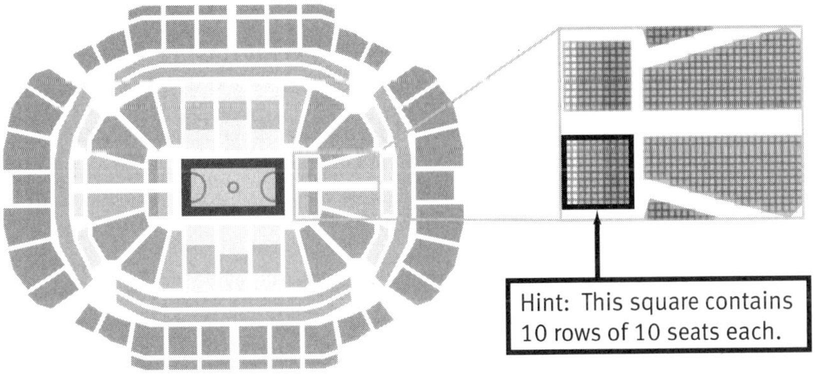

Hint: This square contains 10 rows of 10 seats each.

LESSON 2.1

Multiplying Multiples and Powers of 10

Student Edition • page 48

Find each product.

1. $6 \times 10 =$ ______
2. $60 \times 10 =$ ______
3. $85 \times 10 =$ ______
4. $85 \times 100 =$ ______
5. $100 \times 64 =$ ______
6. $10 \times 64 =$ ______
7. $1{,}000 \times 6 =$ ______
8. $62 \times 100 =$ ______
9. $100 \times 92 =$ ______
10. $1{,}000 \times 4 =$ ______
11. $170 \times 100 =$ ______
12. $10 \times 200 =$ ______
13. $1{,}000 \times 5 =$ ______
14. $10 \times 10 =$ ______
15. $100 \times 10 =$ ______
16. $10 \times 1{,}000 =$ ______
17. $100 \times 100 =$ ______
18. $1{,}000 \times 1{,}000 =$ ______

LESSON 2.1 **Name** ______________________ **Date** __________

Student Edition • page 49

Find each product.

19 $7 \times 3 =$ ______

20 $7 \times 30 =$ ______

21 $7 \times 300 =$ ______

22 $4 \times 9 =$ ______

23 $40 \times 9 =$ ______

24 $400 \times 9 =$ ______

25 $6{,}000 \times 90 =$ ______

26 $200 \times 70 =$ ______

27 $4{,}000 \times 600 =$ ______

28 $60 \times 5{,}000 =$ ______

29 $5{,}000 \times 500 =$ ______

30 $8{,}000 \times 700 =$ ______

31 How many minutes are in

a. one hour? ______

b. one day? ______

c. one week? ______

32 How many seconds are in

a. one minute? ______

b. one hour? ______

c. one day? ______

33 Seth and his sister worked together on a project for health class. They kept track of the amount of time Seth spends watching TV. They found that on weekdays, he watches an average of 4 hours of TV. On weekends, he watches about 6 hours each day. About how many *minutes* of TV per week does Seth watch altogether? ______

34 **Extended Response** At the flea market, Sylvia wants to buy 20 stamps at 10 cents each, 3 drinking glasses at 50 cents each, and 8 packs of batteries at 70 cents a pack. She has $10. Does she have enough money to buy everything? How can she be sure? Explain.

____

____

LESSON 2.2

Multiplying by a One-Digit Number

Student Edition • page 50

Find the number of tiles in a hallway, using the given information. Solve the problems in whatever way you wish.

1. 5 tiles wide and 9 tiles long ____________

2. 7 tiles wide and 8 tiles long ____________

3. 5 tiles wide and 50 tiles long ____________

4. 8 tiles wide and 25 tiles long ____________

5. 5 tiles wide and 59 tiles long ____________

6. 8 tiles wide and 80 tiles long ____________

LESSON 2.2

Name ______________________ Date ____________

Student Edition • page 51

Solve the following problems. Find the number of tiles in a hallway in each case, using the given information.

7. 6 tiles wide and 90 tiles long ____________

8. 8 tiles wide and 53 tiles long ____________

9. 5 tiles wide and 359 tiles long ____________

10. 5 tiles wide and 124 tiles long ____________

11. 9 tiles wide and 578 tiles long ____________

12. 9 tiles wide and 636 tiles long ____________

LESSON 2.2

Student Edition • page 52

Find each product. Check to see whether your answers make sense.

13. 247×3

14. 29×4

15. 855×7

16. 41×9

17. 700×6

18. 800×6

19. 809×6

20. 80×9

21. 79×9

22. 444×2

23. A storekeeper needs to know how much it costs to run her store for a 7-day week. Each day, for 5 days each week, she pays each of her 2 employees $12 per hour for 8 hours of work. She also pays $30 per day, 7 days a week, for rent and an extra $25 per week for other expenses.

- What are her expenses for the week? ______
- If sales for the week were $1,700, did she make a profit or did she lose money for the week? How much? ______

24. **Extended Response** Chuck and Marcus were playing checkers. They had half of the 24 checkers cleared from the board when the bell rang, signaling that recess was over. They had to figure out who won. Marcus claimed he had captured 2 more checker pieces than Chuck had captured. Chuck disagreed, so they decided to count. They found Marcus was correct.

- How many checker pieces did Chuck have? ______
- How many did Marcus have? ______
- How can you know for sure? Explain.

______

______

______

LESSON 2.3

Name ______________________ Date ____________

Multiplying Any Two Whole Numbers

Student Edition • page 55

Find each product. Use shortcuts when you can.

1. $25 \times 25 =$ ______
2. $38 \times 10 =$ ______
3. $11 \times 11 =$ ______
4. $13 \times 9 =$ ______
5. $213 \times 344 =$ ______
6. $216 \times 10 =$ ______
7. $216 \times 100 =$ ______
8. $216 \times 101 =$ ______
9. $216 \times 111 =$ ______
10. $406 \times 23 =$ ______
11. $769 \times 10 =$ ______
12. $514 \times 306 =$ ______
13. $400 \times 100 =$ ______
14. $473 \times 100 =$ ______
15. $100 \times 473 =$ ______
16. $624 \times 1{,}000 =$ ______
17. $1{,}000 \times 624 =$ ______
18. $1{,}001 \times 624 =$ ______
19. $100 \times 76 =$ ______
20. $1{,}000 \times 541 =$ ______
21. $2{,}000 \times 2{,}000 =$ ______
22. $6{,}242 \times 1{,}964 =$ ______

LESSON 2.3

Student Edition • page 55

23 The Hillside School drama club and the glee club are working together to put on a play. The auditorium has 10 rows of 24 seats and 20 rows of 30 seats.

a. How many people can be seated at one time? __________

b. Two rows of 30 seats were empty during the play, but all the other seats were taken. How many people attended the play? __________

c. **Extended Response** If Tara claimed there were 720 people at the play when 2 rows of 30 seats were empty, is she wrong? If so, what error do you think Tara made in her computation? Explain.

____

____

____

24 **Extended Response** The drama club and the glee club decided to perform their next play in the gymnasium. The gymnasium has 50 rows of 15 chairs and 20 rows of 25 bleacher seats. If all 50 rows of 15 chairs and the first 8 rows of 25 bleacher seats have been sold, how many people were in the audience? How much money will be made? How can you tell? Explain.

____

____

____

25 If there are 6 students in the glee club, twice as many students in the drama club, and 1 teacher advisor needed for every 6 students working on the play, how many teacher advisors are needed? __________

LESSON 2.4

Name ______________________ Date ____________

Applying Multiplication

Student Edition • pages 56–57

Use this table to answer Problems 1–10.

Food (serving size)	Calories	Fat (g)	Calcium (mg)	Vitamin A (IU)*
Whole milk (8 oz.)	146	8	291	249
2% milk (8 oz.)	137	5	297	184
Apple (1)	72	0	8	75
Orange (1)	65	0	61	317
Banana (1)	105	0	6	76
Carrots (1 cup)	52	0	42	15,406
White bread (1 slice)	66	1	38	0
Sandwich cookie (1)	82	5	6	1
Apple pie (1 slice)	411	20	11	90

*IU is the symbol for International Unit—a measure of the amount of a vitamin.

A fifth grader's diet should provide about 2,400 calories, 1,000 milligrams of calcium, and 5,000 IU of vitamin A each day, with no more than 60 grams of fat.

1 Every day for one week, Raulito ate 1 apple for dessert. For the same week, his sister Juanita ate 1 slice of apple pie instead. At the end of the week,

a. about how many calories did Juanita consume for dessert? ____________

b. about how many calories did Raulito consume for dessert? ____________

2 Typically, every 4,000 calories that the body does not use for daily activities or during exercise are stored as a pound of fat.

a. Compared with her brother, how many more calories did Juanita consume during the week? ____________

b. If Juanita and Raulito continue eating these desserts for 10 weeks, about how many more calories will Juanita have consumed than Raulito? ____________

c. If Juanita doesn't use the calories through exercise, about how many extra pounds will she likely have gained? ____________

LESSON 2.4

Student Edition • page 57

3. How many sandwich cookies would it take to provide more than a full day's allowance of fat? ______

4. Do 6 sandwich cookies have more calories or fewer calories than a slice of apple pie? ______

5. Would 4 servings of whole milk provide the daily requirement for calcium? If not, how many more servings are needed?

______

6. **Extended Response** Renée estimated that 20 apples would have more calcium than 3 servings of 2% milk. Is she correct? Why or why not?

______

______

7. Do 2 cups of carrots have more calories or fewer calories than 1 banana? ______

8. Which would provide more calcium: 2 slices of white bread or 4 bananas? How much more?

______

9. Would 3 servings of whole milk and 1 slice of apple pie provide more than the daily allowance of fat? ______

10. Morgan calculated that 1 slice of apple pie has more calories than 2 sandwich cookies. Is he correct? What is the difference between the calories in 1 slice of apple pie and the calories in 2 sandwich cookies?

______

______

LESSON 2.5

Name ______________________________ Date ______________

Problem-Solving Applications

Student Edition • page 58

Read the problems and answer the questions.

1. For the school picnic, Amy bought 15 bags of potato chips. They cost 87¢ a bag. She also bought 26 containers of juice. They cost 97¢ each.

   a. How much did she pay for all the potato chips? ____________

   b. How much did she pay for the juice? ____________

   c. How much did she pay for both? ____________

2. Miguel sleeps about 8 hours a night.

   a. About how many hours does Miguel sleep in 1 week? ____________

   b. About how many hours does he sleep in 1 year (365 days)? ____________

   c. About how many hours a week is Miguel awake? ____________

   d. **Extended Response** Explain two ways you can calculate the answer to Problem 2c.

   ____

   ____

   e. About how many hours a year is he awake? ____________

   f. **Extended Response** Give two ways you can calculate how many hours are in 1 year, using some of the information in this set of problems.

   ____

   ____

Student Edition • **page 59**

3. Triangle Park measures about 240 meters on each of its 3 sides.

   a. What is the perimeter of Triangle Park? ______________

   b. Emiko runs around the park twice every morning. About how far does she run? ______________

   c. Victor runs around the park 8 times a day. About how far does he run? ______________

   d. One day, Lisa ran around the park 29 times. About how far did she run? ______________

4. The new bakery puts 12 muffins in each long box. It puts 6 muffins in each short box. Will 11 full long boxes and 4 full short boxes be enough for 80 people to have 2 muffins each? If not, how many more muffins are needed? ______________

5. At work, Carlos is writing and illustrating a narrative based on something funny that happened at a family reunion. He usually works on the story for 2.5 hours each day. If it takes him 10 days to finish the story, how many hours of work should he be paid for?

   ____

6. Mr. McDonald takes 27 papers to the copying service. He needs to make 29 copies of each paper.

   a. How many copies will he make in all? ______________

   b. How much will the copying cost if he pays 5¢ for each copy? ______________

7. Canned tuna is on sale. The sale price is 6 cans for $6.25. How much will a half dozen cans cost? ______________

8. There are about 25 desks in each classroom in Fort Meadow School. There are 14 classrooms in the school. About how many desks are there altogether? ______________

Name ______________________ **Date** ____________

Student Edition • pages 60–61

Problem-Solving Applications Lesson 2.5

Oh, no! Paint has been spilled on this page. In each problem, two of the possible answers are clearly wrong, and one is correct. Choose the correct answer.

9 52 + 5
- **a.** 10
- **b.** 105
- **c.** 150

10 7 + 3 0
- **a.** 700
- **b.** 400
- **c.** 1,090

11 3 × 1
- **a.** 3,663
- **b.** 2,336
- **c.** 9,999

12 2 − 64
- **a.** 412
- **b.** 1,412
- **c.** 2,412

13 7 6 − 3
- **a.** 4,1 7
- **b.** 1,4 7
- **c.** 4

14 73 × 60
- **a.** 7
- **b.** 43
- **c.** 4,38

15 29 + 9 + 11
- **a.** 885
- **b.** 18 5
- **c.** 3 5

16 5 8 − 1234
- **a.** 4,444
- **b.** 444
- **c.** 44

17 8 × 49
- **a.** 5,0 7
- **b.** 4,21
- **c.** 3,21

18 3 × 17
- **a.** 26
- **b.** 54
- **c.** 91

19 46 × 6
- **a.** 2,8 6
- **b.** 2,3 6
- **c.** 2,0 6

20 1 + 8 4
- **a.** 65
- **b.** 26
- **c.** 445

21 × 4
- **a.** 745
- **b.** 748
- **c.** 751

22 × 7
- **a.** 4,249
- **b.** 4,252
- **c.** 4,255

23 × 3
- **a.** 2,852
- **b.** 2,854
- **c.** 2,856

24 111 ×
- **a.** 754
- **b.** 777
- **c.** 802

25 123 ×
- **a.** 738
- **b.** 798
- **c.** 858

26 207 ×
- **a.** 2,077
- **b.** 2,177
- **c.** 2,277

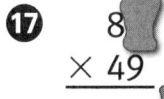

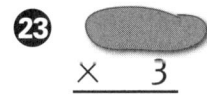

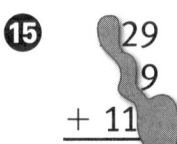

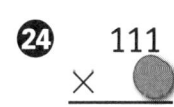

Student Edition • page 62

There are three ways to score points in basketball.

Three-point field goal
a shot from more than 20 feet away, outside the three-point line

Two-point field goal
a shot from less than 20 feet away, inside the three-point line

Free throw (one point)
an unguarded shot from the foul line by a player whose opponent committed a personal or technical foul

This table shows how four players scored their points in the playoffs one year. But some of the numbers are smudged.

Player	Shots Made			Total Points
	3-Point Field Goals	2-Point Field Goals	Free Throws	
Joreen Smith	16	37	35	[redacted]
Nikki Fields	15	29	[redacted]	118
Cheryl Hall	10	[redacted]	8	58
Keesha Phillips	[redacted]	12	25	82

Name ______________________ Date ____________

Student Edition • page 62

Find the numbers and explain how you found them.

1. How many points did Smith score in the playoffs?

____

____

2. How many free throws did Fields make in the playoffs?

____

____

3. How many two-point field goals did Hall make?

____

____

4. How many three-point field goals did Phillips make?

____

____

CHAPTER 2 Exploring Problem Solving

Student Edition • page 63

Rodriguez made 65 baskets in all. How many 3-point field goals did she make? How many 2-point field goals did she make?

Player	Baskets Made			Total Points
	3-Point Field Goals	2-Point Field Goals	Free Throws	
Bea Rodriguez	[redacted]	[redacted]	21	117

James solved the problem this way:

I used the Guess, Check, and Adjust and Make a Table Strategies.

Rodriguez made a total of 44 field goals.

These 44 shots counted for 96 points.

For my first guess, I'll try 20 three-point field goals and 24 two-point field goals.

	3-pt. FGs	2-pt. FGs	Points from Field Goals	Result
1st Guess	20	24	$(20 \times 3) + (24 \times 2) = 60 + 48 = 108$	too high
2nd Guess				

Name ______________________ Date ____________

Student Edition • page 63

Answer the following questions.

5. How does James know Rodriguez made 44 field goals altogether?

____

6. How does James know that those 2- and 3-point field goals add up to 96 points?

____

7. Will James's strategy work? Why or why not?

____

____

8. What numbers do you think James should try next? Why?

____

9. Solve the problem. Use James's strategy or a strategy of your own.

____

____

10. Why did you choose the strategy you did?

____

____

CHAPTER 2

Cumulative Review

Student Edition • page 64

Rounding and Approximating **Grade 4 Lesson 5.5**

Solve.

1. A backyard is about 42 meters long and 58 meters wide. Approximate the area by finding two numbers that the area must be between. Which of these could be the actual area?

   a. 1,856 square meters
   b. 3,056 square meters
   c. 2,436 square meters

In Problems 2–5, two of the answers are clearly wrong and one is correct. Choose the correct answer.

2. 32×17 ______

   a. 264
   b. 544
   c. 914

3. 46×61 ______

   a. 2,806
   b. 2,316
   c. 2,026

4. 28×195 ______

   a. 5,460
   b. 6,140
   c. 7,440

5. 206×38 ______

   a. 5,828
   b. 7,828
   c. 4,828

Multiplying by a One-Digit Number **Lesson 2.2**

Multiply.

6. 74×7

7. 385×8

8. 77×8

9. 976×4

10. 888×7

11. 528×6

Cumulative Review

Name ______________________ Date ____________

Student Edition • page 65

Applying Math **Lesson 1.4**

Solve.

12. Chung's bedroom is 13 feet long and 9 feet wide. What is the area of his room?

____

13. Carpet is sold in rolls measuring 10 feet by 5 feet. How many rolls of carpet will Chung need to cover his bedroom floor?

____

14. What is the perimeter of Chung's room?

____

15. What is the area of a square with a perimeter of 40 inches?

____

16. A rectangle with a perimeter of 62 feet could have which of the following dimensions?

a. 50 feet by 12 feet

b. 30 feet by 2 feet

c. 28 feet by 3 feet

d. 20 feet by 21 feet

Cumulative Review

Student Edition • page 65

Converting Customary Units **Grade 4 Lesson 6.6**

Solve.

17. How many fluid ounces are in 7 cups? ______

18. How many fluid ounces are in 1 pint? ______

19. How many fluid ounces are in 1 quart? ______

20. How many inches are in 8 feet? ______

21. How many feet are in 15 yards? ______

22. In math class, Angie sits 42 inches from Mrs. Packard's computer. Jenny sits 3 feet from Mrs. Packard's computer. Who sits closer to the computer, Angie or Jenny? ______

Applying Multiplication **Lesson 2.4**

Solve.

Eduardo and Ming each do odd jobs after school. Eduardo earns $15 for each lawn mowed and $10 for each car washed. Ming earns $17 per lawn and $8 per car.

23. Eduardo mowed 7 lawns and washed 4 cars. How much did he earn? ______

24. Ming mowed 6 lawns and washed 5 cars. How much did he earn? ______

25. Ming's goal is to earn $200. How can he do it? ______

LESSON 2.6

Name ______________________ Date ____________

Interpreting Remainders

Student Edition • page 67

Divide.

1. $9\overline{)83}$
2. $8\overline{)49}$
3. $7\overline{)19}$
4. $6\overline{)35}$
5. $6\overline{)52}$
6. $8\overline{)29}$
7. $6\overline{)24}$
8. $8\overline{)72}$
9. $5\overline{)46}$
10. $7\overline{)32}$
11. $9\overline{)60}$
12. $3\overline{)18}$
13. $13 \div 4 =$ ____________
14. $56 \div 7 =$ ____________
15. $62 \div 8 =$ ____________

16. **Extended Response** Parents of Fairfield Elementary School students decided to carpool in order to take the greatest number of students to the high school basketball game. If each car can hold 6 students, how many cars are needed to take 26 students to the basketball game? Explain your answer.

____

____

17. The cook in a restaurant wants to make omelets. He uses 3 eggs to make an omelet, and he has 23 eggs.

    a. How many omelets can he make? ____________

    b. **Extended Response** How many eggs will be left over? Explain.

    ____

18. A parcel service has 5,600 kilograms worth of packages that need to be sorted. One pallet will hold 750 kilograms. How many pallets are needed? ____________

LESSON 2.7

Dividing by a One-Digit Divisor

Student Edition • page 69

Divide.

1. $3\overline{)52}$
2. $2\overline{)21}$
3. $5\overline{)43}$
4. $8\overline{)187}$
5. $6\overline{)342}$
6. $6\overline{)345}$
7. $4\overline{)575}$
8. $7\overline{)8145}$
9. $9\overline{)648}$
10. $9\overline{)649}$
11. $9\overline{)650}$
12. $9\overline{)651}$
13. $8\overline{)804}$
14. $5\overline{)6798}$
15. $6\overline{)3798}$
16. $3\overline{)999}$
17. $3\overline{)131}$
18. $4\overline{)1466}$
19. **Extended Response** Mrs. Ogata has 17 students. She must order a computer disk for each student. The disks come 5 to a box. How many boxes should she order? Explain.

____

____

LESSON 2.7 **Name** ______________________ **Date** __________

Student Edition • **pages 69–70**

20. The science class is studying rocks and minerals. The students need to work in groups to do an experiment, but their teacher says that each group may not have more than 3 people. There are 17 students in the class. What is one way to organize the groups? How many students would there be in each group? (Hint: There is more than one possibility.)

____

____

21. Mrs. Ogata lets 5 students go to the school library every hour. How many hours will it take for all 17 students to go to the library? __________

22. To raise money for a trip to the science museum, Mrs. Ogata's class held a car wash and a bake sale. They need $100 to rent a charter bus. The class also needs $45 for food and beverages. Admission to the museum is $4 per student for 17 students. The class raised $220. Is that enough? If so, will they have any money left over? If not, how much more do they need?

____

____

Find the missing digit.

23. 40____ ÷ 4 = 100 R2

24. 4,____07 ÷ 7 = 701

25. 220 ÷ ____ = 44

26. 670 ÷ 4 = 1____7 R2

27. 71 ÷ 8 = 8 R____

28. 360 ÷ ____ = 120

29. ____,403 ÷ 8 = 800 R3

30. 32 ÷ 9 = 3 R____

31. 64 ÷ 7 = ____R1

32. 700 ÷ ____0 = 70

33. 2,505 ÷ ____ = 501

34. 6,613 ÷ 6 = ____,102 R1

Student Edition • **page 70**

35 A basketball league has 475 students to assign to 9-person teams. If all spots must be filled, how many students will not have a team? ______________

36 Pictures of all the students will be printed in the school yearbook. Only 9 pictures will fit on each page. If there are 475 students, how many pages will be needed to print pictures of all the students? ______________

37 Suppose 475 students buy yearbooks for $9 each. How much money will be collected? ______________

38 **Extended Response** Did you notice any similarities between Problems 35–37? Explain what you observed.

____

____

39 **Extended Response** Did you get the same answers for any of these problems? Explain why or why not.

____

____

40 All of the fourth- and fifth-grade students at City School are going to watch a movie in the auditorium. There are 9 seats in each row, and there are 124 students. How many rows of seats will be completely filled? ______________

LESSON 2.8

Name ______________________ Date ______________

Exponents

Student Edition • page 72

Evaluate each expression by multiplying.

1. $3^8 = 3 \times 3 \times 3 \times 3 \times 3 \times 3 \times 3 \times 3 =$ ______________
2. $8^3 = 8 \times 8 \times 8 =$ ______________
3. $2^{10} = 2 \times 2 \times 2 \times 2 \times 2 \times 2 \times 2 \times 2 \times 2 \times 2 =$ ______________
4. $5^6 = 5 \times 5 \times 5 \times 5 \times 5 \times 5 =$ ______________

Write each product by using exponents.

5. $7 \times 7 \times 7 \times 7 =$ ______________
6. $4 \times 4 \times 4 =$ ______________
7. $5 \times 5 \times 5 \times 5 \times 5 =$ ______________
8. $3 \times 3 \times 3 \times 3 \times 3 \times 3 =$ ______________

Evaluate the following by using multiplication or your calculator if you have one.

9. $3^8 =$ ______________
10. $8^3 =$ ______________
11. $2^{10} -$ ______________
12. $5^6 =$ ______________
13. $3^4 =$ ______________
14. $3^8 \times 3^4 =$ ______________

LESSON 2.8

Student Edition • page 73

Use the facts in the following table to do the exercises below. Do *not* use your calculator. Write your answers in standard form (without exponents).

$7^1 =$	7	$7^2 =$	49	$7^3 =$	343
$7^4 =$	2,401	$7^5 =$	16,807	$7^6 =$	117,649
$7^7 =$	823,543	$7^8 =$	5,764,801	$7^9 =$	40, 353,607
$7^{10} =$	282,475,249	$7^{11} =$	1,977,326,743	$7^{12} =$	13,841,287,201

15. $7^2 \times 7^3 =$ ______

16. $7^7 \times 7^4 =$ ______

17. $7^6 \times 7^6 =$ ______

18. $7^5 \times 7^4 =$ ______

19. $7^1 \times 7^1 =$ ______

20. $7^{10} \times 7^2 =$ ______

21. $7^3 \times 7^4 =$ ______

22. $7^4 \times 7^4 =$ ______

23. $16{,}807 \times 823{,}543 =$ ______

24. $2{,}401 \times 823{,}543 =$ ______

25. $343 \times 823{,}543 =$ ______

26. $49 \times 117{,}649 =$ ______

27. $117{,}649 \times 343 =$ ______

28. $2{,}401 \times 2{,}401 =$ ______

29. $7 \times 5{,}764{,}801 =$ ______

30. $343 \times 49 =$ ______

LESSON 2.8 **Name** ______________________ **Date** ______________

Student Edition • page 73

Check **to see what your calculator does with large numbers.**

31 Use your calculator to find 8^2, 8^3, 8^4, and so on.

a. **Extended Response** When does the calculator stop displaying numbers in standard form? What does it show instead?

____

b. What is the greatest exponent of 6 that will allow an answer to be displayed in standard form on your calculator?

____

32 Two fifth-grade classrooms had a competition to see who could collect the most canned-food items in one month. Here are Classroom A's results: Week 1: 38, Week 2: 31, Week 3: 33, Week 4: 18. Here are Classroom B's results: Week 1: 40, Week 2: 35, Week 3: 30, Week 4: 27. What is each classroom's average number of cans collected?

____

____

LESSON 2.9

Prime and Composite Numbers

Student Edition • page 75

Write all the factors for the following numbers.

1. 32 ______
2. 15 ______
3. 29 ______
4. 80 ______
5. 100 ______
6. 295 ______
7. How can you decide whether a number has a factor of 5?

______

8. How can you decide whether a number has a factor of 2?

______

9. How can you decide whether a number is divisible by 6? (Hint: Think about other factors.)

______

Decide whether each of the following numbers is a prime number or a composite number. If it is prime, write *P*. If it is composite, write the number in factored form, using exponents when there are two or more factors of a prime number.

For example, $35 = 5 \times 7$. No exponents are needed.
$36 = (2 \times 2 \times 3 \times 3) = 2^2 \times 3^2$. You must use exponents. $37 = P$

10. 2 ______
11. 8 ______
12. 24 ______
13. 51 ______
14. 12 ______
15. 9 ______
16. 29 ______
17. 111 ______
18. 11 ______
19. 387 ______
20. 1,000 ______
21. 7,000 ______
22. 800 ______
23. 10,000 ______
24. 7,000,000 ______

Name ______________________ Date ____________

Student Edition • page 75

25 Write every number from 1 to 100. After each number, write *prime* if the number is prime. If the number is composite, write the number as a product of prime factors, using exponents to show multiples of a factor (for example, $24 = 2 \times 2 \times 2 \times 3 = 2^3 \times 3$).

26 Using the rules you have learned about identifying numbers that have factors of 2, 3, 5, 9, and 10, every whole number less than 100 (besides 1) is either a prime number or can easily be shown to be a composite number except for one number. Which number is the exception? What are its factors? What is the next composite number that is not obviously composite? What are its factors?

LESSON 2.10

Applications Using Customary Measurement

Student Edition • pages 77–78

In some of the following situations, an incorrect measurement has been given. If the unit is appropriate, write "yes." If the unit is inappropriate, write an appropriate unit.

1. The envelope is 7 feet long. ______________
2. The envelope and letter together weigh a little less than 1 ton. ______________
3. The dog weighs 16 pounds. ______________
4. Kevin ran 7 inches today. ______________
5. That person is 62 centuries old. ______________
6. The basketball hoop is 10 miles high. ______________
7. A basket of apples weighs about 5 ounces. ______________
8. The front door is 1 yard wide. ______________
9. My dad's truck weighs 2 pounds. ______________
10. The United States is more than 2 millennia old. ______________
11. Mr. Ramirez rode his bike 4 miles yesterday. ______________
12. The bike path is 10 inches long. ______________

Answer the following questions.

13. Professional baseball fields have 90 feet between bases. How many feet does a player run if he hits a home run? ______________
14. Monica said that her birthday will be in 20 days. If she said that on June 14, what is her birthday? Is there another famous birthday on that day? ______________
15. Jong-Hyun said that he was strong enough to carry 10,000 pencils. Could he be right? Explain.

____

____

Name ______________________ Date ____________

Student Edition • pages 78–79

16. Juanita said that her birthday will be in 14 months. Could she be right? Explain.

____

____

17. How many ounces are in 16 pounds? ____________

18. Is it possible to have 53 Mondays and 53 Tuesdays in the same year? Explain.

____

____

19. Is it possible to have 53 Mondays, 53 Tuesdays, and 53 Wednesdays all in the same year? ____________

20. Is it possible to have 53 Mondays, 53 Tuesdays, 53 Wednesdays, and 53 Thursdays in the same year? ____________

Use a calculator and any other necessary tools (such as a ruler or tape measure), and work with another student to answer these questions.

21. How many days old are you? Do not forget leap years. ____________

22. About how many minutes old are you? ____________

23. Without measuring, estimate the length of your classroom in feet. ____________

24. Measure the length of the classroom in feet. How close was your estimate in Problem 23? ____________

Extended Response **Use a calendar to answer the following questions.**

25. Why do April 1 and July 1 fall on the same day of the week? Do they always?

____

____

26. Why do September 1 and December 1 fall on the same day of the week? Do they always?

____

____

Student Edition • page 79

27 Why do January 1 and October 1 fall on the same day of the week? Do they always?

____

____

28 Why do February 1 and March 1 fall on the same day of the week? Do they always?

____

____

29 For which three months does the first day of the month fall on the same day of the week? Why? Will they always?

____

____

30 Carrie and Sophia went to a movie. The movie was 97 minutes long and started at 5:30. If Carrie's mom arrived to pick them up at 7:15, was she on time, early, or late? Is there a way to tell without doing any arithmetic? Explain.

____

____

31 Sabina had 210 minutes on her calling card. She used 42 minutes talkingto her friend Casey. Then she talked to her cousin for 1 hour and 13 minutes. Her mom then added 2 hours to the card. How many minutes can she use so she will have exactly 1 hour of talking time left? ______

32 **Extended Response** A holiday that is important to many people of Mexican heritage is the Day of the Dead. It is celebrated during the first two days of November. Luis is going to Mexico on November 1st to celebrate the Day of the Dead. He will be in Mexico for 42 days. After Luis leaves Mexico, he will go on two business trips that will last a total of 11 days. Will he be back home in time to celebrate his birthday on December 29th? Explain.

____

____

LESSON 2.11

Name ______________________ Date ____________

Temperature

Student Edition • pages 80–81

Use the table below, which shows mean (or average) temperatures (in degrees Fahrenheit) for three United States cities, to answer the following questions.

	JAN	FEB	MAR	APR	MAY	JUN	JUL	AUG	SEP	OCT	NOV	DEC
A	22	25	35	47	56	66	71	69	61	49	39	28
B	−14	−16	−14	−1	20	35	40	39	31	15	−1	−11
C	54	58	63	70	79	89	93	91	86	75	62	54

1. What is the coldest month in City A? In City B? In City C?

2. What is the warmest month in each city?

3. **Extended Response** Where do you think City B is? Explain.

4. **Extended Response** Where do you think City C is? Explain.

Student Edition • page 81

5 **Extended Response** Where do you think City A is? Explain.

____

____

6 Which city has the greatest difference between its highest and lowest mean monthly temperature? __________

7 Which city has the least difference between its highest and lowest mean monthly temperature? __________

8 For the other city, what is the difference between its highest and lowest mean monthly temperature? __________

9 Which city do you think would be most comfortable in June? __________

Which would be most comfortable in January? __________

10 Which city has the greatest difference in mean temperatures between two consecutive months? __________

What is that difference? __________

Exploring Problem Solving

Name ____________________ Date ____________

Student Edition • pages 82–83

Player	Team	Games Played	Shots Made			Total Points
			3-pt. FGs	2-pt. FGs	FTs	
Krystal Moore	Los Angeles Lightning	3	1	17	13	50
Mai Li	North Carolina Flyers	8	6	17	16	68
Tameeka Wright	Arizona Roadrunners	3	7	10	15	56
Joy Engle	Cleveland Rocks	3	4	14	14	54
Emily Young	Atlanta Thunderbirds	5	13	29	4	101
Angela Perez	New York Defenders	6	2	26	17	75
Roberta Collins	Sacramento Stars	8	4	26	43	107
Char DeLaura	Nevada Nighthawks	2	0	10	4	24

Solve the following problems. Use the information in the table to help you.

1. How many shots did Roberta Collins make during the playoffs? ____________

2. How does that add up to 107 points? ____________________

3. On average, how many points did Char DeLaura score in each playoff game?

   ____

4. If you wanted players on your team who scored a lot of points, which two of these players would you choose first? Why?

   ____

   ____

5. The abbreviation *ppg* stands for *points per game*. This is the average number of points a player scores in a game. What formula could you write to show how to calculate the *ppg* for a player? Explain what each abbreviation in your formula means.

   ____

   ____

Student Edition • pages 83–84

6 What other data might help you decide if a player is a good scorer?

---

7 What other data might help you decide how good a player is overall?

In basketball and other sports, teams keep records of how every player performs. This table shows more information about the playoff shooting of the players listed on page 71.

Player	3-pt. FGs		2-pt. FGs		Free Throws	
	Made (A)	Tried (B)	Made (C)	Tried (D)	Made (E)	Tried (F)
Moore	1	4	17	37	13	13
Li	6	20	17	41	16	21
Wright	7	20	10	26	15	16
Engle	4	13	14	32	14	15
Young	13	33	29	45	4	5
Perez	2	9	26	77	17	22
Collins	4	11	26	54	43	53
DeLaura	0	2	10	14	4	4

Imagine you are a coach and want to compare the shooting ability of your players. You create a formula to calculate a number that will help you compare. Call this number "S" to stand for *Shooting Index.*

Shooting Index: $S = (A + C) \div E$ $S = A + C + E$

Name ______________________ Date ____________

Student Edition • page 84

Solve the following problems.

8. Which formula do you think does a better job of describing a player's shooting ability? Why?

____

____

9. Which scoring statistics are most important to you? Which are least important?

____

____

10. Create your own formula for the shooting index. Use your formula to calculate the shooting index for the eight players in the table on page 72.

____

____

11. Record the shooting index you calculate for each player. Use the shooting indexes to rank the players from 1 to 8; the player with the highest index is 1, the next highest is 2, and so on.

____

____

12. Compare your formula and your results. Did all groups agree?

____

____

Cumulative Review

Student Edition • page 85

Interpreting Remainders Lesson 2.6

Solve.

1. For his family reunion, Chet needs enough buns for 50 hamburgers and 75 hot dogs. Hamburger rolls come in 8-packs; hot dog rolls come in 10-packs. How many packages of each type of bun does Chet need? ____________

There are 32 fans who need to be transported to a football game.

2. If 5-person cars are available, how many cars are needed? ____________
3. If 7-person vans are available, how many vans are needed? ____________

There are 43 students interested in playing basketball.

4. How many 5-person teams can be selected? ____________
5. How many more students are needed so that an equal number of 5-person teams can be selected? ____________

Dividing by a One-Digit Divisor Lesson 2.7

Divide.

6. $8\overline{)66}$
7. $7\overline{)89}$
8. $9\overline{)775}$
9. $6\overline{)125}$

Exponents Lesson 2.8

Write each answer in standard form.

10. $5 \times 10^2 =$ ____________
11. $10^3 =$ ____________
12. $22 \times 10^1 =$ ____________
13. $7 \times 10^5 =$ ____________
14. $9 \times 10^6 =$ ____________
15. $8 \times 10^2 =$ ____________

Cumulative Review

Name ______________________ Date ______________

Student Edition • pages 85–86

Write each in exponential form.

16. 5,000 ______
17. 3,000,000 ______
18. 1,300 ______
19. 10,000 ______
20. 45,000,000 ______
21. 600 ______

Prime and Composite Numbers **Lesson 2.9**

For each of the following numbers, write *P* if the number is prime. If it is composite, write the number in factored form using exponents when there are two or more factors of a prime number.

22. 47 ______
23. 17 ______
24. 87 ______
25. 143 ______
26. 1,500 ______
27. 79 ______
28. 370 ______
29. 315 ______

Cumulative Review

Student Edition • page 86

Applying Math Lesson 1.4

Solve.

30. Alayna's 30th birthday was in 2005. In what year was her 10th birthday? ______

31. Ron bought 11 pencils. Each pencil cost 7¢. He gave the storekeeper 80¢. How much change should he get? ______

32. David paid 63¢ for 7 pears. How much did each pear cost? ______

33. Five pounds of beans cost $2.00. If Terri buys 20 pounds, how much does she spend? ______

34. A theater has 50 rows of seats. Each row has 33 seats. Can 1,700 people sit in the theater? ______

35. How can you make 74¢ using 9 coins? ______

Adding and Subtracting Multidigit Numbers Lessons 1.7–1.8

Add or subtract.

36. 556 + 444 = ______

37. 3,000 − 1,645 = ______

38. 2,000 − 857 = ______

39. 4,001 − 1,960 = ______

40. 567 + 123 = ______

CHAPTER 2 Key Ideas Review

Name ____________________ Date ____________

Student Edition • page 87

Select the appropriate answer.

1. $25 \times 12 =$ ________
   a. 301
   b. 300
   c. 325

2. $19 \times 7 =$ ________
   a. 133
   b. 140
   c. 126

3. $395 \div 8 =$ ________
   a. 4 R93
   b. 49
   c. 49 R3

4. $1,396 \div 3 =$ ________
   a. 456 R1
   b. 465 R1
   c. 46 R51

Answer the following questions.

5. What is a shortcut you can use when computing 36×7?

____

____

6. How are multiplication and division used to convert between customary units? Provide an example in your answer.

____

____

Key Ideas Review

Student Edition • **page 87**

7. What does 9^3 mean? What does 9^3 equal?

8. Is 91 a prime or composite number? Explain how you came to your conclusion.

9. How can you check quotients that have remainders?

10. How does knowing how to multiply by powers of 10 help when multiplying numbers such as 22×17?

CHAPTER 2 Chapter Review

Name ______________________ Date ______________

Student Edition • page 88

Multiply. Lessons 2.1–2.3

1. $\begin{array}{r} 7 \\ \times\ 8 \\ \hline \end{array}$

2. $\begin{array}{r} 8 \\ \times\ 9 \\ \hline \end{array}$

3. $\begin{array}{r} 24 \\ \times\ 16 \\ \hline \end{array}$

4. $\begin{array}{r} 100 \\ \times\ 65 \\ \hline \end{array}$

5. $\begin{array}{r} 30 \\ \times\ 40 \\ \hline \end{array}$

6. $\begin{array}{r} 243 \\ \times\ 378 \\ \hline \end{array}$

7. $\begin{array}{r} 66 \\ \times\ 77 \\ \hline \end{array}$

8. $\begin{array}{r} 170 \\ \times\ 98 \\ \hline \end{array}$

9. $\begin{array}{r} 345 \\ \times\ 534 \\ \hline \end{array}$

Solve. Lesson 2.4

10. Pencils cost 18¢ and erasers cost 12¢.

    a. How much do 4 pencils and 3 erasers cost? ______________

    b. How much do 6 pencils and 5 erasers cost? ______________

    c. Is $2 enough money to buy one dozen pencils? ______________

11. Mark wants to buy 4 books at $15 each. He has $70. Does he have enough money to buy all 4 books if the total tax is about $4? ______________

CHAPTER 2 Chapter Review

Student Edition • pages 88–89

Divide. Lessons 2.6–2.7

12. $4\overline{)36}$
13. $4\overline{)37}$
14. $8\overline{)560}$
15. $2\overline{)324}$
16. $9\overline{)2133}$
17. $6\overline{)1656}$
18. $7\overline{)9024}$
19. $8\overline{)7540}$

For each of the following numbers, write *P* if the number is prime. If it is composite, write the number in factored form using exponents when there are two or more factors of a prime number. Lessons 2.8–2.9

20. 37 ________
21. 71 ________
22. 57 ________
23. 187 ________
24. 500 ________
25. 97 ________
26. 270 ________
27. 784 ________

Answer the following questions. Lesson 2.10

28. Melinda placed her baseball bat next to a yardstick. The bottom end of the bat was at the 3-inch mark. The top of the bat was aligned with the other end of the yardstick. How long was the bat? ________
29. **Extended Response** Diego's birthday is June 15, which is a Wednesday in 2005. On what day of the week will his birthday fall in 2010? Explain your answer.

____

____

30. How many seconds are in $4\frac{1}{2}$ hours? ________
31. If the average class lasts 45 minutes, how many classes will fit in 6 hours? ________
32. Jerome cut a 7-ounce piece from a $2\frac{1}{2}$ pound chunk of cheese. How many ounces of cheese are left? ________

Practice Test

Name ______________________ Date __________

Student Edition • page 90

Solve the following problems.

1. Evaluate 6^4 by using multiplication.

____

2. Write all the factors for 36.

____

3. How many minutes are in 2 weeks?

____

4. How many yards are in 3 miles?

____

5. A restaurant orders 2 aprons for each waiter. There are 37 waiters in the restaurant. Aprons come 6 to a package. How many packages does the restaurant need to order?

____

6. An average of 240 people go to the grocery store every day. How many people go to the store over 10 days?

____

7. For the movie night at school, Mr. Davies bought 16 liters of juice. Each liter cost 99¢. How much did Mr. Davies pay for all the juice?

____

8. The auditorium at school can fit 22 rows of 18 seats each. How many people can be seated at one time?

____

Choose the correct answer.

9. 675×7

Ⓐ 4,225 Ⓑ 4,295

Ⓒ 4,695 Ⓓ 4,725

10. $120 \times 100 =$ _______________

Ⓐ 120 Ⓑ 1,200

Ⓒ 12,000 Ⓓ 120,000

11. Milk spilled on Kevin's paper. Which answer could be the correct product?

4  × 26 = _______________

Ⓐ 1,300 Ⓑ 1,275

Ⓒ 1,092 Ⓓ 1,000

12. 325×74

Ⓐ 24,050 Ⓑ 23,030

Ⓒ 3,575 Ⓓ 1,300

Chapter 2 Practice Test

Student Edition • page 91

Choose the correct answer.

13. $6\overline{)434}$

Ⓐ 82 R4

Ⓑ 72 R2

Ⓒ 70 R4

Ⓓ 62 R2

14. About 48 people enter the subway station in 1 hour. At that rate, about how many people enter the subway station in 4 hours?

Ⓐ 192

Ⓑ 182

Ⓒ 162

Ⓓ 122

15. Felicity invited 28 people to her birthday party and gave each person 2 balloons. Balloons come in packages of 5. How many packages of balloons did Felicity buy?

Ⓐ 28

Ⓑ 12

Ⓒ 6

Ⓓ 5

16. Which answer shows the prime factors of 30?

Ⓐ 22 32

Ⓑ 2 3 5

Ⓒ 5 6

Ⓓ 1 103

17. $4^3 =$ ____________

Ⓐ 64

Ⓑ 32

Ⓒ 12

Ⓓ 8

18. Melody bought a 6-pound bag of sugar. How many ounces did she buy?

Ⓐ 36

Ⓑ 60

Ⓒ 72

Ⓓ 96

19. Which number is the greatest?

Ⓐ 55,500

Ⓑ 55,005

Ⓒ 55,505

Ⓓ 55,055

Practice Test

Name ______________________ Date ____________

Student Edition • page 92

Choose the correct answer.

20. Samantha and her 2 friends bought 2 bags of pretzels. Each bag has about 18 pretzels. If they share the bags equally, how many pretzels will each person get?

Ⓐ 6

Ⓑ 8

Ⓒ 12

Ⓓ 18

21. $\begin{array}{r} 573 \\ +\ 532 \\ \hline \end{array}$

Ⓐ 1,105

Ⓑ 1,106

Ⓒ 1,006

Ⓓ 1,005

22. $\begin{array}{r} 854 \\ 765 \\ \hline \end{array}$

Ⓐ 81

Ⓑ 89

Ⓒ 111

Ⓓ 199

23. Giorgio saved all his allowance for 6 weeks to buy a pair of jeans that cost $36. How much does he get for an allowance each week?

Ⓐ 216

Ⓑ 18

Ⓒ 7

Ⓓ 6

24. Which answer shows 100,000 + 6,000 + 4 in standard form?

Ⓐ 160,004

Ⓑ 106,004

Ⓒ 100,604

Ⓓ 1,604

25. Solve for n: $16 + (3 \times 2) = n$

Ⓐ $n = 26$

Ⓑ $n = 11$

Ⓒ $n - 10$

Ⓓ $n = 8$

Practice Test

Student Edition • page 93

Use the provided information to solve the following problems. Show your work.

26. Extended Response Kerwick Elementary School is having a picnic. About 350 students and 180 adults are expected to attend. Hamburger buns come 8 to a package, and hot dog buns come 6 to a package.

a. About how many people are expected to attend the picnic altogether? ___________

b. If each adult eats 2 hamburgers, how many hamburgers will the adults eat altogether? ___________

c. If each person at the picnic eats 1 hot dog, how many packages of hot dog buns will be opened? Explain how you found your answer.

____

____

____

d. If each student eats 1 hamburger, how many packages of hamburger buns will be opened for the students? Explain how you found your answer.

____

____

____

Name ____________________ Date ____________

Decimals

Student Edition • page 95

Look at these two photos of Machu Picchu and its surroundings.

A

B

Answer the following questions.

1. A distance in Photo A appears many times greater than the same distance in Photo B. How many times greater? Choose the best estimate. ____________

   a. 2 **b.** 10 **c.** 100 **d.** 1,000,000

2. How did you decide which estimate is best? ____________

3. If a wall is 10 centimeters long in Photo A, how long would it be in Photo B? ____________

4. Could you measure that distance with a standard centimeter ruler? ____________

LESSON 3.1

Decimals and Money

Student Edition • page 96

Write the amount of money shown by using a dollar sign and a decimal point.

1  ______

2  ______

3  ______

4  ______

5  ______

6  ______

Use >, <, or = to complete each statement.

7 5.04 ______ 4.05

8 6.40 ______ 0.64

9 643.00 ______ 643

10 101.01 ______ 110.11

11 0.51 ______ 51

12 16.05 ______ 16.50

13 69.77 ______ 697.70

14 3,015.13 ______ 3,105.31

15 0.07 ______ 0.70

16 505.05 ______ 505.50

17 140.00 ______ 140

18 1.10 ______ 110

LESSON 3.1 **Name** ______________________ **Date** ______________

Student Edition • pages 97—98

Add or subtract. Watch the signs.

19. $14.53 + 27.99

20. $216.22 + 132.80

21. $0.96 + 1.04

22. $275.70 + 65.60

23. $40.61 + 61.22

24. $52.25 + 35.10

25. $76.70 + 16.45

26. $705.25 + 861.88

Solve for n.

27. \$622.17 − \$446.18 = n ______________

28. \$48.12 + \$19.12 = n ______________

29. \$146.64 + \$24.46 = n ______________

30. \$4.40 − \$1.50 = n ______________

31. \$67.26 − \$13.14 = n ______________

32. \$37.25 − \$12.15 = n ______________

33. \$0.23 + \$66.79 = n ______________

34. \$94.20 + \$0.76 = n ______________

35. \$77.63 − \$18.13 = n ______________

36. \$19.90 + \$12.56 = n ______________

37. \$312.20 + \$22.13 = n ______________

Student Edition • page 98

Solve the following problems.

38 Raymond bought three packages of hamburger at the store. They cost $3.01, $3.25, and $2.49. How much did the hamburger cost altogether?

____

39 **Extended Response** A basketball costs $7.16, including tax. Brooke gave the clerk some money and got $2.84 in change. How much money did Brooke give the clerk? Explain some different ways to show that amount.

____

____

____

40 Enrique's father gives Enrique the money he saves from using coupons when he shops. During October, he gave Enrique $1.25, $0.75, $1.00, and $0.73. How much money did Enrique get altogether?

____

LESSON 3.2

Name ______________________ Date ____________

Place Value and Decimals

Student Edition • page 101

Write <, >, or = to complete the following statements.

1. 5.2 __________ 5.4
2. 17.63 __________ 17.64
3. 8.12 __________ 8.120
4. 8.09 __________ 8.12
5. 8.9 __________ 8.12
6. 4.34 __________ 4.7
7. 6 __________ 6.000
8. 410 __________ 4.03
9. 4.1 __________ 4.03
10. 12.79 __________ 16.79

Order the following sets of numbers from least to greatest.

11. 0.7, 1.3, 0.09 ______________________
12. 3.49, 3.2, 3.109 ______________________
13. 6.12, 6.8, 6.18 ______________________
14. 1.01, 1.1, 1.11 ______________________
15. 0.4, 1.4, 0.01 ______________________
16. 0.9, 1.0, 0.09 ______________________
17. 3.5, 3.03, 3.1 ______________________
18. 7.007, 7.7, 7.07 ______________________
19. 1.81, 1.80, 1.08 ______________________
20. 0.5, 5.0, 0.0005 ______________________

LESSON 3.3

Comparing and Ordering Decimals

Student Edition • page 102

Write $<$, $>$, or $=$ to make each statement true.

1. 5.2 ________ 5.4
2. 17.63 ________ 17.64
3. 8.12 ________ 8.120
4. 8.09 ________ 8.12
5. 8.9 ________ 8.12
6. 4.34 ________ 4.7
7. 6 ________ 6.000
8. 410 ________ 4.03
9. 4.1 ________ 4.03
10. 12.79 ________ 16.79
11. 12.79 ________ 12.8
12. 1.0001 ________ 1.001
13. 3.04 ________ 3.0068
14. 2.1 ________ 3.1

Write the following sets of numbers in order from least to greatest.

15. 8.7, 8.65, 8.9 ____________________
16. 2.16, 2.3, 2.19 ____________________
17. 1.005, 1.05, 1.0052 ____________________
18. 4.1, 4.2, 4.03 ____________________
19. 0.7, 1.3, 0.09 ____________________
20. 3.49, 3.2, 3.109 ____________________
21. 6.12, 6.8, 6.18 ____________________
22. 1.01, 1.1, 1.11 ____________________
23. 0.4, 1.4, 0.01 ____________________
24. 0.9, 1.0, 0.09 ____________________

LESSON 3.4

Name ______________________ Date ____________

Adding and Subtracting Decimals

Student Edition • page 105

Choose the correct answer.

1. \$38.17 + \$1.65 = ____________
   - **a.** \$54.67
   - **b.** \$38.33
   - **c.** \$39.82

2. \$426.13 + \$7.21 = ____________
   - **a.** \$498.23
   - **b.** \$433.34
   - **c.** \$1,147.13

3. \$652.17 − \$2.81 = ____________
   - **a.** \$649.36
   - **b.** \$654.98
   - **c.** \$624.06

4. 0.63 + 0.56 = ____________
   - **a.** 11.9
   - **b.** 1.19
   - **c.** 0.07

5. 27.3 + 4.6 = ____________
   - **a.** 63.3
   - **b.** 31.9
   - **c.** 319

6. 47.1 − 23.4 = ____________
   - **a.** 70.5
   - **b.** 2.37
   - **c.** 23.7

Solve for *n*. Watch the signs.

7. $34.2 + 16.7 = n$ ____________

8. $34.2 - 16.7 = n$ ____________

9. $107.82 - 69.7 = n$ ____________

10. $107.82 + 69.7 = n$ ____________

11. $1.02 - 0.56 = n$ ____________

12. $0.1 + 1.2 = n$ ____________

13. $0.005 + 0.005 = n$ ____________

14. $0.1 - 0.05 = n$ ____________

Student Edition • page 105

Solve the following problems.

15. Mr. Stein's yard is in the shape of a rectangle. It is 11.75 meters long and 9.25 meters wide. How long a fence does Mr. Stein need if he wants it to go completely around the yard? ______________

16. Sharon is 148.3 centimeters tall. Last year she was 140.2 centimeters tall. How much has she grown since last year? ______________

17. At 6:00 last night, Eliza had a fever of 100.1°F. Three hours later, her temperature was up by 1.1°F. This morning her temperature was 98.9°F. By how much did her temperature go down overnight? ______________

18. **Extended Response** Simon wants to build a frame for a picture he made on his computer. He has 91.44 centimeters of wood he can use to make the frame. What are some possible dimensions the finished frame could have if Simon uses all the wood?

____

____

____

LESSON 3.5

Name ______________________ Date ____________

Applying Math

Student Edition • page 106

Solve the following problems.

1. A local caterer is advertising a special on trays of lasagna. The first tray ordered costs \$14.00, but each additional tray costs only \$8.50. Raphael has \$40 to spend on the party he is planning and would like to get 4 trays of lasagna.

   a. Can Raphael afford 4 trays of lasagna? ____________

   b. How much change will he have left, if any? ____________

2. Norman owns a hot dog stand. He sells only hot dogs and soft drinks. He sells about 500 hot dogs and 700 soft drinks each day. His profit is 60¢ for each hot dog and 50¢ for each soft drink. About how much profit does Norman make each day? ____________

3. Kishi bought 12 stickers for 25¢ each. She sold one sticker to Brenda for 25¢, 3 stickers to Andre for 78¢, and 8 stickers to Jeff for \$1.60. How much profit did Kishi make? ____________

4. Joe was born in 1966. He was 24 years old when he graduated from college and 32 years old when he got married.

   a. In what year did Joe graduate from college? ____________

   b. In what year did he get married? ____________

5. Mr. Tyler's bank account has a balance of \$123.46. How much does he need to deposit in order to have a balance of \$250? ____________

6. **Extended Response** The Deluxe Supermarket advertised a liter of milk for \$2.65. The Best Prices grocery store advertised half a liter of milk for \$1.30. Which is the better buy? Explain.

____

____

____

Student Edition • page 107

Solve the following problems.

7. LizAnne cut a string into 3 equal parts. If 1 piece was 48 centimeters long, how long was the string before LizAnne cut it? ____________

8. Miss Farr owns a fruit stand. Her sales for one week were \$136.75, \$143.00, \$164.25, \$140.10, and \$131.27. Her expenses were \$366.80. How much profit did she make that week? ____________

9. Mr. Chang owns a music store. Last Wednesday he sold 15 CDs for \$12 each and 4 CDs for \$15 each. He makes a profit of \$6 each on the \$12 CDs and a profit of \$7.50 each on the \$15 CDs. How much profit did Mr. Chang make on CDs last Wednesday? ____________

10. José and Dave need to make banners for the school election. They have 15.5 feet of paper to use. José would like to make banners that are 4.5 feet long.

    a. How many 4.5-feet-long banners could José make? ____________

    b. How much paper will be left? ____________

    c. If Dave wants to make 5 banners all the same length, how long can each banner be? ____________

11. The Rogers Elementary School principal has 144 packages of construction paper. If he plans to give each of the 9 teachers the same amount of paper, how many packages will each teacher receive?

    ____

12. The Clark Middle School principal wants to have a conference with each of the 277 students during the early part of the school year. If she can meet with 9 students each day, how many days will it take her to meet with all the students? ____________

LESSON 3.6

Name ______________________ Date ____________

Multiplying and Dividing Decimals

Student Edition • page 108

Find each product.

1. $10 \times 75 =$ ______________
2. $10 \times 62.97 =$ ______________
3. $10 \times 89 =$ ______________
4. $10 \times 9.28 =$ ______________
5. $10 \times 0.06 =$ ______________
6. $10 \times 58.39 =$ ______________
7. $10 \times 95.17 =$ ______________
8. $10 \times 0.975 =$ ______________
9. $100 \times 8 =$ ______________
10. $82.45 \times 100 =$ ______________
11. $100 \times 0.47 =$ ______________
12. $100 \times 9.27 =$ ______________
13. $20.1 \times 100 =$ ______________
14. $67.29 \times 100 =$ ______________
15. $12.3 \times 100 =$ ______________
16. $100 \times 97.31 =$ ______________
17. $10{,}000 \times 0.978 =$ ______________
18. $0.792 \times 100 =$ ______________
19. $0.97653 \times 10{,}000 =$ ______________
20. $1{,}000 \times 63.576 =$ ______________
21. $15.1 \times 1{,}000 =$ ______________
22. $10{,}000 \times 1.17149 =$ ______________
23. $0.36781 \times 1{,}000{,}000 =$ ______________
24. $10 \times 627 =$ ______________

Student Edition • page 109

Find each quotient.

25. 27 ÷ 10 = ____________
26. 0.09 ÷ 10 = ____________
27. 18,390 ÷ 100 = ____________
28. 2.7 ÷ 10 = ____________
29. 0.76 ÷ 10 = ____________
30. 1,839 ÷ 100 = ____________
31. 89.261 ÷ 10 = ____________
32. 36.143 ÷ 1,000 = ____________
33. 42.9 ÷ 100 = ____________
34. 0.9267 ÷ 1,000 = ____________
35. 39 ÷ 1,000 = ____________
36. 6.814 ÷ 100 = ____________

Multiply or divide.

37. 347.26 ÷ 1,000 = ____________
38. 0.07 ÷ 10 = ____________
39. 100 × 47.3 = ____________
40. 1,000 × 0.01 = ____________
41. 66.41 × 1,000 = ____________
42. 280.03 ÷ 100 = ____________

LESSON 3.7

Name ______________________ Date ____________

Metric Units

Student Edition • page 111

Use a dictionary to help answer the following questions.

1. What does the prefix *milli-* mean? ____________
2. How many millimeters are in a meter? ____________
3. How many milliliters are in a liter? ____________
4. What does the prefix *centi-* mean? ____________
5. How many centimeters are in a meter? ____________
6. How many cents are in a dollar? ____________
7. What does the prefix *kilo-* mean? ____________
8. How many grams are in a kilogram? ____________

Find the missing measure.

9. 14 m = ____________ cm
10. 0.001 L = ____________ mL
11. 200 mL = ____________ L
12. 3 dm = ____________ m
13. 16.2 mm = ____________ cm
14. 17.241 km = ____________ m
15. 4,000 g = ____________ kg
16. 1,796 m = ____________ km
17. 17.241 dm = ____________ m
18. 3.02 m = ____________ cm
19. 17.1 kg = ____________ g
20. 17.241 cm = ____________ mm
21. A meter has 1,000 millimeters, and 100 centimeters are in a meter.
    a. Which is longer, a millimeter or a centimeter? ____________
    b. How many times longer? ____________

Solve for *n*.

22. $n + 3.006 = 5.126$ ____________
23. $5.72 - 2.65 = n$ ____________
24. $72.6 - n = 52.9$ ____________
25. $7.421 + n = 10$ ____________

LESSON 3.8

Choosing Appropriate Metric Measures

Student Edition • page 112

Choose the measure that makes the most sense for each sentence.

1. Chad is ______________ tall.

   a. 14 cm **b.** 140 cm **c.** 140 m

2. Nick's cat weighs ______________.

   a. 2 kg **b.** 20 g **c.** 200 mg

3. I drank ______________ of water during the soccer game.

   a. 500 mL **b.** 5 mL **c.** 50 L

4. Courtney's fifth-grade classroom is ______________ long.

   a. 15 cm **b.** 15 km **c.** 15 m

5. Ms. Teal weighs ______________.

   a. 5.2 g **b.** 52 g **c.** 52 kg

6. A basketball weighs about ______________.

   a. 600 g **b.** 60 kg **c.** 600 kg

7. John ran ______________ this morning.

   a. 2 cm **b.** 2 m **c.** 2 km

LESSON 3.8 **Name** ______________________ **Date** ____________

Student Edition • page 113

Choose an appropriate measure.

8 The basket on a basketball court is about __________ above the ground.

a. 30 cm **b.** 3 m **c.** 30 m

9 The glasses are about __________ wide.

a. 12 m **b.** 120 cm **c.** 12 cm

10 A baseball weighs about __________.

a. 14.5 g **b.** 145 g **c.** 14.5 kg

11 The new swimming pool is __________ deep.

a. 1.5 m **b.** 15 m **c.** 5 m

12 A baseball bat is about __________ long.

a. 100 cm **b.** 10 m **c.** 100 m

13 A box of textbooks weighs about __________.

a. 10 kg **b.** 10 g **c.** 1 kg

14 Brian lives __________ from the school.

a. 5 km **b.** 5 m **c.** 5 cm

15 **Extended Response** Explain whether the measurement in the following sentence is appropriate or inappropriate: Suppose your friend says, "The pitcher holds 2 milliliters of water." Does this make sense? If not, what would make more sense?

____

____

____

Student Edition • page 114

You are going to build a scale model of this city for a museum of ancient astronomy. Each length in the model will be 0.01 as long as the actual length. The area of the square base of the Pyramid of the Sun is 46,440 square meters. What area will be covered by the pyramid on your scale model?

Paul solved the problem this way:

I started to Guess, Check, and Adjust.
First I figured out the length of the actual pyramid.

Guess	Check	Result
100	$100 \times 100 = 10,000$	too low
500	$500 \times 500 = 250,000$	too . . .

Think about Paul's strategy. Answer the following questions.

1. How will knowing the length of the actual pyramid help Paul solve the problem?

____

____

2. What would your next guess be if you were using Paul's strategy?

____

3. Would you use Paul's strategy? Why or why not?

____

____

Exploring Problem Solving

Name ______________________ Date ______________

Student Edition • page 115

Gina solved the problem another way:

I decided to Use Simpler Numbers, Make a Table, and Look for a Pattern. First, I will see how length and area are related. I'll start with a small square and see what happens as it grows.

Enlarged figure	Length compared to original length	Area compared to original area
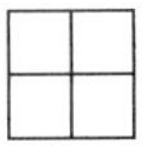	2 times the original	4 times the original
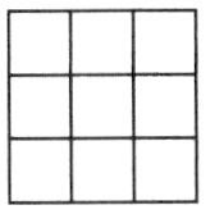	3 times the original	

Think about Gina's strategy, and then answer these questions.

4. What will Gina write about the area of the 3 × 3 square?

____

5. What do you think Gina will draw and write in the next row?

____

6. How would finding a pattern help Gina solve the problem?

____

____

7. Use any strategy you like to solve the problem. Why did you choose the strategy you did?

____

____

____

CHAPTER 3 Cumulative Review

Student Edition • page 116

Place Value Lesson 1.3

Count on or back. Write the missing numbers.

1. 53, 54, 55, ______, ______, ______, ______, ______, ______, ______, 63

2. 507, 506, 505, ______, ______, ______, ______, ______, ______, 498

3. 996; 997; 998; ______; ______; ______; ______; ______; 1,004

4. 9,996; 9,997; 9,998; ______; ______; ______; 10,002

Adding and Subtracting Decimals Lesson 3.4

Solve.

5. Jen has $25 to spend on books. The books cost $5.95 each.

   a. How many books can she buy? ______

   b. How much change will she get? ______

6. Steve rides his bicycle to and from school each day. The school is 2.2 miles from his house.

   a. How many miles does he ride in 1 day? ______

   b. How many miles does he ride in 5 days? ______

   c. How many miles does he ride in 10 days? ______

Cumulative Review

Name ______________________ Date ______________

Student Edition • pages 116–117

Arithmetic Laws Lesson 1.6

Use arithmetic laws to make computation easier.

7. $(45 \times 8) + (5 \times 8) =$ ________

8. $(5 \times 17 \times 4) =$ ________

9. $(16 \times 9) + (9 \times 4) =$ ________

10. $(100 \times 22 \times 0.01) =$ ________

Adding Multidigit Numbers Lesson 1.7

Add.

11. $\begin{array}{r} 27652 \\ +\ 384986 \\ \hline \end{array}$

12. $\begin{array}{r} 37373 \\ +\ 98989 \\ \hline \end{array}$

13. $\begin{array}{r} 896 \\ 432 \\ +\ 175 \\ \hline \end{array}$

Multiplying by a One-Digit Number Lesson 2.2

Multiply.

14. $\begin{array}{r} 659 \\ \times\ \ 9 \\ \hline \end{array}$

15. $\begin{array}{r} 747 \\ \times\ \ 8 \\ \hline \end{array}$

16. $\begin{array}{r} 694 \\ \times\ \ 7 \\ \hline \end{array}$

17. $\begin{array}{r} 876 \\ \times\ \ 4 \\ \hline \end{array}$

Cumulative Review

Student Edition • page 117

Interpreting Remainders **Lesson 2.6**

Solve.

18. There are 3 pizzas with 8 slices each that need to be divided equally among 7 friends. How many whole slices will each person get? If the remaining slices are divided equally, how much more would each person get?

____

____

19. There are 30 fans who need a ride to the football game. They have 7-passenger minivans and 5-passenger cars available to use. What is the minimum number of vehicles needed to transport everyone?

____

Applications Using Customary Measurement **Lesson 2.10**

Solve.

20. Seth has 4 wooden boards at home. Their measurements are 38 inches, 26 inches, and 3 feet. If he needs 24 feet of wood, how much more wood does Seth need to buy? _______________

Cumulative Review

Name ______________________ Date ____________

Student Edition • page 117

21. On June 10, 2007, Abe says he will be 10 years old in 15 months. What month and year will that be? In what year will he be 15?

____

____

Exponents Lesson 2.8

Evaluate.

22. $4^3 =$ ____________

23. $8^2 =$ ____________

24. $3^4 =$ ____________

25. $2^5 =$ ____________

Write in exponential form.

26. $7 \times 7 \times 7 \times 7 =$ ____________

27. $9 \times 9 \times 9 =$ ____________

28. $8 \times 8 =$ ____________

LESSON 3.9

Multiplying Decimals by Whole Numbers

Student Edition • page 120

Multiply. Check your answers to see whether they make sense.

1. $2.4 \times 5 =$ __________
2. $5 \times 2.4 =$ __________
3. $0.02 \times 173 =$ __________
4. $1.02 \times 173 =$ __________
5. $1.2 \times 173 =$ __________
6. $0.12 \times 173 =$ __________
7. $4 \times 0.25 =$ __________
8. $4 \times 2.5 =$ __________
9. $7 \times 0.25 =$ __________
10. $5 \times 0.2 =$ __________
11. $0.75 \times 8 =$ __________
12. $8 \times 7.5 =$ __________
13. $6 \times 54 =$ __________
14. $6 \times 5.4 =$ __________
15. $0.6 \times 54 =$ __________
16. $26 \times 4.2 =$ __________
17. $0.05 \times 20 =$ __________
18. $0.005 \times 20 =$ __________

LESSON 3.9 **Name** ______________________ **Date** ____________

Student Edition • **page 120**

19 1.05 × 10 = ____________

22 6.8 × 9 = ____________

20 10 × 1.5 = ____________

23 4.23 × 2 = ____________

21 9 × 6.08 = ____________

24 0.2 × 423 = ____________

Solve the following problems.

25 Mrs. Lundquist is making shelves from a board that is 5 meters long. Each shelf must be 1.45 meters long. Can she cut 4 shelves from the board? ____________

26 Suppose you must pay $0.05 in sales tax for each dollar that something costs. How much sales tax would you have to pay for something that costs $52? ____________

27 The Last Federal Trust Company pays $0.06 in interest for each dollar that you keep in a savings account for a year. If you keep $250 in a savings account for one year, how much interest will they pay you? ____________

28 **Extended Response** Mandy's father wants to cut 4 pieces of rope to make 2 tree swings in the backyard. Each piece of rope must be 6.5 feet long. He has a piece of rope that is 28 feet long. Does he have enough rope to make the 2 swings? Explain.

____

____

____

LESSON 3.9

Student Edition • page 121

Men's Outdoor Track and Field World Records

Distance	Time	Year	Runner(s)
100 m	9.78 sec	2002	Tim Montgomery, United States
200 m	19.32 sec	1996	Michael Johnson, United States
400 m	43.18 sec	1999	Michael Johnson, United States
800 m	1 min, 41.11 sec	1997	Wilson Kipketer, Denmark
1,000 m	2 min, 12.00 sec	1999	Noah Ngeny, Kenya
10,000 m	26 min, 20.31 sec	1996	Kenenisa Bekele, Ethiopia
4 × 100 m relay	37.40 sec	1992	United States Team
4 × 200 m relay	1 min, 18.68 sec	1994	United States Team

Use the chart above to answer the following questions.

29 Look at the world record for 100 meters.

a. How long would 200 meters take at this pace? ____________

b. How long would 400 meters take at this pace? ____________

30 **Extended Response** How do the records for 200 meters and 400 meters compare to your answers to Problem 29? What are some possible explanations for the differences?

____

____

____

Name ______________________________ **Date** ______________

Student Edition • **page 121**

31. In the 4 × 100-meter relay, 4 sprinters run 100 meters each. If members of the team ran their relay legs in 9.9 seconds, would they beat the world record? ____________

32. **Extended Response** If all the members of the 4 × 100-meter relay team ran at a pace equal to the world record speed for 100 meters, would they beat the record? Why do you think that is?

____

____

33. **Extended Response** In the 4 × 200-meter relay, 4 sprinters run 200 meters each. If all members of a relay team ran at a pace equal to the world record speed for 200 meters, would they beat the record? Why do you think that is?

____

____

34. How much longer is the world record time for 10,000 meters than 10 times the record for 1,000 meters? ____________

LESSON 3.10

Rounding and Approximating Numbers

Student Edition • page 123

Round each number.

1. 67 to the nearest 10 ____________
2. 209 to the nearest 10 ____________
3. 1,255 to the nearest 100 ____________
4. 1,500 to the nearest 1,000 ____________
5. 745 to the nearest 100 ____________
6. 2,561 to the nearest 10 ____________
7. 39,417 to the nearest 1,000 ____________
8. 25 to the nearest 10 ____________
9. 488,965 to the nearest 1,000 ____________
10. 6.8 to the nearest 1 ____________
11. 5.529 to the nearest 0.1 ____________
12. 0.0295 to the nearest 0.01 ____________
13. 7.5602 to the nearest 0.001 ____________
14. 900.77 to the nearest 0.1 ____________
15. 14.3843 to the nearest 0.01 ____________
16. 14.5 to the nearest 1 ____________
17. 0.3329 to the nearest 0.001 ____________
18. 17.76 to the nearest 1 ____________
19. 212.425 to the nearest 0.01 ____________
20. 52.0373 to the nearest 0.001 ____________

LESSON 3.10 **Name** ______________________ **Date** ____________

Student Edition • page 124

Discuss solutions to the following questions. Try to find solutions without doing calculations.

21. The Johnson family will vacation in a city that is 1,578 kilometers from where they live. They plan to spend 2 days driving and would like to drive about the same distance each day. How far should they drive the first day?

____

22. Mrs. Kamata has 29 test papers to correct. She knows that each paper will take about 20 minutes. About how long will it take her to correct all the papers? If she can work on the papers for 3 hours each day, how many days will it take her to finish?

____

____

23. **Extended Response** If Mark saves $1 a week, can he save $100 a year? If he saves $2 a week, can he save $100 a year? Explain why or why not.

____

____

24. **Extended Response** Holly gets an allowance of $4.50 each week. If she saves half her allowance each week, can she save $100 a year? $200 a year? Explain why or why not.

____

____

25. David wants to buy 15 small bags of candy for $1.98 each and a mask for $7.98. He has $35.07 with him.

   a. Will he have enough money? ____________

   b. How many bags of candy can he buy after he buys the mask? ____________

Student Edition • page 125

Solve the following problems without using a calculator or paper and pencil. Discuss your methods with others.

26. Grant measured a filing cabinet that was 91.5 centimeters wide. He wants to put as many filing cabinets as possible along the wall of a room that is 5 meters long. How many cabinets can fit along the wall?

____

27. Ms. Smith has measured the distance from home to work on her car's odometer. The distance is 7.9 miles.

    a. About how long is the round trip to work and back? About how far will she travel in a week if she drives to and from work 5 days a week and does not drive anywhere else? _______________

    b. Ms. Smith estimates that she gets about 25 miles to a gallon of gasoline, and her car's manual says the tank holds 16 gallons of gas. About how many miles can she drive on a full tank of gas?

    ____

    c. If Ms. Smith fills her tank just before going to work on Monday, about how many weeks can she drive before she needs gas again?

    ____

28. Audrey needs to buy 5 tomatoes for $0.79 each, a bag of flour for $1.49, and 3 gallons of milk for $2.29 each. If she has $15.00 in her wallet, does Audrey have enough money to buy everything she needs?

____

29. Kevin earns $23.50 a week delivering newspapers. About how much money does he earn in 15 weeks? _______________

30. Max wants to buy a portable stereo that costs $137.99. If he earns $5 an hour, about how many hours will he have to work to earn enough money to buy the stereo? _______________

LESSON 3.11

Name ______________________ Date ____________

Approximation Applications

Student Edition • page 126

In each exercise, two of the answers are clearly wrong and one is correct. Approximate to select the correct answers.

1. 47.968 + 4.952 = ____________

   a. 25.920
   b. 52.920
   c. 95.220

2. 63.313 − 36.392 = ____________

   a. 26.921
   b. 62.921
   c. 92.621

3. 51.6 × 284 = ____________

   a. 41,654.4
   b. 14,654.4
   c. 61,454.4

4. 55.55 − 19.99 = ____________

   a. 65.53
   b. 35.56
   c. 53.56

5. 5.280 + 6.820 = ____________

   a. 11.100
   b. 10.120
   c. 12.100

6. 965 × 1.01 = ____________

   a. 1,974.65
   b. 9,074.65
   c. 974.65

7. 255 × 2.13 = ____________

   a. 345.15
   b. 543.15
   c. 453.15

8. 56.301 − 19.654 = ____________

   a. 36.647
   b. 46.647
   c. 16.647

9. 1,019.09 + 9,091.01 = ____________

   a. 10,110.10
   b. 1,101.10
   c. 101,010.10

10. 5.2768 + 2.5022 = ____________

    a. 9.7770
    b. 7.7790
    c. 8.3770

11. 2.85 × 29 = ____________

    a. 682.50
    b. 32.85
    c. 82.65

12. 7,654.3 − 1,234.5 = ____________

    a. 5,419.8
    b. 6,419.8
    c. 7,419.8

LESSON 3.11

Student Edition • page 127

Solve each of the following problems by approximating.

13 The Green Thumb Nursery has 6 greenhouses. Each greenhouse has 5 benches. Each bench can hold 495 flowerpots. About how many flowerpots can be held in the Green Thumb's greenhouses? ______________

14 The Green Thumb Nursery sells about 1,500 plants each day. At the end of each day, new plants are brought in to replace the ones that were sold. About how many new plants are put in the greenhouses each day?

____

15 **Extended Response** Pedro had 497 football cards. Melissa said she had about 100 cards. Pedro bought all her cards for $3.50. About how many does Pedro have now? Explain how you arrived at your answer.

____

____

16 The Riverview Library has a total of 87,989 books. The librarian says that about 5,000 books are out on loan at any time. About how many books are in the library at any time? ______________

17 **Extended Response** If a family of 2 adults and 3 children goes to the movies, how much does the family spend on tickets if adult tickets cost $5.75 each and child tickets cost $3.25 each? ______________

18 The length of a garden is 34 feet, 3 inches, and the width is 29 feet, 9 inches. What is the total length of fence needed to go around the garden? ______________

LESSON 3.12

Name ______________________ Date ____________

Understanding Decimal Division Problems

Student Edition • page 129

Divide. Do not use remainders. All the exercises have exact decimal answers. Check your answers by multiplying (or adding if it is easier).

1. $5\overline{)6}$
2. $2\overline{)1}$
3. $4\overline{)2}$
4. $5\overline{)3}$
5. $4\overline{)5}$
6. $2\overline{)4.7}$
7. $4\overline{)5.16}$
8. $5\overline{)4}$
9. $8\overline{)9}$
10. $5\overline{)46}$

11. $8 \div 5 =$ ______
12. $8.4 \div 6 =$ ______
13. $10 \div 8 =$ ______
14. $9.9 \div 9 =$ ______
15. $7.3 \div 2 =$ ______
16. $35.8 \div 2 =$ ______
17. $56 \div 5 =$ ______
18. $15 \div 8 =$ ______
19. $2.4 \div 4 =$ ______
20. $24.1 \div 4 =$ ______

Solve the following problems. Write 0s in the dividend when you need to.

21. $1 \div 8 =$ ______
22. $3 \div 8 =$ ______
23. $1 \div 3 =$ ______
24. $2 \div 6 =$ ______

25. Answer the following questions about Problems 23 and 24.
    a. Were the answers exact after you wrote more 0s to the right of the dividend? ______
    b. Do you think the answers would ever be exact if you continued to write more 0s? ______

LESSON 3.12

Student Edition • pages 130–131

Solve the following problems. Check your answers by multiplying.

26 Josh needs to buy 20 cupcakes for a party. The cupcakes he wants come in packages of 8. How many packages does he need to buy? ______

27 Lydia, Inéz, and Latisha earned $17.50 altogether for shoveling snow. If they want to divide the money equally, how much should each person get?

______

28 Ricardo is cutting short wooden dowels from a long dowel that is 40 centimeters long. How many 6-centimeter dowels can he cut from the long dowel?

______

29 If a stack of 100 cards is 3 centimeters thick, how thick is each card?

______

30 Suppose Yoshi divides 18 paintbrushes equally among 5 friends.

How many paintbrushes will he have left? ______

31 Mark needs 14 folders for school. The folders come in packages of 3.

How many packages does he need to buy? ______

For Problems 32–36 you must divide 34 by 5. Read each problem, and then match the problem with its answer.

a. 6.80	**b.** 6 R4	**c.** 6	**d.** 7	**e.** $6\frac{4}{5}$

32 If 5 people can ride in a car, how many cars will be needed to take 34 people to a picnic? ______

LESSON 3.12 **Name** ______________________ **Date** __________

Student Edition • page 131

33 Mr. Jones can make 1 suit from 5 yards of material. How many suits can he make with 34 yards of material? ____________

34 Suppose 5 people went to lunch together. They agreed to split the bill among them equally. If the bill was exactly \$34, how much should each person pay?

____

35 The Robinson family uses 5 frozen dinners each day. If they have 34 frozen dinners in the freezer, how many days will the dinners last? ____________

36 Suppose 5 people agree to share 34 small rolls of candy equally. The rolls of candy have been cut so that they are easily divided into 5 equal parts. How much candy should each person get? ____________

Notice that the situation in Problem 37 affects what you do with the remainder.

37 **Extended Response** Can you think of any question for which the answer 6.8 might be a reasonable response to "What is 34 ÷ 5"?

____

____

Extended Response **Create your own division word problems for each of the following situations.**

38 The answer must be rounded down to the next whole number.

____

____

39 The answer should be divided to the hundredths place.

____

____

40 The answer should be given as a mixed number.

____

____

LESSON 3.13

Interpreting Quotients and Remainders

Student Edition • page 132

Divide. Do not use remainders. Round answers to the nearest hundredth when needed.

1. $2\overline{)1}$
2. $4\overline{)3}$
3. $7\overline{)6.44}$
4. $5\overline{)11.35}$
5. $3\overline{)46}$
6. $3\overline{)8.25}$
7. $2\overline{)6.28}$
8. $8\overline{)8.8}$
9. $8\overline{)74}$
10. $3\overline{)17}$
11. $4\overline{)37.6}$
12. $7\overline{)2.87}$
13. $9\overline{)21.33}$
14. $5\overline{)92.4}$
15. $7\overline{)43}$
16. $3\overline{)27.9}$
17. $3\overline{)28}$
18. $4\overline{)64.8}$
19. $4\overline{)63}$
20. $6\overline{)8.9}$

Name ______________________ Date ____________

Student Edition • page 133

Solve the following problems by using division. Make sure your answers make sense.

21. Kenji needs 50 buns for the class picnic. Buns come in packages of 8. How many packages does Kenji need to buy? ____________

22. Jeremy wants to bring oranges to share at the picnic. He decides that 100 oranges will be enough for everyone. If the oranges are sold in packages of 30, how many packages does he need to bring to the picnic? How many oranges will be left over? ____________

23. After the picnic, the class decided to play basketball. If 34 students are in the class, how many teams of 5 can play? ____________

24. Luis bought fruit for 9 students in his class. He spent $4.59 for the fruit. If each student shares the cost of the fruit equally, how much should each student pay? ____________

25. Miss Chang needs 57 bags of concrete for some work on the foundation of her house. The warehouse sells concrete in batches of 6 bags. How many batches must she buy? ____________

26. Brian and his 3 sisters want to divide the $487 they earned doing yard work over the summer. They did the same amount of work, so the money should be divided equally. How much should each person receive? ____________

27. Janis plans to set up a row of square tables placed end to end. Each table is 2 meters on a side. How many tables can fit across a room that is 11 meters long? ____________

28. Karen is cleaning her room and packing away some books to store in the closet. She fills square boxes that measure 3 feet on a side. How many boxes can fit along the back wall of a closet that is 8 feet long? ____________

29. Doug bought a birthday gift for his mother. His brother and sister told him they would help pay for the gift, which cost $26.25. If the 3 siblings share the cost of the gift equally, how much should each of them pay? ____________

30. Olivia has 9 DVDs and 14 CDs. She wants to divide them equally among herself and 4 friends. How many DVDs or CDs will each of Olivia's friends receive? ____________

LESSON 3.14

Decimals and Multiples of 10

Student Edition • page 134

Multiply or divide.

1. $79.6 \div 10 =$ ______
2. $79.6 \div 100 =$ ______
3. $0.796 \times 10{,}000 =$ ______
4. $8.35 \div 100 =$ ______
5. $0.835 \times 1{,}000 =$ ______
6. $83.5 \div 10 =$ ______
7. $10 \times 1.0540 =$ ______
8. $1.0540 \times 1{,}000 =$ ______
9. $105.40 \div 100 =$ ______

Solve the following problems.

10. **Extended Response** A 10-pound smoked ham sells for $29.84 at the deli. At this price, how much does 1 pound of smoked ham cost? Explain how you could solve the problem without doing any arithmetic.

______

______

______

11. Jasper, a truck driver, added 100 gallons of diesel fuel to his truck's gas tank. If the total cost of the diesel fuel was $225.70, how much does 1 gallon of diesel fuel cost? ______

Name ______________________ Date ____________

Student Edition • page 136

Divide. Give exact answers. Check your answers to see whether they make sense.

12. $9\overline{)63}$

13. $90\overline{)630}$

14. $900\overline{)6300}$

15. $6\overline{)54}$

16. $6\overline{)540}$

17. $40\overline{)124}$

18. $70\overline{)3752}$

19. $6\overline{)300}$

20. $800\overline{)5600}$

21. $60\overline{)480}$

22. $10\overline{)1600}$

23. $8\overline{)500}$

24. $70\overline{)3500}$

25. $20\overline{)8005}$

26. $40\overline{)156}$

Student Edition • page 137

Solve the following problems. Check to see that your answers make sense.

27. Mr. Ebert must pack 600 books in boxes. He can fit 30 books in each box. How many boxes will he need? ____________

28. **Extended Response** After making 10 equal deposits into her savings account, Cathy saved $555.00. If she made 10 equal deposits and recorded each of those deposits as $5.550, is she correct? Explain.

____

____

____

29. Suppose 30 players on the soccer team want to charter a bus to take them to see a championship game. The bus will cost $600.00.

a. How much should each player pay to cover the cost of the bus?

____

b. Suppose the bus costs $630.00. How much would each player pay?

____

Name ______________________ **Date** ____________

Student Edition • page 137

30 The 42 members of the Healthful Health Club are planning to march from Chicago, Illinois, to Washington, D.C. They want people to know that exercise is important. They know the distance is about 700 miles, and they have 60 days in which to complete the trip.

a. About how many miles must they walk each day? ____________

b. Can healthy adults walk that much in one day? ____________

31 Ms. Jones is part of a team that is putting up fences along a highway. The fencing comes in pieces that are 30 feet long.

a. How many pieces are needed for each mile? ____________

b. Ms. Jones and her work team can put up 4 pieces an hour. How many hours will it take to put up 1 mile of fence? ____________

c. Ms. Jones' team works 8 hours each day, but it takes about 30 minutes in the morning to set up and 30 minutes in the late afternoon to put things away. How many days will it take to put up 1 mile of fence?

____

32 Samuel needs to read a book that has about 600 pages for a class project. He has 10 days to read the book, and he can read about 30 pages in an hour. How many hours per day will Samuel need to read to finish the book?

____

LESSON 3.15

Applying Decimals

Student Edition • page 138

Solve **the following problems by using your addition, subtraction, multiplication, and division skills. You may want to draw pictures to help you solve some of the problems.**

1. Miss Echohawk wants to fence her yard on 3 sides. Her lot is square and measures 31.5 meters per side. How many meters of fencing does she need?

   ____

2. Miss Flores buys items in large quantities for a department store. She buys T-shirts in boxes of 50 shirts per box. A box costs $62.50. How much does each shirt cost the store? ______________

3. Kate runs a restaurant. She can buy a 50-kilogram bag of potatoes for $10.54 from the Farmer's Outlet. She can buy a 20-kilogram bag of potatoes from the Restaurant Supply Company for $5.21. Kate wants to buy 100 kilograms of potatoes. Which supplier gives her the better buy? ______________

4. Isaac bought 3 packages of pens at $1.35 a package and 2 packs of pencils at 63¢ a pack. How much did he pay altogether? ______________

5. Mr. Chu's class is going on a field trip to a museum. It will cost a total of $94.50 to charter a bus. The people going on the trip will equally share the cost.

   a. If 30 people are going, how much should each person pay? ______________

   b. If 20 people are going, how much should each person pay? ______________

Name ______________________ Date ____________

Student Edition • page 139

Solve the following problems.

Darryl and his classmates plan to sell hot dogs, peanuts, and soft drinks at their school's big baseball game. They plan to donate the money they earn to the local hospital. They know that last year 400 people came to the game and bought 190 cans of soda for $0.50 each and 110 hot dogs at $1.25 each.

6. How many dollars worth of soda and hot dogs were sold last year? ____________

They have to decide how many hot dogs and cans of soda to buy this year and how much to charge. The cost of 1 hot dog and a bun is $0.80. If they buy at least 125 hot dogs, they can get free mustard, relish, and napkins. They can buy cans of cola or lemon-lime soda for $0.25 each. They can return any unsold soda, but unsold hot dogs cannot be returned.

7. How many cans of soda should they buy? What other information would be useful for making a decision?

____

____

8. How many hot dogs should they buy? What other information would be useful for making a decision?

____

____

9. **Extended Response** Make a plan for how much of each item you would buy. Explain your reasons in the plan.

____

____

____

LESSON 3.15

Student Edition • **page 139**

Darryl and his friends will buy 125 hot dogs and buns, 150 cans of cola, and 100 cans of lemon-lime soda.

10 How much will they spend? ____________

They will charge $0.75 for each can of soda and $1.00 for each hot dog.

11 **Extended Response** Why do you think they plan to charge these amounts?

____

____

____

At the end of the game, they sold all 125 hot dogs and 78 cans of soda.

12 How much money did they collect? ____________

13 After cleaning up and returning the unsold soda, what was their profit?

____

14 **Extended Response** Do you think they should have bought more hot dogs? Charged more for the hot dogs? Why or why not?

____

____

____

15 **Extended Response** Do you think they charged the right amount for the soda? Could they have made more money by charging less? Why or why not?

____

____

____

Name ______________________ Date ______________

Student Edition • page 141

Behind the leaning slabs of stone, two spirals are carved in the rock face. The larger spiral has $9\frac{1}{2}$ turns in the shape of an ellipse that measures 34 centimeters by 41 centimeters.

On June 21, the first day of summer, a single dagger of sunlight pierces the center of the carved spiral. With each passing day, the light spear moves farther and farther to the right of center. On December 21, the first day of winter, two light daggers touch the outer edges of the carving.

Summer Solstice

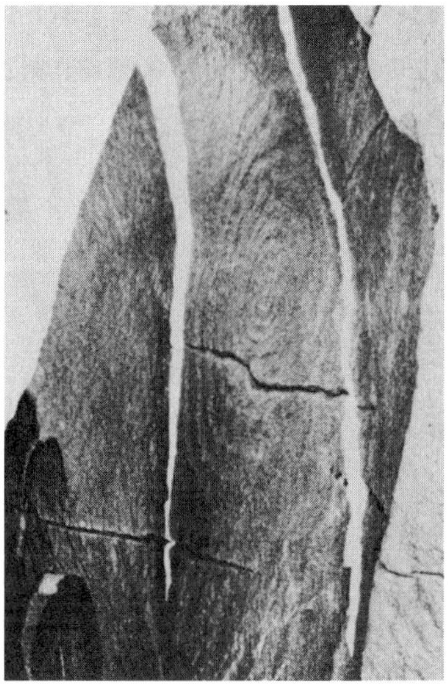

Winter Solstice

Solve these problems.

1. What is the shape and size of the larger of the two spirals carved onto the cliff? ______________

2. About how far is it between two consecutive loops on the large spiral? How did you estimate?

____

____

3. Estimate a different way by drawing a scale diagram.

4. Did your two estimates match? ______________

Student Edition • page 142

Imagine you are part of an archaeological team studying the sun dagger site. You are analyzing this sequence of photos from the site.

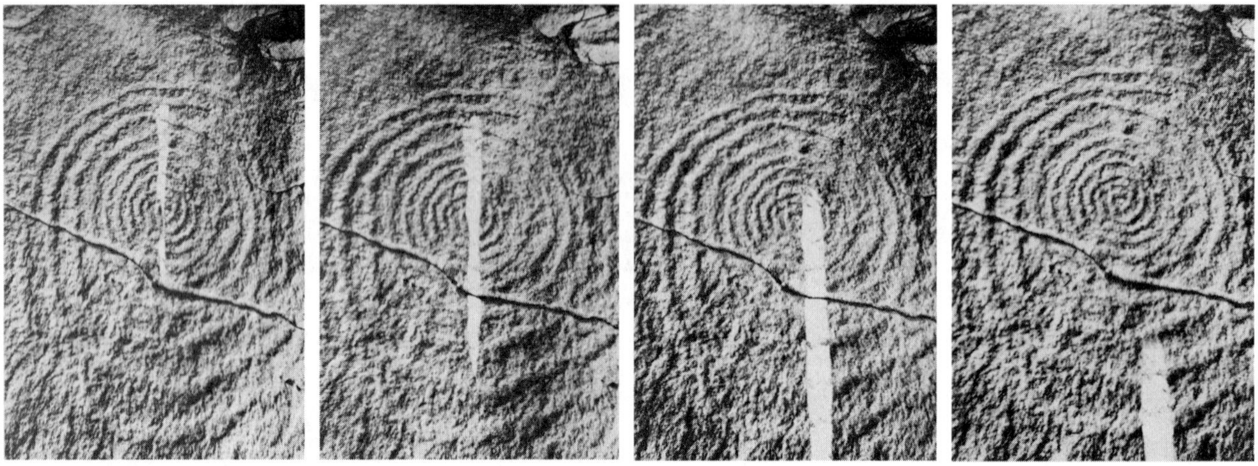

(a) 11:10:45 A.M. (b) 11:13:00 A.M. (c) 11:16:45 A.M. (d) 11:20:45 A.M.

Solve these problems.

5. On what date were these photos taken? How do you know?

6. At what average speed did the top of the dagger move from the time of photo b to the time of photo d?

7. At what speed did it move from the time of photo c to the time of photo d?

8. Four days before the first day of summer, the light dagger is 0.2 cm from the center of the spiral. Would that difference be noticeable?

9. Could you use the information from Problem 8 to predict how long it would be until the first day of summer?

Cumulative Review

Name ______________________ Date ______________

Student Edition • page 143

Subtracting Multidigit Numbers Lesson 1.8

Subtract.

1. $\begin{array}{r} 632417 \\ -\ 28691 \\ \hline \end{array}$

2. $\begin{array}{r} 3998743 \\ -\ 216043 \\ \hline \end{array}$

3. $\begin{array}{r} 75213 \\ -\ 69789 \\ \hline \end{array}$

4. $\begin{array}{r} 12035 \\ -\ 9648 \\ \hline \end{array}$

Multiplying by Two Whole Numbers Lesson 2.3

Multiply.

5. $\begin{array}{r} 654 \\ \times\ 74 \\ \hline \end{array}$

6. $\begin{array}{r} 781 \\ \times\ 44 \\ \hline \end{array}$

7. $\begin{array}{r} 9876 \\ \times\ 789 \\ \hline \end{array}$

8. $\begin{array}{r} 7342 \\ \times\ 89 \\ \hline \end{array}$

Dividing by a One-Digit Divisor Lesson 2.7

Find the missing digit.

9. 20______ ÷ 4 = 51

10. 2______17 ÷ 5 = 563 R2

11. 440 ÷ ______ = 88

12. 350 ÷ 4 = ______7 R2

13. 65 ÷ 9 = 7 R______

14. 160 ÷ ______ = 40

Cumulative Review

Student Edition • page 144

Prime and Composite Numbers Lesson 2.9

Find the prime number.

15. Which of the following numbers is prime?

Ⓐ 49 Ⓑ 399 Ⓒ 29 Ⓓ 99

16. Which of the following numbers is *not* prime?

Ⓐ 91 Ⓑ 79 Ⓒ 89 Ⓓ 107

Factor.

17. 120 ______________

18. 105 ______________

Comparing and Ordering Decimals Lesson 3.3

Write <, >, or = to make a true statement.

19. 5.43 __________ 5.34

20. 4.23 __________ 4.023

21. 4.09 __________ 4.12

22. 1.9 __________ 1.89

23. 9.34 __________ 9.340

24. 6.010 __________ 6.1001

Cumulative Review

Name ______________________ Date ____________

Student Edition • page 144

Applying Addition, Subtraction, and Multiplication **Lessons 1.9 and 2.4**

Driving Distances

From	To	Miles
home	store	5
home	gym	7
home	work	25
gym	store	10
gym	work	20
store	work	22

How many miles does Alex drive if he goes from

25. home to gym to work to home? ____________

26. home to work to store to home? ____________

27. home to gym to work to store to home? ____________

28. home to work and back 5 times in a week? ____________

29. work to gym to home 3 times in a week? ____________

30. If Alex pays $2 for a gallon of gas and buys 13 gallons, how much does he spend altogether? ____________

CHAPTER 3

Key Ideas Review

Student Edition • page 145

Solve for *n*.

1. $32.04 + n = 48.54$ ______

2. $12.025 - 3 = n$ ______

3. $7.95 \times 4 = n$ ______

4. $9.27 \div 6 = n$ ______

Complete each sentence with an appropriate metric unit.

kilometers	meters

5. Cory ran 100 ______ in 20.2 seconds.

6. Cory's mom drove 100 ______ in 3.5 hours.

Solve.

7. When converting within the metric system, we multiply and divide by powers of ten. What operation is being used when a decimal point moves one place value to the right? ______

8. What does it mean to round a number? Why do we round numbers?

______

______

9. Why is it important to align decimal points when adding or subtracting decimal numbers?

______

______

10. How does knowing that 36 divided by 4 equals 9 help to find the quotient to $3,600 \div 400$?

______

Chapter Review

Name _____ **Date** _____

Student Edition • page 146

Add or subtract. Lesson 3.1

❶	$\$35.37$	❷	$\$30.02$	❸	21.67	❹	14.79
	$+\ 1.99$		$-\ 17.11$		$-\ 19.98$		3.57
							$+\ 1.98$

Order these numbers from least to greatest. Lesson 3.2

❺ 0.5, 0.566, 0.56 _____

❻ 5.2, 4.99, 5.01 _____

Multiply or divide. Watch the signs. Lesson 3.6

❼ $199.77 \div 1{,}000$ = _____

❽ $0.8 \div 10$ = _____

❾ 100×3.45 = _____

❿ $1{,}000 \times 0.04$ = _____

⓫ $8.58 \times 1{,}000$ = _____

⓬ $0.0678 \div 100$ = _____

Find the missing measure. Lesson 3.7

⓭ 0.005 L = _____ mL

⓮ 200 mL = _____ L

⓯ 6.34 km = _____ m

⓰ 5,500 g = _____ kg

⓱ 52.34 cm = _____ mm

⓲ 26 m = _____ cm

Solve. Lesson 3.9

⓳ Luz bought 2 hand weights for $9.98 each. She must pay $1.25 in tax. What is the total cost of the 2 weights? _____

⓴ Timmy bought 7 pears that cost 28¢ each. If he gives the clerk a $5 bill, how much change should he get? _____

Chapter Review

Student Edition • page 147

Divide. Lesson 3.12

21. $8\overline{)18}$
22. $5\overline{)17}$
23. $9\overline{)8.19}$
24. $6\overline{)1083}$
25. $4\overline{)25}$
26. $8\overline{)21}$

Divide. Lesson 3.13

Round quotients with remainders to the nearest tenth.

27. $9\overline{)56.4}$
29. $8\overline{)4804}$
28. $7\overline{)81.33}$
30. $3\overline{)5.26}$

Multiply or divide. Lesson 3.14

31. $9{,}876 \times 100 =$ ______________
33. $362.18 \times 10{,}000 =$ ______________
32. $0.24 \times 1{,}000 =$ ______________
34. $6{,}789 \div 100 =$ ______________

Solve. Lesson 3.15

35. Chin bought books at the fair. One book was \$3.99, two were \$4.59 each, and three were \$4.79 each. How much did the books cost altogether?

____

36. Which is the better buy, 5 pounds of flour for \$2.59 or 2 pounds for \$1.10?

____

CHAPTER 3 Practice Test

Name ______________________ Date ______________

Student Edition • page 148

Write <, >, or = to make each statement true.

1. \$42.30 ________ \$42.03
2. 0.478 ________ 0.48
3. \$802.00 ________ \$802
4. 31.14 ________ 31.104

Find each answer.

5. 3.15×502
6. $740.28 + 32.62$
7. $877.5 \div 9$
8. 4210×0.8
9. $42.09 - 7.99$

Find the missing measure.

10. 5,050 mg = ____________ g
11. 2.5 kL = ____________ L

Solve.

12. About 34,500 people can fit into the baseball stadium. If 32,598 people are at the game, how many seats are empty? ____________

Practice Test

Student Edition • page 149

Choose the correct answer.

13. Which measure makes the most sense to complete this statement? The table is ______________ long.

Ⓐ 150 km Ⓑ 15 cm

Ⓒ 1.5 m Ⓓ 0.5 dm

14. Karen spent $12.50 on 5 candles. How much did each candle cost?

Ⓐ $2.08 Ⓑ $2.50

Ⓒ $3.13 Ⓓ $4.17

15. Which is 612.068 rounded to the nearest tenth?

Ⓐ 610 Ⓑ 612.0

Ⓒ 612.06 Ⓓ 612.1

16. Which has the numbers in order from least to greatest?

Ⓐ 1.11, 1.01, 1.111, 1.001

Ⓑ 1.01, 1.111, 1.001, 1.11

Ⓒ 1.001, 1.01, 1.111, 1.11

Ⓓ 1.001, 1.01, 1.11, 1.111

17. Dante has saved $216.68. He deposits $15.75 every week. How much money does he have in his savings account after 2 weeks of deposits?

Ⓐ $248.18 Ⓑ $232.43

Ⓒ $200.93 Ⓓ $185.18

18. It takes Betsy about 3.2 seconds to walk from her desk to the copy machine at work. If she goes to the copy machine 100 times in one day, how many seconds does she spend walking to the copy machine?

Ⓐ 3.2 Ⓑ 32

Ⓒ 320 Ⓓ 3,200

19. Divide.

$4\overline{)5.4}$

Ⓐ 1.3 Ⓑ 1.35

Ⓒ 1.4 Ⓓ 1.45

Practice Test

Name ______________________ **Date** ____________

Student Edition • **page 150**

20. Galen is 152.15 centimeters tall. His brother Isaac is 138.2 centimeters tall. How much taller is Galen than his brother?

Ⓐ 26.15 cm Ⓑ 24.95 cm

Ⓒ 13.95 cm Ⓓ 13.33 cm

21. $\begin{array}{r} 9.99 \\ \times \quad 26 \\ \hline \end{array}$

Ⓐ 259.74 Ⓑ 2,597.4

Ⓒ 25,974 Ⓓ 259,740

22. Which is the following amount written in dollars and cents?

Ⓐ \$2.04 Ⓑ \$2.14

Ⓒ \$2.24 Ⓓ \$2.54

23. $\begin{array}{r} 384 \\ \times \quad 78 \\ \hline \end{array}$

Ⓐ 29,952 Ⓑ 24,122

Ⓒ 5,760 Ⓓ 3,072

24. Which of the following is a prime number?

Ⓐ 4 Ⓑ 3

Ⓒ 9 Ⓓ 27

25. Which number is the greatest?

Ⓐ 55,500 Ⓑ 55,005

Ⓒ 55,505 Ⓓ 55,055

26. Divide.

$7\overline{)828}$

Ⓐ 118 R2 Ⓑ 118

Ⓒ 108 R2 Ⓓ 104

27. Solve for *n*.

$(25 \times 13) \times 4 = n$

Ⓐ $n = 8$ Ⓑ $n = 27$

Ⓒ $n = 36$ Ⓓ $n = 48$

28. 5^3 − ____________

Ⓐ 15 Ⓑ 25

Ⓒ 125 Ⓓ 625

Student Edition • page 151

Use the following information to answer Problem 29. Show your work.

29. The Fun Center Amusement Park charges $12.95 for an adult ticket and $7.95 for children under age 12.

a. How much would a family of 4 spend on tickets if 2 are adults, one child is 10, and the other child is 15? ______________

b. Each summer about 10,000 people go to the Fun Center. What is the maximum amount of money spent on tickets for 10,000 people?

____

c. A group of 20 or more people receives a discount on ticket prices. If 20 children under age 12 pay $130 total, what is the price for one ticket?

____

30. At the same amusement park, vendors sell club sandwiches and smoothies to the customers. If every person buys a smoothie for $0.75 and a club sandwich for $1.50, how much money is spent if 896 people go to the park in one week? ______________

Name ______________________________ Date ______________

Function Rules

Student Edition • page 153

Imagine you are in the command center on Earth, sending signals 200 million miles through space to control a rover on Mars. But the vehicle has malfunctioned and can no longer move on its own. And worse yet, it can only process two motion commands: *Go forward 50 meters* and *Go backward 30 meters.*

Straight ahead of the rover, 260 meters away, is a light-toned rock that you need to analyze. Your mission is to maneuver the rover to this rock.

Solve the following problems.

1. How can you command the rover to accomplish the mission?

____

____

____

2. What is the fewest number of commands you can give to accomplish the mission? Explain.

____

____

____

LESSON 4.1

Using Your Calculator

Student Edition • page 154

Use your calculator to answer the following questions.

1. Where does your calculator get the energy it needs to run? ____________

2. How can you get an error message on your calculator? ____________

____

3. Suppose you are adding 589, 793, and 864. You enter 589 + 793, but instead of 864, you see that you have entered 886. What is the quickest way to correct your mistake and find the correct answer? ____________

4. What is the least number greater than 0 that your calculator can display?

____

5. What is the greatest number that your calculator can display? ____________

6. If your calculator has a key marked y^x, what does that key do? ____________

____

7. How can you store a number in your calculator's memory? How can you delete a number from the memory? ____________

____

8. **Extended Response** A theater group sells 315 tickets to the Friday night performance and 287 tickets to the Saturday performance. Tickets cost $15 each. How much money did the group collect? How would you solve this problem by using your calculator? Explain your answer.

____

____

LESSON 4.1 **Name** ______________________ **Date** ____________

Student Edition • page 155

Race the Calculator

Complete the following exercises as a race between a group of your classmates with calculators and a group without them to see which is quicker. Those using the calculator must push every key.

9. $10 \times 73 = n$ __________
10. $100 \times 73 = n$ __________
11. $1{,}000 \times 73 = n$ __________
12. $10{,}000 \times 73 = n$ __________
13. $100{,}000 \times 73 = n$ __________
14. $10 + 73 = n$ __________
15. $100 + 73 = n$ __________
16. $1{,}000 + 73 = n$ __________
17. $10{,}000 + 73 = n$ __________
18. $100{,}000 + 73 = n$ __________
19. $800 + 500 = n$ __________
20. $800 - 500 = n$ __________
21. $8 \times 5 = n$ __________
22. $7{,}568 \times 0 = n$ __________
23. $84{,}595 \times 0 = n$ __________
24. $730 \div 10 = n$ __________
25. $7{,}300 \div 100 = n$ __________
26. $73{,}000 \div 1{,}000 = n$ __________

Evaluate the following expressions by using each of these rules:

A. Perform the operations in order from left to right.

B. Do multiplications and divisions first, and then additions and subtractions.

C. Do additions and subtractions first, and then multiplications and divisions.

27. $7 + 8 - 3 =$ __________
28. $2 \times 3 \times 4 =$ __________
29. $24 - 4 \div 4 =$ __________
30. $24 \div 4 - 4 =$ __________
31. $3 + 3 \times 3 =$ __________
32. $1 + 1 \times 1 =$ __________

LESSON 4.2

Using Number Patterns to Predict

Student Edition • page 156

Answer each of the following questions.

1 Turn on your calculator. Press [C·CE], then [+], then [2], then [=], and [=] again.

a. What does the display show? ____________

b. Press [=] again. What does the display show? ____________

c. What will the display show if you press [=] again? ____________

d. Keep pressing [=]. Each time, predict what the display will show before you press it. ____________

2 Start with 100. Now press [−], [7], [=], [=].

a. What do you get? ____________

b. Press [=] two times. What do you get each time? ____________

c. Keep pressing [=]. Before you press it each time, predict the number you will get. Eventually you will get down to the number 2. What happens next? ____________

LESSON 4.2 **Name** ______________________ **Date** ____________

Student Edition • page 157

Answer the following questions.

3 Extended Response **a.** If you start at 0 and add 3 each time, will you hit 10 exactly, or will you pass it? ____________

b. How do you know? Explain.

____

____

c. Do you have to do the addition to be sure? ____________

d. Which of these numbers will you hit? 12, 15, 16, 30 ____________

4 **a.** If you start at 0 and add 2 each time, will you hit 20? ____________

b. How do you know?

____

c. Do you have to do the addition to be sure? ____________

d. Which of these numbers will you hit? 100; 101; 200; 1,000 ____________

LESSON 4.2

Student Edition • page 157

5 **a.** Suppose you start at 5 and add 2 each time. Will you hit 15? ______________

b. How do you know? Explain.

____

____

c. Will you hit 20? ______________

d. How do you know? Explain.

____

____

6 **a.** If you start at 24 and subtract 3 each time, will you hit 0? ______________

b. How do you know?

____

c. Do you have to do the subtraction to be sure? ______________

Read the table below. Predict which numbers you will hit and circle them.

	If you start at this number	and you keep doing this	will you hit these numbers?		
7	0	add 4	**a.** 20	**b.** 100	**c.** 105
8	0	add 3	**a.** 90	**b.** 100	**c.** 1,000
9	8	add 5	**a.** 58	**b.** 143	**c.** 200
10	1,000	subtract 2	**a.** 0	**b.** 500	**c.** 470
11	1,000	subtract 3	**a.** 0	**b.** 1	**c.** 2
12	2,000	subtract 4	**a.** 1,000	**b.** 500	**c.** 10

LESSON 4.3

Name ______________________ Date ____________

Repeated Operations: Savings Plans

Student Edition • page 158

Elena and Kevin use different plans for spending and saving money. Look for patterns as you fill in the tables.

Savings Plan A

Elena earns $4.00 each week. Every week she puts half of the money in her savings account and spends the other half. Elena made a table to keep a record of her money.

Complete this table.

1.

Week	Amount Earned	Amount to Spend	Amount to Save	Amount in Savings
1	$4.00	$2.00	$2.00	$2.00
2	$4.00	$2.00	$2.00	$4.00
3	$4.00	$2.00	$2.00	$6.00
4	$4.00	$2.00	$2.00	
5	$4.00	$2.00	$2.00	
6	$4.00	$2.00	$2.00	
7				
8				
9				
10				

2. How much money will Elena have saved at the end of 20 weeks? ____________

3. How much money will she have saved at the end of 52 weeks? ____________

LESSON 4.3

Student Edition • page 159

Savings Plan B

Kevin also earns $4.00 a week; however, he uses a different savings plan. Every week he adds the $4.00 to the money he already has in his savings. He spends half of the total and leaves the other half in his savings. Whenever the division is not exact, he saves the extra cent. Kevin made a table to keep a record of his money.

Complete this table.

4.

Week	Amount at Beginning of Week	Amount Earned	Amount Before Spending	Amount to Spend	Amount Left in Savings
1	$0.00	$4.00	$4.00	$2.00	$2.00
2	$2.00	$4.00	$6.00	$3.00	$3.00
3	$3.00	$4.00	$7.00	$3.50	$3.50
4	$3.50	$4.00	$7.50	$3.75	
5	$3.75	$4.00	$7.75	$3.87	
6	$3.88	$4.00	$7.88	$3.94	
7	$3.94	$4.00	$7.94	$3.97	
8	$3.97	$4.00	$7.97	$3.98	
9		$4.00			
10		$4.00			

5. How much money will Kevin have saved at the end of 20 weeks? ______________

6. How much money will Kevin have saved at the end of 52 weeks? ______________

Name ______________________ Date ____________

Student Edition • page 159

7 Suppose Kevin spent the extra cent when the division was not exact. Create a new table that shows what his record would look like for the first 10 weeks.

Week	Amount at Beginning of Week	Amount Earned	Amount Before Spending	Amount to Spend	Amount Left in Savings
1					
2					
3					
4					
5					
6					
7					
8					
9					
10					

8 **Extended Response** Think about Elena's and Kevin's savings plans, and answer the following questions.

a. How different are Kevin's original table and the second table you made? Explain.

____

____

b. If Elena and Kevin were to compete to see who could save the most money during a year, who would win? Explain your answer.

____

____

LESSON 4.4

Function Machines

Student Edition • pages 160–161

These tables show some numbers that went into a +8 machine.
In each case, write the number that came out.

1 $x \rightarrow (+8) \rightarrow y$

In	Out
10	18
2	
5	

2 $x \rightarrow (+8) \rightarrow y$

In	Out
0	
100	
1,000	

These tables show some numbers that went in and came out of a +8 machine.
Complete the tables.

3 $x \rightarrow (+8) \rightarrow y$

x	y
8	16
	9
4	
	28

4 $x \rightarrow (+8) \rightarrow y$

x	y
22	
	31
	19
5	

 Name ____________________ **Date** ____________

Student Edition • page 161

Find the number that went in *(x)*, the number that came out *(y)*, or an addition rule that each function machine could be using.

5. x → (+6) → 13 ____________

7. 10 → (?) → 100 ____________

6. 5 → (+8) → y ____________

8. y → (+18) → 5 ____________

9. **Extended Response** A sculptor requests an additional 200 pounds of sand to complete his sand sculpture. The next day, he receives 12 buckets, each containing 28 pounds of sand. How can you tell that the sculptor has too much sand without working the problem? Explain.

____

____

____

____

____

____

CHAPTER 4 Exploring Problem Solving

Student Edition • pages 162–163

Imagine you are controlling a rover on the surface of one of Saturn's moons. At 4:17 P.M., you send a signal that commands the rover to start moving toward its target 38 meters away. At 7:53 P.M., you receive a signal from the craft telling you that it has reached its target. You know it takes 67 minutes for a signal to travel one way between the rover and Earth. You want to know how long the rover took to travel those 38 meters.

Juana decided to solve the problem this way:

I Drew a Diagram and Worked Backward.

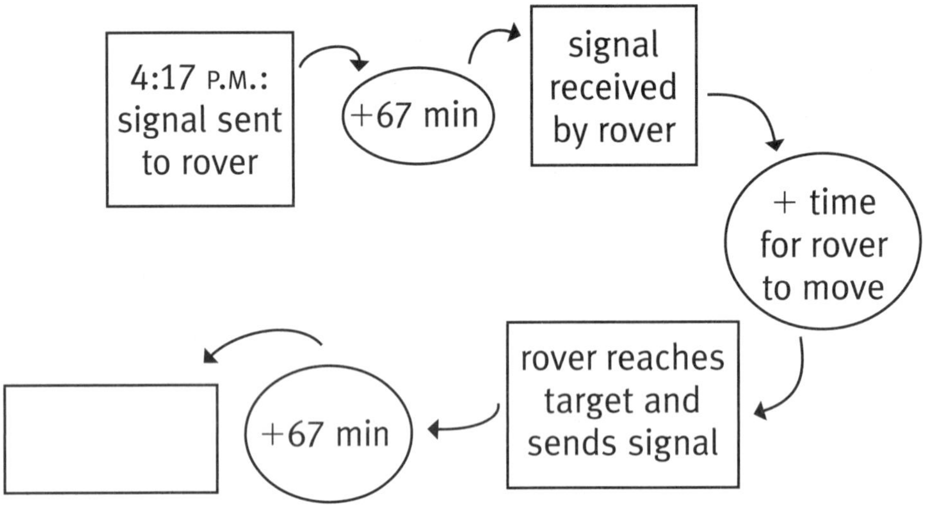

Think about Juana's strategy. Answer the following questions.

1. What do you think Juana will write in the last box? ______________

2. What time was it at the command center when the rover received your signal to start moving? ______________

3. How can Juana work backward to find how long it took the rover to move to the target?

____

____

Name ______________________ Date ____________

Student Edition • page 163

Raj solved the problem in a different way.

I Wrote an Equation.

Total time	=	Time for signal to travel both ways	+	Time for rover to move to target

Think about Raj's strategy. Answer the following questions.

4 Does Raj's equation make sense? Why or why not?

____

____

5 How can Raj figure out the total time?

____

____

Student Edition • **page 163**

6. How can Raj figure out the time for the signal to travel both ways?

____

____

7. Finish solving the problem. Use Juana's strategy, Raj's strategy, or a strategy of your own.

____

8. What strategy did you use? Why?

____

____

9. Was the rover's average speed greater than or less than 0.1 kilometer per hour? Explain.

____

____

CHAPTER 4 Cumulative Review

Name ______________________________ Date ______________

Student Edition • page 164

Multiplying Any Two Whole Numbers Lesson 2.3

Multiply.

1. 265×3
2. 84×35
3. 300×52
4. 175×25
5. 896×7
6. 42×53
7. 375×120
8. 798×114

Dividing by a One-Digit Divisor Lesson 2.7

Divide.

9. $7\overline{)56}$
10. $9\overline{)108}$
11. $8\overline{)560}$
12. $8\overline{)384}$
13. $6\overline{)6565}$
14. $5\overline{)4500}$
15. $3\overline{)7024}$
16. $8\overline{)5496}$

Cumulative Review

Student Edition • pages 164–165

Prime and Composite Numbers Lesson 2.9

For each of the following numbers, write *P* if the number is prime. If it is composite, write the number in factored form.

17. 41 ______
18. 79 ______
19. 87 ______
20. 209 ______
21. 300 ______
22. 101 ______
23. 195 ______
24. 238 ______

Applications Using Customary Measurements Lesson 2.10

Solve.

25. A table has dimensions of $5\frac{1}{2}$ feet by 18 inches. What is the perimeter?

______

26. A quart container of water is used to fill a pint bottle and an 8-ounce measuring cup. How much water is left in the container?

______

Cumulative Review

Name ______________________ Date ______________

Student Edition • page 165

27 A fast runner can run a 1-mile race in about 4 minutes. About how long should it take that runner to run a 440-yard race? (Hint: There are 5,280 feet in 1 mile.)

a. 75 seconds

b. 2 minutes

c. 55 seconds

d. 20 seconds

28 How many 10-ounce glasses can a half-gallon bottle of milk fill?

a. 6

b. 7

c. 8

d. 9

29 What is the area of a tray that is 1 foot 5 inches long and 6 inches wide?

____

30 How many ounces are in 3 pounds of steak?

a. 27

b. 36

c. 54

d. 48

LESSON 4.5

Multiplication Function Rules

Student Edition • page 166

Find a multiplication rule in each case.

Miss Swensen pushed:		The display showed:	
1. 3, =	→	18.	______
2. 1, 5, =	→	30.	______
3. 1, =	→	75.	______
4. 1, 0, 0, =	→	1,100.	______
5. 5, =	→	25.	______
6. 1, 7, =	→	51.	______
7. 2, 5, =	→	75.	______
8. 2, =	→	100.	______
9. 2, =	→	102.	______

 Name ______________________ Date ____________

Student Edition • page 167

Complete each table.

10. $x \xrightarrow{\times 7} y$

in	out
5	
9	
8	
6	

11. $x \xrightarrow{\times 8} y$

in	out
4	
	80
	56
	72

12. $x \xrightarrow{\times 9} y$

in	out
	81
6	
	45
	36

13. $x \xrightarrow{\times 5} y$

in	out
4	
	30
	40
10	

14. $x \xrightarrow{\times 3} y$

in	out
0	
	9
6	
	27

15. $x \rightarrow \bigcirc \rightarrow y$

in	out
0	0
3	18
6	36
9	54

The rule is ____________.

16. **Extended Response** Irial put 3 into a function machine, which then produced 12. She said the rule has to be $\times 4$ because $4 \times 3 = 12$. Paul disagreed and said there is another rule that could result in the machine giving 12 when 3 is put into it. What function could Paul be thinking of? Could Irial and Paul both be correct? How could they find out? Explain.

____

____

LESSON 4.6

Finding Function Rules

Student Edition • page 168

Find an addition or multiplication function rule that works for both pairs of numbers.

1. 10 → ? → 30 ____________
   20 → ? → 40

2. 10 → ? → 30 ____________
   20 → ? → 60

3. 0 → ? → 0 ____________
   7 → ? → 56

4. 0 → ? → 0 ____________
   7 → ? → 7

Find the addition or multiplication rule that the calculator is using.

5. [2], [=] → 10.
   [1], [=] → 5.

   ____

6. [1], [0], [=] → 30.
   [2], [0], [=] → 40.

   ____

7. [1], [0], [=] → 37.
   [0], [=] → 27.

   ____

8. **Extended Response** For which of Problems 5–7 could you have determined the function rule from only one of the pairs of numbers given? Why?

____

____

LESSON 4.7

Name ______________________ Date ____________

Subtraction Rules and Negative Numbers

Student Edition • page 170

Find the subtraction rule in each case.

Miss Swensen pushed:		The display showed:	
1. 3, 7, =	→	31.	________
2. 1, 2, =	→	0.	________
3. 1, 0, 7, =	→	50.	________
4. 5, 8, =	→	57.	________
5. 4, 9, =	→	28.	________
6. 2, 4, =	→	3.	________
7. 1, 0, =	→	2.	________
8. 1, 0, =	→	1.	________
9. 1, 0, =	→	0.	________
10. 1, 0, =	→	–1.	________

LESSON 4.7

Student Edition • page 172

Complete the following tables.

11

Temperature Before Change	Temperature Change	Temperature After Change
10°C	up 5°	
−5°C (5° below 0°C)	down 10°	
−15°C (15° below 0°C)	up 15°	
5°C	down 10°	

Ahmed is scuba diving 20 feet below sea level. He goes down another 15 feet. He is now swimming 35 feet below sea level.

12

Ahmed's Depth	Movement	Ahmed's New Depth
−20 feet	down 5 feet	
−10 feet	up 5 feet	
−15 feet	down 10 feet	
−25 feet	up 20 feet	

Name ______________________ Date ____________

Student Edition • page 173

Add or subtract. Do not use a calculator. Watch for negative numbers.

13. 50 + 10 = ________
14. (−25) + 25 = ________
15. 0 − 15 = ________
16. 15 + 15 = ________
17. 60 − 50 = ________
18. 0 + 10 = ________
19. (−3) + 4 = ________
20. (−6) + 5 = ________
21. 10 + 5 = ________
22. 0 − 10 = ________
23. (−2) + 1 = ________
24. 9 − 12 = ________
25. 15 − 20 = ________
26. 2 − 4 = ________
27. 4 − 6 = ________

Add or subtract. Watch for negative numbers.

28. 10 − 20 = ________
29. (−5) + 10 = ________
30. (−5) − 20 = ________
31. Now use your calculator to do Exercises 28–30 again. See whether the calculator gives the correct answers.

32. **Extended Response** Mr. Marks had $375 in his checking account. He wrote two checks, one for $250 and the other for $320. Then he deposited $120 in his account. What is his account balance now? Explain.

____

____

____

LESSON 4.8

Adding and Subtracting Integers

Student Edition • pages 174–175

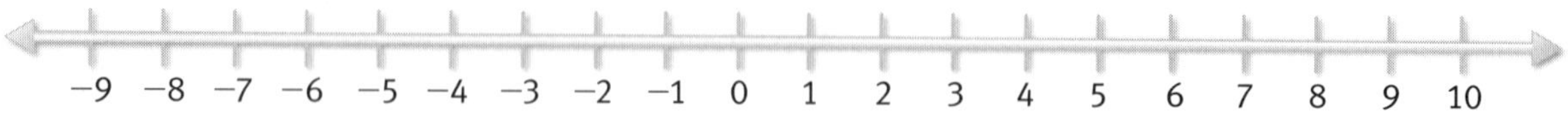

Answer the following questions by using a number line.

1. If you start at 2 and subtract 3 (move 3 places to the left), where will you be?

   $2 - 3 =$ ____________

   If you start at -1 and add 3, where will you be? $-1 + 3 =$ ____________

2. If you start at 0 and move left 3 places, and then move left 2 more places, where will you be? You have added negative 3 and negative 2.

   $(-3) + (-2) =$ ____________

3. You know that subtraction is the inverse of addition; subtraction "undoes" addition. So, if $4 + 5 = 9$, then $9 - 5 = 4$. Therefore, if $-5 + 2 = -3$, what is $-3 - (+2)$? ____________

4. What is $(-5) - (-2)$? ____________

   What can you add to -2 to get -5? ____________

   Would you have gotten the same answer by adding 2 to -5? ____________

5. What is $-6 + 9$? ____________

Complete the following sentences by indicating whether the answer is *positive* or *negative*. These completed sentences may help you when doing arithmetic with integers. Notice the relation of the absolute values in each exercise and answer.

6. If you subtract a positive number from a smaller positive number, the answer is ____________.

   For example, $2 - 10 = -8$. Notice that the distance on the number line from -8 to 2 is 10.

7. If you add a negative number to another negative number, the answer is ____________.

LESSON 4.8

Name ______________________ Date __________

Student Edition • page 175

8. If you subtract a negative number from a negative number with a smaller absolute value, the answer is ______________.

9. If you subtract a negative number from a negative number with a greater absolute value, the answer is ______________.

10. If you subtract a negative number from a positive number, the answer is ______________.

11. If you add a negative number to a positive number with a smaller absolute value, the answer is ______________.

12. If you add a negative number to a positive number with a greater absolute value, the answer is ______________.

Complete each exercise.

13. $(-7) + (-8) =$ ______________

14. $(-7) - (-8) =$ ______________

15. $7 + 8 =$ ______________

16. $7 - 8 =$ ______________

17. $|-5| =$ ______________

18. $| \ 3| \quad | \ 5| =$ ______________

19. $|3| - |-5| =$ ______________

20. $|-3| + |-5| =$ ______________

21. $|-3| + |5| =$ ______________

22. $(8) + 0 =$ ______________

23. $(-8) - 0 =$ ______________

24. $0 + 8 =$ ______________

25. $0 - (-8) =$ ______________

26. $(\ 473) \quad (\ 473) =$ ______________

27. $(-473) + (-473) =$ ______________

28. **Extended Response** Ana's family has 9 pairs of shoes that they no longer wear. Her father donated 11 pairs to a homeless shelter. How many pairs of shoes do they have left? Explain.

____

____

LESSON 4.9

Multiplying and Dividing Integers

Student Edition • page 177

Complete the following exercises. Watch the signs.

1. $-7 \times 4 =$ ______
2. $-7 \times (-4) =$ ______
3. $4 \times (-7) =$ ______
4. $8 \div (-2) =$ ______
5. $-8 \div (-2) =$ ______
6. $-8 \div 2 =$ ______
7. $5 + (-12) =$ ______
8. $-5 + 12 =$ ______
9. $-17 + (-8) =$ ______
10. $-17 - 8 =$ ______
11. $9 \times (-9) =$ ______
12. $-81 \div 9 =$ ______

13. In golf, players count the number of strokes they take to get the ball in the hole. "Par" is a number of strokes that seems reasonable to officials. If a player has a score below par, it is a good score. At the end of the third day of a tournament, Tiger Woods had a three-day total of 11 under par (−11). His score on the third day was 3 under par (−3). What was his score at the beginning of the third day? ______

14. Early one winter morning, the thermometer read −16° F. By late afternoon, the temperature had risen by 12°. What was the temperature then? What did you have to do to find the answer? ______

______

15. Cecilia has a new cell phone plan that allows 60 minutes of free long distance time. She talks on Wednesday for 11 minutes, on Friday for 7 minutes, and on Sunday for 23 minutes. Does she have enough minutes left for a 10-minute phone conversation, or will she exceed her time limit? If she has enough minutes, how many will she have left after the conversation? ______

______

16. **Extended Response** A group of friends set up a lemonade stand one hot summer day. They spent \$7 on lemonade mix, \$3 on paper cups, \$4 on a pitcher, and \$2 on ice. Over the first weekend, they had sales of \$14. Did they make a profit, or did they lose money? Explain.

______

LESSON 4.10

Name ______________________ Date ____________

Patterns

Student Edition • page 178

Describe each pattern in your own words.

1. 36   28   20   12   4   −4   −12   −20

____

2. 18   54   162   486   1,458   4,374

____

3. 

____

4. 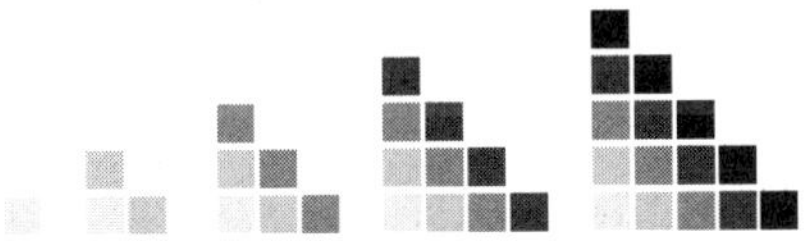

____

5. 

____

Student Edition • page 179

Write or draw the missing shapes or numbers of the pattern in each blank. Then tell what the pattern is.

6. 

____

7. 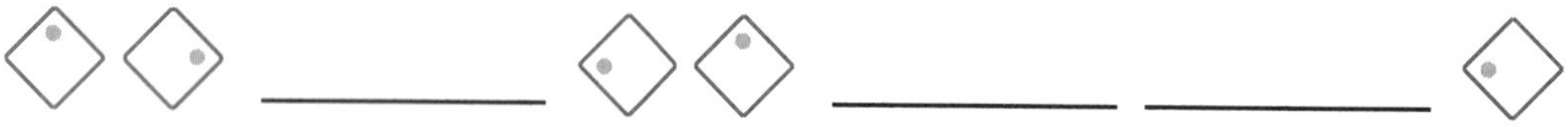

____

8. −19, −14, −9, ______, ______, ______, ______, 16

____

9. 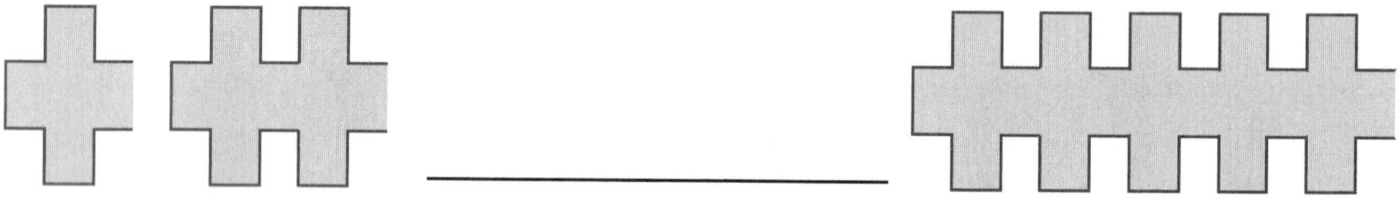

____

Name ______________________ Date ____________

Student Edition • page 179

10. −72, −24, __________, −2.7, −0.9, __________, __________, −0.03

____

11. Yenfen put the number 5 into a function machine and got 9. Cory took the 9 and put it into a second function machine, and 7 came out. Yenfen put −2 into her function machine and got 2, and when Cory put 2 into his machine, he got 0. What pattern was being used?

____

12. **Extended Response** Write or draw a sequence that uses a particular pattern. Then find a partner. Describe your pattern but do not let your partner see it; have him or her draw, write, or act out that pattern. Then have your partner describe his or her pattern so you can draw it, write it, or act it out.

Student Edition • page 180

Where No Spacecraft Has Gone Before

The space probe *Huygens* made history as it survived its landing on Saturn's largest moon. After a seven-year voyage in space, piggybacked on the *Cassini* spacecraft, the cone-shaped *Huygens* ejected from its mother ship, smashed into Titan's dense atmosphere, and parachuted safely to the surface. Sixty-seven minutes later, its faint signals reached Earth, setting off a long-awaited celebration in mission control.

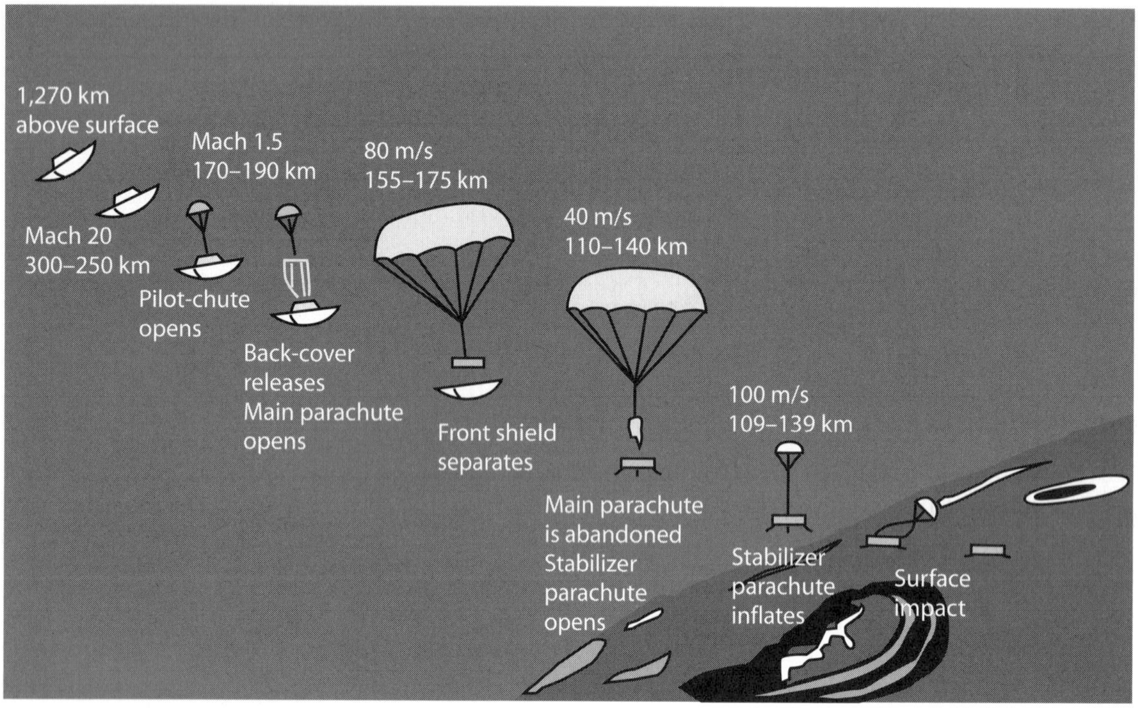

Huygens's descent

Mach 2.0 means "two times the speed of sound." What do you think *Mach 1.5* means? ____________________

Name ______________________ Date ______________

Student Edition • page 181

As it sped through the upper atmosphere of Titan, the *Huygens* craft had to withstand extreme temperatures. When its main parachute opened, the probe had slowed down enough to safely discard its heat shield, enabling its electronic sensors to work.

Each detail of the descent was carefully planned. This time line shows just a few of the hundreds of steps necessary for a successful landing.

Scheduled Time Line of Events for *Huygens's* Descent

Time (compared to time of entry)	Event
−20d 07h	*Huygens* probe separates from Orbiter
−07d 00h	Probe relay critical sequence begins
−02h 40m	Set Solid State Recorder pointers for probe recording
−02h 28m	Transition to thruster control for relay
−02h 16m	Turn on probe receivers
−00h 22m	Probe turns transmitters on; Low power mode
00h 00m	Probe reaches entry altitude (1,270 km)
+00h 03m	Pilot chute deployed at 170–190 km altitude
+00h 04m	Probe begins transmission to Orbiter; Release front shield
+00h 19m	Main parachute separation; Deploy stabilizer chute; 110–140 km altitude
+00h 36m	Surface proximity sensor activated at 60 km altitude
+02h 21m	Surface impact; End descent phase

Solve the following problems. Use the information in the timetable and the descent diagram.

1. How long were the probe's transmitters turned on before they began transmitting to the Orbiter? ______________

2. How long after *Huygens* separated from the Orbiter were its receivers turned on? ______________

Student Edition • pages 181–182

3. How long had the probe been separated from the Orbiter when it hit the surface of Titan? ______________

4. How long did it take the probe to slow down from $1\frac{1}{2}$ times the speed of sound (about 331 meters per second) to about 80 meters per second? ______________

Imagine you are planning a mission that will send a spacecraft past Saturn and beyond Pluto. The table shows what the temperature of your spacecraft will be at different distances from the sun.

Distance from sun (millions of miles)	Temperature (K)
100	300
200	212
400	150
800	106
1,600	

Work in groups. Give your spacecraft a name. Then discuss and solve the following problems.

5. If you add 273 to convert from degrees Celsius to Kelvin, what should you do to convert from Kelvin to degrees Celsius? ______________

____

6. What will be the temperature of your craft in degrees Celsius when it is 200 million miles from the sun? ______________

7. What will be the temperature of your craft in Kelvin when it is 1,600,000,000 miles from the sun? (Hint: You might look for a pattern.)

____

8. What is your answer to Problem 7 in degrees Celsius? ______________

Cumulative Review

Name ______________________ Date ______________

Student Edition • page 183

Adding and Subtracting Decimals **Lesson 3.4**

Solve.

Lunch Menu

Sandwich	Side	Drink
Hamburger $1.99	Fries $0.89	Milk $0.59
Chicken $2.69	Beans $0.79	Lemonade $1.09
Fish $2.99	Cole slaw $0.59	Juice $0.79

1. Colleen has $5 for lunch. Can she afford to buy chicken, beans, and lemonade? ______________

2. Shenita has $4. She wants fish, fries, and juice. Can she afford those? If not, does Colleen have enough change to loan her? ______________

3. Shenita really wants the fish, but can she buy a side and drink too? ______________

4. How much is the cheapest combo of sandwich, side, and drink? ______________

5. How much is the most expensive combo of sandwich, side, and drink? ______________

Cumulative Review

Student Edition • page 183

Comparing and Ordering Decimals Lesson 3.3

Write these numbers in order from least to greatest.

6. 9.16, 9.3, 9.19 ______

7. 3.027, 3.27, 3.0272 ______

8. 3.888, 3.88, 3.088 ______

9. 0.5, 2.1, 0.07 ______

10. 3.23, 3.3, 3.33 ______

Multiplying and Dividing Decimals by Powers of 10 Lesson 3.6

Multiply or divide. Watch the signs.

11. $88.41 \times 1{,}000 =$ ______

12. $244.03 \div 100 =$ ______

13. $357.76 \div 1{,}000 =$ ______

14. $0.07 \div 10 =$ ______

15. $0.7 \div 100 =$ ______

16. $3{,}000 \times 0.01 =$ ______

Cumulative Review

Name ______________________ Date ____________

Student Edition • page 184

Order and Parentheses Lesson 1.5

Solve for *n*.

17 $6 \times (5 + 2) = n$ ____________

18 $(6 \times 5) + 2 = n$ ____________

19 $5 + (8 \times 7) = n$ ____________

20 $(9 + 1) \times (5 - 3) = n$ ____________

21 $24 \div (4 + 3 + 1) = n$ ____________

22 $(2 + 4) \div (13 - 7) = n$ ____________

Interpreting Quotients and Remainders Lesson 3.13

Solve.

23 A camp counselor plans to have 2 hot dog buns and 2 hot dogs for each of the 25 campers attending a cookout. If hot dogs come in packages of 10 and buns come in packages of 8, how many packages of hot dogs and buns are needed? ____________

24 Which is the better buy, 8 pounds of dog food for $14.40 or 9 pounds for $15.40? ____________

Cumulative Review

Student Edition • **page 184**

25 Twenty-five students want to divide into 6-person dodgeball teams. How many more students are needed to form an even number of teams?

____

26 Four boys want to share 14 cookies. How many should each one get?

____

Repeated Operations: Savings Plans **Lesson 4.3**

Carlos began the year with $40 and saves $9 each week toward his goal of $500. Lilla began the year with $65 and saves $4 each week toward her goal of $300.

27 About how many months will it take for Carlos to reach his goal? _______________

28 About how many months will it take for Lilla to reach her goal? _______________

29 If Carlos continues saving at the same rate, will he have $900 in 24 months? _______________

30 If Lilla continues saving at the same rate, will she have $500 in 24 months? _______________

CHAPTER 4

Key Ideas Review

Name ______________________ Date ____________

Student Edition • page 185

Use the calendar to answer the questions.

Shane's mom labels his calendar so he knows what is taking place each day.

☼ = Shane has a football game.

■ = Shane helps with dinner.

▲ = Shane cleans his room.

SUN	MON	TUE	WED	THU	FRI	SAT
	1 ■	2	3 ■	4 ▲	5 ■	6 ☼
7 ■	8 ▲	9 ■	10	11 ■	12 ▲	13 ■☼
14	15 ■	16 ▲	17 ■	18	19 ■	20 ☼▲

Describe a pattern for the following symbols.

1. ☼ ______________________
2. ■ ______________________
3. ▲ ______________________
4. If this month has 31 days, what symbol will appear on the 28th day?

   ____

5. Which event occurs most frequently throughout the month? ____________

Solve the following problems.

6. Using the constant function on a calculator, start with -3 and add 2. At what point will you reach the first multiple of 3? ____________
7. Takara entered $3 + 6 \times 4$ on a calculator and got an answer of 27. How is this possible?

   ____

   ____

8. Explain how to multiply and divide integers.

   ____

   ____

CHAPTER 4

Chapter Review

Student Edition • page 186

Lesson 4.2

	If you start at this number	and you keep doing this	will you hit these numbers?
1	5	add 2	**a.** 100 ____ **b.** 105 ____ **c.** 150 ____
2	3	add 3	**a.** 10 ____ **b.** 45 ____ **c.** 75 ____
3	1,000	subtract 4	**a.** 500 ____ **b.** 100 ____ **c.** 10 ____

Lesson 4.3

4. Maddie is saving her allowance to buy a jacket that costs $60. She normally receives $3 per week, but if she does additional chores she can earn an extra $2 per week. How much sooner can she purchase the jacket if she does extra chores every week? Explain.

____

5. Maddie decides to do the extra chores each week, but wants to spend $1 per week on snacks. How long will it be before she will have enough to buy the jacket? ____________

In each problem, find the number that went in *(x)*, the number that came out *(y)*, or an addition rule that the function machine could be using. **Lesson 4.4**

6. 7 → (+11) → *y* ____________

7. *x* → (+9) → 13 ____________

8. 5 → (?) → 17 ____________

Chapter Review

Name ______________________ **Date** ______________

Student Edition • pages 186–187

9 5 → (+7) → y ______________

10 11 → (+12) → y ______________

11 5 → (+14) → y ______________

Find a function rule that works for both pairs of numbers for each function. **Lessons 4.5–4.6**

12 12 → (?) → 18 18 → (?) → 24 ______________

13 5 → (?) → 15 8 → (?) → 24 ______________

14 17 → (?) → 9 16 → (?) → 8 ______________

Chapter Review

Student Edition • page 187

Solve. Lessons 4.7–4.9

15. $10 - 15 =$ ______
16. $-8 \times 9 =$ ______
17. $|7| - |-9| =$ ______
18. $-8 + 8 =$ ______
19. $6 - (-7) =$ ______
20. $-7 \times (-5) =$ ______
21. $-10 \div 5 =$ ______
22. $-10 \div |-5| =$ ______
23. $-56 \div -8 =$ ______
24. Alexis received $50 for her birthday. She bought 3 pairs of socks for $3 each and 1 hat. She had $21 left. How much did the hat cost? ______
25. If the temperature is −9° C and goes up 5°, what will the new temperature be? ______
26. If the temperature is −6° C and goes up 10°, what will the new temperature be? ______

Find the pattern and fill in the missing numbers. Lesson 4.10

27. 5, 8, 11, ______, 17, 20, ______, ______, 29

    The pattern is ______.

28. 20, ______, 8, 2, ______, −10, ______, −22, −28

    The pattern is ______.

CHAPTER 4 Practice Test

Name ______________________________ Date ______________

Student Edition • page 188

Find the unknown for each problem. It may be the number that went in *(x)*, the number that came out *(y)*, or the addition rule that the function machine is using.

1. 8 → (+5) → y ________

2. x → (+9) → 21 ________

3. 7 → (?) → 17 ________

4. 22 → (+6) → y ________

Complete each table by using the given function rule.

5. $x \xrightarrow{\times 7} y$

in	out
2	
4	
6	
8	

6. $x \xrightarrow{\times 5} y$

in	out
	5
	30
8	
	100

7. $x \xrightarrow{\times 9} y$

in	out
2	
	36
9	
	99

Solve.

8. $3 - 7 =$ ____________

9. $(-4) + 6 =$ ____________

10. $-3 \times 4 =$ ____________

11. $12 \div -4 =$ ____________

Practice Test

Student Edition • **page 189**

Choose the correct answer.

12. If you start at 0 and keep adding 7 on a calculator, which number will you reach?

Ⓐ 12 Ⓑ 22

Ⓒ 32 Ⓓ 42

13. Becca earns \$4.00 a week. Each week she saves \$1.50. How much will she have saved after 5 weeks?

Ⓐ \$7.50 Ⓑ \$5.50

Ⓒ \$3.50 Ⓓ \$1.50

14. The temperature at noon is 12°F. The temperature at midnight is −2°F. By how many degrees did the temperature fall?

Ⓐ 10° Ⓑ 12°

Ⓒ 14° Ⓓ 16°

15. Which function rule works for both pairs of numbers?

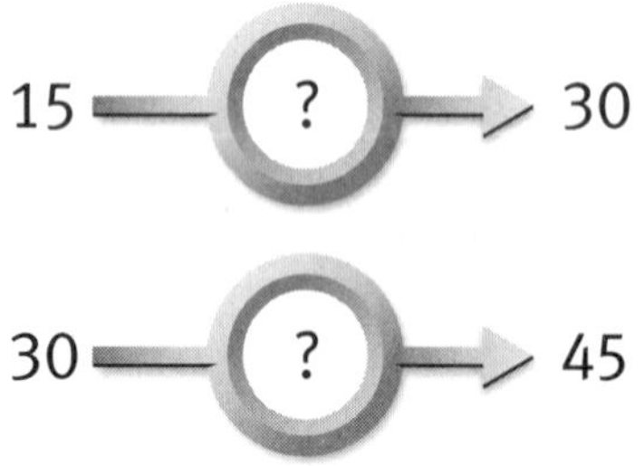

Ⓐ ×2 Ⓑ ×3

Ⓒ +10 Ⓓ +15

16. What is the next number in the following pattern?

−10, −6, −2

Ⓐ −1 Ⓑ 2

Ⓒ 4 Ⓓ 6

17. The rule for a function machine is −8. If 2 comes out of the function machine, which number went in?

Ⓐ −6 Ⓑ 6

Ⓒ 10 Ⓓ 16

18. If you start at 100 and keep subtracting 3 on a calculator, which number will you hit?

Ⓐ 90 Ⓑ 80

Ⓒ 70 Ⓓ 60

19. Solve for *n*.
$7 - (-5) = n$

Ⓐ $n = 12$ Ⓑ $n = 2$

Ⓒ $n = -2$ Ⓓ $n = -12$

20. The rule for a function machine is +5. If 2 went into the function machine, what number will come out?

Ⓐ 7 Ⓑ 8

Ⓒ 9 Ⓓ 10

Practice Test

Name ______________________ Date ____________

Student Edition • page 190

Choose the correct answer.

21. Solve for n.
$6 \times (-3) = n$

Ⓐ $n = -24$ Ⓑ $n = -18$
Ⓒ $n = -2$ Ⓓ $n = 18$

22. Miguel pushed [5], [=] on his calculator, and the display showed 35. What is the multiplication rule for this function?

Ⓐ ×10 Ⓑ ×9
Ⓒ ×8 Ⓓ ×7

23. About 2,100 students take the bus to school. Only 410 students walk. How many more students take the bus than walk to school?

Ⓐ 2,510 Ⓑ 2,390
Ⓒ 1,690 Ⓓ 1,600

24. Greta is 128.15 centimeters tall. Her brother Nate is 124.2 centimeters tall. How much taller is Greta than her brother?

Ⓐ 4.15 cm Ⓑ 3.95 cm
Ⓒ 15.73 cm Ⓓ 23.95 cm

25. Which number is the greatest?

Ⓐ 800,500 Ⓑ 808,005
Ⓒ 880,500 Ⓓ 808,055

26. Ricky spent $20.50 on 5 books. How much did each book cost if they cost the same amount?

Ⓐ $4.01 Ⓑ $4.10
Ⓒ $5.10 Ⓓ $5.13

27. Write the number 3,002,202 in expanded form.

Ⓐ 3,000,000 + 2,000 + 200 + 2
Ⓑ 3,000,000 + 20,000 + 200 + 2
Ⓒ 300,000 + 2,000 + 200 + 2
Ⓓ 300,000 + 20,000 + 200 + 2

28. Which of the following sets of numbers is in order from least to greatest?

Ⓐ 2.52, 2.05, 2.205, 2.002
Ⓑ 2.05, 2.205, 2.002, 2.52
Ⓒ 2.002, 2.05, 2.52, 2.205
Ⓓ 2.002, 2.05, 2.205, 2.52

Student Edition • **page 191**

Solve.

29. **Extended Response** Rachel drew the following pattern:

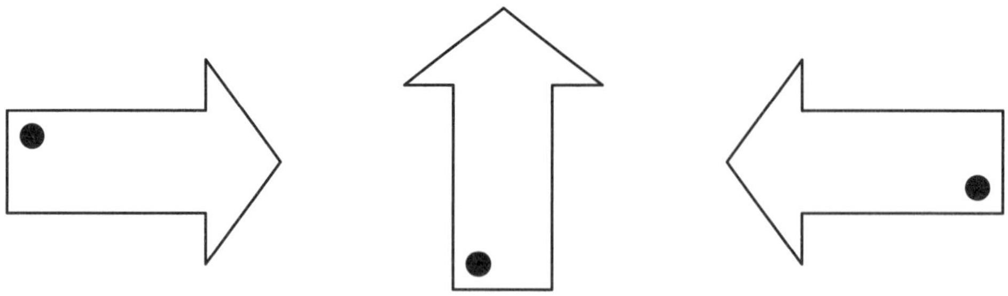

a. Describe the next two shapes in the pattern. ______________________

____

b. Describe the pattern in your own words.

____

____

30. **Extended Response** Find an addition or multiplication function rule that works for both pairs of numbers in each problem.

a. 1 → ? → 10   10 → ? → 100 ____________

b. 0 → ? → 25   10 → ? → 35 ____________

c. 4 → ? → 16   8 → ? → 20 ____________

d. For which pair could you have determined the function rule by looking at only the first pair of numbers given? Why?

____

____

Name ______________________ Date ______________

Graphing Functions

Student Edition • page 193

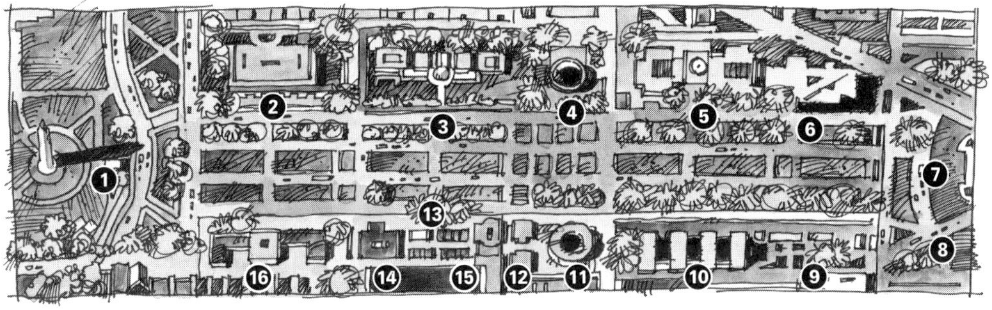

Complete the following questions. Compare the aerial illustration with the map below to help you.

1. The address of the National Museum of African Art is 950 Independence Avenue. Which of the buildings in the illustration could it be? ____________

2. Examine the four addresses on the map. What pattern do you think is used for addresses in this part of Washington, D.C.?

____

3. According to that system, which of the buildings in the illustration is most likely the National Museum of African Art? ____________

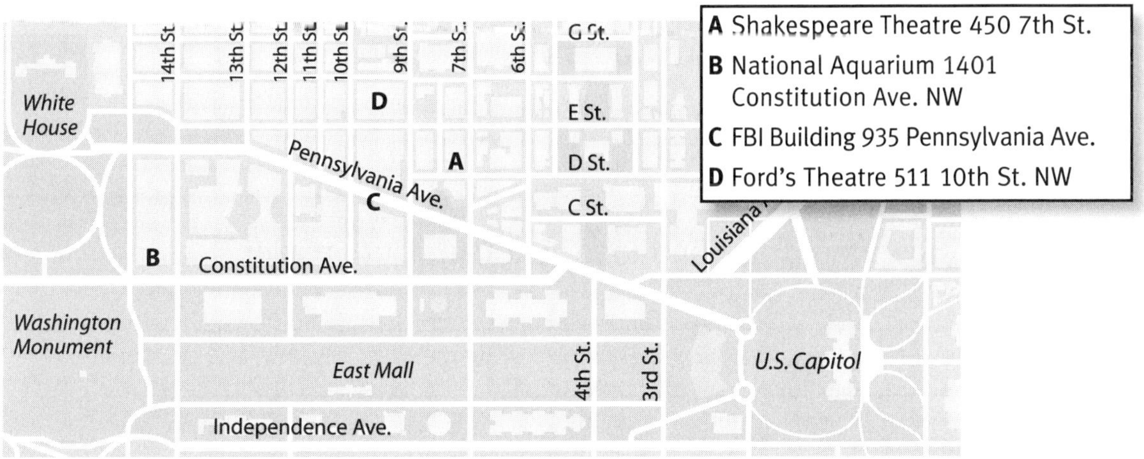

LESSON 5.1 Coordinates

Student Edition • pages 194–195

Graph City was planned with numbered streets running east and west and numbered avenues running north and south.

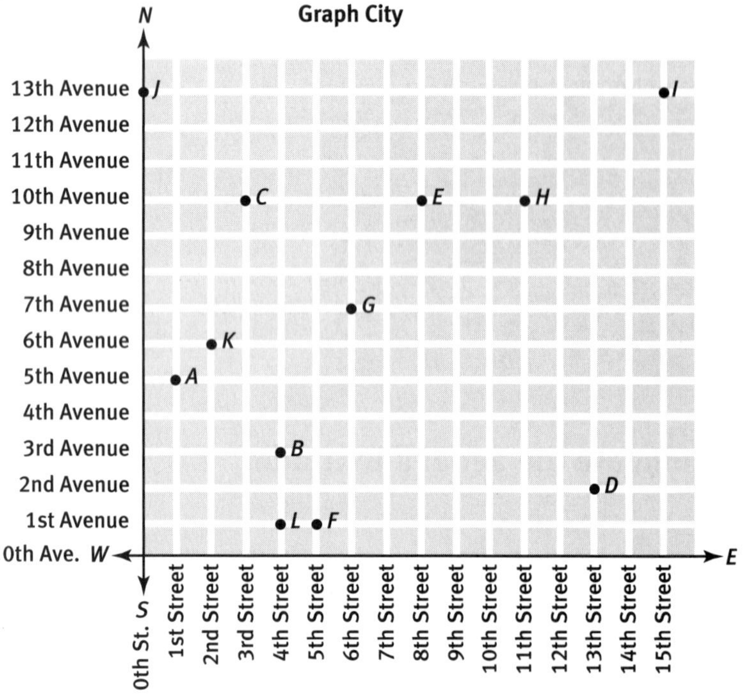

Look at the map of Graph City. Answer the following questions.

1. The corner of 1st Street and 5th Avenue is at point *A*. Where is point *B?*

   ____

2. Suppose José asked you to meet him at the corner of 1st and 5th in Graph City. Where would you go? ______________

3. If José was not where you went, where do you think he might be?

   ____

4. Extended Response How would you find José? Explain your answer.

   ____

   ____

LESSON 5.1 **Name** ______________________ **Date** ____________

Student Edition • page 195

When describing a location, the people of Graph City have agreed to always give the street name first and the avenue name second. Answer the following questions.

5. Where is the corner of 1st and 5th? ______________

6. Where is the corner of 5th and 1st? ______________

7. How many blocks would you have to walk to get from 1st and 5th to 5th and 1st? (You must walk along streets or avenues.) ______________

8. **Extended Response** Is there more than one way to get from 1st and 5th to 5th and 1st by walking only 8 blocks? See how many ways you can find.

____

____

____

9. Suppose you walk only along streets or avenues, and you do not walk in a wrong direction on purpose.

   a. Do all ways of getting from 1st and 5th to 5th and 1st require walking exactly 8 blocks? ______________

   b. Is there a shorter way? ______________

   c. What must you do to make the path longer? ______________

10. How many blocks would you have to walk to get from 7th and 7th to 7th and 7th? ______________

11. How many blocks would you have to walk to get from 5th and 8th to 9th and 3rd? ______________

   a. In what direction would you walk to get from 5th Street to 9th Street? ______________

   b. In what direction would you walk to get from 8th Avenue to 3rd Avenue? ______________

12. How many blocks would you have to walk to get from 2nd and 3rd to 12th and 4th? ______________

Student Edition • pages 195–196

13. How many blocks would you have to walk to get from 15th and 13th to 11th and 6th? ______

14. Give the location of all the points (*A*–*L*) on the map of Graph City. Always give the street name first and the avenue name second.

______

______

______

______

______

Answer the following questions by using the graph on page 187.

15. What are the coordinates of point *Q*? ______
16. What are the coordinates of point *U*? ______
17. What are the coordinates of point *A*? ______
18. What are the coordinates of point *R*? ______
19. What are the coordinates of point *K*? ______
20. What are the coordinates of point *G*? ______
21. What are the coordinates of point *P*? ______
22. What are the coordinates of point *N*? ______
23. What are the coordinates of point *T*? ______
24. What are the coordinates of point *Z*? ______
25. What are the coordinates of point *V*? ______

Name ______________________ Date ______________

Student Edition • page 197

Answer these questions by writing the correct letter for each of the coordinates.

26. What bird can spot a rabbit three kilometers away?
(0, 5); (1, 2); (11, 12); (14, 10); (13, 2); (2, 13)
(13, 2); (6, 6); (0, 5); (11, 12); (13, 2)

____

27. What is the largest bird alive today?
(1, 2); (3, 10); (0, 12); (10, 7); (7, 10); (5, 13); (1, 11) ______________________

28. What bird beats its wings up to 90 times per second?
(1, 11); (12, 11); (8, 3); (8, 3); (7, 10); (2, 13); (0, 5);
(3, 8); (7, 10); (10, 7); (14, 10)

____

29. Which bird has the most feathers (more than 25,000)?
(3, 10); (5, 2); (6, 6); (2, 13)

____

30. What bird gets its pink color from the brine shrimp that it eats?
(2, 1); (11, 12); (6, 6); (8, 3);
(7, 10); (2, 13); (0, 5); (1, 2)

____

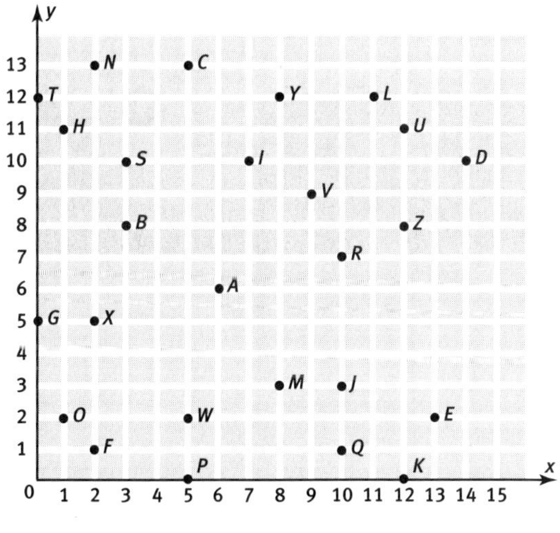

Make up more questions. Share them with a friend.

____

____

____

LESSON 5.2

Functions and Ordered Pairs

Student Edition • page 198

Copy each list of ordered pairs, but replace the *x* or *y* with the correct number. The first one is done for you.

1. $x \rightarrow (+5) \rightarrow y$

   (7, 12); (12, *y*); (15, *y*); (0, *y*); (*x*, 7)

   ____
   ____
   ____
   ____
   ____

2. $x \rightarrow (-9) \rightarrow y$

   (11, *y*); (20, *y*); (25, *y*); (*x*, 0); (*x*, 8); (*x*, 9)

   ____
   ____
   ____
   ____
   ____

3. $x \rightarrow (\times 0) \rightarrow y$

   (7, *y*); (12, *y*); (50, *y*); (2,589, *y*); (*x*, 0)

   ____
   ____
   ____
   ____
   ____

Complete these function machine tables.

4. $x \rightarrow (-7) \rightarrow y$

in	out
9	
11	
14	
	21

5. $x \rightarrow (\div 4) \rightarrow y$

in	out
4	
	4
12	
16	

6. $x \rightarrow (\times 5) \rightarrow y$

in	out

LESSON 5.2

Name ______________________ Date ____________

Student Edition • page 199

Find three ordered pairs for each function rule and graph them.

7. $x \rightarrow \boxed{\times 2} \rightarrow y$

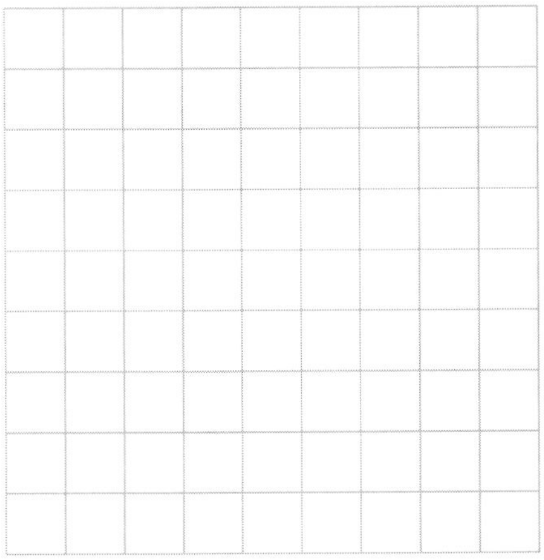

____

____

____

8. $x \rightarrow \boxed{\times 1} \rightarrow y$

____

____

____

9. $x \rightarrow \boxed{\div 2} \rightarrow y$

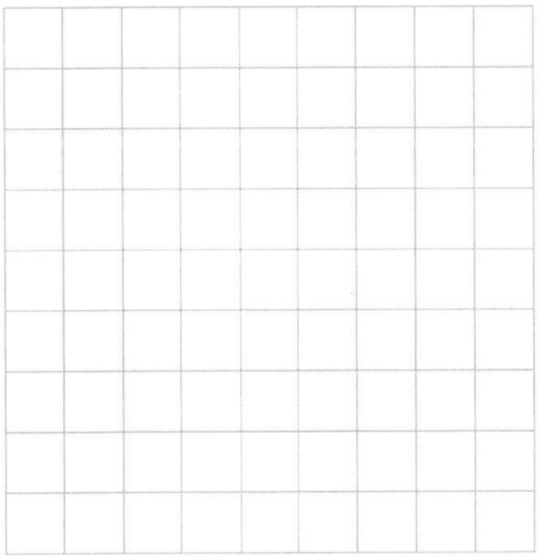

____

____

____

10. $x \rightarrow \boxed{\times 0} \rightarrow y$

____

____

____

Student Edition • **page 199**

11 Jorge got a $500 paycheck on Friday. By the following Monday, he had spent $56 from his checking account. On Tuesday, Jorge wrote checks to pay bills, which totaled $147. On Wednesday he wrote a $225 check for a new stereo. By that time, Jorge had $1,378 in his checking account. How much money did he have before he got paid? ______________

12 **Extended Response** Sarah put 6 into a $\times 7$ function machine. She claimed that the ordered pair she got was (7, 42). Juan disagreed. Sarah said that $6 \times 7 = 42$, and that there could be no other ordered pair. Who is correct and why? Explain.

____

____

____

____

____

LESSON 5.3

Name ______________________ Date ____________

Composite Functions

Student Edition • pages 200–201

Complete this table. Then graph the ordered pairs.

1.

Number of checks cashed during the month (x)	0	1	2	3	4	5	6	7	8	9	10	15	20	30	40
Charge for the month in dollars (y)															

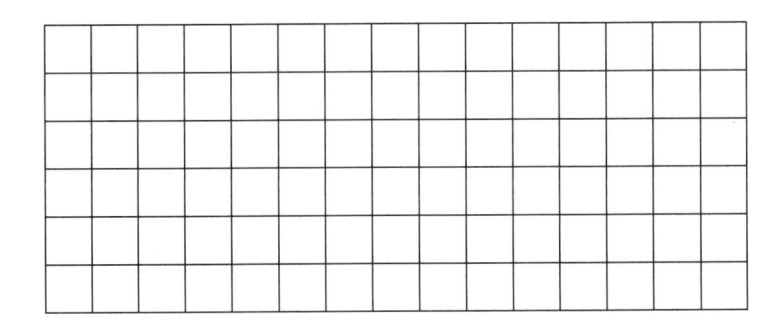

Work individually or in small groups. For each composite function, complete the table. Then graph the ordered pairs.

2. 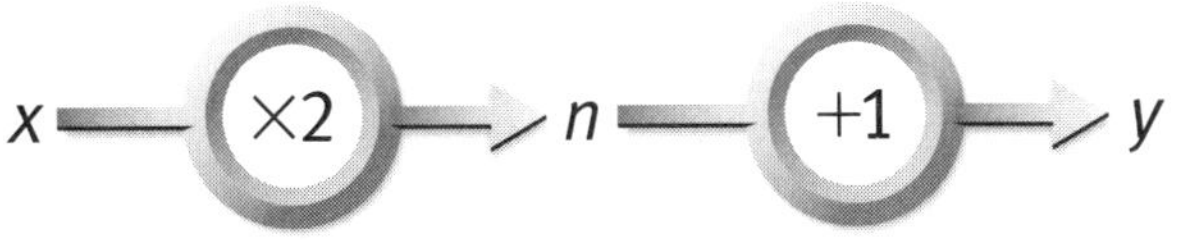

x	0	1	2	3	4	5
y						

Student Edition • page 201

3 $x \rightarrow (\times 4) \rightarrow n \rightarrow (+2) \rightarrow y$

x	0	1	2	3	4	5
y						

4 **Extended Response** Does the order of the steps in a composite function make a difference? For example, is $x \rightarrow (\times 8) \rightarrow n \rightarrow (+3) \rightarrow y$ the same as $x \rightarrow (+3) \rightarrow n \rightarrow (\times 8) \rightarrow y$? Explain how to check your answer.

LESSON 5.4

Name ______________________ Date ____________

Graphing in Four Quadrants

Student Edition • page 202

You saw Graph City in Lesson 5.1. Since then, the city has grown.

The people of Graph City wanted all their roads—even the new ones—to have numbers and to be in order. E. 1st St. stands for East 1st Street, W. stands for West, N. for North, and S. for South.

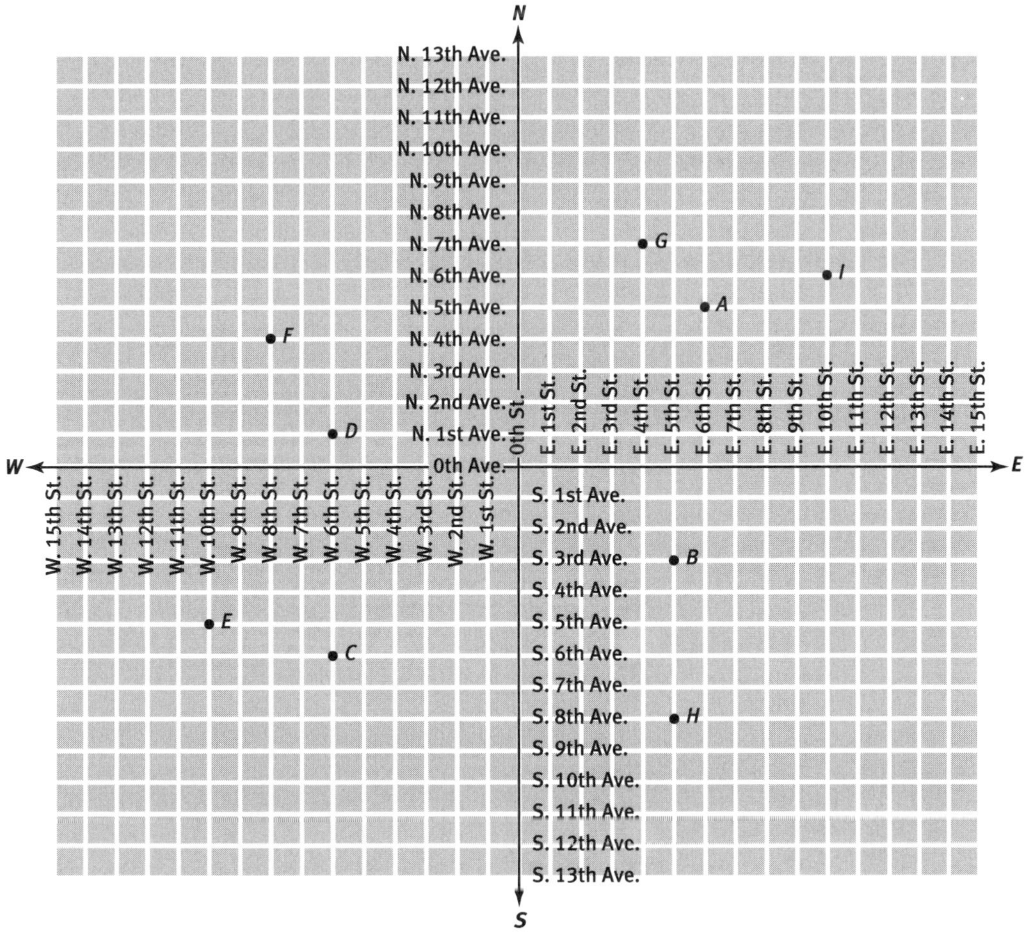

Give the locations of these points.

1. *A* ______________
2. *B* ______________
3. *C* ______________
4. *E* ______________

Student Edition • page 203

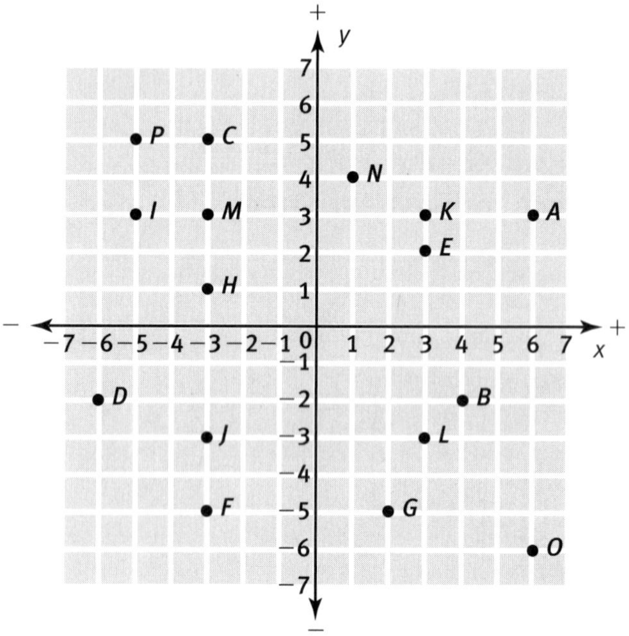

Find the coordinates of the following points.

5. *E* ______
6. *F* ______
7. *G* ______
8. *H* ______
9. *I* ______
10. *J* ______

Find the points with the following coordinates.

11. (3, −3) ______
12. (−3, 3) ______
13. (1, 4) ______
14. (3, 3) ______
15. (6, −6) ______
16. (−5, 5) ______

Name ______________________ **Date** ____________

Student Edition • page 203

Complete these tables. Then graph the ordered pairs.

17 x → (−5) → y

x	0	2	5	6	−2
y	−5				

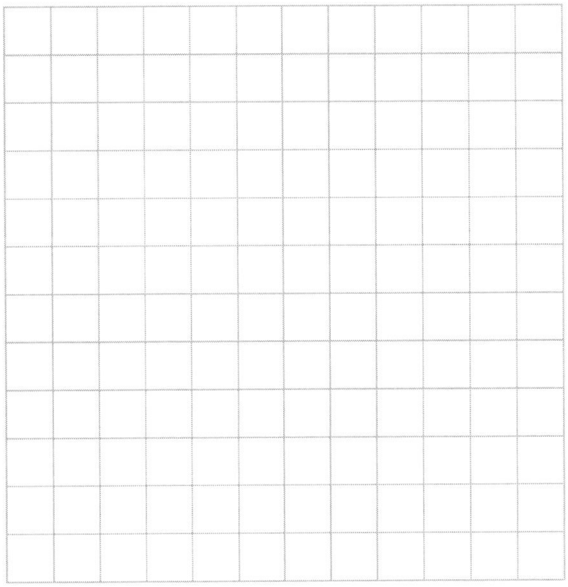

18 x → (+5) → y

x	1	2	3	4	5
y	6				

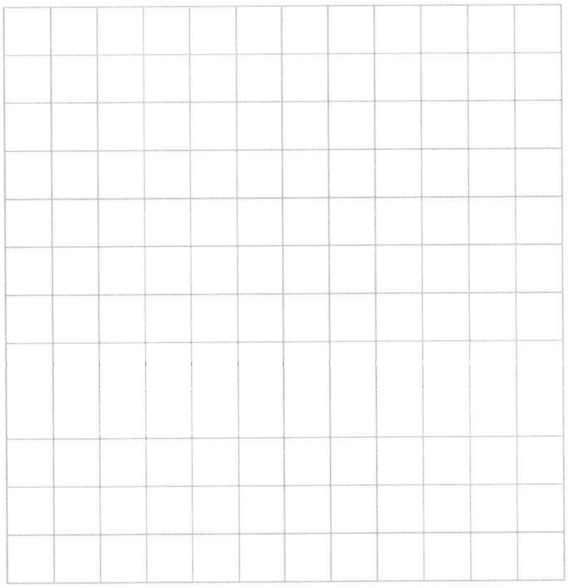

LESSON 5.5

Making and Using Graphs

Student Edition • pages 206–207

To figure out his profit for the week, Mr. Schultz subtracts $240 from the money he makes on the haircuts. The function rule for his profit looks like this:

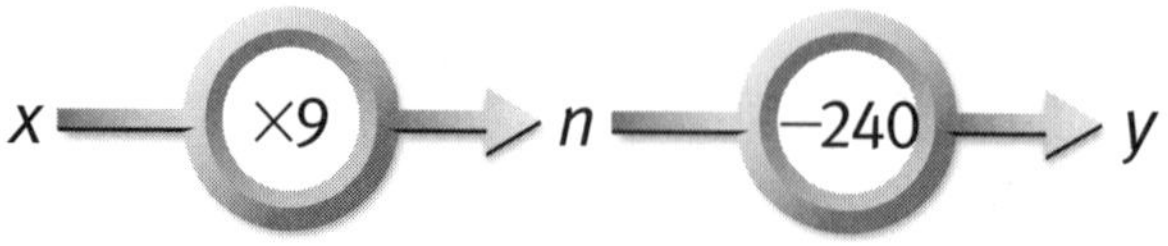

Complete this table by using the function rule above.

1.

Number of haircuts during the week	0	1	2	5	10	15	20	30	50	70
Profit for the week (dollars)										

2. Complete Mr. Schultz's graph below. Graph the ordered pairs from the table in Problem 1. The first few points are plotted to help you check your answers.

3. **Extended Response** How many haircuts must Mr. Schultz give to break even for the week? To break even means to make exactly enough money to pay all expenses and have a profit of $0. Explain your answer.

____

____

____

____

4. About how much profit will Mr. Schultz make if he gives 40 haircuts during one week?

____

Mr. Schultz's Profit for Different Numbers of Haircuts

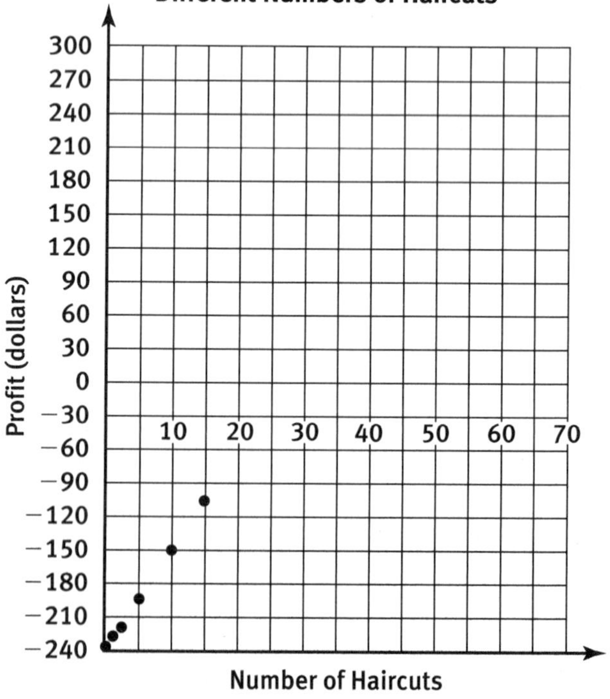

Name ______________________ **Date** ______________

Student Edition • page 208–209

Imagine you are in charge of a remote-control robot that guards a museum at night. All is well until the robot malfunctions. It can no longer move any way you want it to. It can follow only these eight commands:

Command	Meaning	Example
$x + 7$	Add 7 to x-coordinate.	If the robot is at (−3, 5), it will go to (4, 5).
$x - 7$	Subtract 7 from x-coordinate.	If the robot is at (7, −4), it will go to (0, −4).
$y + 7$	Add 7 to y-coordinate.	If the robot is at (−1, −1), it will go to (−1, 6).
$y - 7$	Subtract 7 from y-coordinate.	If the robot is at (3, 0), it will go to (3, −7).

The other four commands are $x + 13$, $x - 13$, $y + 13$, and $y - 13$.

Suddenly something at coordinate (3, 6) triggers an alarm. You need to maneuver the robot from its current position at (−2, −5) to the trouble point. What series of commands will move the robot to where it needs to go?

Rachel solved the problem this way:

I Made a Physical Model.

Command	Location
$x + 7$	(5, −5)
$y + 13$	

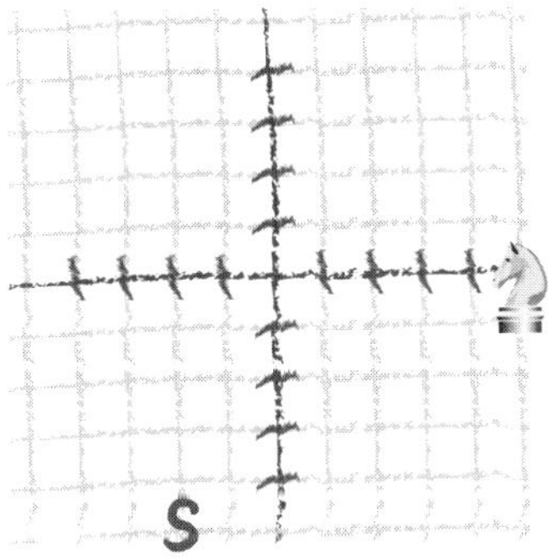

Think about Rachel's strategy, and answer the following questions.

❶ What is Rachel doing to try to solve the problem?

____

____

Student Edition • **page 209**

❷ What do you think Rachel will write next?

❸ Will Rachel's strategy work?

Ernesto solved the problem another way.

I Thought of a Related Problem I had already solved.

This reminds me of a problem I solved in the Chapter 4 Introduction.

First I'll move the robot back and forth until it's at point *A*.

Then I'll move the robot up and down to get to the target.

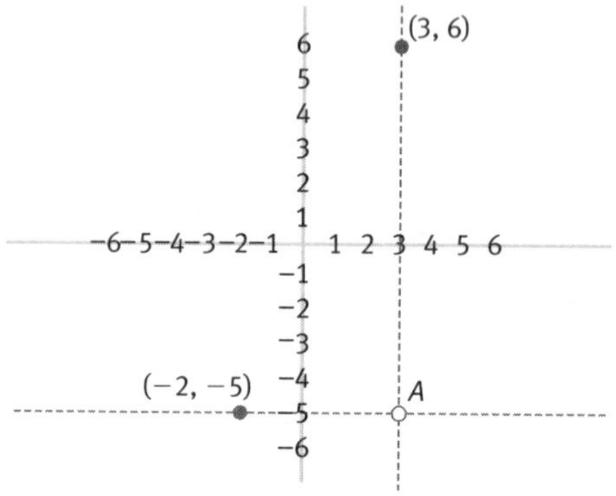

Think about Ernesto's strategy, and answer the following questions.

❹ How is this problem like the one Ernesto is thinking of? How is it different?

❺ How far from point *A* does the robot start?

❻ Do you think Ernesto's strategy will work? Why or why not?

❼ Finish solving the problem. Use Rachel's strategy, Ernesto's strategy, or a strategy of your own. What strategy did you use? Why?

CHAPTER 5 Cumulative Review

Name ______________________ Date ____________

Student Edition • page 210

Savings Plans Lesson 4.3

Solve.

Abdul and Caitlin are both saving money to buy bicycles for $100 each. Each week, Abdul gets $5 but spends $2 of that, and Caitlin gets $4 and spends $2 of that.

1. How many weeks will it take for each person to save enough money to buy a bicycle? ____________

2. How much sooner will they have enough money if they each spend only $1 each week? ____________

3. How many weeks will it take for each person to save enough money if they do not spend any? ____________

Function Rules Lesson 4.6

Find a function rule that works for both pairs of numbers.

4. 20 → ? → 50

   15 → ? → 45

   ____

5. 7 → ? → 21

   8 → ? → 24

   ____

6. 50 → ? → 30

   40 → ? → 20

   ____

7. 20 → ? → 4

   100 → ? → 20

   ____

Cumulative Review

Student Edition • page 211

Decimals and Money Lesson 3.1

Solve.

8. Jimmy was at the ballpark and wanted a hot dog ($2.50), chips ($1.50), and a drink ($1.75). His mother had only a $5 bill and a $10 bill.
   - **a.** Was the $5 bill enough or did Jimmy need the $10 bill? ______
   - **b.** How much change did he get? ______
9. Renee's lunch at school this week will cost between $2.25 and $3.00 each day. How much money does she need to be sure to have enough to pay for all her lunches this week? ______
10. Fara had $10. She loaned her friends Jay and Peggy $2.75 each to buy snacks. How much did Fara have left? ______

Metric Units Lesson 3.7

Find the missing measure.

11. 350 mL = ______ L
12. 50 dm = ______ m
13. 16.2 mm = ______ cm
14. 17.241 km = ______ m
15. 4,000 g = ______ kg
16. 1,796 m = ______ km
17. 17.241 dm = ______ m
18. 25 m = ______ cm
19. 0.050 L = ______ mL

Adding and Subtracting Integers Lesson 4.8

Complete each exercise.

20. $(-4) - (-5) =$ ______
21. $9 + 8 =$ ______
22. $3 - 8 =$ ______
23. $|-7| =$ ______
24. $-|-5| =$ ______
25. $|-8| - |-5| =$ ______

LESSON 5.6

Name ______________________ Date ____________

Inverse Functions

Student Edition • pages 212–213

Write the inverse of each of these functions.

❶ 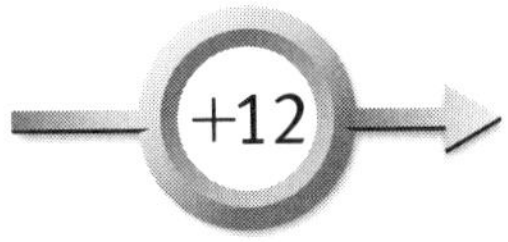

____

❷ 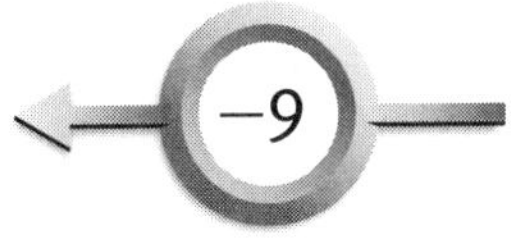

____

❸ 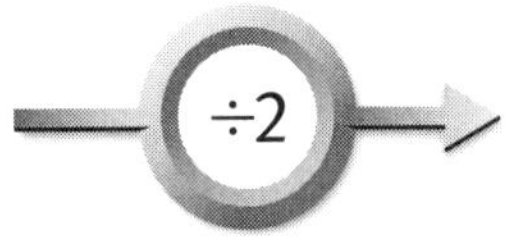

____

Find the value of *x* in each case. If it helps you, use the inverse function.

❹ 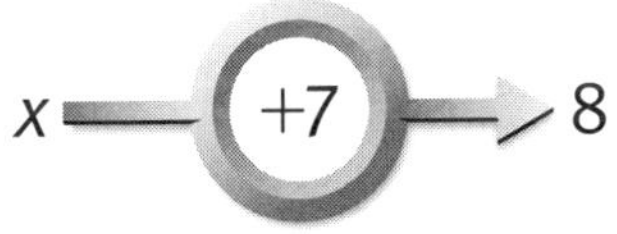

____

❺ 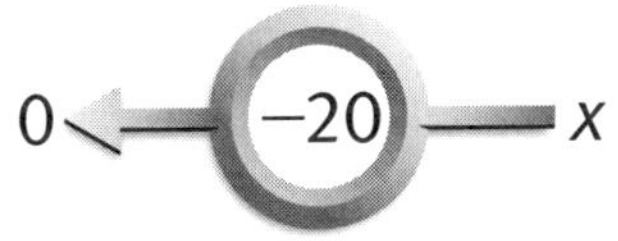

____

❻ 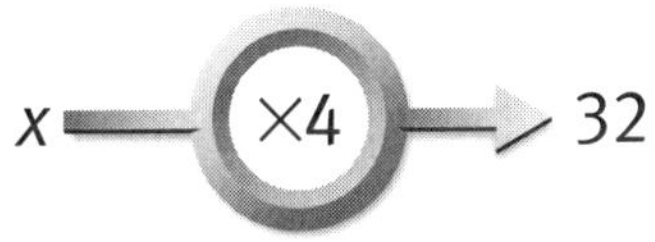

____

Answer the following questions.

Tickets to the Apple County Fair cost $4 each.

❼ How would you find the cost of 4 tickets? ______________________

❽ How would you find the cost of *x* tickets? ______________________

❾ The Gartner family spent $20 on tickets. Write the function rule to find the cost of *x* tickets. How many did they buy? ______________________

____

LESSON 5.6

Student Edition • **page 213**

Groups can make advance reservations for fair tickets by calling the ticket office. There is a $3 service charge added to the total cost for orders taken over the phone.

10 The Ramirez family's ticket order cost $31.

a. Write the function rule to find the cost of x tickets with the service charge. ______

b. What was the cost before the service charge? ______

c. How many tickets did the Ramirez family order? ______

11 The Hilltown softball team's ticket order cost $51.

a. What was the cost before the service charge? ______

b. How many tickets did the team order? ______

12 The Girl Scout troop's ticket order was $83. At the last minute, the troop had to order 5 more tickets, which included another service charge.

a. What was the cost of the first order before the service charge? ______

b. How many tickets did the troop order the first time? ______

c. What was the cost of the second order, including the service charge?

______

d. What was the total amount spent on tickets for the Girl Scout troop?

______

LESSON 5.7

Name ____________________ Date ____________

Inverse of a Composite Function

Student Edition • pages 214–215

Write the inverse function of each of these functions.

❶ $x \rightarrow (+2) \rightarrow n \rightarrow (\times 3) \rightarrow y$

____

❷ $y \leftarrow (\times 4) \leftarrow n \leftarrow (+8) \leftarrow x$

____

Put each of the numbers below into the function rule $x \rightarrow (\times 2) \rightarrow n \rightarrow (+4) \rightarrow y$.

Put that result into the inverse function $y \rightarrow (-4) \rightarrow n \rightarrow (\div 2) \rightarrow x$.

❸ 0 ____________

❹ 2 ____________

❺ 22.7 ____________

❻ 10 ____________

Rewrite each composite function rule as a one-step function that does the same thing, if possible. Give the inverse of each function.

❼ $x \rightarrow (+5) \rightarrow n \rightarrow (+3) \rightarrow y$

____

____

❾ $x \rightarrow (\times 2) \rightarrow n \rightarrow (\times 4) \rightarrow y$

____

____

❽ $x \rightarrow (-2) \rightarrow n \rightarrow (+5) \rightarrow y$

____

____

❿ $x \rightarrow (\times 3) \rightarrow n \rightarrow (+2) \rightarrow y$

____

____

Student Edition • pages 215–216

11. $y \rightarrow (\div 2) \rightarrow n \rightarrow (-1) \rightarrow x$

____

____

13. $y \rightarrow (+9) \rightarrow n \rightarrow (\div 3) \rightarrow x$

____

____

12. $y \rightarrow (+7) \rightarrow n \rightarrow (-4) \rightarrow x$

____

____

14. $y \rightarrow (\times 7) \rightarrow n \rightarrow (\div 7) \rightarrow x$

____

____

15. What is a rule for the identity function that uses only one operation?

____

16. Give as many rules as you can think of for an identity function that uses exactly two operations. For example:

$x \rightarrow (+5) \rightarrow n \rightarrow (-5) \rightarrow y$

____

____

____

____

Name ______________________ **Date** ____________

Student Edition • **pages 216–217**

17 Give three rules for an identity function that uses three different operations. For example:

x → (+3) → n → (−3) → n → (×1) → y

____

____

____

18 **Extended Response** Is this a rule for the identity function? Explain why or why not.

x → (+3) → n → (÷2) → y

____

____

____

19 If you put a number into the function machine in Problem 18, do you get the same number back? Try some numbers.

a. If you put in 1, what number comes out of the function machine? ____________

b. If you put in 2, what number comes out of the function machine? ____________

c. If you put in 3, what number comes out of the function machine? ____________

d. When you put 3 into the function machine, do you get the same number back? ____________

LESSON 5.7

Student Edition • page 217

Look at this function:

$$x \xrightarrow{\times 2} n \xrightarrow{-6} y$$

20 Is there a number that you can put into this function machine and get out the same number? Is there another number? ______________

____

For each function, find a number that you can put in and get out the same number.

21 $x \xrightarrow{\times 2} n \xrightarrow{-7} y$

____

24 $y \xrightarrow{\times 3} n \xrightarrow{-10} x$

____

22 $x \xleftarrow{-4} n \xleftarrow{\times 3} y$

____

25 $y \xrightarrow{\times 4} n \xrightarrow{-6} x$

____

23 $x \xrightarrow{\times 2} n \xrightarrow{-5} y$

____

26 $y \xleftarrow{-4} n \xleftarrow{\times 5} x$

____

LESSON 5.8

Name ______________________ Date ____________

Using Composite Functions

Student Edition • page 218

Odessa wants to make a table that will tell her the total charge for different numbers of bracelets ordered.

Answer the following questions.

$x \rightarrow \boxed{\times 3} \rightarrow n \rightarrow \boxed{+0.50} \rightarrow y$

1 Help Odessa. Complete the table by filling in the correct amounts.

Number of bracelets ordered							7
Total charge	$3.50		$9.50				

2 Extended Response Shiro ordered some bracelets and then told Odessa he should be charged $5.00. Could that be right? Explain.

____

____

3 Odessa found a bill she was supposed to send to Celia. The bill was for $12.50. How many bracelets had Celia ordered? ____________

4 Odessa received an order for bracelets. The order form listed the total for the order as $27.50, but the number of bracelets was not listed. How many bracelets were ordered? ____________

5 Extended Response Tom and Elise each wanted a bracelet. Elise had an idea. "Tom," she said, "let me order both bracelets." Why did Elise think this was a good idea? Explain.

____

____

6 Extended Response During one month, Odessa sold 26 bracelets. During that same month her expenses were $23.64. Without knowing anything else, can you figure out the most profit she might have made? Can you figure out the least profit she might have made? Explain how you found your answer.

____

____

LESSON 5.8

Student Edition • page 219

Odessa keeps records of her bracelet business. This table shows her records for the first year she was in business.

Month	Number of Bracelets Sold	Total Income (Sales)	Total Expenses	Total Profit
January	0	0	0	0
February	0	0	0	0
March	1	$3.50	$37.50	−$34.00
April	7	$24.00	0	$24.00
May	12	$37.00	$18.23	$18.77
June	5	$17.00	$8.04	$8.96
July	6	$21.00	0	$21.00
August	10	$34.50	0	$34.50
September	8	$26.50	$10.13	$16.37
October	3	$10.00	$7.88	$2.12
November	7	$22.00	$6.38	$15.62
December	9	$29.00	$14.21	$14.79

Study the table. Then work in small groups to discuss answers to the following questions.

7. In what month do you think Odessa started her business? ______________

8. Do you think she started near the beginning of the month or near the end of the month? ______________

9. In which month were Odessa's expenses the highest? ______________

 Name ______________________ **Date** __________

Student Edition • page 219

10 Why do you think Odessa had the most expenses that month?

____

____

11 **a.** In which two-month period did Odessa have the most profit?

____

b. **Extended Response** What might have happened during those two months to account for this?

____

____

12 **Extended Response** In which month did Odessa have the most customers? (This need not be the month in which the most bracelets were sold.) Explain how you found your answer.

____

____

LESSON 5.9

Temperature Conversions

Student Edition • pages 220–221

$C \rightarrow (\times 1.8) \rightarrow n \rightarrow (+32) \rightarrow F$

This function converts Celsius temperatures to Fahrenheit temperatures.

Answer the following questions.

1. Normal body temperature for most people is said to be about 37°C. What is the same temperature on the Fahrenheit scale? ______

2. **Extended Response** What is the inverse function of the composite function that converts Celsius temperatures to Fahrenheit temperatures? What would this new composite function do? Explain.

______

______

3. Instead of 1.8, which we used in the composite function for converting from Celsius to Fahrenheit, some people use $\frac{9}{5}$. What would the function rule be in that case? ______

4. Using the fraction rather than the decimal, what would the inverse function rule be? ______

5. Use either form of the function rule and its inverse to complete the following table:

Celsius temp.	−10		10		30		40	50	100
Fahrenheit temp.		32		68		98.6			212

Some people use a different function to estimate conversions between Fahrenheit and Celsius temperatures. That function rule is

$C \rightarrow (\times 2) \rightarrow n \rightarrow (+30) \rightarrow F.$

The inverse of the composite function shown above looks like this:

$F \rightarrow (-30) \rightarrow n \rightarrow (\div 2) \rightarrow C$

LESSON 5.9

Name ______________________ Date ____________

Student Edition • page 221

Use **the estimating function and its inverse to answer the following questions.**

6. If C is 0, about what is F? ____________

7. If C is 100, about what is F? ____________

8. If C is 10, about what is F? ____________

9. If C is 37, about what is F? ____________

10. Using the estimating rule and its inverse, complete the following table:

Celsius temp.	−10	0			30	37	40	50	100
Fahrenheit temp.		30	50	68		104		130	

11. **a.** For what Celsius temperature do the exact function and the "estimating" function give the same Fahrenheit temperature? ____________

    b. **Extended Response** For which values of C are the estimates reasonably close? For which are they pretty far apart? Explain.

    ____

    ____

12. Using the horizontal axis for C and the vertical axis for F, with C ranging from −10° to 100° and F ranging from 0° to 230°, graph the table of the function on page 210 and the table of the estimating function above.

LESSON 5.10

Standard Notation for Functions

Student Edition • pages 222–223

Complete each table.

1. $y = x + 3$

x	0		4	
y	3	5		2

3. $y = x + 10$

x	1	4		20
y	11		19	

2. $y = x - 6$

x	10	8		4
y	4		0	

Complete each table.

4. $y = 9x$

x	2			8	
y	18	36	54		90

6. $y = \frac{x}{5}$

x	0	5		40	
y			4		9

5. $y = \frac{x}{3}$

x	3	6	11	15	
y	1				6

LESSON 5.11

Name ______________________ Date ____________

Composite Functions in Standard Notation

Student Edition • pages 224–225

Complete each table.

1. $y = 4x - 7$

x	8		2	1	
y		13			−7

2. $y = 7x + 3$

x		2	7		5
y	66			31	

3. $y = 6x + 9$

x		3	8		
y	39			33	21

4. $y = 5x - 6$

x	8	2		6	
y			9		19

Complete each table.

5. $y = \frac{x}{2} + 7$

x	0			8	4
y		15	8		

6. $y = \frac{x}{3} + 4$

x				3	6
y	9	7	4		

7. $y = 4x + 5$

x	0	6			7
y			17	9	

8. $y = \frac{x}{5} - 3$

x	20		10	15	
y		3			4

Student Edition • pages 225–226

9 $y = 2x - 1$

x		5		4	1
y	5		3		

10 $y = 6x + 3$

x	4	0			5
y			15	39	

11 **Extended Response** Doug put 3 into a composite function machine and out came 24. Write two possible composite functions in standard notation that make Doug's output true. In your answer, tell what numbers were put into the machine (the value of x).

____

____

____

12 **Extended Response** Give an example of a real-life situation in which you would use the function rule $y = 6x - 5$.

____

____

____

Solve the following problems.

13 Ms. Chee runs a computer repair service. She charges $50 to make a service call plus $60 for each hour she spends working on a computer.

a. If she works on a computer for 3 hours, how much will Ms. Chee charge? ____________

b. What is a function rule for her charges? Make a table showing how much she charges *(y)* for any number of hours *(x)* from 1–10. ____________

Name ______________________ **Date** ____________

Student Edition • page 226

c. Graph the data from your table. Be careful to choose your scale so that the graph will fit on your paper.

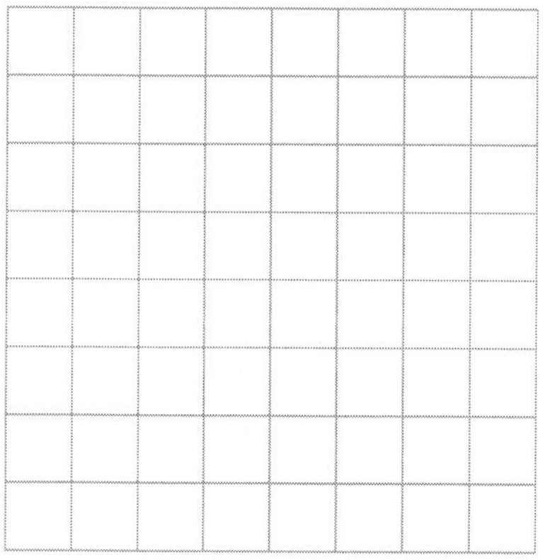

14 Mr. Alexander also runs a computer repair service. He charges only $30 per hour while he is working on a computer, but he charges $100 to make a service call.

a. If he works on a computer for 3 hours, how much will he charge?

____

b. Make a function rule for Mr. Alexander's charges. Make a table showing how much he charges for any number of hours from 1–10.

____

c. Graph the data from this table on the same graph that you used for Ms. Chee's charges.

15 **Extended Response** Which of the two computer services costs less? Explain.

____

____

____

LESSON 5.11

Student Edition • pages 226–227

Complete each function table and graph the ordered pairs for each on a sheet of graph paper.

16. $y = 4x - 2$

x	y
2	
1	
	10

17. $y = \frac{x}{4} + 1$

x	y
8	
	4
4	

18. $y = \left(\frac{2}{3}\right)x + 3$

x	y
3	
0	
	7

Choose three *x*-values to put into the following function rules. Then graph the ordered pairs.

19. $y = 2x - 4$ ____________

20. $y = 3x + 1$ ____________

21. $y = \frac{x}{2} + 5$ ____________

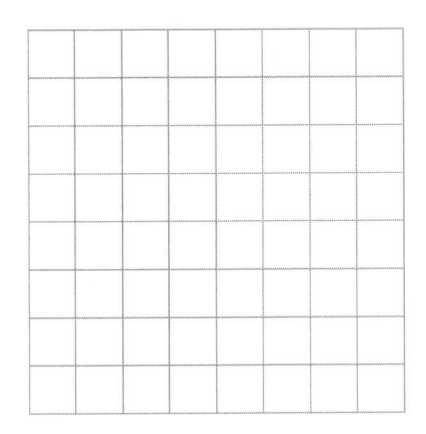

Complete the following exercises.

22. $7 \times 3 =$ ____________

23. $7 - 3 =$ ____________

24. $7 \div 3 =$ ____________

25. $9 \times 6 =$ ____________

26. $9 + 6 =$ ____________

27. $9 \div 6 =$ ____________

28. $7 \times 8 =$ ____________

29. $7 + 8 =$ ____________

Name ______________________ Date ____________

Student Edition • page 227

Solve for n.

30. $10 \times 5 = n$ ____________
31. $10 - n = 5$ ____________
32. $10 + 5 = n$ ____________
33. $10 \div n = 2$ ____________
34. $10 \times 2 = n$ ____________
35. $n \div 2 = 10$ ____________
36. $8 \times 4 = n$ ____________
37. $8 \div n = 2$ ____________
38. $8 + 4 = n$ ____________

Divide. Round answers to the nearest hundredth. Look for patterns that will help you.

39. $7\overline{)1.54}$
40. $6\overline{)34.2}$
41. $3\overline{)1}$
42. $3\overline{)2}$
43. $10\overline{)43.21}$
44. $4\overline{)36}$
45. $400\overline{)3600}$
46. $40\overline{)3600}$
47. $40\overline{)36}$
48. $39\overline{)3600}$
49. $39\overline{)360}$
50. $39\overline{)36}$

51. **Extended Response** Give an example of a real-life situation for which you would use the function rule $y = 4x$.

____

____

52. Darla and Hong are playing a game in which they get 6 points for every time one of them kicks a ball past a certain line. Which rule fits this situation if x is the number of times they kick the ball past the line? ____________

a. $y = x + 6$ **b.** $y = 6x$ **c.** $y = x - 6$

LESSON 5.12

Linear Equations

Student Edition • page 228

Evaluate each equation by solving for either x or y.

1. $5x - 7 = 33$ ______
2. $4x + 12 = 52$ ______
3. $12(3) - 34 = y$ ______
4. $\frac{x}{9} \times 6 = 48$ ______
5. $x + 6(7) = 63$ ______
6. $\frac{12}{4} - 56 = y$ ______
7. $12x + 6 = 78$ ______
8. $32 - 8(4) = y$ ______
9. $17x - 26 = -77$ ______
10. $25(8) + 31 = y$ ______
11. $7x - 63 = 21$ ______
12. $\frac{x}{3} + 25 = 67$ ______
13. $24.5x + 39 = 186$ ______
14. $7x - 46 = -67$ ______
15. $36(9) - 176.8 = y$ ______
16. $-16.4x + 51 = 51$ ______
17. $45(5) - 69 = y$ ______
18. $\frac{x}{8} - 56 = 36.5$ ______
19. $4x + 1{,}245 = 1{,}577$ ______
20. $-6x + (-19) = -49$ ______
21. $32(3) - 32 = y$ ______
22. $12.6x + 43 = -20$ ______

LESSON 5.12

Name ______________________ Date __________

Student Edition • page 229

Solve the following problems.

23 Jason took a cab home from the airport. The sign on the side of the cab said that the charge would be \$2.00 to start the trip plus 35¢ for each $\frac{1}{5}$ of a mile. The trip cost \$18.45. Jason noticed that the meter said \$2.35 as soon as the cab started. Jason wanted to know how far it is from the airport to his home. What is the answer? He was pretty sure the distance was less than 10 miles. Is he right? Is your answer exactly right? If not, what is the range of possible distances?

____

____

24 **Extended Response** Choose one equation from this lesson and graph the *x*- and *y*-values. Then put three different *x*-values into the equation and graph those ordered pairs too. What are your observations of the graph you made?

25 Look at the following equations. Would you expect them to have the same answer? Why? **a.** $3(x + 5) = 18$ **b.** $3x + 15 = 18$

____

____

____

Student Edition • page 230

How Many Museums in a Mile?

In New York City is El Museo del Barrio, a museum that showcases Latino culture. Across the street is Central Park. Each year 50,000 people enjoy music, artwork, and free admission to El Museo and eight other museums—all within a twenty-three block stretch of Fifth Avenue. No wonder they call this the "Museum Mile."

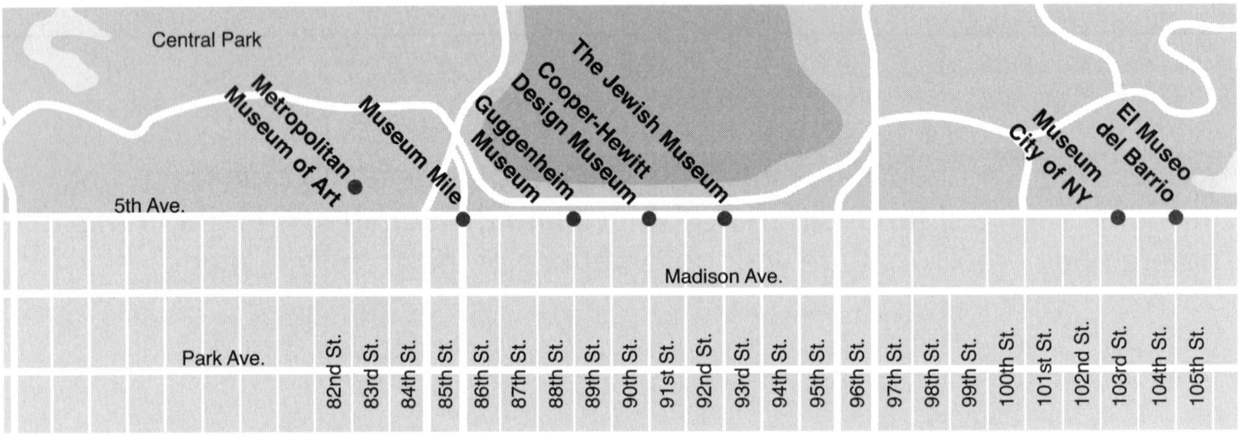

Do you see why the outlined section of Fifth Avenue is called the "Museum Mile"? Explain.

____

____

____

CHAPTER 5 Exploring Problem Solving

Name ______________________________ Date ______________

Student Edition • page 231

You can get to El Museo del Barrio and the rest of the Museum Mile Festival in several ways, including by bus or by train. This map shows only a part of the extensive subway network that weaves under the streets of New York City.

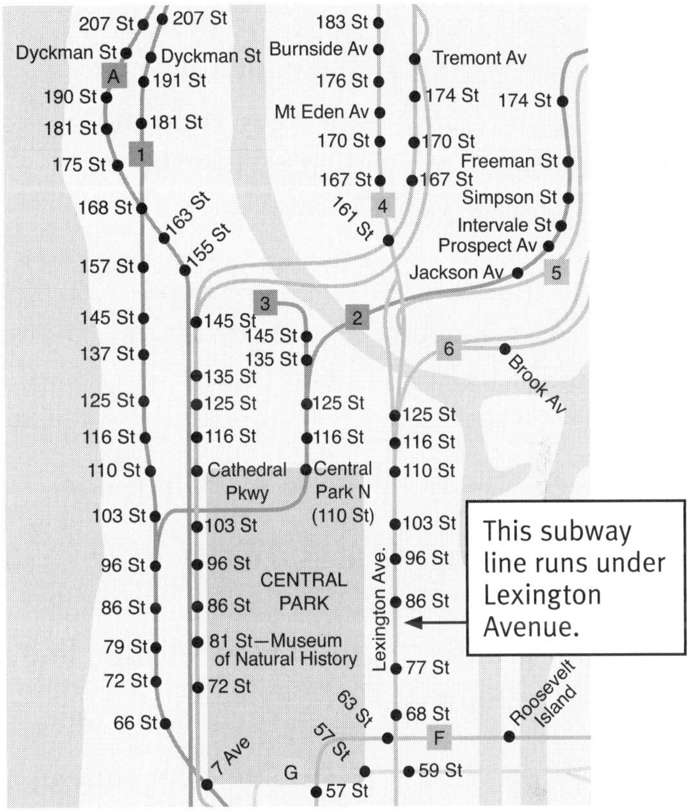

Answer the following questions.

❶ How is the layout of the streets near Museum Mile similar to the layout of Graph City on page 193? How is it different?

____

____

❷ Which subway station is closest to El Museo del Barrio? ______________

❸ Suppose you walked at an average speed of 3 miles per hour. About how long would it take to walk to El Museo del Barrio from the nearest subway station? Explain how you made your estimate.

____

____

Student Edition • page 232

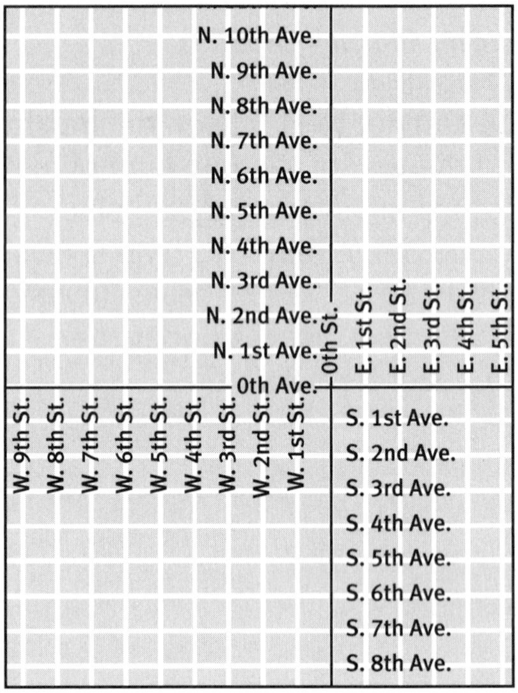

Imagine you work for the Graph City Rapid Transit Department. The Historical Society is erecting a new multicultural museum, and you are going to help plan a subway line from the airport to the museum entrance.

- The museum entrance will be at (−4, −5), which is the corner of West 4th Avenue and South 5th Street.
- The subway will go in a straight line.
- The subway will pass directly under (3, 9).

Work in groups to graph your subway line, and then discuss and solve the following problems.

4 List three other intersections the subway will pass directly under. Write each pair of coordinates in a table.

____

5 Will the subway pass directly under (0, 0)? How do you know? ______________________________

____

6 What equation could be used to represent the path of the subway?

____

Name ______________________ **Date** ____________

Student Edition • page 232

7. Take the first pair of x- and y-values from your table. What happens if you use them in place of x and y in your equation? ____________

____

8. List an intersection the subway will not pass under. ____________

9. What happens if you use those values for x and y in your equation?

____

____

10. What happens if you take other pairs of x- and y-values from your table and use them in your equation?

____

____

11. Explain why you agree or disagree with each of the following statements:

- If an intersection is along the subway line, then its coordinates make the equation true.

  ____

  ____

- If an intersection is not along the subway line, then its coordinates make the equation false.

  ____

  ____

CHAPTER 5 Cumulative Review

Student Edition • page 233

Multiplying and Dividing Integers Lesson 4.9

Solve.

1. $-6 \times 4 =$ ____________
2. $-4 \times (-8) =$ ____________
3. $4 \times (-9) =$ ____________
4. $25 \div (-5) =$ ____________
5. $63 \div (-9) =$ ____________
6. $-27 \div 3 =$ ____________
7. $9 + (-15) =$ ____________
8. $-10 + 17 =$ ____________

Functions and Ordered Pairs Lesson 5.2

Find three ordered pairs for each function rule, and graph them.

9. $x \longrightarrow$ ×4 $\longrightarrow y$

____

____

____

10. $x \longrightarrow$ +7 $\longrightarrow y$

____

____

____

Cumulative Review

Name ______________________ Date ______________

Student Edition • page 233

11 $x \rightarrow \boxed{\div 3} \rightarrow y$

____

____

____

12 $x \rightarrow \boxed{-5} \rightarrow y$

____

____

____

Patterns **Lesson 4.10**

Use the pattern to find the missing numbers.

13 7, 10, 13, ________, ________, 22, ________, ________

14 1, 3, 9, ________, ________, 243

15 100, 85, 70, ________, ________, 25, ________

16 40, 50, 45, 55, 50, ________, ________, 65, ________, ________

Cumulative Review

Student Edition • pages 233–234

Multiplying Decimals by Whole Numbers Lesson 3.9

Multiply.

17. $\begin{array}{r} 542 \\ \times\ 2.6 \\ \hline \end{array}$

18. $\begin{array}{r} 74.62 \\ \times\ 68 \\ \hline \end{array}$

19. $\begin{array}{r} 3.176 \\ \times\ 24 \\ \hline \end{array}$

20. $\begin{array}{r} 25.24 \\ \times\ 9 \\ \hline \end{array}$

Interpreting Quotients and Remainders Lesson 3.13

Divide. Do not use remainders. Round answers to the nearest hundredth when needed.

21. $10\overline{)5}$

22. $8\overline{)6}$

23. $7\overline{)8.24}$

24. $3\overline{)38.25}$

Solve.

25. Aaron, Eric, and Iris shoveled their neighbor's driveway and were given $20 to share. How much should each person get? __________

26. The Lima School seventh- and eighth-grade classes were going together on a field trip. Each bus has 40 seats. If there are 56 seventh graders and 68 eighth graders, how many buses are needed? __________

Cumulative Review

Name ______________________ Date ____________

Student Edition • page 234

Rounding and Approximating **Lesson 3.10**

Round to the nearest hundredth.

27. 102.548 ____________

29. 107,589 ____________

28. 99.966 ____________

30. 89,348.27 ____________

Solve.

31. A bottle of juice costs $2.19. If Jerry has $10, how many bottles can he purchase? ____________

32. Don's van holds 18 gallons of gas and gets about 20 miles per gallon. He plans to travel about 400 miles. Can he make the trip without stopping for gas? If not, about how far would he get? ____________

____

____

Customary Measurements **Lesson 2.10**

Solve.

33. Beth says she is 7 years and 3 months old. Josh says he was born 80 months ago. Who is older? ____________

34. 4 feet = ____________ inches

35. 3 tons = ____________ pounds

CHAPTER 5 Key Ideas Review

Student Edition • page 235

Use the graph below to answer the following questions.

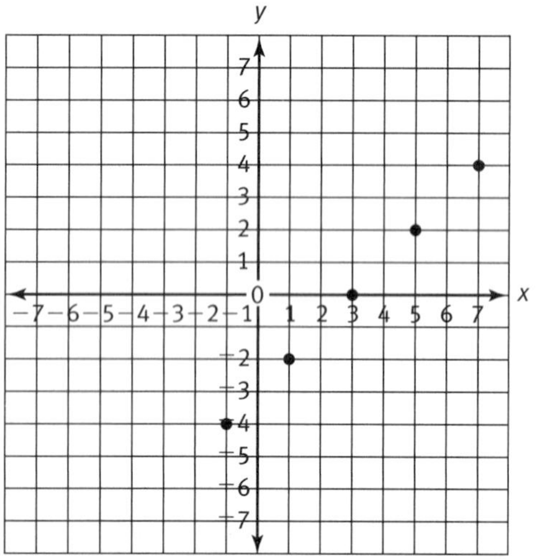

1. Name two points on the graph.

____

2. Use the points on the graph to describe the function represented.

____

Use the following composite function to answer the questions below.

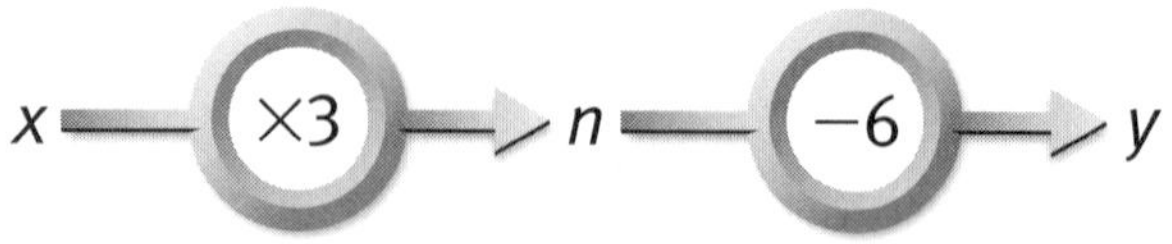

3. What number can be put into the function to get the same number out?

____

4. Write the inverse of the composite function above.

____

Solve the following problems.

5. If a Celsius thermometer reads 24°, what is the temperature in Fahrenheit degrees? __________

6. $6x - 7 = 53$ __________

7. $\frac{36}{4} - 15 = y$ __________

8. $12(x) + 12 = 72$ __________

Chapter Review

Name ______________________ Date ______________

Student Edition • page 236

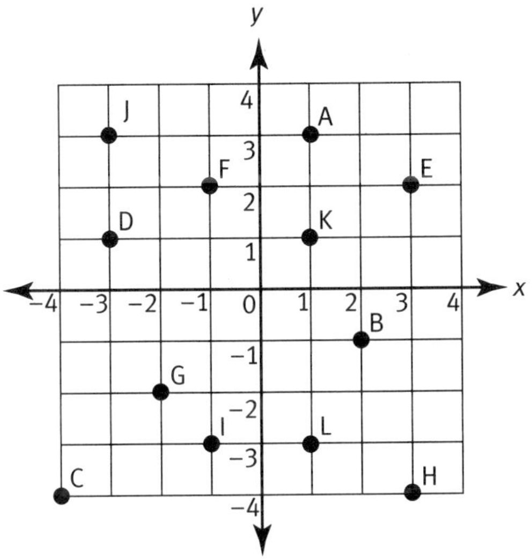

Give the coordinates of these points. **Lessons 5.1 and 5.4**

1. *A* ______________
2. *B* ______________
3. *C* ______________
4. *D* ______________

Give the correct letter for each of these coordinates.

5. (1, −3) ______________
6. (−3, 3) ______________
7. (−2, −2) ______________
8. (3, 2) ______________

Chapter Review

Student Edition • page 236

Complete each table. Make a graph of each set of ordered pairs. **Lessons 5.2 and 5.3**

9. $x \rightarrow (\times 3) \rightarrow y$

x	y
−1	
	0
1	
2	
	9

10. $x \rightarrow (+3) \rightarrow n \rightarrow (\times 2) \rightarrow y$

x	y
−2	
−1	
	6
2	
	14

Write the inverse of each function. **Lesson 5.6**

11. $\rightarrow (+8) \rightarrow$ __________

12. $\rightarrow (\div 5) \rightarrow$ __________

Chapter Review

Name ______________________ **Date** ______________

Student Edition • page 237

Write the inverse of each function. **Lesson 5.7**

13. $x \rightarrow (+1) \rightarrow n \rightarrow (\div 9) \rightarrow y$

____

14. $x \rightarrow (-6) \rightarrow n \rightarrow (\times 3) \rightarrow y$

____

For each function, find a number that you can put in to get out the same number.

15. $x \rightarrow (\times 2) \rightarrow n \rightarrow (-5) \rightarrow y$

____

16. $x \rightarrow (+14) \rightarrow n \rightarrow (\div 3) \rightarrow y$

____

Solve. **Lesson 5.12**

17. $x - 8 = 15$ ______________
18. $4x + 6 = 30$ ______________
19. $3x - 20 = 100$ ______________
20. $\frac{x}{4} - 10 = 4$ ______________
21. $\frac{x}{2} + 8 = 40$ ______________
22. $x + 10 = 8$ ______________

Practice Test

Student Edition • page 238

Use the graph to find the coordinates of each point or to find the letters that match the given coordinates.

1. *B* ____________
2. *G* ____________
3. (−5, 2) ____________
4. (0, −2) ____________
5. (−5, −3) ____________

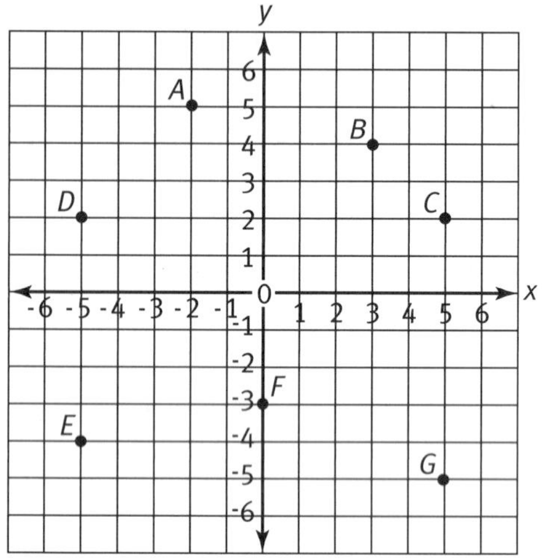

Complete the table for each composite function. Then graph the ordered pairs.

6. *x* → (×2) → *n* → (+3) → *y*

x	0	1	2	3	4
y					

7. *x* → (÷2) → *n* → (−1) → *y*

x	2	4	6	8	10
y					

Use the inverse function rule to find the value of *x*.

8. *x* → (÷4) → 20 ____________

9. *x* → (+14) → 11 ____________

Chapter 5 Practice Test

Name ______________________ Date ______________

Student Edition • page 239

Choose the correct answer.

10. What is the inverse function of the following composite function?

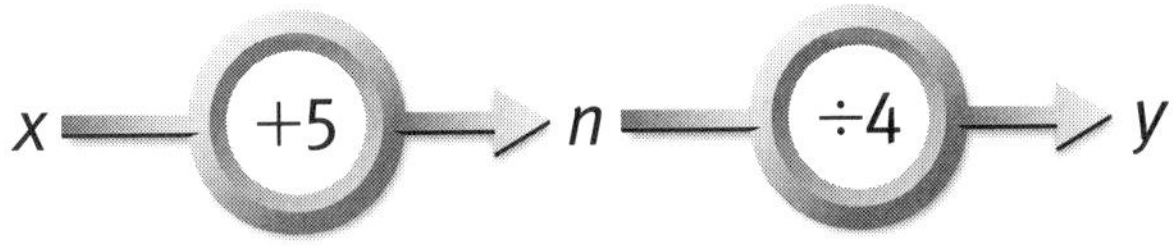

Ⓐ $x \leftarrow (+4) — n \leftarrow (\div 5) — y$

Ⓑ $x \leftarrow (\div 4) — n \leftarrow (+5) — y$

Ⓒ $x \leftarrow (\times 4) — n \leftarrow (-5) — y$

Ⓓ $x \leftarrow (-5) — n \leftarrow (\times 4) — y$

11. In $5x + 6 = y$, if y is 21, what is x?

Ⓐ $x = 3$ Ⓑ $x = 4$

Ⓒ $x = 5.4$ Ⓓ $x = 7$

12. What does $3x$ mean?

Ⓐ $3 + x$ Ⓑ $3 - x$

Ⓒ $3 \times x$ Ⓓ $3 : x$

13. If the temperature is 18°C, what is a good estimate of the temperature in Fahrenheit?

Ⓐ 76°F Ⓑ 68°F

Ⓒ 48°F Ⓓ 36°F

14. Using the function

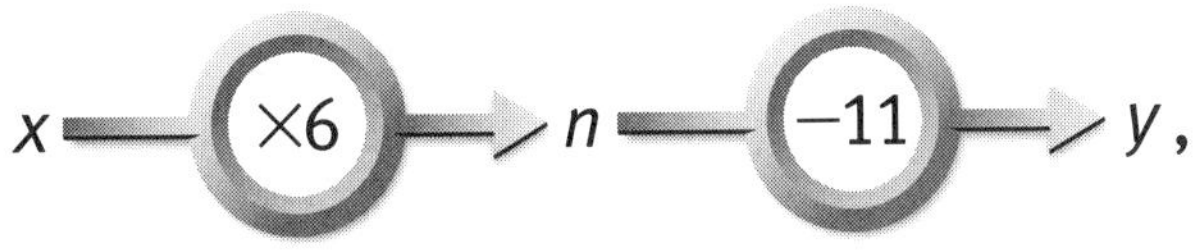

if x is 4, what is y?

Ⓐ $y = 12$ Ⓑ $y = 13$

Ⓒ $y = 19$ Ⓓ $y = 21$

15. Which ordered pair does *not* satisfy this function rule?

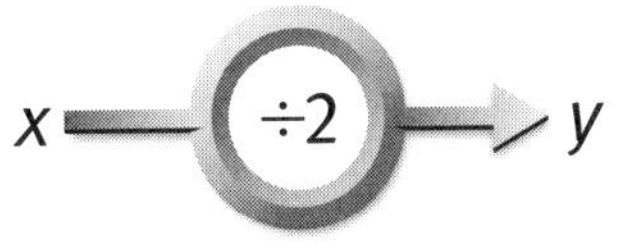

Ⓐ (10, 5) Ⓑ (14, 7)

Ⓒ (18, 10) Ⓓ (22, 11)

16. Janis sells boxes of cookies for \$2 each. If she sells \$140 worth of cookies in one day, how many boxes of cookies does she sell?

Ⓐ 90 Ⓑ 80

Ⓒ 70 Ⓓ 60

17. Which equation matches this composite function?

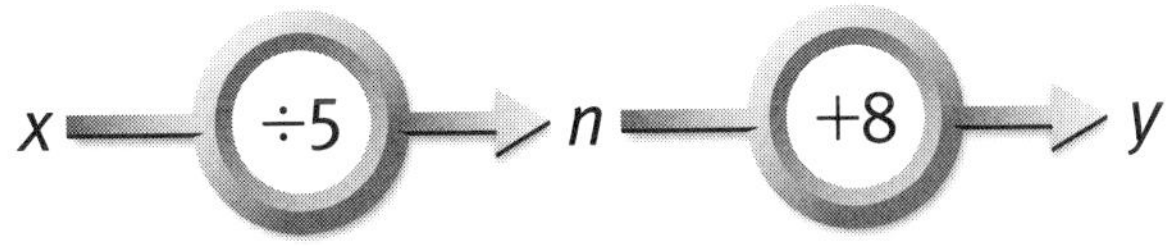

Ⓐ $y = \frac{x}{5} + 8$ Ⓑ $y = 5x + 8$

Ⓒ $y = \frac{x}{8} + 5$ Ⓓ $y = 8x + 5$

Student Edition • page 240

18. Which of the following is an identity function?

Ⓐ

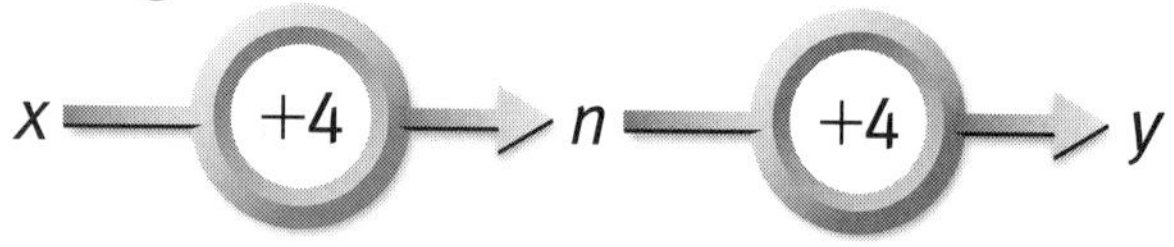

Ⓑ

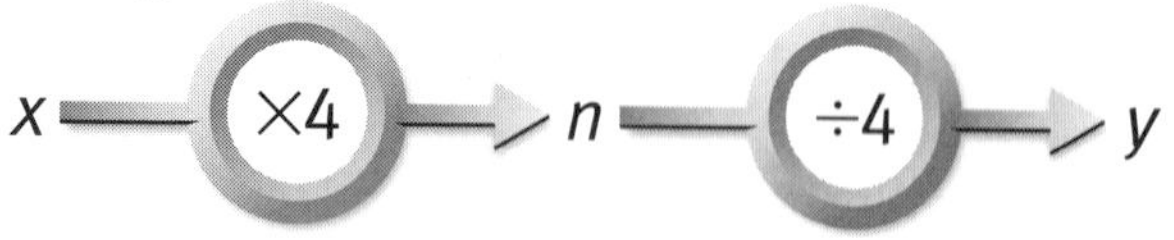

Ⓒ

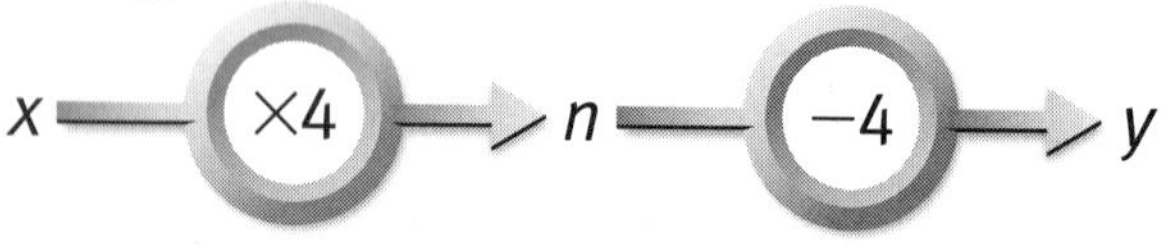

Ⓓ

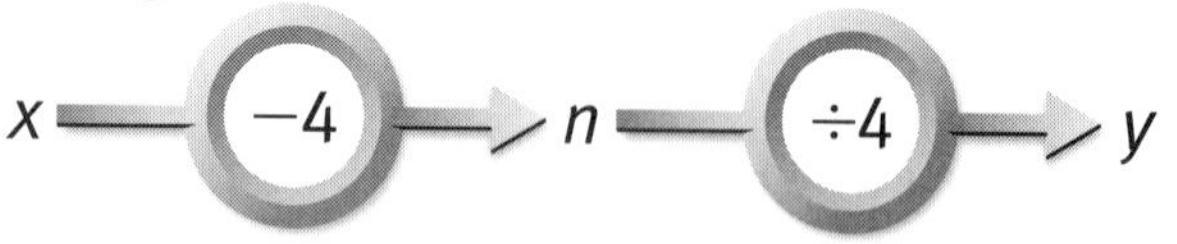

Choose the correct answer.

19. In the equation $\frac{x}{6} - 2 = y$, if x is 36, what is y?

Ⓐ $y = 34$ Ⓑ $y = 6$

Ⓒ $y = 4$ Ⓓ $y = 2$

20. The temperature at midnight is −6°F. If the temperature at noon is 12°F, by how many degrees did the temperature rise?

Ⓐ 20° Ⓑ 18°

Ⓒ 12° Ⓓ 6°

21. Solve for n.
$3 \times (58 + 15) = n$

Ⓐ $n = 45$ Ⓑ $n = 129$

Ⓒ $n = 189$ Ⓓ $n = 219$

22. Choose the measure that makes the most sense for this sentence: The book is ____________ long.

Ⓐ 3,000 m Ⓑ 300 km

Ⓒ 30 cm Ⓓ 3 m

23. Each section of the auditorium has 44 chairs. If there are 12 sections, how many chairs are in the auditorium?

Ⓐ 528 Ⓑ 428

Ⓒ 132 Ⓓ 88

24. What is 1,264.029 rounded to the nearest hundredth?

Ⓐ 1,264 Ⓑ 1,300

Ⓒ 1,264.1 Ⓓ 1,264.03

25. What is the next number in the pattern 18, 12, 6, 0?

Ⓐ 6 Ⓑ −6

Ⓒ 8 Ⓓ 12

26. $5^4 =$ ____________

Ⓐ 20 Ⓑ 125

Ⓒ 625 Ⓓ 3,125

Practice Test

Name ______________________ **Date** ______________

Student Edition • page 241

Extended Response **Answer** the following questions by using the given information.

27. Jasmine makes and sells cakes. She spends about $20 a month on ingredients. She charges $12 for each cake. To figure her profit, she uses the following function rule:

$x \rightarrow (\times 12) \rightarrow n \rightarrow (-20) \rightarrow y$

a. Complete the table by using the given function rule.

Number of Cakes Sold	Profit for the Month (dollars)
0	
1	
5	
10	
20	

b. Plot the ordered pairs from the table above.

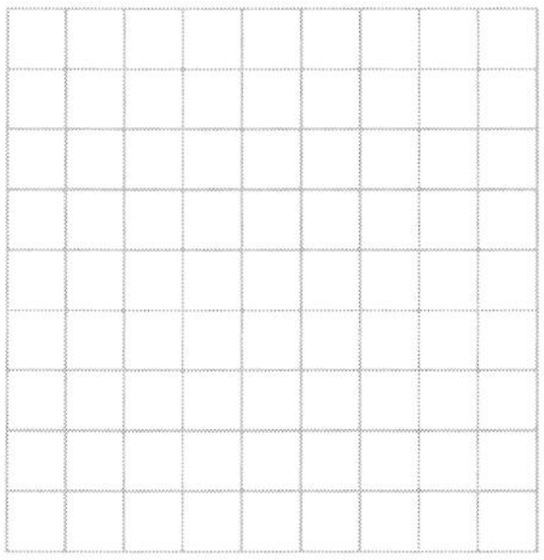

c. How many individual cakes must Jasmine sell in order to break even for the month?

____

d. How much profit will Jasmine make if she sells 30 cakes?

____

28. Jasmine charges an additional $10 for orders of 5 cakes or more. To determine how much to charge for each order, she uses the following function rule:

$x \rightarrow (\times 12) \rightarrow n \rightarrow (+10) \rightarrow y$

a. Jasmine received an order for 5 cakes. How much money did she charge?

____

b. A bakery received a bill from Jasmine for $310. How many cakes did the bakery order?

____

Fractions

Student Edition • page 243

These circle graphs show the nutritional breakdown for the dishes below.

Recipe	Type of Food	Fat	Carbohydrates	Protein
arroz con pollo	Puerto Rican	22 g	85 g	39 g
gumbo	Creole	3 g	7 g	16 g
lentil curry	Indian	9 g	26 g	5 g
hot pot (sin-su-lo)	Korean	24 g	126 g	44 g

A.
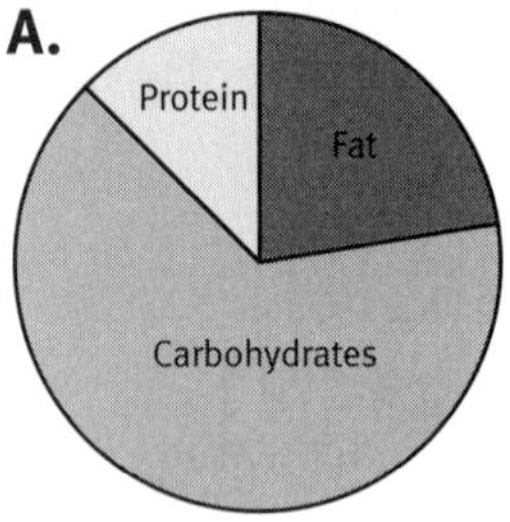

B.
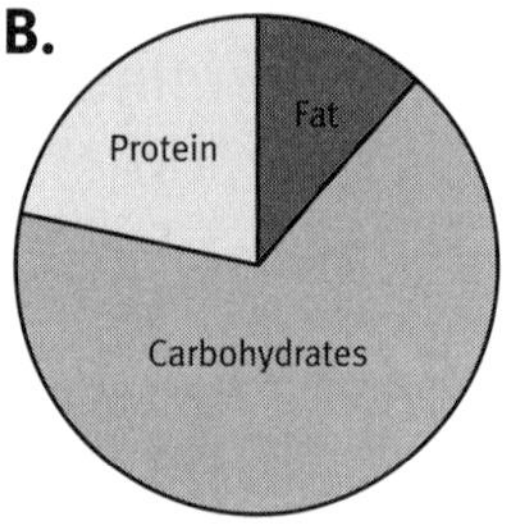

C.
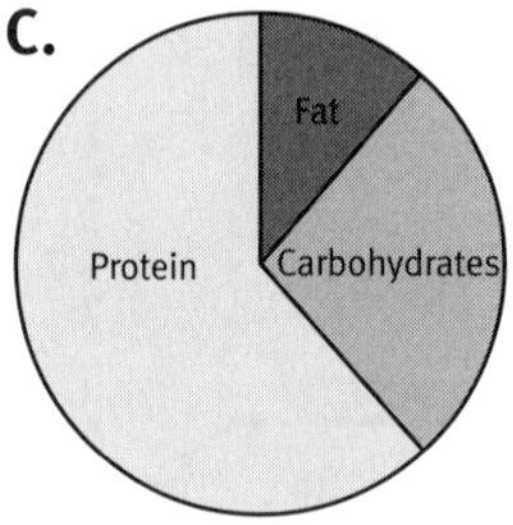

D.
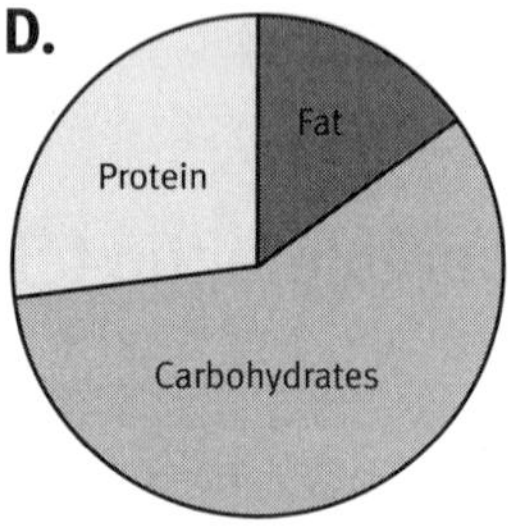

Work in groups to answer the following questions.

1. Which graph represents which dish?

____

____

2. How did you decide which foods go with Graphs A and C?

____

____

3. Graphs B and D look alike. How did you match each of these graphs with the correct dish?

____

____

LESSON 6.1

Name ______________________ Date ____________

Fractions of a Whole

Student Edition • page 245

Solve the following problems.

1. Mr. Estrada just made a raspberry pie. He cut it into 8 equal pieces. He gave a piece to Miss Wu and ate a piece himself.

   a. What fraction of the pie is left? ____________

   b. What fraction of the pie did Miss Wu eat? ____________

   c. What fraction of the pie did Mr. Estrada and Miss Wu eat altogether? Draw a picture that shows your answer.

2. Ramon bought 12 bagels. He ordered 6 sesame bagels, 4 garlic bagels, and 2 onion bagels.

   a. What fraction of Ramon's bagels are sesame bagels? ____________

   b. What fraction of the bagels are garlic? ____________

   c. What fraction are onion? ____________

3. Rob had $14.00. He bought a puzzle for $4.50 and a pen for $3.00. Did he spend more than $\frac{1}{2}$ of his money? ____________

4. Lydia and her parents went out for pizza last week. They ordered a large pizza with pepperoni and cheese. The cook cut the pizza into 12 slices. Lydia ate 3 slices, her father ate 4, and her mother ate 3.

   a. What fraction of the pizza did Lydia eat? ____________

   b. What fraction of the pizza did her father eat? ____________

   c. What fraction of the pizza did her mother eat? ____________

   d. What fraction of the pizza was eaten altogether? ____________

   e. What fraction of the pizza was left over? ____________

LESSON 6.1

Student Edition • page 247

Solve for *n*.

5. $\frac{1}{3}$ of 15 = *n* ______
6. $\frac{2}{3}$ of 15 = *n* ______
7. $\frac{3}{3}$ of 15 = *n* ______
8. $\frac{1}{5}$ of 15 = *n* ______
9. $\frac{1}{5}$ of 30 = *n* ______
10. $\frac{1}{5}$ of 60 = *n* ______
11. $\frac{2}{5}$ of 30 = *n* ______
12. $\frac{2}{5}$ of 60 = *n* ______
13. *n* = $\frac{2}{6}$ of 90 ______
14. *n* = $\frac{1}{6}$ of 90 ______
15. *n* = $\frac{0}{6}$ of 90 ______
16. *n* = $\frac{4}{6}$ of 90 ______
17. *n* = $\frac{4}{6}$ of 60 ______
18. *n* = $\frac{2}{3}$ of 60 ______
19. *n* = $\frac{2}{5}$ of 120 ______
20. *n* = $\frac{4}{10}$ of 120 ______
21. *n* = $\frac{4}{8}$ of 64 ______
22. *n* = $\frac{2}{4}$ of 64 ______
23. *n* = $\frac{1}{4}$ of 36 ______
24. *n* = $\frac{2}{4}$ of 36 ______
25. *n* = $\frac{4}{5}$ of 30 ______
26. *n* = $\frac{2}{5}$ of 45 ______
27. *n* = $\frac{1}{8}$ of 24 ______
28. *n* = $\frac{6}{8}$ of 36 ______

Answer the following questions. You may wish to draw a picture of each answer choice to help you decide on the correct fraction.

29. Chen asked the 30 people in his class to name their favorite flower. If 9 people said they liked roses best, then what fraction of the class chose roses?

a. $\frac{2}{5}$ **b.** $\frac{1}{2}$ **c.** $\frac{3}{10}$

30. Holly has read 6 pages of a 24-page research paper. What fraction of the research paper has Holly read?

a. $\frac{1}{2}$ **b.** $\frac{1}{4}$ **c.** $\frac{2}{3}$

LESSON 6.2

Name ______________________ Date ______________

Fractions of Fractions

Student Edition • page 249

Multiply.

1. $\frac{4}{7} \times \frac{2}{5} =$ ______________

2. $\frac{2}{7} \times \frac{2}{5} =$ ______________

3. $\frac{7}{7} \times \frac{2}{5} =$ ______________

4. $\frac{3}{7} \times \frac{2}{5} =$ ______________

5. $\frac{2}{5} \times \frac{4}{7} =$ ______________

6. $\frac{3}{5} \times \frac{2}{7} =$ ______________

7. $\frac{1}{5} \times \frac{4}{7} =$ ______________

8. $\frac{3}{5} \times \frac{5}{7} =$ ______________

9. $\frac{1}{5} \times \frac{1}{7} =$ ______________

10. $\frac{5}{5} \times \frac{7}{7} =$ ______________

11. $\frac{4}{5} \times \frac{3}{7} =$ ______________

12. $\frac{3}{5} \times \frac{4}{7} =$ ______________

Write <, >, or = to make each statement true.

13. $\frac{1}{2} \times$ ______________ $= \frac{1}{12}$

14. $\frac{3}{4}$ of ______________ $= \frac{6}{16}$

15. $\frac{4}{5} \times$ ______________ $= \frac{8}{45}$

16. $\frac{2}{9}$ of ______________ $= \frac{8}{45}$

17. $\frac{3}{4}$ of ______________ $= \frac{6}{12}$

18. $\frac{5}{8} \times$ ______________ $= \frac{10}{56}$

LESSON 6.3

Decimal Equivalents of Fractions

Student Edition • page 252

For each fraction, give the decimal equivalent or an approximation to the nearest thousandth. To help you check your answers, each fraction is placed above its corresponding point on a number line. Work in groups.

$\frac{1}{2}$

_____

$\frac{1}{3}$ $\frac{2}{3}$

_____ _____

$\frac{1}{4}$ $\frac{2}{4}$ $\frac{3}{4}$

_____ _____ _____

$\frac{1}{5}$ $\frac{2}{5}$ $\frac{3}{5}$ $\frac{4}{5}$

_____ _____ _____ _____

$\frac{1}{6}$ $\frac{2}{6}$ $\frac{3}{6}$ $\frac{4}{6}$ $\frac{5}{6}$

_____ _____ _____ _____ _____

$\frac{1}{7}$ $\frac{2}{7}$ $\frac{3}{7}$ $\frac{4}{7}$ $\frac{5}{7}$ $\frac{6}{7}$

_____ _____ _____ _____ _____ _____

$\frac{1}{8}$ $\frac{2}{8}$ $\frac{3}{8}$ $\frac{4}{8}$ $\frac{5}{8}$ $\frac{6}{8}$ $\frac{7}{8}$

_____ _____ _____ _____ _____ _____ _____

$\frac{1}{9}$ $\frac{2}{9}$ $\frac{3}{9}$ $\frac{4}{9}$ $\frac{5}{9}$ $\frac{6}{9}$ $\frac{7}{9}$ $\frac{8}{9}$

_____ _____ _____ _____ _____ _____ _____ _____

$\frac{1}{10}$ $\frac{2}{10}$ $\frac{3}{10}$ $\frac{4}{10}$ $\frac{5}{10}$ $\frac{6}{10}$ $\frac{7}{10}$ $\frac{8}{10}$ $\frac{9}{10}$

_____ _____ _____ _____ _____ _____ _____ _____ _____

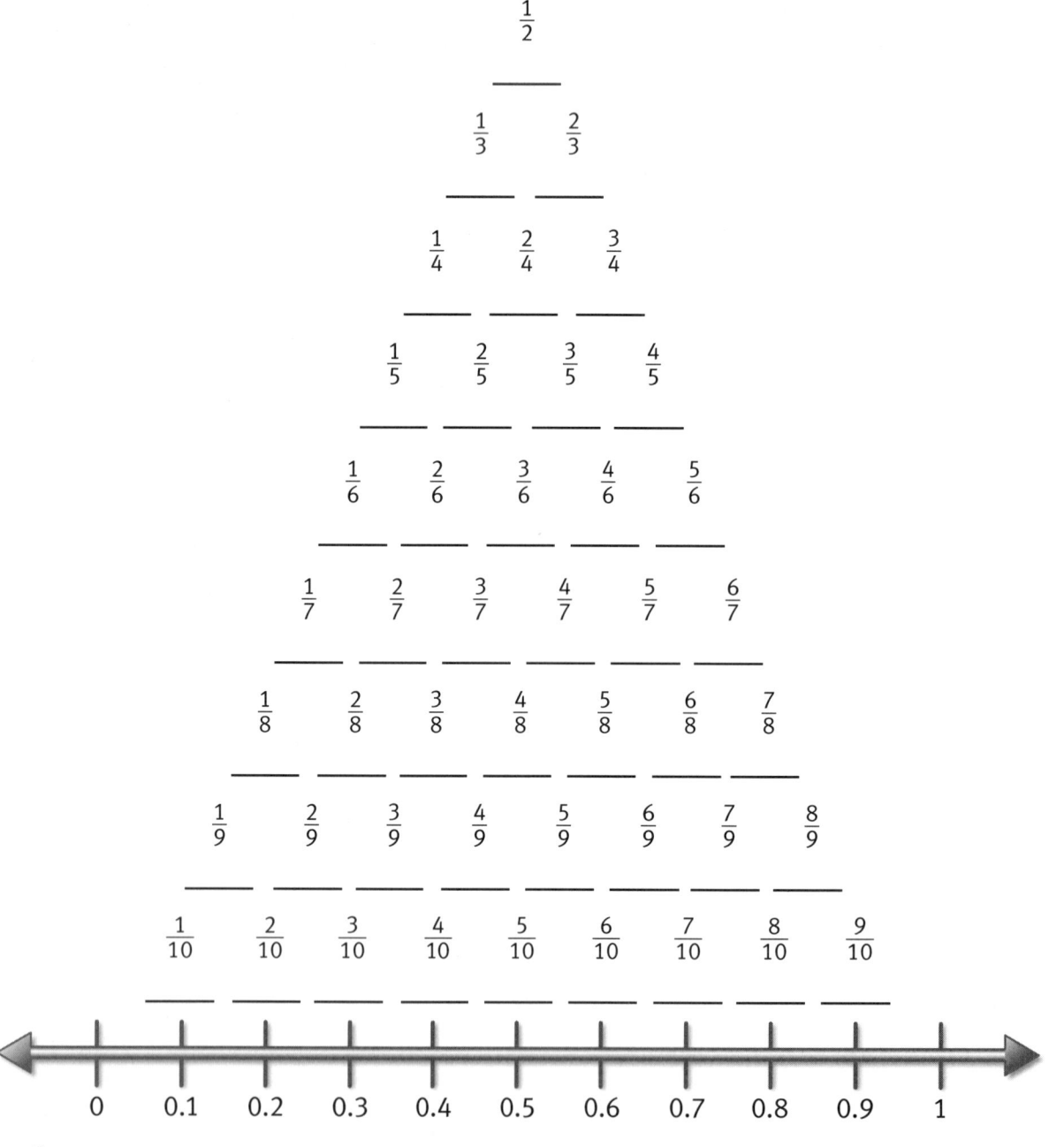

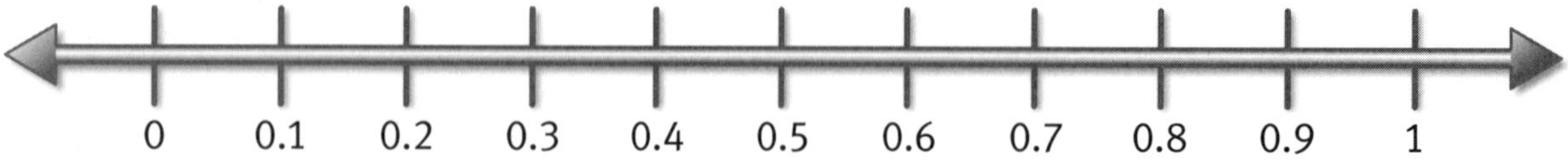

When you are finished, draw a table on a separate sheet of paper to organize the fractions and their decimal equivalents or approximations. Save your table. You will find it useful when you play the **Up to 1 Game.**

LESSON 6.4

Name ______________________________ Date ______________

Equivalent Fractions

Student Edition • page 256

Find the missing numerator or denominator.

1. $\frac{1}{3} = \frac{}{12}$ ______________

2. $\frac{}{20} = \frac{3}{5}$ ______________

3. $\frac{2}{3} = \frac{10}{}$ ______________

4. $\frac{1}{2} = \frac{}{18}$ ______________

5. $\frac{}{12} = \frac{2}{3}$ ______________

6. $\frac{}{24} = \frac{5}{6}$ ______________

7. $\frac{20}{} = \frac{2}{3}$ ______________

8. $\frac{5}{7} = \frac{20}{}$ ______________

9. $\frac{3}{4} = \frac{}{12}$ ______________

10. $\frac{1}{7} = \frac{3}{}$ ______________

11. $\frac{}{8} = \frac{3}{4}$ ______________

12. $\frac{1}{} = \frac{3}{9}$ ______________

13. $\frac{3}{} = \frac{1}{5}$ ______________

14. $\frac{3}{4} = \frac{}{20}$ ______________

15. $\frac{1}{2} = \frac{}{16}$ ______________

LESSON 6.4

Student Edition • page 257

Reduce each of the following fractions to lowest terms.

16. $\frac{17}{34} =$ ______
17. $\frac{16}{80} =$ ______
18. $\frac{16}{64} =$ ______
19. $\frac{9}{27} =$ ______
20. $\frac{9}{36} =$ ______
21. $\frac{27}{36} =$ ______
22. $\frac{18}{36} =$ ______
23. $\frac{12}{30} =$ ______
24. $\frac{9}{30} =$ ______
25. $\frac{18}{30} =$ ______
26. $\frac{5}{30} =$ ______
27. $\frac{5}{35} =$ ______
28. $\frac{15}{35} =$ ______
29. $\frac{25}{35} =$ ______
30. $\frac{20}{35} =$ ______

Write three equivalent fractions for each of the following fractions.

31. $\frac{1}{3}$ ______
32. $\frac{1}{5}$ ______
33. $\frac{1}{7}$ ______
34. $\frac{4}{7}$ ______
35. $\frac{1}{4}$ ______
36. $\frac{3}{5}$ ______
37. $\frac{3}{7}$ ______
38. $\frac{4}{9}$ ______
39. $\frac{3}{5}$ ______
40. $\frac{5}{9}$ ______

LESSON 6.5

Name ______________________ Date ____________

Fractions with the Same Denominator

Student Edition • pages 259–260

Add or subtract.

1. $\frac{3}{4} + \frac{1}{4} =$ ____________
2. $\frac{2}{5} + \frac{2}{5} =$ ____________
3. $\frac{4}{8} - \frac{2}{8} =$ ____________
4. $\frac{1}{3} + \frac{1}{3} =$ ____________
5. $\frac{6}{12} - \frac{2}{12} =$ ____________
6. $\frac{2}{3} - \frac{1}{3} =$ ____________
7. $\frac{5}{7} + \frac{2}{7} =$ ____________
8. $\frac{9}{10} - \frac{4}{10} =$ ____________

Add or subtract. Write your answers in lowest terms.

9. $\frac{1}{7} + \frac{2}{7} =$ ____________
10. $\frac{5}{6} - \frac{4}{6} =$ ____________
11. $\frac{4}{7} - \frac{3}{7} =$ ____________
12. $\frac{7}{12} - \frac{6}{12} =$ ____________
13. $\frac{3}{6} + \frac{2}{6} =$ ____________
14. $\frac{5}{6} - \frac{5}{6} =$ ____________
15. $\frac{6}{8} - \frac{3}{8} =$ ____________
16. $\frac{4}{12} - \frac{3}{12} =$ ____________
17. $\frac{8}{8} - \frac{3}{8} =$ ____________
18. $\frac{1}{9} + \frac{2}{9} =$ ____________
19. $\frac{6}{9} - \frac{4}{9} =$ ____________
20. $\frac{3}{10} + \frac{2}{10} =$ ____________
21. $\frac{4}{5} - \frac{2}{5} =$ ____________
22. $\frac{6}{6} - \frac{3}{6} =$ ____________
23. $\frac{2}{3} + \frac{1}{3} =$ ____________
24. $\frac{7}{9} - \frac{4}{9} =$ ____________
25. $\frac{8}{15} + \frac{4}{15} =$ ____________
26. $\frac{12}{16} + \frac{2}{16} =$ ____________
27. $\frac{5}{10} + \frac{3}{10} =$ ____________
28. $\frac{5}{11} + \frac{3}{11} =$ ____________
29. $\frac{12}{18} - \frac{6}{18} =$ ____________

LESSON 6.5

Student Edition • page 261

Solve the following problems.

30 Mike baked a pie, and then cut it into 8 equal parts.

a. What fraction of the whole pie was each part? ______

b. Mike ate $\frac{3}{8}$ of the pie, and Ana ate $\frac{2}{8}$ of the pie. How much did they eat altogether? ______

c. How much of the pie was left? ______

31 Mr. and Mrs. Cosby drove across the country. They started in Portland, Maine, and drove to Portland, Oregon, which is about 3,100 miles away. They divided the trip into 10 equal parts and drove 1 part each day.

a. What fraction of the trip did the Cosbys complete on the first day?

______

b. How many miles is that? ______

c. What fraction of the trip did the Cosbys complete in 1 week (7 days)?

______

32 **Extended Response** Bob and 4 friends decided to fill a tub with water from his well. Each of the 5 people brought a bucket full of water. Each bucket had enough water to fill $\frac{1}{4}$ of the tub. How full was the tub after they all poured their buckets into it? Explain.

______

______

LESSON 6.6

Name ______________________ Date ____________

Practice with Fractions

Student Edition • page 262

Look along the length of the ruler, between the 0" mark and the 1" mark, at the lines of different lengths. Answer the following questions.

1. What length does the longest of those lines represent? ____________

2. There are two lines that are shorter than the $\frac{1}{2}$" mark but longer than any of the other lines. What lengths do they stand for? ____________

3. **Extended Response** Find the marks for $\frac{1}{8}$", $\frac{3}{8}$", $\frac{5}{8}$", and $\frac{7}{8}$" on the ruler. Where are the marks for $\frac{2}{8}$", $\frac{4}{8}$", and $\frac{6}{8}$"? How are the odd-numbered eighths different from the even-numbered eighths? Why are they marked this way?

____

____

4. The shortest marks on this ruler stand for sixteenths of an inch. For each of the following, tell whether the given mark corresponds to the marks for $\frac{1}{2}$", $\frac{1}{4}$", $\frac{1}{8}$", or whether it is one of the shortest marks:

a. $\frac{1}{16}$ ________	b. $\frac{2}{16}$ ________	c. $\frac{3}{16}$ ________
d. $\frac{4}{16}$ ________	e. $\frac{5}{16}$ ________	f. $\frac{6}{16}$ ________
g. $\frac{7}{16}$ ________	h. $\frac{8}{16}$ ________	i. $\frac{9}{16}$ ________
j. $\frac{10}{16}$ ________	k. $\frac{11}{16}$ ________	l. $\frac{12}{16}$ ________
m. $\frac{13}{16}$ ________	n. $\frac{14}{16}$ ________	o. $\frac{15}{16}$ ________

LESSON 6.6

Student Edition • page 263

Decide which fraction in each of the following pairs is greater. Write a <, >, or = symbol.

5. $\frac{1}{2}$ ______ $\frac{3}{4}$

6. $\frac{5}{16}$ ______ $\frac{3}{8}$

7. $\frac{7}{8}$ ______ $\frac{3}{4}$

8. $\frac{1}{4}$ ______ $\frac{1}{2}$

9. $\frac{2}{16}$ ______ $\frac{1}{8}$

10. $\frac{15}{16}$ ______ $\frac{3}{4}$

11. $\frac{6}{8}$ ______ $\frac{11}{16}$

12. $\frac{1}{2}$ ______ $\frac{10}{16}$

13. $\frac{2}{4}$ ______ $\frac{8}{16}$

14. $\frac{4}{16}$ ______ $\frac{2}{8}$

15. $\frac{7}{16}$ ______ $\frac{3}{8}$

16. $\frac{7}{16}$ ______ $\frac{1}{2}$

17. $\frac{1}{8}$ ______ $\frac{3}{16}$

18. $\frac{12}{16}$ ______ $\frac{7}{8}$

19. $\frac{7}{8}$ ______ $\frac{14}{16}$

20. $\frac{9}{16}$ ______ $\frac{1}{2}$

Name ______________________ Date ____________

Student Edition • page 264

Burrito Bonito offers a variety of burritos on their menu.
What fraction of the burritos contain beef?

Build Your Own Burrito!

Welcome to BURRITO BONITO

CHOOSE ALL 3 FILLINGS, ANY 2, OR JUST 1.

FILLINGS

•MEAT* •CHEESE •BEANS

*Meat Choices are shredded beef or chicken

Rita solved the problem this way:

I Made an Organized List. I used a system to make sure I listed every possibility.

First I listed all the burritos with beef.	Then I listed all the burritos with chicken.	Then I listed all the burritos with no meat.
beef + cheese + beans	chicken + cheese + beans	beans+ cheese
beef + cheese	chicken + cheese	beans only
beef + beans	chicken + beans	cheese only
beef only	beef only	

Think about Rita's strategy. Answer the following questions.

1. What system did Rita use to help her make the list in an organized way?

____

____

____

____

Student Edition • pages 264–265

2. How does organizing help to make sure that nothing is missed and nothing is listed twice?

____

____

3. What answer will Rita get? Why?

____

____

DeShawn solved this problem another way:

I Made an Organized List and Used Logical Reasoning.

I listed 7 types of burritos. Because 4 of them have meat, that means $\frac{4}{7}$ of the burritos have meat. Because $\frac{1}{2}$ of the meat burritos have beef, that means $\frac{1}{2}$ of $\frac{4}{7}$ of the burritos have beef.

With meat	**Without meat**
meat, cheese, & beans	beans & cheese
meat & cheese	beans only
meat & beans	cheese only
meat only	

Think about DeShawn's solution. Answer the following questions.

4. How did DeShawn organize his list?

____

____

5. What answer will DeShawn get if he continues? ____________________

____

Name ______________________ Date ______________

Student Edition • page 265

6 Will DeShawn get the same answer as Rita? Explain.

____

7 Do you agree with DeShawn's statement that $\frac{4}{7}$ of the burritos have meat? Why or why not?

____

____

8 What is your answer to the problem? Explain.

____

____

____

Solve **the following problems. Explain how you solved them.**

9 Suppose Burrito Bonito now offers two choices of bean filling. Now what fraction of the burritos have beef? ______________

____

10 Do a greater fraction of the burritos have beef now that there are two kinds of beans?

____

Build Your Own Burrito!

Welcome to BURRITO BONITO

CHOOSE ALL 3 FILLINGS, ANY 2, OR JUST 1.

FILLINGS

•MEAT* •CHEESE •BEANS

*Shredded beef or chicken •Plain or refried

Cumulative Review

Student Edition • page 266

Decimals and Money Lesson 3.1

Add or subtract.

1
```
  $24.17
+  36.84
```

2
```
  $121.83
-   87.98
```

3
```
  $300.00
-   94.87
```

Using Number Patterns to Predict Lesson 4.2

	If you start at this number	and you keep doing this,	which number or numbers will you hit?
4	10	add 20	**a.** 100 **b.** 150 **c.** 650
5	3	add 6	**a.** 27 **b.** 45 **c.** 72
6	500	subtract 3	**a.** 400 **b.** 300 **c.** 200

Function Machines Lesson 4.4

Solve.

7 A function machine gives 10 as the answer when 30 is put in. You could program your calculator to do this in two ways. What are they?

____

Find the number that came out *(y)* or the function machine rule.

8 17 → (?) → 9

____

9 7 → (×8) → y

____

Cumulative Review

Name ______________________ **Date** ______________

Student Edition • page 267

Graphing in Four Quadrants **Lesson 5.4**

Complete these tables. Then graph the ordered pairs.

10 x → -3 → y

x	0	2	5	6	−2
y	−3				

11 x → $\times 4$ → y

x	1	2	3	4	5
y	4				

Cumulative Review

Student Edition • page 267

Multiplying and Dividing by Powers of 10 Lesson 3.6

Multiply or divide.

12 $3.624 \times 100 =$ ______

13 $36.24 \div 100 =$ ______

14 $0.6789 \times 1{,}000 =$ ______

15 $9.876 \div 1{,}000 =$ ______

Applying Decimals Lesson 3.15

Solve.

16 Nathan buys a hot dog for $2.75, a drink for $1.75, and chips for $1.25 at the ball game.

a. What is Nathan's change if he pays with a $10 bill? ______

b. What is Nathan's change if he pays with a $20 bill? ______

17 The XYZ Store buys T-shirts in boxes of 100. Each box costs $350. If the shirts are sold for $6 each, how much profit will the store make on each shirt? ______

LESSON 6.7

Name ____________________ Date ____________

Comparing Fractions

Student Edition • pages 269–270

Find a common denominator for each of the following pairs of fractions.

1. $\frac{2}{3}, \frac{1}{6}$ ____________
2. $\frac{1}{10}, \frac{3}{5}$ ____________
3. $\frac{1}{2}, \frac{1}{4}$ ____________
4. $\frac{1}{8}, \frac{3}{4}$ ____________
5. $\frac{1}{3}, \frac{2}{5}$ ____________
6. $\frac{1}{4}, \frac{2}{3}$ ____________
7. $\frac{1}{6}, \frac{3}{8}$ ____________
8. $\frac{4}{9}, \frac{1}{2}$ ____________
9. $\frac{1}{12}, \frac{3}{10}$ ____________
10. $\frac{1}{2}, \frac{4}{5}$ ____________
11. $\frac{3}{4}, \frac{1}{6}$ ____________
12. $\frac{1}{4}, \frac{5}{8}$ ____________

Find a common denominator for each of the following sets of fractions.

13. $\frac{1}{3}, \frac{5}{6}, \frac{1}{8}$ ____________
14. $\frac{5}{9}, \frac{3}{4}, \frac{13}{16}$ ____________
15. $\frac{8}{12}, \frac{3}{4}, \frac{1}{2}$ ____________
16. $\frac{4}{5}, \frac{3}{15}, \frac{7}{45}$ ____________
17. $\frac{1}{6}, \frac{3}{5}, \frac{2}{3}$ ____________
18. $\frac{1}{9}, \frac{2}{3}, \frac{4}{27}$ ____________

Write <, >, or = to make each comparison correct.

19. $\frac{1}{3}$ ____________ $\frac{4}{12}$
20. $\frac{1}{3}$ ____________ $\frac{2}{7}$
21. $\frac{2}{3}$ ____________ $\frac{4}{6}$
22. $\frac{11}{22}$ ____________ $\frac{33}{44}$
23. $\frac{1}{6}$ ____________ $\frac{1}{2}$
24. $\frac{8}{13}$ ____________ $\frac{20}{39}$
25. $\frac{2}{6}$ ____________ $\frac{1}{8}$
26. $\frac{3}{4}$ ____________ $\frac{2}{8}$

LESSON 6.7

Student Edition • pages 270—271

27. $\frac{1}{7}$ ______ $\frac{3}{12}$

28. $\frac{1}{3}$ ______ $\frac{2}{3}$

29. $\frac{2}{9}$ ______ $\frac{1}{3}$

30. $\frac{9}{12}$ ______ $\frac{3}{4}$

31. $\frac{2}{9}$ ______ $\frac{9}{18}$

32. $\frac{1}{2}$ ______ $\frac{4}{5}$

33. $\frac{3}{4}$ ______ $\frac{14}{16}$

34. $\frac{2}{6}$ ______ $\frac{1}{4}$

Order the following sets of fractions from least to greatest.

35. $\frac{1}{2}, \frac{1}{4}, \frac{3}{8}, \frac{5}{8}, \frac{3}{4}$ ______

36. $\frac{7}{10}, \frac{2}{5}, \frac{1}{4}, \frac{4}{5}, \frac{3}{4}$ ______

37. $\frac{7}{9}, \frac{1}{3}, \frac{3}{6}, \frac{2}{3}, \frac{5}{9}$ ______

38. $\frac{1}{15}, \frac{5}{5}, \frac{2}{3}, \frac{7}{15}, \frac{1}{5}$ ______

39. $\frac{3}{16}, \frac{1}{5}, \frac{1}{4}, \frac{7}{16}, \frac{2}{4}$ ______

40. $\frac{5}{10}, \frac{1}{2}, \frac{3}{5}, \frac{4}{10}, \frac{1}{5}$ ______

Name ____________________ Date __________

Student Edition • page 271

Solve the following problems.

41. Sara, Mark, and Laura all took the same math test, which had fewer than 50 questions. Sara missed $\frac{1}{5}$ of the questions, Mark missed $\frac{3}{10}$ of the questions, and Laura missed $\frac{1}{8}$ of the questions.

   a. Who had the greatest score? __________

   b. How many questions were on the test? __________

42. Rebecca wants to buy $\frac{1}{2}$ of a pie that is divided into 16 equal parts. How many pieces will she get? __________

43. The Lopez family drove $\frac{1}{3}$ of the way to their vacation spot on Monday and $\frac{3}{8}$ of the way on Tuesday. On which day did they drive farther? __________

44. Hector usually finishes his homework in $\frac{3}{4}$ of an hour. Sara usually finishes her homework in $\frac{5}{8}$ of an hour. Who takes less time?

   ____

45. Pamela read about $\frac{2}{3}$ of a book on Monday and about $\frac{1}{6}$ of the same book on Tuesday. On which day did she read more? __________

LESSON 6.8

Counting Possible Outcomes

Student Edition • page 273

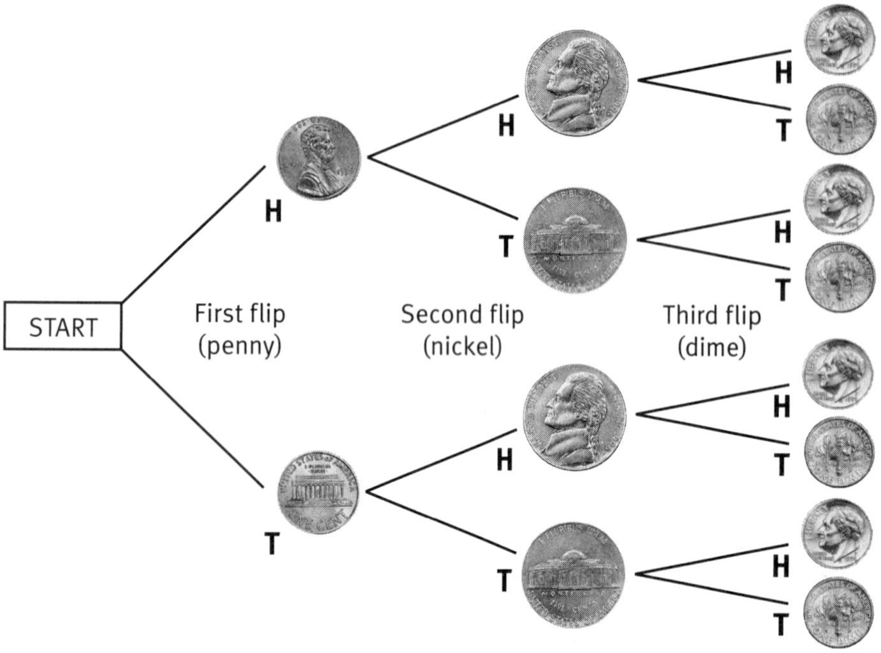

Answer the following questions using the tree diagram.

1. How many total outcomes are there for 3 flips? ______________

2. How many outcomes have 3 heads? ______________

3. How many outcomes have 3 tails? ______________

4. How many outcomes have 2 heads and 1 tail? Write the different letter combinations.

____

____

Name ______________________ Date __________

Student Edition • page 273

5. How many combinations have 1 head and 2 tails? Write the different letter combinations.

____

____

6. Which of the following events do you think will occur most often: 3 heads, 2 heads and 1 tail, 1 head and 2 tails, or 3 tails?

____

____

7. Would you be surprised if it did not occur? ______________

8. **Extended Response** Try to list all the possible ways that two 0–5 ***Number Cubes*** could be rolled. You may wish to list outcomes in a logical order (0, 0; 0, 1; 0, 2;...) or by using a tree diagram. (You should start with six branches.)

Keep your list for the outcomes of the experiment using two 0–5 ***Number Cubes.*** You will need it in the next lesson.

LESSON 6.9

Probability and Fractions

Student Edition • page 274

Answer the following questions.

1. How many marbles are in the box? ______________

2. Suppose you choose one marble without looking. Which shade—light, medium, or dark—are you most likely to choose? ______________

3. Which shade are you least likely to choose? ______________

4. How many marbles are dark? ______________

5. What is the probability of choosing a dark marble? ______________

6. What is the probability of choosing a medium marble? ______________

7. What is the probability of choosing a light marble? ______________

8. What is the probability of not choosing

   a. a dark marble? ______________

   b. a medium marble? ______________

   c. a light marble? ______________

LESSON 6.9

Name ______________________ **Date** ______________

Student Edition • page 275

Perform the probability experiment from Lesson 6.8 in which a penny, nickel, and dime are flipped one at a time.

With a partner, flip the three coins 40 times. While one person flips coins, the other person should keep records, like the example table shown. Tally how often you get 3 heads, 2 heads, 1 head, and 0 heads. Write the totals as fractions of 40. After about 20 flips, switch jobs.

Complete the table, and then answer the questions.

Event	Tallies	Total	Fraction of 40
3 Heads		7	$\frac{7}{40}$
2 Heads		17	$\frac{17}{40}$
1 Head			
0 Heads			

9 Which two events happened most often during your experiment? Were these the same two events that happened most often in Lesson 6.8?

____

____

10 **Extended Response** Are the results what you expected? Why or why not?

____

____

LESSON 6.9

Student Edition • page 276

Find the probability of the following events when flipping 3 coins. Write your answers both as a fraction with a denominator of 8 and as an equivalent fraction with a denominator of 40.

11. 3 heads ______
12. 1 head and 2 tails ______
13. 3 tails ______
14. 4 heads ______
15. 2 heads or 1 head ______
16. 0 heads, 1 head, 2 heads, or 3 heads ______
17. Use the above information to answer these questions.
    a. What is the least a number can be for a probability? ______
    b. What is the greatest a number can be for a probability? ______
18. Extended Response How did the results of your experiment compare to the calculated probabilities?

______

______

Calculate the following probabilities. Use the list you made in Lesson 6.8 for the possible outcomes when rolling two 0–5 ***Number Cubes.***

19. What is the probability of the two numbers rolled having a sum of

a. 0? ______ **b.** 1? ______ **c.** 2? ______

d. 3? ______ **e.** 4? ______ **f.** 5? ______

g. 6? ______ **h.** 7? ______ **i.** 8? ______

j. 9? ______ **k.** 10? ______ **l.** 11? ______

20. Why do the middle sums occur more often than the other sums?

______

______

LESSON 6.10

Name ______________________ Date ____________

Adding Fractions

Student Edition • pages 278–279

Add the following fractions. Write your answers in lowest terms.

1. $\frac{1}{4} + \frac{3}{8} =$ ______________
2. $\frac{5}{8} + \frac{1}{4} =$ ______________
3. $\frac{2}{9} + \frac{3}{6} =$ ______________
4. $\frac{3}{10} + \frac{1}{5} =$ ______________
5. $\frac{1}{2} + \frac{1}{2} =$ ______________
6. $\frac{1}{4} + \frac{1}{2} =$ ______________
7. $\frac{4}{15} + \frac{2}{5} =$ ______________
8. $\frac{1}{3} + \frac{1}{5} =$ ______________
9. $\frac{1}{7} + \frac{1}{2} =$ ______________
10. $\frac{3}{5} + \frac{1}{10} =$ ______________
11. $\frac{3}{8} + \frac{6}{12} =$ ______________
12. $\frac{1}{3} + \frac{1}{4} =$ ______________
13. $\frac{7}{15} + \frac{2}{5} =$ ______________
14. $\frac{2}{9} + \frac{2}{3} =$ ______________
15. $\frac{1}{4} + \frac{1}{8} =$ ______________
16. $\frac{2}{12} + \frac{3}{6} =$ ______________
17. $\frac{3}{7} + \frac{1}{2} =$ ______________
18. $\frac{9}{18} + \frac{1}{9} =$ ______________
19. $\frac{1}{2} + \frac{1}{6} =$ ______________
20. $\frac{2}{9} + \frac{1}{2} =$ ______________
21. $\frac{3}{5} + \frac{1}{6} =$ ______________
22. $\frac{1}{8} + \frac{1}{3} =$ ______________
23. $\frac{4}{7} + \frac{1}{3} =$ ______________
24. $\frac{4}{14} + \frac{2}{7} =$ ______________

LESSON 6.10

Student Edition • page 279

Solve the following problems.

25 Mrs. Sanchez walked $\frac{1}{5}$ mile from her house to Route 20 and then $\frac{3}{10}$ mile to her downtown office. How far did she walk altogether?

____

26 Paul bought $\frac{1}{4}$ pound of peanuts and $\frac{5}{8}$ pound of cashews.

How many pounds of nuts did he buy? ______________

27 Javier sold $\frac{2}{5}$ of the tickets to the play at school. Henry sold $\frac{3}{10}$ of the tickets while he was at the skate park. What fraction of the tickets did the two boys sell altogether? ______________

28 Linda needs $\frac{1}{4}$ teaspoon of salt for her rolls and $\frac{1}{8}$ teaspoon of salt to make muffins. How much salt does she need altogether? ______________

29 Doug walked $\frac{3}{6}$ mile to the store and $\frac{1}{3}$ mile farther to the theater. How far has Doug walked? ______________

30 The home team fans filled $\frac{2}{3}$ of the stadium, and the visiting team fans filled $\frac{1}{6}$ of the stadium. How much of the stadium was filled altogether? ______________

LESSON 6.11

Name ______________________ Date ____________

Subtracting Fractions

Student Edition • pages 280–281

Add or subtract. Write your answers in lowest terms.

1. $\frac{1}{2} + \frac{1}{3} =$ ______________

2. $\frac{1}{2} - \frac{1}{3} =$ ______________

3. $\frac{5}{8} + \frac{1}{4} =$ ______________

4. $\frac{5}{8} - \frac{1}{4} =$ ______________

5. $\frac{3}{5} - \frac{1}{2} =$ ______________

6. $\frac{3}{5} + \frac{1}{4} =$ ______________

7. $\frac{5}{6} - \frac{1}{3} =$ ______________

8. $\frac{5}{6} - \frac{1}{2} =$ ______________

9. $\frac{4}{7} - \frac{1}{2} =$ ______________

10. $\frac{2}{7} + \frac{1}{4} =$ ______________

11. $\frac{5}{9} + \frac{2}{9} =$ ______________

12. $\frac{3}{7} - \frac{2}{7} =$ ______________

Solve the following problems.

19. **Extended Response** Bob and Roland baked a pie. Each boy cut a slice and ate it. Bob's slice was about $\frac{1}{4}$ of the pie. Roland's slice was about $\frac{1}{3}$ of the pie.

   a. About what fraction of the pie did they eat altogether? ______________

   b. Suppose someone told you that Hank later ate $\frac{1}{2}$ of the original pie. What would you think?

   ____

   ____

LESSON 6.11

Student Edition • **page 281**

20 Rayette, Luz, and Patty decided to fill a barrel with water from the lake. Rayette used a pail that holds enough water to fill $\frac{1}{2}$ of the barrel. Luz used a pail that holds enough water to fill $\frac{1}{4}$ of the barrel. Patty used a pail that holds enough water to fill $\frac{1}{3}$ of the barrel.

a. Whose pail holds the most water? ______________

b. Whose pail holds the least water? ______________

c. If all three people filled their pails and emptied them into the barrel, how full would the barrel be? ______________

d. Which two pails together can hold the most water? How full would just those two pails of water fill the barrel?

____

____

21 Mrs. Wong began a trip with a full tank of gas. When she was about $\frac{2}{3}$ of the way to her destination, she saw that her gas tank was only $\frac{1}{4}$ full.

a. Do you think she should try to finish the trip without stopping for gas?

____

b. Suppose she had started the trip with only $\frac{1}{2}$ tank of gas and was about $\frac{2}{3}$ of the way to her destination when she saw that her gas tank was only $\frac{1}{4}$ full. Could she finish the trip without stopping for gas?

____

22 Anna ate $\frac{3}{8}$ of the pizza, and Luis ate $\frac{1}{2}$ of the pizza.

a. About what fraction of the pizza did they eat altogether? ______________

b. How much of the pizza was left over? ______________

LESSON 6.12

Name ____________________ Date ____________

Applying Fractions

Student Edition • page 282

Add or subtract.

1. $\frac{2}{3} - \frac{1}{4} =$ ____________

2. $\frac{3}{5} + \frac{1}{5} =$ ____________

3. $\frac{5}{6} + \frac{1}{4} =$ ____________

4. $\frac{1}{3} - \frac{1}{4} =$ ____________

5. $\frac{3}{5} - \frac{2}{5} =$ ____________

6. $\frac{1}{2} - \frac{1}{3} =$ ____________

7. $\frac{5}{6} - \frac{3}{7} =$ ____________

8. $\frac{1}{5} + \frac{5}{7} =$ ____________

9. $\frac{3}{6} + \frac{1}{5} =$ ____________

10. $\frac{1}{3} - \frac{1}{8} =$ ____________

11. $\frac{1}{2} + \frac{1}{3} =$ ____________

12. $\frac{5}{6} - \frac{6}{9} =$ ____________

LESSON
6.12

Student Edition • page 282

Solve the following problems.

13 Annette promised to give $\frac{1}{4}$ of her pencils to Percy, $\frac{2}{3}$ to Inez, and $\frac{1}{4}$ to James. Can she keep this promise? ____________

14 Ms. Dixon is driving from Springfield to Princeton and back. She started with a full tank of gasoline. She is halfway to Princeton and has $\frac{1}{4}$ of a tank of gasoline left.

a. What fraction of a tank of gas has Ms. Dixon used so far? ____________

b. If she fills the tank, what fraction of a tank of gas will she have left when she gets to Princeton? ____________

c. About how many tanks of gas will Ms. Dixon use in getting from Springfield to Princeton? ____________

d. About how many tanks of gas will she use for the entire round trip? ____________

15 Mrs. Lindsey had a piece of birch wood that was $\frac{2}{3}$ foot long. She cut off $\frac{1}{6}$ foot to use as the pedestal for a model airplane. How much wood is left? ____________

16 Erin has $\frac{3}{4}$ pound of jelly beans. Shannon has $\frac{2}{8}$ pound of jelly beans. How much do they have altogether? ____________

Name ______________________ Date ______________

Student Edition • page 285

Chicken Suqaar (yields 8 servings)			
1 lb or 4 cups	cooked chicken, diced	1 cup	green pepper, chopped
$\frac{1}{4}$ cup	cilantro, chopped	1 tsp	chicken base
$\frac{3}{4}$ cup	onion, chopped	1 tsp	garlic, minced
1 cup	carrots, frozen or fresh, sliced	$\frac{1}{8}$ cup	vegetable oil

Saute all ingredients except chicken in oil until tender. Add chicken. Mix well. Heat ingredients to 165 degrees.

Answer and discuss the following questions.

1. How many cups of carrots are in each serving of chicken suqaar? ______________

2. How many cups of carrots would be needed to make 800 servings of chicken suqaar? ______________

3. How many cups of diced cooked chicken are in a single serving? How many pounds is that? ______________

4. How many pounds of diced cooked chicken would be needed to make 800 servings of chicken suqaar? ______________

5. If the diced cooked chicken comes in 10-pound bags, how many bags would be needed for 800 servings? ______________

Student Edition • page 286

Imagine you are in charge of ordering food for your school cafeteria. You are ordering ingredients to make Hmong beef fried rice.

Hmong Beef Fried Rice
(yields approximately 7 one-cup servings)

ground beef	1 lb
garlic powder	2 tbsp
sugar	1 tsp
salt	$\frac{1}{2}$ tsp
rice, cooked	4 cups
eggs	2

For toppings or garnish, use cilantro sprigs, peas, and chopped scallions.

You know that about $\frac{2}{3}$ of the students in the school will order Hmong beef fried rice when it is on the menu. There are 1,054 students in the school.

To help order the rice, assume the following:

- $\frac{1}{3}$ cup of dry rice makes 1 cup of cooked rice
- 1 cup of dry rice weighs about $\frac{1}{2}$ pound

Work in groups to solve the following problems.

6 Complete the order form.

Item	Quantity
10-pound bag of ground beef	
carton of 48 eggs	
25-pound bag of dry rice	

7 Explain how you figured out how much of each item to order.

____

____

____

8 Create your own problem based on the information on this page and page 267. Exchange your problem with a classmate.

____

____

____

CHAPTER 6 Cumulative Review

Name ______________________ Date ______________

Student Edition • page 287

Multiplying and Dividing Integers **Lesson 4.9**

Multiply or divide.

1. $-9 \times 4 =$ ________
2. $-8 \times (-4) =$ ________
3. $-6 \times (-7) =$ ________
4. $28 \div (-4) =$ ________
5. $48 \div (-8) =$ ________
6. $-56 \div -7 =$ ________

Functions and Ordered Pairs **Lesson 5.2**

Copy each list of ordered pairs, but replace the *x* or *y* with the correct number.

7. $x \rightarrow (-5) \rightarrow y$ (12, 7); (15, y); (x, 5); (0, y); (−1, y)

____

____

8. $x \rightarrow (\div 3) \rightarrow y$ (12, 4); (21, y); (x, 5); (0, x); (x, 8); (−6, y)

____

____

CHAPTER 6

Cumulative Review

Student Edition • page 287

Composite Functions in Standard Notation **Lesson 5.11**

Complete each function table and graph the ordered pairs for each.

9 $y = 3x + 1$

x	y
2	
1	
	10

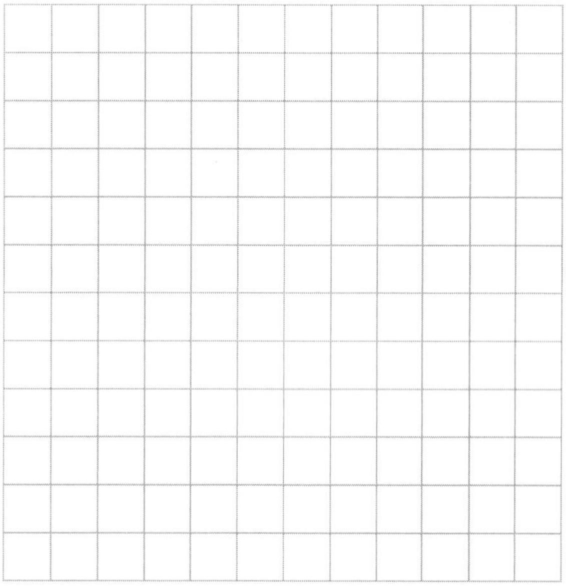

10 $y = \frac{x}{2} - 1$

x	y
10	
0	
	2

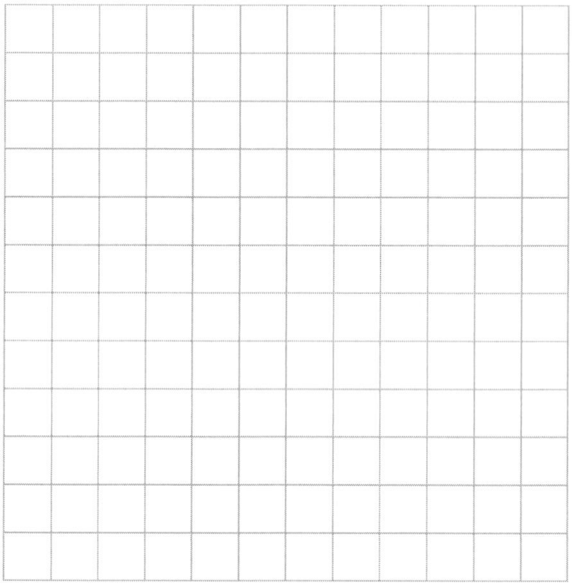

Cumulative Review

Name ______________________ Date ____________

Student Edition • page 288

Linear Equations **Lesson 5.12**

Evaluate each equation by solving for either x or y.

11. $3x - 5 = 25$ ____________

12. $5x + 2 = 42$ ____________

13. $11(3) - 22 = y$ ____________

14. $\frac{x}{7} \times 6 = 30$ ____________

15. $4(x) + 7 = 23$ ____________

16. $\frac{85}{5} - 20 = y$ ____________

Fractions of a Whole **Lesson 6.1**

Solve for n.

17. $\frac{1}{3}$ of $30 = n$ ____________

18. $\frac{2}{3}$ of $60 = n$ ____________

19. $\frac{3}{4}$ of $100 = n$ ____________

20. $\frac{4}{5}$ of $80 = n$ ____________

Decimal Equivalents of Fractions **Lesson 6.3**

For each fraction, give the decimal equivalent or approximation correct to three decimal places (to the nearest thousandth).

21. $\frac{2}{3}$ ____________

22. $\frac{1}{8}$ ____________

23. $\frac{3}{7}$ ____________

24. $\frac{4}{9}$ ____________

25. $\frac{1}{6}$ ____________

26. $\frac{2}{5}$ ____________

Key Ideas Review

Student Edition • page 289

Complete the following exercises.

1. $\frac{2}{9}$ of $54 =$ ______
2. $\frac{2}{7} + \frac{3}{4} =$ ______
3. $\frac{2}{3} - \frac{1}{2} =$ ______
4. $\frac{4}{8} \times \frac{2}{8} =$ ______

Answer the following questions.

5. Create a number line with the following fractions, listed from least to greatest and having the same denominator.

   $\frac{1}{2}$, $\frac{6}{8}$, $\frac{4}{4}$, $\frac{4}{16}$, and $\frac{0}{7}$

   ______

6. Explain why all decimals can be written as fractions, but not all fractions can be written as decimals.

   ______

   ______

List three equivalent fractions for each number.

7. $\frac{3}{9}$ ______
8. $\frac{4}{7}$ ______

Use the sums from the two spinners to answer the following questions.

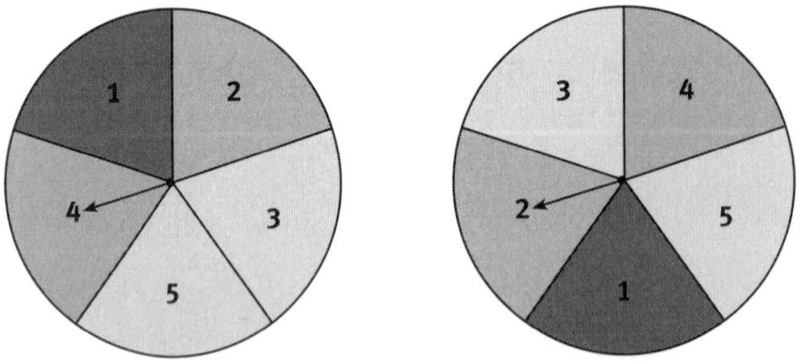

Suppose you spun both spinners and added the two numbers together.

9. What is the probability of spinning a sum that is an even number? ______
10. What is the probability of spinning a sum that is a multiple of 3? ______

CHAPTER 6

Chapter Review

Name ______________________ Date ______________

Student Edition • page 290

Solve. Lesson 6.1

1. $\frac{1}{4}$ of $20 = n$ ______

2. $\frac{3}{4}$ of $20 = n$ ______

3. $\frac{1}{3}$ of $45 = n$ ______

4. $\frac{3}{5}$ of $45 = n$ ______

5. $\frac{1}{6}$ of $18 = n$ ______

6. $\frac{5}{6}$ of $30 = n$ ______

Multiply. Lesson 6.2

7. $\frac{4}{7} \times \frac{2}{9} =$ ______

8. $\frac{2}{3} \times \frac{2}{5} =$ ______

9. $\frac{2}{5} \times \frac{3}{7} =$ ______

10. $\frac{2}{3} \times \frac{4}{7} =$ ______

Fill in the blank to make each statement true.

11. $\frac{1}{3} \times$ ______ $= \frac{1}{12}$

12. $\frac{3}{4}$ of ______ $= \frac{6}{12}$

13. $\frac{3}{5} \times$ ______ $= \frac{9}{25}$

14. $\frac{2}{7}$ of ______ $= \frac{8}{35}$

Find the missing numerator or denominator. Lesson 6.4

15. $\frac{2}{5} = \frac{10}{}$ ______

16. $\frac{1}{2} = \frac{}{16}$ ______

17. $\frac{5}{7} = \frac{15}{}$ ______

18. $\frac{1}{6} = \frac{}{24}$ ______

Chapter Review

Student Edition • pages 290—291

Order the fractions from least to greatest. **Lesson 6.7**

19. $\frac{1}{3}, \frac{1}{2}, \frac{5}{6}, \frac{2}{3}, \frac{1}{6}$ ________________

20. $\frac{5}{8}, \frac{1}{4}, \frac{3}{4}, \frac{1}{2}, \frac{3}{8}$ ________________

21. $\frac{4}{15}, \frac{5}{5}, \frac{2}{3}, \frac{11}{15}, \frac{1}{5}$ ________________

22. $\frac{3}{10}, \frac{1}{2}, \frac{4}{5}, \frac{7}{10}, \frac{3}{5}$ ________________

Solve. Lesson 6.9

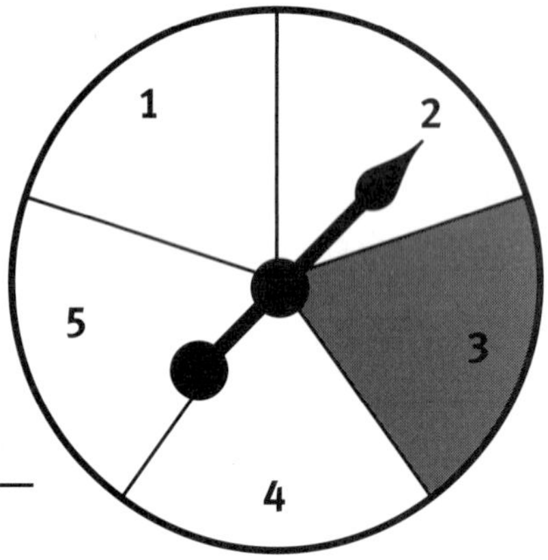

23. A spinner with the numbers 1–5 has an equal chance of landing on any number. What is the probability of it

a. landing on a number less than 2? __________

b. landing on a number greater than 3? __________

c. landing on an odd number? __________

24. What is the probability of it landing on a number greater than 5?

a. $\frac{1}{5}$ **b.** $\frac{1}{2}$ **c.** 0

Chapter Review

Name ______________________ Date ______________

Student Edition • page 291

Add or subtract. Write your answers in lowest terms. **Lessons 6.10–6.11**

25 $\frac{1}{2} + \frac{3}{7} =$ ______________

27 $\frac{1}{3} + \frac{1}{5} =$ ______________

26 $\frac{4}{5} - \frac{3}{10} =$ ______________

28 $\frac{11}{12} - \frac{1}{4} =$ ______________

Solve. **Lesson 6.12**

29 Krystin started the day with $\frac{3}{4}$ of a tank of gas in her car. She used $\frac{1}{8}$ to go to work and another $\frac{1}{16}$ to drive to the store. How much gas did she have left when she got to the store? ______________

30 Kobe lives $\frac{5}{6}$ of a mile from school. On the way home, he stopped at a friend's house $\frac{1}{2}$ mile from school. How far from home was Kobe? ______________

CHAPTER 6 Practice Test

Student Edition • page 292

Find the missing numerator or denominator.

1. $\frac{3}{4} = \frac{}{20}$ ______________
2. $\frac{21}{} = \frac{7}{8}$ ______________
3. $\frac{3}{7} = \frac{15}{}$ ______________
4. $\frac{}{25} = \frac{1}{5}$ ______________
5. $\frac{4}{5} = \frac{}{30}$ ______________
6. $\frac{5}{6} = \frac{15}{}$ ______________
7. $\frac{7}{9} = \frac{42}{}$ ______________
8. $\frac{1}{9} = \frac{}{36}$ ______________

Solve for *n*. Write your answers in lowest terms.

9. $\frac{3}{5} + \frac{1}{3} = n$ ______________
10. $\frac{1}{4} + \frac{4}{8} = n$ ______________
11. $\frac{3}{4} - \frac{2}{16} = n$ ______________
12. $\frac{1}{4} \times \frac{2}{7} = n$ ______________
13. $\frac{1}{2} \times \frac{3}{4} = n$ ______________
14. $\frac{2}{5} + \frac{5}{9} = n$ ______________
15. $\frac{5}{7} - \frac{1}{4} = n$ ______________
16. $\frac{3}{8} \times \frac{4}{6} = n$ ______________

Decide which fraction in each of the following pairs is greater. Fill in the blank with <, >, or =.

17. $\frac{3}{10}$ ______________ $\frac{5}{12}$
18. $\frac{1}{4}$ ______________ $\frac{1}{5}$
19. $\frac{2}{5}$ ______________ $\frac{4}{10}$
20. $\frac{5}{7}$ ______________ $\frac{2}{3}$
21. $\frac{9}{18}$ ______________ $\frac{1}{2}$
22. $\frac{4}{6}$ ______________ $\frac{12}{18}$
23. $\frac{1}{2}$ ______________ $\frac{1}{4}$
24. $\frac{6}{20}$ ______________ $\frac{10}{24}$

Practice Test

Name ______________________ Date ____________

Student Edition • page 293

Choose the correct answer.

25. Which decimal is equivalent to the fraction $\frac{2}{5}$?

Ⓐ 0.2 Ⓑ 0.4

Ⓒ 0.5 Ⓓ 0.7

26. Hilton has $\frac{3}{4}$ of his drink left, and Evelyn has $\frac{1}{5}$ of her drink left. How much more of his drink does Hilton have than Evelyn has?

Ⓐ $\frac{2}{5}$ Ⓑ $\frac{4}{7}$

Ⓒ $\frac{11}{20}$ Ⓓ $\frac{19}{20}$

27. Ms. Ying has 12 flowers in her window box. There are 4 marigolds, 3 petunias, and the rest are pansies. What fraction of the flowers are pansies?

Ⓐ $\frac{1}{12}$ Ⓑ $\frac{3}{12}$

Ⓒ $\frac{4}{12}$ Ⓓ $\frac{5}{12}$

28. Which fraction is equivalent to $\frac{3}{8}$?

Ⓐ $\frac{4}{9}$ Ⓑ $\frac{6}{11}$

Ⓒ $\frac{6}{16}$ Ⓓ $\frac{11}{16}$

29. Which of the following sets shows the fractions in order from greatest to least?

Ⓐ $\frac{5}{6}, \frac{4}{5}, \frac{1}{2}, \frac{1}{3}$ Ⓑ $\frac{4}{5}, \frac{5}{6}, \frac{1}{3}, \frac{1}{2}$

Ⓒ $\frac{1}{3}, \frac{1}{2}, \frac{4}{5}, \frac{5}{6}$ Ⓓ $\frac{1}{2}, \frac{1}{3}, \frac{4}{5}, \frac{5}{6}$

30. Quinn put 6 colored counters into a bag; 2 are red, 1 is blue, and 3 are green. What is the probability that Quinn will pull out a blue counter?

Ⓐ $\frac{6}{6}$ Ⓑ $\frac{3}{6}$

Ⓒ $\frac{2}{6}$ Ⓓ $\frac{1}{6}$

31. What fraction will make the following statement true?

$\frac{4}{5} \times _____ = \frac{8}{15}$

Ⓐ $\frac{4}{10}$ Ⓑ $\frac{2}{3}$

Ⓒ $\frac{2}{10}$ Ⓓ $\frac{4}{3}$

32. Devon put $\frac{2}{3}$ of her vacation pictures into a photo album and framed $\frac{1}{5}$ of them. What fraction of her pictures did *not* go into the album or get framed?

Ⓐ $\frac{2}{15}$ Ⓑ $\frac{3}{8}$

Ⓒ $\frac{1}{2}$ Ⓓ $\frac{13}{15}$

Practice Test

Student Edition • **page 294**

33. What is a common denominator for the following fractions?

$\frac{4}{5}, \frac{6}{7}, \frac{1}{2}$

Ⓐ 10 Ⓑ 14

Ⓒ 35 Ⓓ 70

34. What is $\frac{4}{5} \times \frac{7}{8}$?

Ⓐ $\frac{11}{13}$ Ⓑ $\frac{14}{20}$

Ⓒ $\frac{19}{40}$ Ⓓ $\frac{3}{3}$

35. The rule for a function machine is subtract 3. If 7 comes out of the function machine, which number went in?

Ⓐ 4 Ⓑ 6

Ⓒ 10 Ⓓ 21

36. $3x - 4 = y$. If y is 20, what is x?

Ⓐ $x = 5$ Ⓑ $x = 8$

Ⓒ $x = 20$ Ⓓ $x = 56$

37. Which number is greatest?

Ⓐ 100,101 Ⓑ 101,001

Ⓒ 110,100 Ⓓ 101,011

38. Felicia spent $25.50 on 5 jump ropes. How much did each jump rope cost?

Ⓐ $5.50 Ⓑ $5.10

Ⓒ $4.10 Ⓓ $4.01

39. x — ($\times 2$) → n — (-8) → y

If x is 3, what is y?

Ⓐ $y = -2$ Ⓑ $y = 2$

Ⓒ $y = 5.5$ Ⓓ $y = 14$

40. $350 \times 1{,}000 =$ ______

Ⓐ 35 Ⓑ 3,500

Ⓒ 35,000 Ⓓ 350,000

41. What is 79.174 rounded to the nearest hundredth?

Ⓐ 79 Ⓑ 79.1

Ⓒ 79.17 Ⓓ 79.18

42. If you start at the point (1, 4) and move right 2 steps and down 2 steps, at what point would you be?

Ⓐ (4, 1) Ⓑ (3, 2)

Ⓒ (2, 3) Ⓓ (−1, 2)

Practice Test

Name ______________________ **Date** ____________

Student Edition • page 295

Extended Response **Answer** the following questions.

43. This tree diagram shows the outcomes of tossing two pennies and rolling one 0–5 ***Number Cube.***

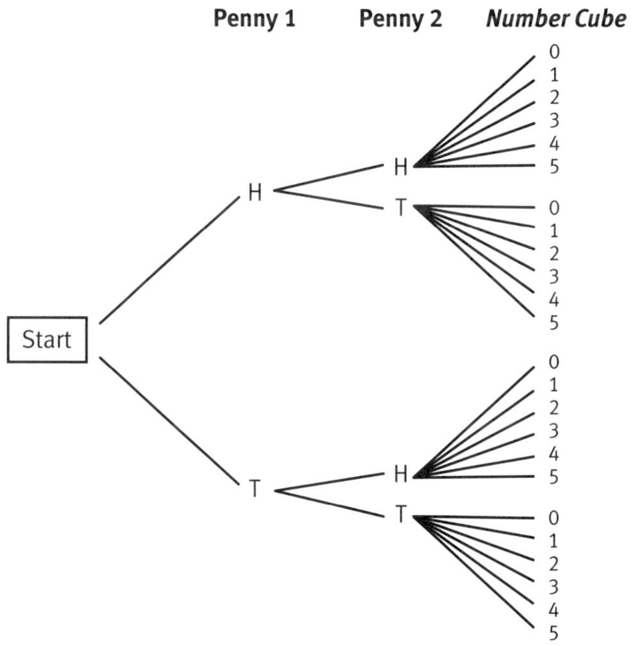

a. How many possible outcomes are there for tossing 2 pennies and rolling the ***Number Cube?*** ______________

b. How many outcomes have 2 heads? Write the combinations.

____

c. How many outcomes have 1 head, 1 tail, and the number 1? Write the combinations.

____

Student Edition • page 295

d. What is the probability (in lowest terms) of rolling a 2? ______

e. What is the probability of tossing 2 heads and rolling an even number? Write your answer in lowest terms. ______

f. What is the probability of tossing a head, a tail, and rolling an odd number? Write your answer with a denominator of 24 and also in lowest terms. ______

44. Which would you expect to happen more frequently: 2 heads and a 1 or a head, a tail, and a 1? Explain why.

______

______

______

______

Name ______________________ Date __________

Mixed Numbers and Improper Fractions

Student Edition • page 297

A **April 18, 10:00 P.M.** Revere orders the lantern signal to be sent. **10:15 P.M.** Revere hurries from his house and heads to Charlestown.

B **11:00 P.M.** Revere sets off for Lexington.

C **11:30 P.M.** Revere reaches Medford and awakens the captain of the Minute Men.

D **April 19, 12:05 A.M.** Revere reaches Lexington. Another messenger, William Dawes, arrives about $\frac{1}{2}$ hour after Revere. The two riders soon set off for Concord together.

Use the record below to solve these problems.

From	To	Distance	Time
Lechmere Point	Lexington	11 miles	3–4 hours
Lexington	Concord	6–7 miles	2–3 hours
Concord	Lexington	6–7 miles	2–3 hours
Lexington	Charlestown	11 miles	3–4 hours

1. What are the least and the greatest total distances that the British soldiers could have marched? ______________________

2. What are the least and the greatest total times that the British soldiers marched? ______________________

3. What can you say about the average speed of the British soldiers?

____

LESSON 7.1 Mixed Numbers and Improper Fractions

Student Edition • page 299

Complete each expression with an equivalent improper fraction or mixed number.

1. $2\frac{1}{3} =$ ____________
2. $2\frac{3}{5} =$ ____________
3. $1\frac{1}{2} =$ ____________
4. $3\frac{2}{3} =$ ____________
5. $\frac{7}{4} =$ ____________
6. $\frac{11}{6} =$ ____________
7. $\frac{8}{3} =$ ____________
8. $\frac{5}{4} =$ ____________

Solve.

9. **Extended Response** Taylor is counting distance markers along the highway. She has counted 33 of them so far. Her parents told her there is $\frac{1}{10}$ of a mile between each marker. How many miles has Taylor traveled since she started counting? Explain why the answer is not $\frac{33}{10}$.

____

____

____

10. Ms. Blair is conducting an experiment with her chemistry class. Each pair of students needs $\frac{1}{4}$ meter of plastic tubing. If there are 11 pairs of students, how much tubing does Ms. Blair need for the whole class? Give your answer as both a mixed number and an improper fraction. ____________

LESSON 7.2

Name ______________________ Date ____________

Multiplying Mixed Numbers

Student Edition • page 301

Multiply. Check to see that your answers make sense.

1. $2\frac{1}{3} \times 5\frac{2}{7} =$ ____________
2. $\frac{7}{8} \times 2\frac{1}{6} =$ ____________
3. $2\frac{2}{5} \times 4\frac{1}{6} =$ ____________
4. $3\frac{1}{8} \times 2\frac{1}{6} =$ ____________
5. $1\frac{2}{3} \times 2\frac{1}{6} =$ ____________
6. $\frac{4}{7} \times 5\frac{1}{4} =$ ____________
7. $4\frac{1}{3} \times 3\frac{4}{7} =$ ____________
8. $3\frac{4}{5} \times \frac{5}{7} =$ ____________
9. $1\frac{3}{4} \times 2\frac{2}{7} =$ ____________
10. $1\frac{1}{2} \times 2\frac{1}{4} =$ ____________
11. $\frac{2}{3} \times \frac{3}{8} =$ ____________
12. $\frac{2}{3} \times 3\frac{3}{8} =$ ____________
13. $\frac{2}{3} \times \frac{2}{5} =$ ____________
14. $2\frac{2}{3} \times 1\frac{1}{6} =$ ____________
15. $\frac{3}{4} \times \frac{2}{3} =$ ____________
16. $1\frac{3}{4} \times 1\frac{2}{3} =$ ____________

Solve the following problems.

17. Lee worked $1\frac{1}{2}$ hours overtime on each of 3 days last week. How many overtime hours did Lee work altogether last week? ____________

18. Mark went to the local indoor rock-climbing facility. His first 3 climbs were each $16\frac{3}{4}$ feet. How many total feet did Mark climb on his first 3 attempts? ____________

LESSON 7.3

Adding Mixed Numbers

Student Edition • page 303

Add.

1. $3\frac{5}{8} + 1\frac{1}{4} =$ ______

2. $5\frac{1}{2} + 2\frac{2}{3} =$ ______

3. $4\frac{3}{4} + 1\frac{5}{6} =$ ______

4. $1\frac{1}{3} + 3\frac{2}{3} =$ ______

5. $3\frac{1}{2} + 2\frac{3}{4} =$ ______

6. $3\frac{6}{7} + 4\frac{1}{4} =$ ______

7. $1\frac{1}{2} + 2\frac{4}{5} =$ ______

8. $4\frac{1}{6} + 2\frac{2}{3} =$ ______

9. $4\frac{3}{4} + 3\frac{3}{4} =$ ______

10. $5\frac{2}{3} + 3\frac{1}{3} =$ ______

11. $4\frac{11}{15} + 5\frac{2}{3} =$ ______

12. $5\frac{2}{3} + 3\frac{2}{3} =$ ______

13. $12\frac{2}{3} + 4\frac{2}{9} =$ ______

Solve.

14. A plumber bought 5 pipes. Two were $3\frac{1}{2}$ feet long, and the others were $1\frac{3}{8}$ feet. What was the total length of pipe purchased? ______

15. For a school project, Drew needs $4\frac{1}{4}$ feet of rope, and Owen needs $5\frac{2}{3}$ feet of rope. How much rope do they need altogether? ______

16. Clara had $5\frac{3}{4}$ cups of blueberries and $2\frac{5}{8}$ cups of strawberries. How many cups of berries did she have altogether? ______

LESSON 7.4

Name ______________________ Date ______________

Subtracting Mixed Numbers

Student Edition • page 305

Subtract.

1. $5\frac{7}{9} - 3\frac{4}{6} =$ ______________

2. $4\frac{5}{7} - 2\frac{1}{2} =$ ______________

3. $3\frac{1}{4} - 2\frac{5}{8} =$ ______________

4. $3\frac{1}{2} - 2\frac{1}{4} =$ ______________

5. $5\frac{2}{7} - 3\frac{6}{7} =$ ______________

6. $8\frac{5}{6} - 3\frac{1}{3} =$ ______________

7. $5\frac{3}{5} - 2\frac{1}{3} =$ ______________

8. $2\frac{4}{5} - 1\frac{1}{2} =$ ______________

9. $4\frac{1}{6} - 2\frac{2}{3} =$ ______________

10. $5\frac{6}{10} - 1\frac{1}{5} =$ ______________

11. $5\frac{2}{3} - 3\frac{1}{3} =$ ______________

12. $3\frac{2}{3} - 1\frac{1}{3} =$ ______________

13. $7\frac{2}{3} - 2\frac{1}{4} =$ ______________

14. $5\frac{2}{3} - 3\frac{2}{3} =$ ______________

Student Edition • page 305

Add or subtract.

15 $5\frac{4}{9} + 2\frac{2}{3} =$ ______

16 $15\frac{1}{3} - \frac{2}{3} =$ ______

17 $1\frac{7}{8} + 3\frac{1}{4} =$ ______

18 $3\frac{1}{4} - 1\frac{7}{8} =$ ______

19 $10\frac{1}{2} + 10\frac{1}{2} =$ ______

20 $2\frac{1}{2} + 3\frac{4}{7} =$ ______

21 $5\frac{4}{9} - 2\frac{2}{3} =$ ______

22 $15\frac{1}{3} - 1\frac{2}{3} =$ ______

Solve the following problems.

23 Tom weighs $142\frac{1}{2}$ pounds. His wrestling opponent weighs $140\frac{3}{4}$ pounds. By how much does Tom outweigh his opponent? ______

24 Amy lives $1\frac{3}{4}$ miles from the baseball field. Tony lives $1\frac{2}{3}$ miles from the same field. How much farther is Amy's round trip than Tony's round trip? ______

25 Daniel ran $7\frac{1}{2}$ miles on Monday and $8\frac{3}{5}$ miles on Tuesday. How much farther did Daniel run on Tuesday? ______

26 A bolt of fabric contains $7\frac{1}{3}$ yards of material. If Mr. Walker cuts $4\frac{2}{5}$ yards from the bolt to make a suit, how many yards will be left? ______

LESSON 7.5

Name ____________________ Date ____________

Addition and Subtraction Applications

Student Edition • page 306

Abigail is making a piece of furniture that will be 30 inches tall. The base, or bottom portion, and the crown, or top portion, are each to be $4\frac{1}{2}$ inches high. There will be 4 drawers and 3 spaces between the drawers. The spaces between the drawers will each be $\frac{1}{4}$ inch high.

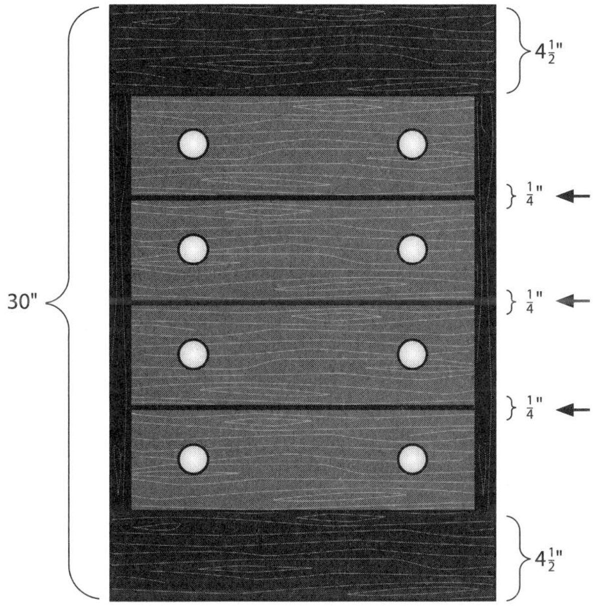

Solve.

1. How much space is left for drawers? ____________

2. If the 2 bottom drawers are each $4\frac{1}{4}$ inches high, how much space is left for the other 2 drawers? ____________

3. If the bottom 3 drawers are each $4\frac{1}{4}$ inches high, how much space is left for the top drawer? ____________

4. **Extended Response** If the bottom 3 drawers are each 7 inches high, how much space is left for the top drawer? Explain.

____

____

5. If all 4 drawers are equal in height, how high should each of them be? ____________

Student Edition • page 307

Solve the following problems.

6. If it is a quarter after 2 now, what time will it be in $3\frac{1}{2}$ hours? ______

7. Lia is $10\frac{1}{2}$ years old. In how many years will she be 18 years old? ______

8. Mrs. Harris earns $8 per hour. She gets time and a half for overtime. That means she is paid $1\frac{1}{2}$ times her usual wage when she works overtime.

   a. How much does Mrs. Harris earn per hour when she works overtime?

   ______

   b. Last week, Mrs. Harris worked 40 hours at her regular hourly rate plus 10 hours of overtime. How much money did she earn last week?

   ______

   c. This week, Mrs. Harris worked 40 hours at her regular hourly rate and $12\frac{1}{2}$ hours of overtime. How much did she earn? ______

   d. Mrs. Harris usually works until 4:30 P.M. Today she worked until 8:00 P.M. How many hours of overtime did she put in today? ______

   e. Mrs. Harris worked until 6:30 P.M. on Thursday and until 7:00 P.M. on Friday. How many hours of overtime did she work in those two days?

   ______

9. Both Maria and Derek collect miniature cars. Maria has $1\frac{1}{2}$ times as many cars as Derek does. If Derek has 20 cars, how many does Maria have?

   ______

10. Diego gets a $\frac{1}{2}$-hour lunch and a 20-minute break each day at his job. How many hours of break time does he get during his 5-day work week?

   ______

Name ______________________ Date ______________

Student Edition • pages 308–309

Stan is building a model of Paul Revere's house. The instructions say that if you measure and cut very carefully, the seven pieces listed below can be cut from a single 16-inch by 12-inch sheet of foam board. How can that be done?

Instructions

Rectangles	Right Triangles
$12\frac{1}{4}$ in. by $2\frac{5}{8}$ in.	$9\frac{3}{8}$ in. by $6\frac{3}{4}$ in.
$9\frac{1}{4}$ in. by $2\frac{5}{8}$ in.	$9\frac{3}{8}$ in. by $6\frac{3}{4}$ in.
$6\frac{3}{4}$ in. by $3\frac{3}{4}$ in.	
$6\frac{3}{4}$ in. by $5\frac{1}{2}$ in.	
$3\frac{3}{4}$ in. by $2\frac{5}{8}$ in.	

Olivia solved the problem this way:

I decided to Make a Physical Model.

I decided to cut the pieces from two sheets of foam board. Then I looked at a photo of the house and glued the pieces together.

Think about Olivia's strategy, and answer these questions.

1. Why doesn't Olivia need to make her model from a 16-inch × 12-inch piece of foam board?

____

____

Student Edition • page 309

2 How can Olivia use her model to try to solve the problem?

3 Would you use Olivia's strategy? Why or why not?

Diego solved the problem another way:

I decided to Break the Problem into Parts, Use Logical Reasoning, and Make a Diagram.

First, I figured out what to do with the triangles. Next, I looked for pieces that have the same length or same width.

Then, I looked for measurements that added to whole numbers, especially 12 or 16.

Think about Diego's strategy, and answer the following questions.

4 How do you think the triangles should be arranged?

5 Why might it help to find pieces that have a side the same length?

Exploring Problem Solving

Name ______________________ Date ______________

Student Edition • page 309

❻ Why might it help to find measurements that add to whole numbers?

____

____

❼ Would you use Diego's strategy? Why or why not?

____

____

❽ Solve the problem. Use any strategy you think will work.

____

____

❾ What strategy did you use? Why?

____

____

❿ Write a problem like the one on page 289. Then trade with a partner and solve.

____

____

Cumulative Review

Student Edition • page 310

Using Composite Functions **Lesson 5.8**

Solve.

Livio opened a lemonade stand. He purchased a large jug of lemonade for $20, and sold glasses at $1.25 apiece.

1. Write a function rule to calculate Livio's profit *(y)* if he sells *x* glasses.

   ____

2. What will his profit or loss be if he sells 10 glasses? ______________
3. What will his profit or loss be if he sells 20 glasses? ______________

Equivalent Fractions **Lesson 6.4**

Reduce each of the following fractions to lowest terms.

4. $\frac{35}{49}$ ______________
5. $\frac{54}{63}$ ______________
6. $\frac{48}{72}$ ______________

For each of the following fractions, write three equivalent fractions.

7. $\frac{3}{4}$ ______________
8. $\frac{2}{5}$ ______________
9. $\frac{1}{6}$ ______________
10. $\frac{5}{7}$ ______________

Counting Possible Outcomes **Lesson 6.8**

If the spinner is spun 3 times, how many ways can the combination be

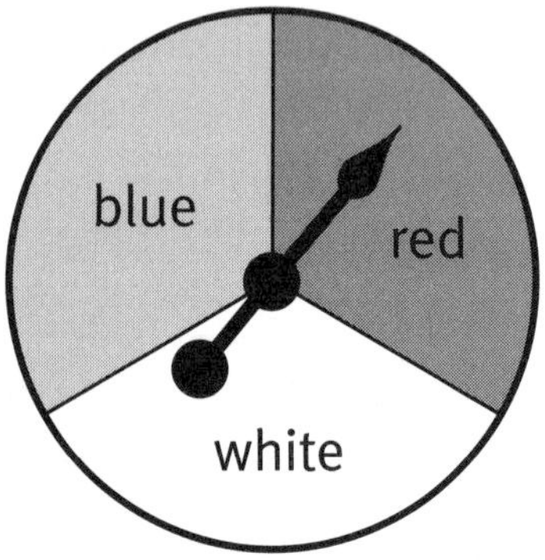

11. red, white, and blue? ______________
12. red, red, and blue? ______________
13. red, red, and red? ______________

Cumulative Review

Name ______________________ Date ______________

Student Edition • page 311

Addition and Subtraction of Fractions Lessons 6.10 and 6.11

Add or subtract.

14. $\frac{1}{2} + \frac{1}{3} =$ ______

15. $\frac{2}{3} - \frac{1}{4} =$ ______

16. $\frac{1}{4} + \frac{1}{6} =$ ______

17. $\frac{1}{2} - \frac{1}{3} =$ ______

18. $\frac{3}{8} + \frac{1}{3} =$ ______

19. $\frac{1}{6} - \frac{1}{8} =$ ______

20. $\frac{1}{2} + \frac{1}{4} =$ ______

21. $\frac{3}{5} + \frac{1}{3} =$ ______

22. $\frac{5}{9} - \frac{3}{8} =$ ______

23. $\frac{4}{7} - \frac{1}{2} =$ ______

24. $\frac{1}{8} + \frac{1}{4} =$ ______

25. Abu walked $\frac{1}{4}$ mile to school and $\frac{3}{10}$ mile to the store. How far did he walk altogether?

______

Multiplying Decimals by Whole Numbers Lesson 3.9

Multiply.

26. $648.25 \times 43 =$ ______

27. $869 \times 51.6 =$ ______

28. $9,755 \times 54.2 =$ ______

29. $865.4 \times 997 =$ ______

30. $23.65 \times 51 =$ ______

31. $341.88 \times 62 =$ ______

32. $156 \times 96.3 =$ ______

33. $369 \times 45.32 =$ ______

34. $574.09 \times 68 =$ ______

35. If 1 lunch costs $4.98, how much would 75 lunches cost?

______

LESSON 7.6

Dividing Fractions

Student Edition • pages 312–313

Divide. Reduce whenever possible.

1. $12 \div \frac{2}{3} =$ ______
2. $\frac{1}{2} \div \frac{1}{3} =$ ______
3. $16 \div \frac{4}{5} =$ ______
4. $\frac{2}{5} \div \frac{3}{7} =$ ______
5. $\frac{5}{8} \div \frac{5}{4} =$ ______
6. $\frac{5}{12} \div \frac{10}{3} =$ ______

Fill in the blank for each of the following to make a correct statement.

7. $\frac{7}{5} \times \frac{2}{3} =$ ______
8. $\frac{14}{15} \div \frac{7}{5} =$ ______
9. $\frac{14}{15} \div \frac{2}{3} =$ ______
10. $6\frac{1}{4} \div$ ______ $= 3\frac{3}{4}$
11. ______ $\div 4\frac{1}{3} = \frac{33}{65}$
12. $8\frac{1}{3} \div$ ______ $= 5$

Answer the following questions.

13. Reuben teaches art in an elementary school. He has $2\frac{1}{2}$ large containers of blue acrylic paint for his students to use. If about $\frac{3}{10}$ of a container is used for each day's lesson, about how many lessons can Reuben teach with the paint available? ______

14. **Extended Response** Orlando needed to measure salt for a recipe. The recipe called for $\frac{1}{4}$ teaspoon of salt, but Orlando did not have a measuring spoon that small. Instead he used two $\frac{1}{2}$-teaspoons of salt. Was this correct? Explain why Orlando might have done that.

______

______

LESSON 7.7

Name ______________________ Date ______________

Fractions and Decimals

Student Edition • page 315

In the table below, each number across the top stands for the numerator. Each number down the left side stands for the denominator.

Fill in the blanks. Find the decimal equivalents or approximations and round to the nearest thousandth.

Denominator \ Numerator	1	2	3	4	5	6	7	8	9	10
1										
2										
3										
4				1					2.25	
5										
6										
7	0.143									
8			0.375							
9								0.889		
10										

Solve the following problems in two ways—by finding a common denominator and by using decimals to approximate. For each problem, show that the two answers you get are equivalent or nearly equivalent.

1. $\frac{2}{5} - \frac{1}{3} =$ ______________
2. $\frac{2}{3} - \frac{1}{6} =$ ______________
3. $\frac{5}{9} - \frac{1}{3} =$ ______________
4. $\frac{4}{4} - \frac{3}{4} =$ ______________
5. $\frac{3}{8} - \frac{1}{4} =$ ______________
6. $\frac{1}{2} - \frac{1}{4} =$ ______________
7. $\frac{1}{3} + \frac{5}{9} =$ ______________
8. $\frac{2}{3} - \frac{3}{5} =$ ______________

LESSON 7.8

Decimal Equivalents of Rational Numbers

Student Edition • page 317

Solve the following problems in two ways. For each problem, check to see that your two answers are equivalent or about equivalent. Round your answers to four decimal places, if necessary.

1. $1\frac{4}{9} + 3\frac{1}{3} =$ ______
2. $2\frac{1}{3} + \frac{5}{6} =$ ______
3. $5\frac{8}{9} + 8\frac{1}{6} =$ ______
4. $7\frac{3}{8} + 6\frac{1}{2} =$ ______
5. $6\frac{3}{4} - 4\frac{1}{2} =$ ______
6. $\frac{4}{5} + \frac{1}{3} =$ ______
7. $9\frac{1}{4} - 4\frac{2}{3} =$ ______
8. $8\frac{2}{3} - 2\frac{2}{5} =$ ______
9. $3\frac{1}{6} - 2\frac{2}{3} =$ ______
10. $1\frac{4}{5} - \frac{1}{3} =$ ______
11. $8\frac{5}{6} + 3\frac{1}{3} =$ ______
12. $1\frac{3}{8} + 1\frac{3}{4} =$ ______
13. $4\frac{3}{5} - 2\frac{7}{10} =$ ______
14. $6\frac{1}{9} + 2\frac{8}{9} =$ ______
15. $4\frac{2}{3} - 2\frac{3}{4} =$ ______
16. $8\frac{5}{9} + 6\frac{2}{3} =$ ______
17. $5\frac{3}{8} + \frac{5}{6} =$ ______
18. $6\frac{3}{8} + 1\frac{1}{4} =$ ______
19. $5\frac{1}{4} - 2\frac{11}{12} =$ ______
20. $5\frac{1}{3} - 3\frac{4}{9} =$ ______

Name ______________________ Date ____________

Student Edition • page 318

For each fraction, write the decimal equivalent or approximation to the nearest thousandth. Each fraction is placed above its corresponding point on the number line. Work in small groups. Use a calculator when you need it. The table on page 295 should also help.

$\frac{10}{10}$ ______

$\frac{9}{9}$ ______ $\frac{10}{9}$ ______

$\frac{8}{8}$ ______ $\frac{9}{8}$ ______ $\frac{10}{8}$ ______

$\frac{7}{7}$ ______ $\frac{8}{7}$ ______ $\frac{9}{7}$ ______ $\frac{10}{7}$ ______

$\frac{6}{6}$ ______ $\frac{7}{6}$ ______ $\frac{8}{6}$ ______ $\frac{9}{6}$ ______ $\frac{10}{6}$ ______

$\frac{5}{5}$ ______ $\frac{6}{5}$ ______ $\frac{7}{5}$ ______ $\frac{8}{5}$ ______ $\frac{9}{5}$ ______ $\frac{10}{5}$ ______

$\frac{4}{4}$ ______ $\frac{5}{4}$ ______ $\frac{6}{4}$ ______ $\frac{7}{4}$ ______ $\frac{8}{4}$ ______

$\frac{3}{3}$ ______ $\frac{4}{3}$ ______ $\frac{5}{3}$ ______ $\frac{6}{3}$ ______

$\frac{2}{2}$ ______ $\frac{3}{2}$ ______ $\frac{4}{2}$ ______

$\frac{1}{1}$ ______ $\frac{2}{1}$ ______

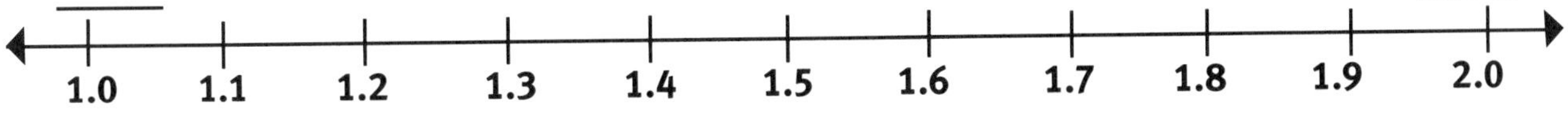

LESSON 7.9

Using Mixed Numbers

Student Edition • page 320

Solve the following problems.

1. Mindy charges \$20.00 per hour for tutoring high-school students in algebra. She tutored Gerald twice this week, once for $\frac{3}{4}$ hour, and once for $\frac{1}{2}$ hour. How much money does Gerald owe Mindy? ______

2. Mr. LaRue earns about \$37,000 per year. He spends about \$120 each week on groceries. About what fraction of his income is spent on groceries? ______

3. Ava was downloading a program to her computer. It took 12 minutes to download $\frac{3}{4}$ of the program. At that rate, how many more minutes will it take to finish downloading? ______

4. **Extended Response** Judy's grades put her in the top $\frac{1}{5}$ of her graduating class. If there were 125 students in the class, could she have had the 30th highest grade average? Explain.

______

5. **Extended Response** Juanita was told to practice her piano lessons for at least 5 hours each week.

   a. If she practices for $\frac{3}{4}$ hour each day, will she have practiced at least 5 hours? Explain.

   ______

   b. If she practices $1\frac{1}{4}$ hour each day, will she have practiced at least 5 hours? Explain.

   ______

Name ______________________ Date ____________

Student Edition • **page 321**

6 **Extended Response** Janice, Patti, and Becky worked together in their garden for about $\frac{1}{2}$ hour each day, sharing the work equally. At the end of the week, about what fraction of the work did Becky do? Explain.

____

____

7 **Extended Response** The Palaez family was driving from Hartville to Mason City, a distance of about 64 miles. When they had driven about 40 miles, Juanita exclaimed that they were $\frac{8}{5}$ of the way there. Could Juanita be right? Why or why not? If not, what mistake did she likely make?

____

____

8 Ms. Yonteff's fifth-grade class raised money so they could go on a trip to Bunker Hill. Their goal was to raise $9,000. They were able to raise $10,000. About what fraction of their goal did they reach? ____________

9 Thornwell Elementary School sought donations so that they could purchase new computers. The goal was to raise $30,000. At the end of the year, the principal reported that they had raised $\frac{5}{4}$ of their goal. Is that possible? If so, about how much did they raise? ____________

10 Mr. Pickwick's job is to sell dishes, pots, pans, and glasses to restaurants. He earns $\frac{1}{20}$ of his total sales as a commission. He also has a sales goal. If he reaches the sales goal, he receives a bonus of $5,000. If he reaches $\frac{12}{10}$ of the goal, he earns an additional bonus of $10,000.

a. If Mr. Pickwick's sales goal is $200,000, how much will he earn if he reaches his goal?

____

b. How much will he earn if he reaches $\frac{12}{10}$ of his goal?

____

Student Edition • pages 322–323

Racing to Boston

April 20 An explosive dash in the final seconds catapulted Louise Sauvage to a Boston Marathon victory on a day honoring the beginning of America's fight for independence.

Reaching speeds of more than 35 miles per hour, Sauvage kept battling seven-time champion Jean Driscoll for the lead. At one point, Sauvage trailed so far behind she could not even see Driscoll in front of her. But with only 70 yards left in the 26-mile race, Sauvage lunged to the most thrilling finish in marathon history—so close that both racers ended with the same official time of 1:41:19.

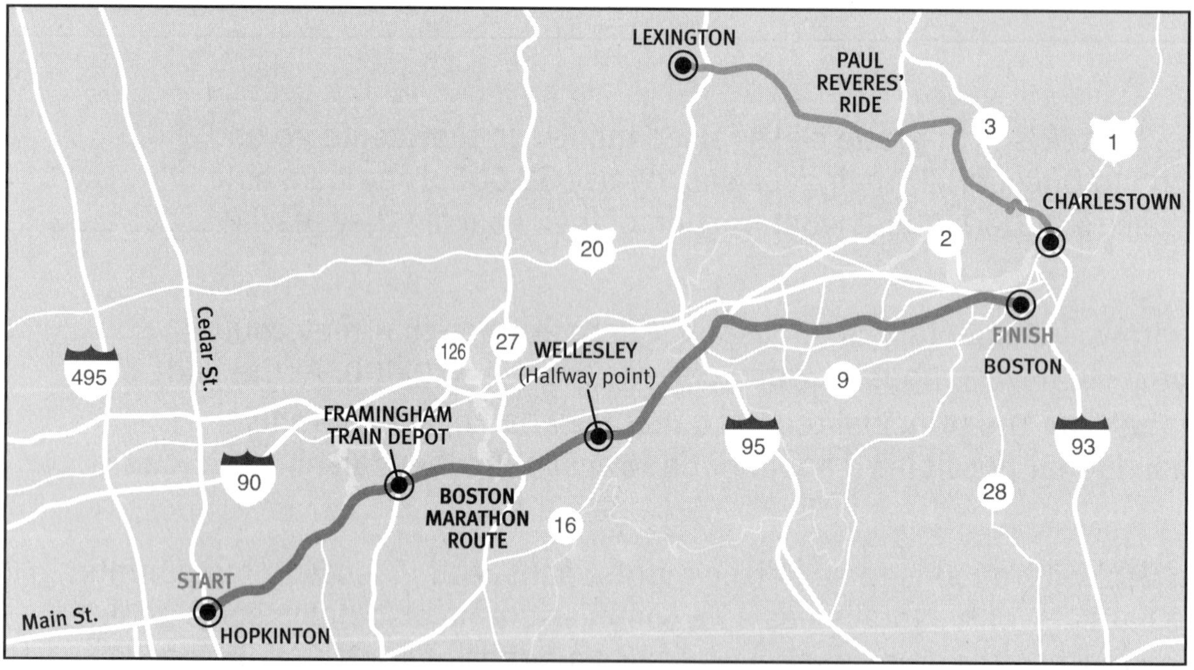

Answer these questions. Use the information above.

1. How could Louise Sauvage have won even though both racers finished with the same official time? Explain with an example.

____

____

Name ______________________________ **Date** ______________

Student Edition • pages 323–324

❷ What is the greatest amount of time that Sauvage could have won by?

____

____

❸ Is the last 70 yards more or less than $\frac{1}{50}$ of the entire $26\frac{1}{5}$-mile marathon? How do you know?

____

____

❹ About what fraction of the Boston Marathon distance was Paul Revere's ride from Charlestown to Lexington?

____

Marathon racing has its ups and downs, as you can see from this graph of the Boston Marathon course. Whether running or propelling a wheelchair, going uphill is a lot harder than going downhill. One uphill stretch of the Boston course is so grueling it is called Heartbreak Hill.

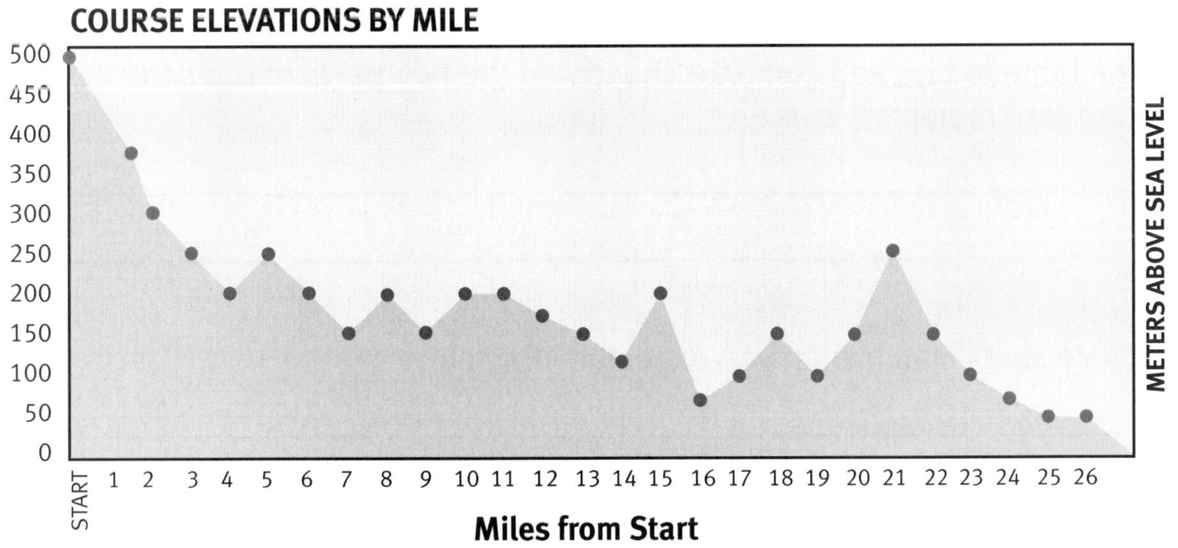

Exploring Problem Solving

Student Edition • page 324

How much do hills affect runners? To find out, you can use the graph on page 301 and the table to the right. The table shows the approximate times for the lead runners at different points of the 104th Boston Marathon.

Mile Mark	Time	Place Name
2	12:09	Ashland
$4\frac{1}{3}$	12:20	Uphill
5	12:24	Framingham
$7\frac{2}{5}$	12:36	Natick
$10\frac{1}{10}$	12:49	Natick Center
$12\frac{2}{5}$	1:00	Wellesley College
$15\frac{2}{5}$	1:15	Wellesley Hills
$16\frac{3}{5}$	1:21	Route 128 Crossing
$17\frac{1}{2}$	1:25	Newton Hills
$20\frac{3}{5}$	1:40	Top of Heartbreak Hill
21	1:42	Boston College
$22\frac{1}{5}$	1:48	Cleveland Circle
$23\frac{1}{3}$	1:53	Coolidge Corner

Work **in groups to discuss and solve these problems.**

5. Based on the graph, on which part of the Boston Marathon course do you think racers go the slowest? Why?

____

____

6. Based on the graph, on which part are racers fastest? Why?

____

____

7. Use the table to find and compare speeds on the two parts of the course you selected for Problems 5 and 6.

____

____

8. Did your results match what you expected? Explain.

____

____

Cumulative Review

Name ______________________________ **Date** ________________

Student Edition • page 325

Temperature Conversions **Lesson 5.9**

Solve.

The relationship between degrees Fahrenheit and degrees Celsius can be written as a function rule:

C → (×1.8) → n → (+32) → F

1 Which temperature in degrees Celsius would you expect in a classroom?

a. 10° **b.** 20° **c.** 45°

2 Which temperature in degrees Celsius is closest to 100°F?

a. 20° **b.** 30° **c.** 40°

3 What is the inverse of the function rule given above?

____

4 Which temperature in degrees Fahrenheit is closest to 5°C?

a. 40° **b.** 32° **c.** 50°

5 If a thermometer reads 86°F, what is the same temperature in degrees Celsius? ____________

Cumulative Review

Student Edition • page 326

Probability **Lesson 6.9**

Solve.

A pool table uses balls that are numbered 1–15. A player "breaks" by taking the first shot. If a ball drops into a pocket, what is the probability that the number of the ball is

6. greater than 9? ______
7. an even number? ______
8. a multiple of 4? ______

Adding and Subtracting Mixed Numbers **Lessons 7.3 and 7.4**

9. $1\frac{7}{8} + 3\frac{1}{4} =$ ______
10. $4\frac{1}{4} - 2\frac{1}{3} =$ ______
11. $2\frac{1}{3} + 3\frac{4}{5} =$ ______
12. $5\frac{1}{6} - 4\frac{3}{4} =$ ______

Graphing in Four Quadrants **Lesson 5.4**

Write the coordinates of the following points.

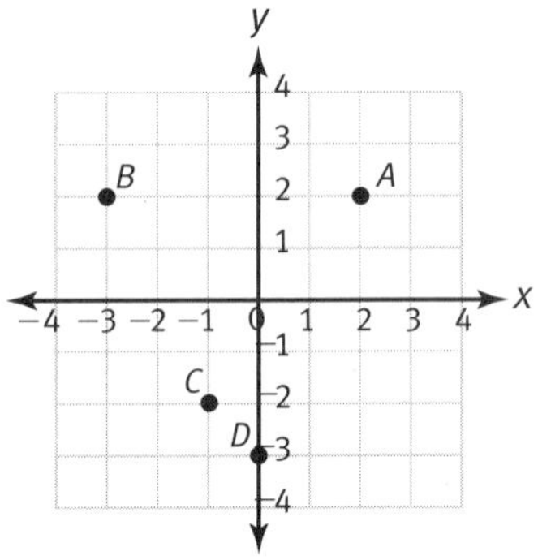

13. *A* ______
14. *B* ______
15. *C* ______
16. *D* ______
17. If you can only walk along the grid lines, which is closer to *D, A* or *B?* ______
18. If you can only walk along the grid lines, which is closer to *C, A* or *B?* ______

Key Ideas Review

Name ______________________ Date ______________

Student Edition • page 327

Answer the following questions.

1. Explain how to convert a mixed number to an improper fraction and provide an example.

____

____

2. Solve the following expression:

$_______ \div \frac{2}{3} = 7\frac{1}{4}$

Explain how you found your answer.

____

____

Write the decimal equivalent of the following fractions.

3. $9\frac{5}{10} =$ ______________

5. $7\frac{5}{8} =$ ______________

4. $3\frac{6}{8} =$ ______________

Solve the following exercises by providing the answer as a fraction and decimal equivalent or approximation.

6. $2\frac{2}{3} \times 1\frac{1}{2} =$ ______________

9. $\frac{1}{2} \div \frac{3}{9} =$ ______________

7. $4\frac{3}{9} + 5\frac{1}{4} =$ ______________

10. $3\frac{3}{4} \times 2\frac{3}{6} =$ ______________

8. $10\frac{4}{6} - 8\frac{1}{2} =$ ______________

CHAPTER 7 Chapter Review

Student Edition • page 328

Replace each mixed number with an equivalent improper fraction. **Lesson 7.1**

1. $2\frac{1}{6}$ ______
2. $1\frac{1}{8}$ ______
3. $4\frac{1}{5}$ ______
4. $3\frac{5}{7}$ ______
5. $7\frac{1}{8}$ ______
6. $6\frac{1}{7}$ ______

Replace each improper fraction with a mixed number.

7. $\frac{5}{2}$ ______
8. $\frac{7}{3}$ ______
9. $\frac{11}{3}$ ______
10. $\frac{9}{4}$ ______
11. $\frac{10}{7}$ ______
12. $\frac{21}{5}$ ______

Multiply. Check to see that your answers make sense. **Lesson 7.2**

13. $3\frac{1}{3} \times 4\frac{2}{7} =$ ______
14. $1\frac{5}{8} \times 1\frac{3}{5} =$ ______
15. $1\frac{2}{5} \times 3\frac{1}{7} =$ ______
16. $4\frac{1}{2} \times 3\frac{1}{9} =$ ______

Add. **Lesson 7.3**

17. $3\frac{5}{8} + 1\frac{1}{4} =$ ______
18. $5\frac{1}{2} + 2\frac{2}{3} =$ ______
19. $4\frac{3}{4} + 1\frac{5}{6} =$ ______
20. $4\frac{3}{5} + 1\frac{1}{3} =$ ______

Subtract. **Lesson 7.4**

21. $5\frac{7}{9} - 3\frac{4}{6} =$ ______
22. $4\frac{1}{4} - 2\frac{3}{8} =$ ______
23. $3\frac{1}{5} - 1\frac{2}{3} =$ ______
24. $5\frac{4}{5} - 2\frac{1}{6} =$ ______

Chapter Review

Name ______________________ Date ____________

Student Edition • page 329

Divide. Reduce when possible. **Lesson 7.6**

25 $12 \div \frac{2}{3} =$ ____________

26 $1\frac{3}{4} \div 2\frac{1}{3} =$ ____________

27 $2\frac{1}{5} \div 3\frac{2}{3} =$ ____________

28 $3 \div \frac{2}{3} =$ ____________

Complete each exercise and write the answer as a mixed number and as a decimal. For each exercise, check to see that your two answers are equivalent or almost equivalent. Round your answers to four decimal places if necessary. **Lesson 7.8**

29 $1\frac{2}{7} + 3\frac{1}{3} =$ ____________

30 $2\frac{3}{8} + 5\frac{3}{4} =$ ____________

31 $1\frac{3}{5} + 4\frac{1}{5} =$ ____________

32 $4\frac{1}{5} + 2\frac{2}{9} =$ ____________

Solve. **Lesson 7.9**

33 Lilla earns \$10 per hour doing errands. On Monday, she worked $2\frac{1}{4}$ hours and on Friday she worked $1\frac{1}{2}$ hours. How much did Lilla earn for those 2 days? ____________

34 Abby walks to raise money. After 6 miles, she had completed $\frac{3}{5}$ of the walk. How many miles were left to go? ____________

35 Gil starts each work week with \$50. He spends about \$3 each day on lunches. About what fraction of his weekly money is spent on lunch? ____________

CHAPTER 7 Practice Test

Student Edition • page 330

Write each improper fraction as a mixed number.

1. $\frac{7}{4}$ ________________

2. $\frac{21}{5}$ ________________

3. $\frac{15}{2}$ ________________

Write each mixed number as an improper fraction.

4. $3\frac{3}{5}$ ________________

5. $2\frac{5}{6}$ ________________

6. $5\frac{8}{9}$ ________________

Solve for *n*. Watch the signs. Reduce when possible.

7. $2\frac{3}{5} + 3\frac{2}{3} = n$ ________________

8. $\frac{3}{4} \div \frac{3}{8} = n$ ________________

9. $2\frac{5}{6} - 2\frac{1}{8} = n$ ________________

10. $4\frac{1}{4} \times \frac{2}{9} = n$ ________________

11. $4\frac{1}{2} \times 3\frac{2}{3} = n$ ________________

12. $1\frac{5}{7} + 4\frac{3}{5} = n$ ________________

13. $1\frac{5}{6} \div 4 = n$ ________________

14. $6\frac{2}{5} - 2\frac{3}{4} = n$ ________________

15. $3\frac{9}{10} + 1\frac{1}{4} = n$ ________________

16. $2\frac{1}{5} \times 1\frac{3}{5} = n$ ________________

Practice Test

Name ______________________________ Date ________________

Student Edition • page 331

Choose the correct answer.

17. Sangi ate $4\frac{3}{4}$ graham crackers with his lunch and $2\frac{1}{2}$ more as a snack. How many graham crackers did Sangi eat?

   Ⓐ $2\frac{1}{4}$ Ⓑ $6\frac{1}{4}$
   Ⓒ $6\frac{2}{3}$ Ⓓ $7\frac{1}{4}$

18. Travis read $1\frac{2}{3}$ chapters of his book in 5 days. How much of 1 chapter did he read each day?

   Ⓐ $\frac{1}{3}$ Ⓑ $\frac{6}{15}$
   Ⓒ $5\frac{2}{3}$ Ⓓ $8\frac{1}{3}$

19. Which decimal approximation is equivalent to the sum of $\frac{7}{10}$ and $\frac{2}{3}$?

   Ⓐ 1.4 Ⓑ 1.367
   Ⓒ 0.692 Ⓓ 0.033

20. Beth's cat weighs 9 pounds. Her dog weighs $25\frac{1}{2}$ pounds. How many times as big as her cat is her dog?

   Ⓐ $229\frac{1}{2}$ Ⓑ $16\frac{1}{2}$
   Ⓒ $2\frac{5}{6}$ Ⓓ $1\frac{7}{18}$

21. Mike works $5\frac{3}{4}$ hours 4 days a week. How many hours does he work in 2 weeks?

   Ⓐ $11\frac{1}{2}$ Ⓑ $19\frac{1}{2}$
   Ⓒ 23 Ⓓ 46

22. Which mixed number will make the following statement true?

   $\frac{4}{5} \times$ ______ $= 1\frac{1}{15}$

   Ⓐ $1\frac{5}{12}$ Ⓑ $1\frac{1}{3}$
   Ⓒ $\frac{2}{3}$ Ⓓ $\frac{4}{15}$

23. The Pifalos are sailing their boat in a race from Marblehead, MA, to Halifax, Nova Scotia. If they have sailed $210\frac{5}{8}$ nautical miles and the race is 360 nautical miles long, how many more miles do they have to sail?

   Ⓐ $149\frac{3}{8}$ Ⓑ $150\frac{3}{8}$
   Ⓒ $569\frac{5}{8}$ Ⓓ $579\frac{3}{8}$

Practice Test

Student Edition • page 332

24. The historical society needs to raise $25,000 to restore an old home. They raised $1\frac{1}{8}$ of their goal. How much money did they raise?

Ⓐ $31,250 Ⓑ $28,125

Ⓒ $21,875 Ⓓ $3,125

25. $3\frac{4}{5} \times 3\frac{7}{8} =$

Ⓐ $9\frac{7}{10}$ Ⓑ $14\frac{7}{10}$

Ⓒ $14\frac{29}{40}$ Ⓓ 15

26. Josiah did some computation and got a rounded answer of 6.2667. Which exercise did he solve?

Ⓐ $6 + \frac{2}{3}$ Ⓑ $8\frac{2}{3} - 2\frac{2}{5}$

Ⓒ $8\frac{2}{5} - 2\frac{4}{15}$ Ⓓ $3\frac{3}{5} + 3\frac{4}{15}$

27. Which of the following equations matches this composite function?

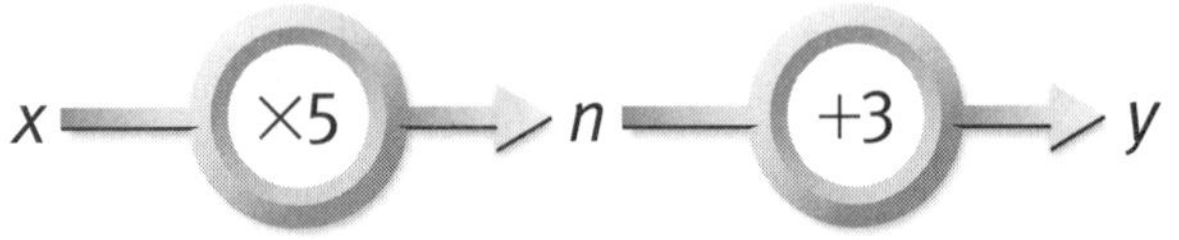

Ⓐ $y = \frac{x}{5} + 3$ Ⓑ $y = 5x + 3$

Ⓒ $y = \frac{x}{3} + 5$ Ⓓ $y = 3x + 5$

28. Which of the following numbers is a common denominator for the fractions $\frac{1}{4}$, $\frac{5}{8}$, and $\frac{5}{6}$?

Ⓐ 16 Ⓑ 24

Ⓒ 32 Ⓓ 42

29. If you start at 100 on a calculator and keep subtracting 6, which number will you hit?

Ⓐ 90 Ⓑ 80

Ⓒ 70 Ⓓ 60

30. Subtract: $7 - (10) = n$.

Ⓐ $n = 17$ Ⓑ $n = 3$

Ⓒ $n = -3$ Ⓓ $n = -17$

31. Which of the following fractions is equivalent to $\frac{15}{40}$?

Ⓐ $\frac{3}{8}$ Ⓑ $\frac{1}{3}$

Ⓒ $\frac{3}{10}$ Ⓓ $\frac{5}{8}$

32. Ellen rolled a ***Number Cube*** labeled with the numbers 5 through 10. What is the probability that she rolled an even number?

Ⓐ $\frac{6}{6}$ Ⓑ $\frac{3}{6}$

Ⓒ $\frac{2}{6}$ Ⓓ $\frac{1}{6}$

33. Paint spilled on Gene's paper. Which answer could be the correct product?

2 ___ × 38 =

Ⓐ 1,140 Ⓑ 1,112

Ⓒ 836 Ⓓ 750

CHAPTER 7

Practice Test

Name ________________________ Date ____________

Student Edition • page 333

Extended Response **Solve** the following problems.

34. Jen sells advertisement space in the newspaper. She earns $\frac{1}{15}$ of her total sales as a commission. She also has a sales goal every month. If she reaches her goal, she receives a bonus of $3,000. If she reaches $\frac{5}{4}$ of her goal, she receives an additional $1,000.

a. If her sales goal is $120,000, how much will Jen earn if she reaches her goal? Explain your answer.

____

____

b. How much will Jen earn if she reaches $\frac{5}{4}$ of her goal? Explain your answer.

____

____

35. Keith had the plans to construct this bookcase. All the measurements are shown below, but the measurement for the heights of the wooden separators, which are equal, are missing.

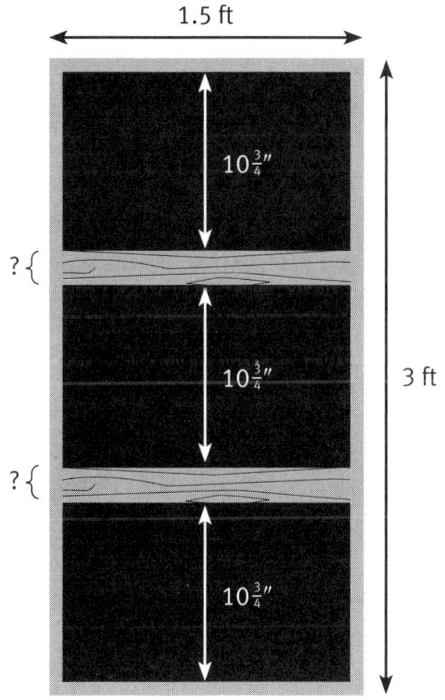

a. How could you find the missing measurements? Explain.

____

____

____

____

b. What is the height of each separator?

____

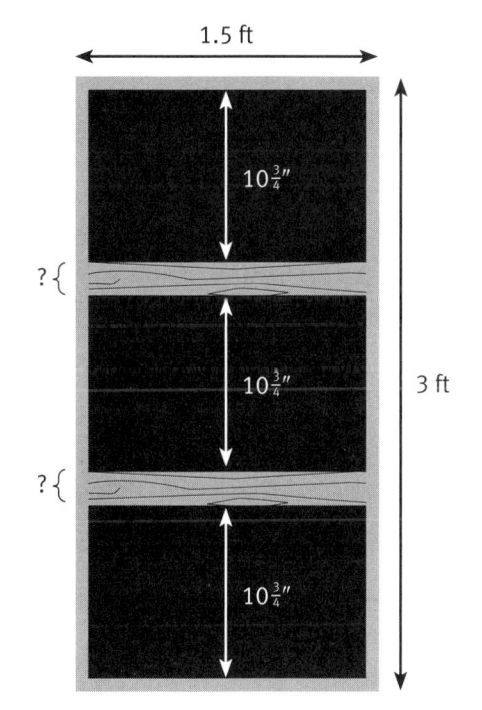

CHAPTER 8 Problem Solving

Division and Ratios

Student Edition • page 335

In any language, some letters occur more often than others, as the following graph shows.

JYVES NMFS YXX FSW RLVEW QLH EYU JHPFWV. YUULQ FSW WUWJQ YP JHES YP ZLPPMKXW. YF FSW PYJW FMJW QLH YVW VWQHWPFWO ULF FL HPW YJJHUMFMLU HUUWEPPYVMXQ. PSLLF LUXQ NSWU QLH SYCW Y PHVW FYVBWF. FVQ

LESSON 8.1

Name ______________________ Date ____________

Averages

Student Edition • pages 336–337

Find the averages.

1. 4, 3, 5, 9, 4 ____________
2. 12, 15, 18, 15 ____________
3. 2, 3, 8, 7 ____________
4. 9, 10, 11, 12, 13 ____________
5. 22, 21, 25, 20 ____________
6. 4, 6, 6, 10, 10 ____________
7. 20, 30, 40, 50 ____________
8. 2, 4, 6, 8, 10 ____________
9. 32, 34, 36, 38, 40 ____________
10. 52, 54, 56, 58, 60 ____________
11. 72, 74, 76, 78, 80 ____________
12. 100, 107, 109, 113 ____________
13. 10, 18, 19, 23, 26 ____________
14. 15, 25, 30, 40 ____________
15. 75, 85, 86, 90, 92 ____________

Amalia kept a record of her test scores at school and recorded them on the following table. On all tests a perfect score is 100.

Date	Test Subject	Score	Date	Test Subject	Score
9/10	mathematics	91	11/20	history	79
9/14	spelling	48	12/1	spelling	55
9/30	history	65	12/4	mathematics	100
10/15	mathematics	95	12/7	history	90
10/19	spelling	53	12/15	mathematics	96
11/2	spelling	49	12/16	spelling	60
11/4	history	75	12/17	history	95
11/6	mathematics	97	12/18	mathematics	96

Student Edition • pages 337–338

Answer the following questions, rounding to the nearest tenth.

16 What was the average of all of Amalia's test scores? ______________

17 **Extended Response** How well does the average describe Amalia's test results?

____

____

18 What was Amalia's average score in mathematics? ______________

19 What was her average score in history? ______________

20 What was Amalia's average score in spelling? ______________

21 **Extended Response** How well do the individual averages describe Amalia's test results? If you were her teacher, how would you report Amalia's results?

____

____

Amalia decided to make a table for her test scores in each subject. This is what her table for history looked like:

History Test Scores

Date	Score
9/30	65
11/4	75
11/20	79
12/7	90
12/17	95

Study Amalia's test scores. Round your answers to the nearest tenth.

22 **Extended Response** Do you think the average score tells how well Amalia is doing in history? Why or why not?

____

____

Name ______________________ Date ____________

Student Edition • pages 338

23 Extended Response If you were Amalia's teacher, what grade would you give her in history? Explain your answer.

____

____

24 What score would Amalia need on her next spelling test to have an average of 60?

____

25 What is the greatest average she could have after her next mathematics test?

____

26 Extended Response Sarah received scores of 75, 80, 82, and 87 on four quizzes. She estimates her average to be 80. Is she correct? Why or why not?

____

____

27 Alan is reading a book for his geography project. He read 32 pages the first night, 24 pages the next night, 28 pages the third night, and 36 pages the fourth night. What is the average number of pages Alan read each night?

____

28 Juan's times, in minutes and seconds (MM:SS), to get home from school this week were 12:00, 9:25, 10:40, 8:35, and 11:20. What was his average time in minutes and seconds? __________

LESSON 8.2

Mean, Median, Mode, and Range

Student Edition • page 340

The Great Long-Jump Contest

Tomeo and Barry had a contest to see who could jump farther. They took five jumps each. The winner would have the longest average of the five jumps.

Jump Number	Distance of Jump (Measured to the nearest centimeter)	
Jump	**Tomeo**	**Barry**
1	140	143
2	141	158
3	139	144
4	143	102
5	138	149

Study **the contest results.**
Then answer the questions that follow.

1. What was the average distance of Tomeo's jumps? ______________

2. What was the average distance of Barry's jumps? ______________

3. Who won the contest, Tomeo or Barry? ______________

4. Do you think the averages describe how well Tomeo and Barry can jump?

____

____

5. If Tomeo and Barry were to have a second contest with only one jump each, who would be more likely to win? ______________

6. **Extended Response** What information did you use to answer the previous question?

____

____

7. **Extended Response** How could you make the judging more favorable for Barry?

____

____

LESSON 8.2

Name ______________________ Date ____________

Student Edition • page 341

As part of a research project to learn about students' study habits, Tom conducted a survey of the 61 fifth-grade students in his school. All students were given survey forms that asked how many hours they spent on homework each week and whether they were A students, B students, C students, or students who usually had grades lower than a C.

Fifty-four students returned their surveys. Tom recorded his results in this way:

8-B, 10-L, 12-A, 6-C, 12-A, 12-A, 8-C, 7-B, 2-B, 15-B, 12-A, 8-C, 5-B, 9-L, 13-A, 9-C, 9-B, 9-A, 3-C, 10-A, 6-C, 8-B, 8-C, 8-A, 10-B, 13-A, 1-L, 8-B, 9-C, 7-A, 10-C, 10-A, 9-B, 12-A, 8-C, 2-L, 7-C, 7-B, 6-C, 9-L, 8-C, 8-B, 9-B, 9-A, 13-A, 17-A, 1-L, 5-C, 8-B, 5-C, 14-A, 8-L, 13-B, 6-C

8. According to Tom's results, what do you think 10-A means?

____

9. What does 2-L mean?

____

10. What does 5-C mean?

____

11. **Extended Response** Was this a useful way for Tom to record his results? What are some other ways?

____

____

Tom decided to find out how much homework A students did. He separated the surveys of the A students and recorded the time they spent on homework each week this way:

12, 12, 12, 12, 13, 9, 10, 8, 13, 7, 10, 12, 9, 13, 17, 14

12. How many students thought of themselves as A students? ____________

13. On average, how many hours a week did they say they do homework?

____

LESSON 8.2

Student Edition • pages 341–342

In order from least to greatest, the numbers are:
7, 8, 9, 9, 10, 10, 12, 12, 12, 12, 12, 13, 13, 13, 14, 17

14 What is the median? ____________

Complete this table by using data from Tom's survey. Use a calculator to find the mean. Round answers to the nearest tenth. Then discuss the meaning of the results.

	A Students	B Students	C Students	Lower Than C Students	All Students
Number of Students	16	15	16	7	54
Mean	11.4				
Median	12				
Mode	12				
Range	10 (7–17)				
Clipped Range	6 (8–14)				

15 **Extended Response** Which method gives the best description of the results of Tom's survey? Explain your answer.

____

____

16 **Extended Response** If you wanted to find out about the study habits of students in your school, how would you conduct your survey? How would you report the results?

____

____

LESSON 8.3

Name ______________________ Date ____________

Interpreting Averages

Student Edition • page 344

The Census Bureau of Humboldt County says that the average number of children per family is 1.8.

1. Is it possible for one family to have 1.8 children? ____________
2. Is it possible for 100 families to have an average of 1.8 children per family?

   ____

3. About how many children would you expect there to be if you surveyed 100 families in Humboldt County? ____________

The Census Bureau of Shelby County says that the average number of children per family is 3.4.

4. Is it possible for one family to have 3.4 children? ____________
5. Is it possible for a number of families to have an average of 3.4 children each?

   ____

6. About how many children would you expect there to be if you surveyed 100 families in Shelby County? ____________

Suppose a family from each of those counties were to visit you.

7. Which family do you think would probably have more children? Can you be certain without knowing the families?

   ____

   ____

Suppose 10 families from each county were to visit you.

8. Which group would probably have more children? Would you be surprised if they didn't?

   ____

   ____

LESSON 8.3

Student Edition • pages 344–345

There are 10,578 families in Orange County. They have 23,269 children altogether.

9 What would you suppose is the average number of children per family? What is the actual average number of children per family? (Use a calculator. Give the answer to the nearest tenth.)

____

For each situation, decide whether the mean, median, or mode would be most appropriate. Explain your answer.

10 Extended Response The Rockville Rockets basketball team has players with the following heights: 5'9", 5'9", 6'11", 5'8", 5'7", 5'8", 5'7", 5'9", 5'7", and 5'8". A newspaper wants the average height of the players. If you were a reporter, how might you report the average height, and why?

____

____

____

11 In order to install a traffic light at an intersection, a city requires an average of 5,000 vehicles to pass through the intersection each day. In one week the following numbers of vehicles were counted: Sunday–1,812; Monday–6,213; Tuesday–5,935; Wednesday–6,086; Thursday–6,113; Friday–6,184; Saturday–2,593. The city claims the average number of cars is approximately 4,991, so the intersection does not need a light. A neighborhood group claims the average number of cars is 6,086 and that there should be a light. How is each group finding its average?

____

____

____

Name ______________________ Date ____________

Student Edition • page 345

12 **Extended Response** A magazine columnist conducted a survey to find the average number of hours her readers watched television each day. Based on the responses, how might she find the average? Explain your reasoning.

____

____

____

13 A school district wants to report the average number of school days cancelled due to bad weather each year for the past decade. Over the past 10 years, school has been cancelled 0, 2, 1, 0, 1, 7, 1, 1, 1, and 0 days. What method would you suggest to the district for reporting the average number of days that were missed?

____

____

____

14 Douglas played three games of miniature golf. His score was 57 in the first game, 63 in the second game, and 63 in the third game. Which method of finding the average would give him the smallest average score, and what is that score?

____

____

____

15 **Extended Response** Michiko has kept track of her grades on her last five math tests. Her scores were 85, 87, 84, 43, and 86. (She accidentally skipped a page on her fourth test.) What would be the best average to use in predicting her score on her next test? What would you predict her next score to be?

____

____

____

LESSON 8.4

Ratios and Rates

Student Edition • page 347

Decide which is the most useful way to report the information in each statement.

1. Sam bought a sports card for 5¢ and sold it for 10¢.

____

____

2. Harry bought a lot of sports cards for 5¢ each and sold them for 10¢ each.

____

____

3. It costs Mrs. Wu 15¢ per kilometer to drive her small car and 45¢ per kilometer to drive her large car.

____

____

4. Cindy is 140 centimeters tall, and Nikki is 138 centimeters tall.

____

____

5. It takes Kevin 10 minutes to walk home from school. It takes Brian 15 minutes to walk home from school.

____

____

6. A math book has 640 pages. A geography book has 520 pages.

____

____

Name ______________________ Date ____________

Student Edition • pages 347 and 349

7. Rishi spent 25¢ for his bottle of water, which he bought in bulk. Vahagn paid $1 for his bottle of water from the vending machine.

____

____

8. Aileen made $15 delivering papers to her 25 customers for 6 days this week. Justin made $2.50 for delivering to the same customers on Sunday.

____

____

Use a calculator if needed. Check your answers to see that they make sense.

9. A 750-gram box of Crunchy Corn cereal costs $2.10, and a 500-gram box costs $1.50.

   a. How much per gram is the cereal in the 750-gram box? ____________

   b. How much per gram is the cereal in the 500-gram box? ____________

   c. Which box is the better buy?

   ____

   ____

   ____

LESSON 8.4

Student Edition • **page 349**

10 Miss Carroll drove about 800 kilometers in 12 hours and used 70 liters of gasoline.

a. What was her average speed? ______

b. On average, about how many kilometers per liter of gasoline did she get?

______

c. If she continued at the same speed, about how far could she have gone in 15 hours? ______

d. About how much more gasoline would Miss Carroll need to drive 200 kilometers further if she continued using gas at the same rate? ______

e. **Extended Response** How did you figure out the answer to the previous question?

______

______

11 Jeff's car gets 25 miles per gallon of gasoline. His cabin is 190 miles away, and he wants to drive directly there without stopping for gas.

a. How many gallons of gas will he need to get there? ______

b. **Extended Response** Suppose his friend's sport utility vehicle gets 19 miles per gallon and has 9 gallons of gas in it. Jeff's car has only 8 gallons of gas. Does it matter whose car they take? Explain.

______

______

12 An office supply store sells 3 pencils for 96¢. If the rate remains the same, how much will 10 pencils cost? ______

LESSON 8.5

Name ______________________________ Date ____________

Comparing Ratios

Student Edition • pages 351–352

1. Mark wrote $\frac{3}{4}$ of his history paper over the weekend. Doug wrote $\frac{2}{3}$ of his history paper over the weekend. Who finished more of the assignment? If they both needed to write a 12-page paper, how many pages did each person write?

____

____

2. Which team has the better record, the Whitewater Blue Sox with 21 wins out of 43 games or the Prairie Creek Pups with 17 wins out of 33 games? How many more games will the team with fewer wins need to win to beat the other team's record?

____

____

3. According to the meteorologist, it has been snowing at a rate of 2 inches per hour for the past 12 hours and is expected to continue doing so for the next 12 hours. How many inches of snow have fallen in the past 12 hours? How many inches will have fallen in 24 hours if the meteorologist's prediction is correct?

____

Fill each blank with <, >, or =. Use a calculator only when necessary.

4. $\frac{3}{7}$ ________ $\frac{4}{7}$

5. $\frac{3}{8}$ ________ $\frac{3}{9}$

6. $\frac{7}{15}$ ________ $\frac{9}{16}$

7. $\frac{4}{9}$ ________ $\frac{4}{7}$

8. $\frac{5}{6}$ ________ $\frac{4}{6}$

9. $\frac{3}{5}$ ________ $\frac{4}{9}$

10. $\frac{1}{3}$ ________ $\frac{1}{4}$

11. $\frac{1}{2}$ ________ $\frac{13}{27}$

12. $\frac{1}{2}$ ________ $\frac{14}{28}$

13. $\frac{1}{4}$ ________ $\frac{3}{7}$

LESSON 8.5

Student Edition • pages 352–353

14 $\frac{1}{2}$ ______ $\frac{15}{29}$

15 $\frac{13}{27}$ ______ $\frac{14}{28}$

16 $\frac{38}{47}$ ______ $\frac{39}{48}$

17 $\frac{23}{39}$ ______ $\frac{24}{40}$

18 $\frac{71}{89}$ ______ $\frac{72}{88}$

19 $\frac{16}{22}$ ______ $\frac{12}{25}$

20 $\frac{51}{101}$ ______ $\frac{60}{100}$

21 $\frac{58}{61}$ ______ $\frac{45}{90}$

Fill each blank with <, >, or = as you complete each statement below. Compare the division problems as you would compare ratios. You do not have to calculate the quotients.

22 8 ÷ 2 ______ 8 ÷ 3

23 6 ÷ 4 ______ 6 ÷ 3

24 60 ÷ 4 ______ 60 ÷ 3

25 517 ÷ 4 ______ 517 ÷ 3

26 517 ÷ 4 ______ 517 ÷ 7

27 1,000 ÷ 9 ______ 1,000 ÷ 10

28 1,000 ÷ 28 ______ 1,000 ÷ 26

29 6 ÷ 2 ______ 8 ÷ 2

30 12 ÷ 3 ______ 14 ÷ 3

31 427 ÷ 3 ______ 421 ÷ 3

32 1,000 ÷ 17 ______ 2,000 ÷ 17

33 9 ÷ 5 ______ 13 ÷ 6

34 19 ÷ 13 ______ 14 ÷ 18

35 10 ÷ 7 ______ 100 ÷ 42

36 100 ÷ 47 ______ 1,000 ÷ 620

37 212 ÷ 31 ______ 612 ÷ 31

38 **Extended Response** Which is the least expensive per kilogram, 2 kilograms of Kitty Kitchen cat food for $2.50 or 1 kilogram of Kitty Kitchen for $1.29? If you needed only 3 kilograms, what would you do and why?

____

____

____

LESSON 8.6

Name ______________________ Date ____________

Using Approximate Quotients

Student Edition • pages 354–355

This table tells how many people, houses, and certain kinds of businesses are in each of three towns: Redhill, Whitetree, and Bluefield.

Some Facts about Three Towns

Type of Information	Redhill	Whitetree	Bluefield
Population	25,075	20,455	9,800
Houses (including apartment buildings)	2,054	4,123	1,987
Automobile service stations	32	37	10
Grocery stores	19	18	4
Restaurants	42	29	18

1. In Whitetree, about how many people are there for each grocery store? In Bluefield?

____

____

2. **Extended Response** In which town do you think a new grocery store would have the best chance of success? How did you decide?

____

____

3. **Extended Response** Why do you think this is a good piece of information on which to base your decision?

____

____

LESSON 8.6

Student Edition • pages 354–355

4 **Extended Response** What other types of information might be helpful in making a decision on where to build a new grocery store?

____

____

5 About how many people are there per restaurant in Redhill? In Whitetree? In Bluefield?

____

____

____

6 **Extended Response** How did you find your answer to Problem 5?

____

____

7 **Extended Response** In which town do you think a new restaurant would have the best chance of success? How did you decide?

____

____

Name ______________________ Date ____________

Student Edition • pages 355–356

8 **Extended Response** In which town do you think a new service station would have the best chance of success? How did you decide?

____

____

9 In which town, on the average, is the highest ratio of people per house?

____

10 **Extended Response** How did you find your answer to the previous question?

____

____

11 **Extended Response** Which town do you think has the most apartment buildings? Why?

____

____

Write a division problem that you could use to approximate ratios in the following situations. Show the corresponding multiplication problem.

12 Suppose you and your 4 friends had 21 party favors. How could you split them fairly?

____

____

Student Edition • page 356

13. How could you seat 178 people at 30 equally-sized tables?

14. A vendor had 422 hot dogs to sell. How could she distribute them to her 6 workers?

15. There were only 5 water fountains for a group of 251 tourists. How many people were there per water fountain?

16. How would you distribute 2,411 bottles of water among 800 relief workers?

17. If 19 boys and 20 girls went on an egg hunt for 603 eggs, what was the average number of eggs found by each child?

18. A casserole had 225 grams of fat and contained 20 servings in all. How many fat grams were there per serving?

LESSON 8.7

Name ______________________ Date ____________

Approximating Quotients

Student Edition • pages 358–359

Find approximate answers.

1. $44 \div 20 =$ ____________
2. $920 \div 19 =$ ____________
3. $158 \div 37 =$ ____________
4. $280 \div 71 =$ ____________
5. $180 \div 60 =$ ____________
6. $542 \div 9 =$ ____________
7. $1{,}600 \div 40 =$ ____________
8. $728 \div 91 =$ ____________
9. $48 \div 24 =$ ____________
10. $8{,}015 \div 51 =$ ____________
11. $341 \div 19 =$ ____________
12. $512 \div 32 =$ ____________
13. $732 \div 16 =$ ____________
14. $121 \div 31 =$ ____________
15. $198 \div 21 =$ ____________
16. $486 \div 98 =$ ____________

Work in groups. You can do these problems without finding exact answers. When you have finished discussing and solving each problem, write an explanation for each answer on your own.

17. **Extended Response** Mr. Cruz owns a grocery store. On an average day, he sells about 35 boxes of Big Oats cereal. He has 725 boxes of this cereal in stock, and his next shipment will arrive in 2 weeks. Is he likely to run out of stock on this item? (Mr. Cruz's store is open 6 days a week.) How do you know?

____

____

Student Edition • page 359

18 Extended Response Mr. Watkins wants to drive from New York City to San Francisco, California, a distance of 4,753 kilometers. He plans to drive about 700 kilometers each day. If he leaves New York City on Wednesday morning, will he be in San Francisco in time to have dinner on Saturday evening of the same week? How do you know?

____

____

19 Extended Response Miss Flores owns a restaurant. On an average day, she sells about 18 sirloin steaks. She has 272 of these steaks in the freezer, and her next shipment will arrive in 3 weeks. If the restaurant is open 7 days per week, is she likely to run out of sirloin steaks before her next shipment? How do you know?

____

____

20 Julie's parents agreed to let her work at her uncle's farm over the summer. She worked weekdays from 3 P.M.–5 P.M. for 3 weeks in a row. Her uncle paid her $148.67, the cost of a new snowboard she wanted.

a. How many hours did Julie work? __________

b. About how much did she make per hour? __________

c. What multiplication or division equation did you use to figure this out?

____

LESSON 8.8

Name ____________________ Date ____________

Dividing by a Two-Digit Number

Student Edition • pages 362–363

For each problem, approximate an answer, and then do the long division. (Round answers to the nearest whole number.)

1. $62\overline{)4973}$ ________
2. $38\overline{)3960}$ ________
3. $23\overline{)966}$ ________
4. $12\overline{)3237}$ ________
5. $81\overline{)7412}$ ________
6. $56\overline{)23128}$ ________
7. $78\overline{)2140}$ ________
8. $35\overline{)3810}$ ________
9. $41\overline{)33456}$ ________
10. $37\overline{)3293}$ ________
11. $15\overline{)4620}$ ________
12. $21\overline{)1466}$ ________
13. $52\overline{)25614}$ ________
14. $77\overline{)1008}$ ________
15. $46\overline{)2342}$ ________

In each exercise, two of the answers are clearly wrong and one is correct. Choose the correct answer.

16. $54\overline{)47088}$

  a. 82 **b.** 872 **c.** 8,722

17. $54\overline{)2646}$

  a. 9 **b.** 49 **c.** 409

LESSON 8.8

Student Edition • page 363

18 $7\overline{)6909}$

a. 97 b. 987 c. 9,087

19 $43\overline{)199133}$

a. 41 b. 461 c. 4,631

20 $654\overline{)5437356}$

a. 834 b. 8,314 c. 83,614

21 $111\overline{)83583}$

a. 73 b. 753 c. 7,543

22 $9\overline{)394434}$

a. 486 b. 4,386 c. 43,826

23 $43826\overline{)394434}$

a. 9 b. 89 c. 889

24 $872\overline{)47088}$

a. 4 b. 54 c. 504

25 $49\overline{)26460}$

a. 40 b. 540 c. 4,540

26 $3\overline{)369669}$

a. 232 b. 1,232 c. 123,223 d. 123,223.5

27 The 1910 census reported that about 92,200,000 people lived in the United States. The debt of the United States government at that time was about $1,100,000,000. Approximately what was the debt per person?

a. $1 b. $12 c. $120 d. $1,200 e. $12,000

28 The 1940 census reported that about 132,200,000 people lived in the United States. The debt of the United States government at that time was about $43,000,000,000. Approximately what was the debt per person?

a. $3 b. $32 c. $325 d. $3,250 e. $32,500

29 The 1980 census reported that about 226,500,000 people lived in the United States. The debt of the United States government at that time was about $907,700,000,000. Approximately what was the debt per person?

a. $4 b. $40 c. $400 d. $4,000 e. $40,000

30 The 2000 census reported that about 281,400,000 people lived in the United States. The debt of the United States government at that time was about $5,628,700,000,000. Approximately what was the debt per person?

a. $2 b. $20 c. $200 d. $2,000 e. $20,000

CHAPTER 8

Exploring Problem Solving

Name ______________________________ **Date** ______________

Student Edition • page 364

Imagine you are a code breaker assigned to decode the three-word phrase below. You know the number 1 stands for *A,* 2 for *B,* 3 for *C,* and so on. But there are no numbers on the paper, only a table that gives clues about the numbers.

Message: ___ ___ ___ ___   ___ ___ ___ ___   ___ ___ ___ ___

Letters of	Mean	Median	Mode	Range
1st word	$15\frac{3}{4}$	$14\frac{1}{2}$	none	12
2nd word	$19\frac{3}{4}$	$19\frac{1}{2}$	none	10
3rd word	10	10	none	9

Wei solved the problem this way:

I used the Guess, Check, and Adjust Strategy.
I'll start with the first word. I'll guess some easy letters.

Guess	Mean	Mode	Range	Result
A, B, C, D 1 2 3 4	$1 + 2 + 3 + 4 = 10$ $\frac{10}{4} - 2\frac{1}{2}$			Mean is way too low.
X, x, x, x 1 2 3 4	$1 + 2 + 3 + 4 = 10$ $\frac{10}{4} = 2\frac{1}{2}$			Mean is still too low.

Student Edition • page 365

Think about Wei's strategy. Answer the following questions.

1. Is there only one combination of 4 numbers with a mean of $15\frac{3}{4}$?

____

____

2. What will Wei need to check once she finds 4 numbers with a mean of $15\frac{3}{4}$?

____

____

3. Would you use Wei's strategy? Why or why not?

____

____

Kareem solved the problem another way.

I Used Logical Reasoning and Number Sense.
First word:

What I Know		What That Tells Me		What Else That Means
The median is $14\frac{1}{2}$.	→	The number $14\frac{1}{2}$ is halfway between the middle two numbers.	→	The two middle numbers add up to 29.
The mean is $15\frac{3}{4}$.	→	The total is $4 \times 15\frac{3}{4}$, which is 63.	→	The high and low numbers add up to 34.
The range is 12.	→	The largest number minus the smallest number is 12.	→	The high and low numbers have a difference of 12.

Exploring Problem Solving

Name ______________________ Date ____________

Student Edition • page 365

Think about Kareem's strategy. Answer the following questions.

4. What do you think Kareem means when he writes "middle numbers"? How does he know that these numbers add up to 29?

5. How does Kareem know that the high and low numbers add up to 34?

6. What conclusion can you draw from the fact that there is no mode for any of the words?

7. Why do you think Kareem's strategy will or will not work?

8. Solve the problem by decoding the phrase. Use any strategy you think will work. What strategy did you use? Why?

CHAPTER 8 Cumulative Review

Student Edition • page 366

Adding and Subtracting Decimals Lesson 3.4

Solve for n. Watch the signs.

1. $28.4 + 13.9 = n$ ______________
2. $28.4 - 13.9 = n$ ______________
3. $187.82 - 105.5 = n$ ______________
4. $67.99 + 49.14 = n$ ______________

Repeated Operations: Savings Plans Lesson 4.3

Solve.

Each week, Enrique earns \$20 and spends \$13.

5. How many weeks will it take for Enrique to save \$100? ______________
6. How many weeks will it take for Enrique to save \$300? ______________

Adding and Subtracting Integers Lesson 4.8

Complete each of the following exercises.

7. $(-5) + (-9) =$ ______________
8. $(-8) - (-4) =$ ______________
9. $5 + 11 =$ ______________
10. $7 - 10 =$ ______________
11. $|-8| =$ ______________
12. $|-6| - |-9| =$ ______________
13. $|7| - |-6| =$ ______________
14. $|-6| + |-5| =$ ______________

CHAPTER 8

Cumulative Review

Name ______________________ Date ____________

Student Edition • page 366–367

Patterns **Lesson 4.10**

Write the missing numbers in each pattern. Then tell what the pattern is.

15. 14, 11, ____, ____, 2, ____, ____, −7, −10

____

16. −64, 32, −16, ____, −4, 2, ____

____

Linear Equations **Lesson 5.12**

Evaluate each equation by solving for either *x* or *y*.

17. $7x - 7 = 35$ ____________

19. $11(4) - 34 = y$ ____________

18. $2x + 27 = 49$ ____________

20. $\frac{x}{2} \times 6 = 42$ ____________

Fractions of Fractions **Lesson 6.2**

21. $\frac{1}{2} \times$ ____________ $= \frac{1}{10}$

24. $\frac{2}{9}$ of ____________ $= \frac{6}{36}$

22. $\frac{3}{4}$ of ____________ $= \frac{6}{20}$

25. $\frac{3}{4}$ of ____________ $= \frac{9}{16}$

23. $\frac{4}{5} \times$ ____________ $= \frac{8}{35}$

26. $\frac{5}{6} \times$ ____________ $= \frac{10}{42}$

Cumulative Review

Student Edition • page 367

Practice with Fractions Lesson 6.6

Solve.

Mrs. May's fifth-grade class was assigned a book to read. So far, Josh has read $\frac{2}{3}$ of the book, Chen has read $\frac{3}{4}$, and Tai has read $\frac{7}{10}$.

27. Who has read the most pages? ______________

28. Who has read the fewest pages? ______________

Decide which fraction in each of the following pairs is greater. Fill the blank with a $<$, $>$, or $=$ symbol.

29. $\frac{1}{3}$ ________ $\frac{1}{4}$

30. $\frac{9}{16}$ ________ $\frac{1}{2}$

31. $\frac{5}{8}$ ________ $\frac{3}{4}$

32. $\frac{1}{3}$ ________ $\frac{2}{5}$

Multiplying Mixed Numbers Lesson 7.2

Multiply. Check to be sure your answers make sense.

33. $3\frac{2}{3} \times 1\frac{1}{7} =$ ______________

34. $\frac{5}{6} \times 4\frac{1}{3} =$ ______________

35. $3\frac{2}{5} \times 1\frac{2}{6} =$ ______________

36. $3\frac{1}{8} \times 1\frac{1}{5} =$ ______________

LESSON 8.9

Name ______________________ Date ____________

Practice with Division

Student Edition • pages 368–369

In each problem, two of the answers are clearly wrong and one is correct. Choose the correct answer.

1. $26\overline{)1352}$

   a. 520 **b.** 52 **c.** 5.2

2. $25\overline{)1625}$

   a. 65 **b.** 100 **c.** 6.5

3. $5\overline{)1005}$

   a. 201 **b.** 202 **c.** 203

4. $12\overline{)1632}$

   a. 1,360 **b.** 13.6 **c.** 136

5. $8\overline{)1168}$

   a. 200 **b.** 146 **c.** 14.6

6. $10\overline{)2160}$

   a. 200 **b.** 216 **c.** 217

7. $26\overline{)1794}$

   a. 6.9 **b.** 69 **c.** 690

8. $15\overline{)2355}$

   a. 156 **b.** 157 **c.** 158

9. Create eight more multiple-choice division questions of your own, using Exercises 1–8 above as a guide. Include three answer choices for each question. Remember that one answer must be correct. You must be able to see that the other two answers are wrong, but don't make the problems too easy.

____

____

____

____

____

Student Edition • page 369

10 The total weight of 12 people is 1,560 pounds.

What is their average weight? ____________

11 Mr. Jackson drove his car 14,062 miles last year. His car averaged 23 miles per gallon of gas. About how many gallons of gas did his car use during that year? ____________

12 Thirty-six people can ride the roller coaster at one time.

a. How many times does the roller coaster have to run in order to give rides to 432 people? ____________

b. **Extended Response** If there were 450 people, how many trips would be necessary? Explain your answer.

____

____

____

____

____

____

____

____

LESSON 8.10

Name ______________________ Date __________

Dividing by a Three-Digit Number

Student Edition • page 370

The annual cost of the health club is $1,533.

Solve the following problems.

1. Approximate the daily cost of becoming a yearly member and using the club the following number of times.

   a. once a week (assume 52 weeks in 1 year) ______________

   b. twice a week ______________

   c. 5 times a month ______________

   d. 10 times a month ______________

   e. every other day ______________

Student Edition • page 371

Approximate first, and then divide. Round quotients to the nearest whole number.

2. $52\overline{)1508}$ ________
3. $245\overline{)6370}$ ________
4. $28\overline{)3154}$ ________
5. $46\overline{)1426}$ ________
6. $173\overline{)2595}$ ________
7. $122\overline{)427}$ ________
8. $162\overline{)1134}$ ________
9. $205\overline{)1291}$ ________
10. $107\overline{)3436}$ ________
11. $115\overline{)690}$ ________
12. $216\overline{)1080}$ ________
13. $314\overline{)7065}$ ________
14. $315\overline{)2116}$ ________
15. $459\overline{)9785}$ ________
16. $136\overline{)1455}$ ________

17. **Extended Response** A box of 144 pencils costs $21.60. What is the cost of one pencil? If a box of 25 pencils costs $4.98 and you need only a limited number of pencils, when would it be more cost effective to buy the larger box?

____

____

____

____

Name ______________________ **Date** __________

Student Edition • page 371

18. The running track is an oval that is exactly 440 yards around. There are 1,760 yards in 1 mile. How many times must Sarah run around the track to run 2 miles? __________

19. It costs $125 to buy an evergreen tree that is 10 feet tall. The Chang family has $730 in their budget to buy new trees this year. How many evergreens can they buy at this price? __________

20. Rob did yard work after school, on weekends, and during vacation last spring and summer and earned $3,648. He knows he worked 105 days. On average, about how much did he earn per day? Round to the nearest dollar. __________

21. A city telephone book has 48,415 names. There are about 323 names on each page in the book. About how many pages are there altogether? __________

22. **Extended Response** Jenna's last 4 math test scores were 87, 89, 92, and 88. What score does she need on the fifth test to have an average of 90? Explain how you got your answer.

____

____

____

____

LESSON 8.11

Batting Averages and Other Division Applications

Student Edition • pages 372–374

Solve the following by using the information in the table.

Player	Official Times at Bat	Hits
Luis	62	27
Lamont	72	27
Chris	90	29

1. Approximate the batting averages for Lamont and Chris. __________

2. Now calculate their batting averages. Carry out the division to four decimal places, and then round to the nearest thousandth. __________

Solve the following problems.

For $118, you can get a season pass to use the Wakefield skating rink. If you don't have a pass, you have to pay $2.95 each time you use the rink.

Suppose you expect to use the rink about 30 times during the season.

3. Which is cheaper—buying a season pass or paying each time? __________

4. About how much would you save per visit if you used the cheaper method? (Hint: Find the ratio of cost to visits in each case.) __________

Suppose you use the rink only 24 times.

5. Which method is cheaper? __________

6. How much cheaper is it per visit? __________

Suppose you use the rink 80 times during the season.

7. Which method is cheaper? __________

8. By how much per visit? __________

LESSON 8.11 **Name** ______________________ **Date** ____________

Student Edition • pages 374–375

For each exercise, approximate an answer, divide, and then check your answer by multiplying. (Round answers to the nearest whole number.)

9. $36\overline{)2478}$ ____________

12. $21\overline{)287}$ ____________

10. $91\overline{)4588}$ ____________

13. $13\overline{)2547}$ ____________

11. $53\overline{)8139}$ ____________

14. $78\overline{)6324}$ ____________

15. A bottle of Slow-Red Ketchup contains 280 grams and costs $1.35. A bottle of Thick-Tomato Ketchup contains 200 grams and costs $1.08.

    a. Which brand costs less per gram? ____________

    b. How much cheaper is it per gram? ____________

16. Cho is driving from Boston, Massachusetts, to Washington, D.C., a distance of about 690 miles. She wants to make the trip in 13 hours.

    a. About how many miles per hour must Cho average? ____________

    b. After 5 hours of travel Cho has gone 300 miles. Must she go faster for the rest of the trip, or can she go slower and still get there in 13 hours? ____________

LESSON 8.11

Student Edition • **page 375**

17. The team's new player has 37 hits. In his other 86 times at bat, he was out.

    a. What fraction of his times at bat has he made hits? ______________

    b. What is his batting average? ______________

18. What is the batting average of a player who has 44 hits and who has been out 106 times? ______________

19. What is the batting average of a player who has been at bat 20 times and has made 12 hits? ______________

20. **Extended Response** Melissa needs 8 ballpoint pens. She can buy a package of 8 pens for $14.96, or she can buy the same pens for $1.75 each. How can she determine which is the better buy? What is the better buy?

____

____

____

____

____

LESSON 8.12

Name ______________________ Date ____________

Average Heights

Student Edition • page 376

The students in Latoya's class have measured their heights again and made a new table.

Name	Height (cm)	Name	Height (cm)	Name	Height (cm)	Name	Height (cm)
Judy	135	Aretha	143	Latoya	146	Melba	150
Chen	135	Joan	144	Kareem	145	Donna	151
Tami	136	Marco	144	Frank	145	Herb	152
Myra	137	Carlos	144	Pedro	146	Gene	153
Florence	138	Steve	145	Melvin	147	Min-ja	153
José	140	Liz	146	Lance	145	Ana	154
Marie	142	Carmen	147	Tiwa	150		

1. What was the average height of the students in Latoya's class at the beginning of the year? (See the table on page 3.) ____________

2. What was the range in heights at the beginning of the year? Remember, the range of a set of numbers is the difference between the greatest and least values. ____________

3. Inspect the tables on this page and on page 3. Who grew the most? Who grew the least?

____

____

4. Estimate the average amount of growth during this period. ____________

5. What is the range of heights in Latoya's class now? ____________

6. Make an estimate of the average height of Latoya's class now. ____________

Student Edition • page 377

Latoya has made another bar graph to show her classmates' heights.

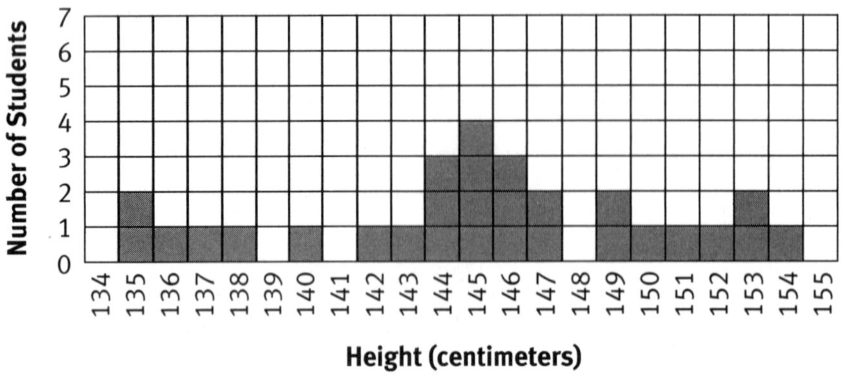

7 **Extended Response** How is the new graph like the one Latoya made at the beginning of the year? (See page 3.) How is it different?

____

____

Work in groups. Measure each person's height to the nearest centimeter.

8 Make a table and record the height of each person in your class.

Name ______________________ Date ____________

Student Edition • page 377

9 Compare your table with the one you made at the beginning of the year (when you completed page 3).

a. What was the average height of the students in your class at the beginning of the year? ____________

b. What was the range in heights of the students in your class at the beginning of the year? ____________

c. Who has grown the most? Who has grown the least? Estimate the average amount of growth since the beginning of the year.

____

____

d. What is the range of heights in your class now? ____________

e. Estimate the average height of your class now. Does your estimate make sense?

____

____

10 Use your table to make a bar graph of the heights of the students in your class now.

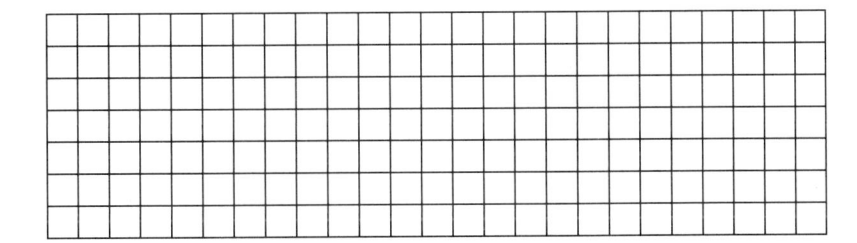

Use your new graph to answer Problems 11–14.

11 How many students are below the class's average height? Above the class's average height? ____________

12 How many students are the same height as the class's average height? ____________

LESSON 8.12

Student Edition • pages 377–378

13 **Extended Response** How is the new graph similar to the one you made earlier in the year?

______

______

14 **Extended Response** How is the new graph different from the earlier one?

______

______

15 Look at the graphs of Latoya's class and of your class.

a. Can you determine the mean of the heights by looking at the graphs?

______

b. Can you tell the median of the heights from the graphs? ______

c. Can you tell the mode of the heights from the graphs? ______

d. **Extended Response** Suppose you included your teacher's height in the graph for your class. Which would be affected the most—the mean, median, mode, or range? Would any of these stay the same?

______

______

Latoya's friend Sergio also collected information from his class. The heights, in centimeters, of the 25 students in Sergio's class are in the following list.

135	138	142	146	147
136	138	144	146	147
137	138	145	146	148
137	140	145	146	150
137	141	145	146	155

Name ______________________ **Date** ____________

Student Edition • page 378

Use **Sergio's information from page 352 to answer the following questions.**

16 Find the median, mode, and range of these heights.

____

17 **Extended Response** Do you think the mean of the heights of the students in Sergio's class will be the same as the mean of the heights of the students in Latoya's class? Why or why not?

____

____

____

18 Make a graph of the heights in Sergio's class like the graph Latoya made of the heights in her class.

19 Based on the graph you made, do you think the mean of the heights in Sergio's class will be greater than, less than, or about the same as the mean of the heights in your class?

____

____

LESSON 8.12

Student Edition • page 379

There are errors in four of the nine problems below. Find the errors, and then do each calculation correctly.

20
$$\begin{array}{r} 2.92 \\ 21\overline{)61.32} \\ -42 \\ \hline 193 \\ -189 \\ \hline 42 \\ -42 \\ \hline 0 \end{array}$$

21
$$\begin{array}{r} 2.08 \\ 32\overline{)62.56} \\ -64 \\ \hline 256 \\ -256 \\ \hline 0 \end{array}$$

22
$$\begin{array}{r} 3.04 \\ 46\overline{)139.84} \\ -138 \\ \hline 18 \\ -0 \\ \hline 184 \\ -184 \\ \hline 0 \end{array}$$

23
$$\begin{array}{r} 1.11 \\ 25\overline{)52.50} \\ -25 \\ \hline 27 \\ -25 \\ \hline 25 \\ -25 \\ \hline 0 \end{array}$$

24
$$\begin{array}{r} 2.35 \\ 17\overline{)39.95} \\ -34 \\ \hline 59 \\ -51 \\ \hline 85 \\ -85 \\ \hline 0 \end{array}$$

25
$$\begin{array}{r} 99 \\ 99\overline{)9801} \\ -891 \\ \hline 891 \\ -891 \\ \hline 0 \end{array}$$

26
$$\begin{array}{r} 3.825 \\ 16\overline{)47.320} \\ -48 \\ \hline 132 \\ -132 \\ \hline 0 \end{array}$$

27
$$\begin{array}{r} 3.02 \\ 24\overline{)36.48} \\ -36 \\ \hline 48 \\ -48 \\ \hline 0 \end{array}$$

28
$$\begin{array}{r} 2.45 \\ 52\overline{)127.40} \\ -104 \\ \hline 234 \\ -208 \\ \hline 260 \\ -260 \\ \hline 0 \end{array}$$

LESSON 8.13

Name ______________________ Date ____________

Using Rates to Make Predictions

Student Edition • pages 380–381

Answer the following questions about continuing at the same rate.

Miss Bluehouse has been driving for 6 hours and has gone 331 miles.

1. At about what average speed is Miss Bluehouse traveling? ____________
2. About how far do you think she will have driven altogether after 10 hours?

   ____
3. About how far will she have driven after 8 hours? ____________
4. About how far do you think Miss Bluehouse drove in the first 4 hours?

   ____
5. If Miss Bluehouse was traveling at an average speed of 45 miles per hour, about how far would she have driven after 10 hours? After 8 hours?

   ____

Solve these problems.

6. Jill's car went 371 miles after she filled the gas tank. Then she stopped at a station and filled the tank again. It took 17 gallons of gas to fill the tank.

   a. About how many miles per gallon did Jill's car travel? ____________

   b. Jill's tank holds 20 gallons of gas. If she starts with a full tank, about how far can Jill go before the car runs out of gas? ____________

   c. Jill has driven 250 miles since she last bought gas. About how many gallons of gas has she used? ____________

   d. Jill has a half tank of gas in her car. Can she drive the 230 miles to the state capital without stopping for gas? ____________

LESSON 8.13

Student Edition • pages 381–382

To find the *daily mean temperature* for a community, we find the average of the high and low temperatures for the day.

7. If the high temperature in Jamestown today was 7°C and the low was 1°C, what was the daily mean temperature in Jamestown? __________

8. If the high temperature in Kingsville today was 28°C and the low was 20°C, what was the daily mean temperature in Kingsville? __________

9. If the high temperature in Greensburg today was 15°F and the low was −5°F, what was the daily mean temperature in Greensburg? __________

10. If the high temperature in Portstown today was 81°F and the low was 52°F, what was the daily mean temperature in Portstown? __________

11. If the high temperature in Fairbanks was −15°F and the low was −40°F, what was the daily mean temperature in Fairbanks? __________

Here are the daily mean temperatures (in °C) for January in Jamestown:

0, 2, 1, 6, 1, 0, 3, 7, 8, 10, 4, 0, 0, 1, 1, 1, 3, 7, 12, 15, 16, 4, 2, 3, 5, 4, 2, 1, 1, 6, 0

12. What was the average mean temperature in Jamestown in January to the nearest tenth of a degree? __________

Try to decide whether average values are useful in the situations described below. Discuss your decisions with other students.

13. **Extended Response** Mr. Miller is planning a trip to New York City in October. He learns that the temperature during October averages about 15°C. Knowing this, Mr. Miller decides not to take a warm coat.

    a. Does Mr. Miller have enough information to make a sound decision? __________

Name ____________________ Date ____________

Student Edition • **pages 382–383**

b. If so, did he make a good decision? If not, what are some other kinds of information he could use?

____

____

14 **Extended Response** Mrs. Soo lives in New York City. To help plan her household budget for October, she wants to estimate the cost for heating her home. Will knowing the average temperature for October in New York City help Mrs. Soo? Explain your answer.

____

____

15 **Extended Response** The visitor's center in New York City created a poster inviting people to spend their vacations enjoying what the city has to offer. On the poster, the average temperature for the summer months is given as 24.8°C. Is this enough information to help people decide what types of clothing to pack when planning a trip to New York City? Explain your answer.

____

____

For the following problems, refer to the **Golf Game** in Lesson 2 on ***Student Edition*** page 343.

16 Suppose Steve had nine more turns with scores of 3, 5, 6, 3, 4, 12, 6, 5, and 4. What are the mean, median, mode, and range for this set of 10 scores (including the 9 from the first turn)? How would you decide what the mode is? Are there several? How many? If the median is found to be two numbers, remember that we use the average of those two numbers.

____

____

LESSON 8.13

Student Edition • page 383

17 Three other players played the **Golf Game.** The other players got the following scores:

Player	Scores	Mean	Median	Mode	Range
Andaiye	5, 5, 6, 4, 4, 3, 4, 3, 7, 3				
Yan-Ping	6, 5, 4, 6, 7, 5, 7, 4, 6, 3				
Cuneyt	5, 9, 4, 5, 7, 7, 8, 5, 6, 8				

Complete the table above by calculating the mean, median, mode, and range for each set of scores.

18 If the four players were competing for the lowest score, who would win if they used means? Who would win if they used medians? Who would win if they used modes? Who would win if they used the smallest range?

____

____

19 **Extended Response** If you had to decide in advance whether to use the mode, median, or mean to decide the winner, which do you think would be the most reasonable to use? Why?

____

____

20 Play the game with ten turns. Keep track of the ten scores. Calculate the mean, median, mode, and range. Compare these figures with the mean, median, mode, and range that your friends got. Who had the best average? Does it matter whether you used the mean, median, or mode?

____

____

LESSON 8.14

Name ______________________ Date ____________

Population Density

Student Edition • page 384

Classes at Centerville School

Teacher	Number of Students	Number of Tables	Number of Chairs	Students per Table	Chairs per Table	Students per Chair
Mr. Burke	22	5	24			
Ms. Ruiz	25	6	28			
Miss Stamos	18	6	24			
Mrs. Davis	20	5	21			
Mr. Asari	23	5	22			
Mr. Gomez	25	5	25			
Ms. Golden	24	6	24			

Use a calculator to solve the following problems. Give your answers to the nearest hundredth.

1. In Ms. Golden's class, how many students are there per table? How many chairs are there per table? How many students are there per chair?

   ____

2. In Mr. Burke's class, how many students are there per table? How many chairs are there per table? How many students are there per chair?

   ____

3. Complete the last three columns in the table above. Round numbers to the nearest hundredth.

4. Determine the total number of students in Centerville School. What is the average number of students per class? __________

5. **Extended Response** Is there anything else you can observe about classes in Centerville School based on the table?

   ____

   ____

LESSON 8.14

Student Edition • page 385

According to the 2000 census, the population of Alaska was 626,932, and its area was 571,951 square miles. The population of the District of Columbia was 572,059, and its area was 61 square miles.

Use this information to answer the following questions.

6. Which was more crowded, Alaska or the District of Columbia—that is, which had more people per square mile? ______________

7. About how many people were there per square mile in Alaska? ______________

8. Is that more or less than 1 person per square mile? ______________

9. About how many people were there per square mile in the District of Columbia?

____

10. Is that more or less than 10,000 people per square mile? ______________

11. Look at the table below. Write the population density (number of people per square mile) for each state. Then, rank the states in order from greatest to least population density. Round to the nearest tenth.

State	2000 Population	Area in Square Miles	Population Density	Rank
California	33,871,648	155,959		
Georgia	8,186,453	57,906		
Massachusetts	6,349,097	7,840		
New York	18,976,457	47,214		
Rhode Island	1,048,319	1,045		
Texas	20,851,820	261,797		
Wyoming	493,782	97,100		

12. According to the 2000 census, the population of the United States was 281,421,906 and its area was 3,537,438 square miles. About how many people were there per square mile in the United States in 2000? ______________

LESSON 8.15

Name ______________________ Date ____________

Using Ratios

Student Edition • page 386

Solve the following problems.

1. Michael is 178 centimeters tall. When he holds out his arms, the distance from fingertip to fingertip is 182 centimeters. What is the ratio of the distance between his fingertips to his height? ____________

2. Sarah is 65 inches tall. When she holds out her arms, the distance from fingertip to fingertip is 63 inches. What is the ratio of the distance between her fingertips to her height? ____________

3. Measure your height and fingertip distance. Find the ratio of your fingertip distance to your height. ____________

4. Find full-body pictures of some animals that walk on land (for example, a cat, a dog, a gerbil).

   a. Measure the fingertip distance up one front leg or arm, across the shoulder, and down the other front leg or arm.

   b. Measure each animal's length by starting at the tip of the nose and measure along the back to the tip of the tail.

   c. What is the ratio of the fingertip distance to the length for each walking animal you measured?

   ____

   ____

5. Find some full-body pictures of flying animals (a bird or a bat, for example).

   a. Measure the fingertip distance from the tip of one wing, across the back, to the tip of the other wing.

   b. Measure the length from the tip of the beak or head, along the back, to the tip of the tail.

   c. Find the ratio of the fingertip distance to the length for each flying animal you measured.

   ____

   ____

Student Edition • page 387

6 Find some full-body pictures of swimming animals (such as a fish, a dolphin, or a whale).

a. Measure the fingertip distance from the tip of one flipper, fin, or front leg across the back to the other flipper, fin, or front leg.

b. Measure the length from the tip of the head to the tip of the tail.

c. What is the ratio of fingertip distance to length for each swimming animal you measured?

____

____

7 Work in groups to organize the data you collected. Make separate tables showing animals with ratios less than, greater than, and equal to 1.

8 **Extended Response** What do the animals in each table have in common?

____

____

9 Suppose you found the skeleton of an animal that had a fingertip distance of 342 centimeters and a length of 351 centimeters. From those measurements, what could you tell about how the animal moved?

____

____

10 If five animals had the dimensions shown in the table below, what could you conclude about how they moved?

____

____

Animal	A	B	C	D	E
Fingertip Distance (cm)	72	41	145	25	104
Length (cm)	74	10	141	92	33

CHAPTER 8 Exploring Problem Solving

Name ______________________ **Date** ____________

Student Edition • pages 388–389

Benedict Arnold based his code on a published book. Arnold would search in this "key" book for each word he wanted to use. Then, instead of writing the word, he wrote the page number, line number, and the position of the word from the left. For example, the second word in this letter of July 12, 1780, is "293. 9 .7," which stands for "wrote."

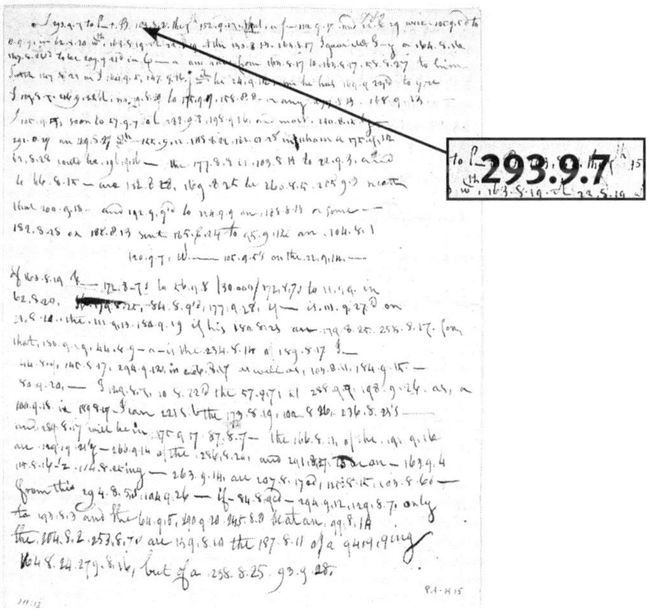

At times, the British would use a trick called a *mask* to hide their secrets.

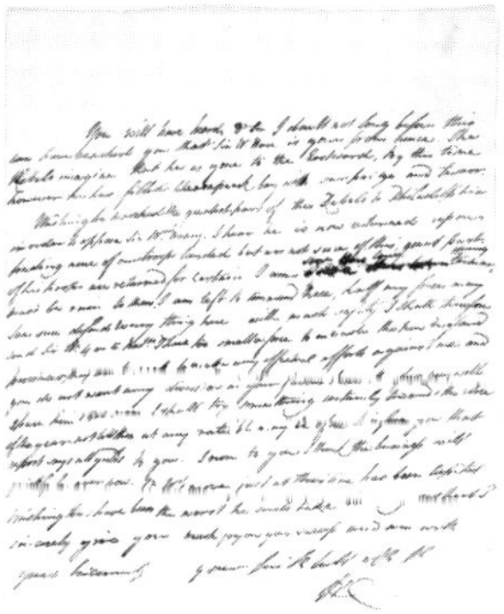

If anyone intercepted the note, it would look and read like an ordinary letter. In fact, it might intentionally give false information.

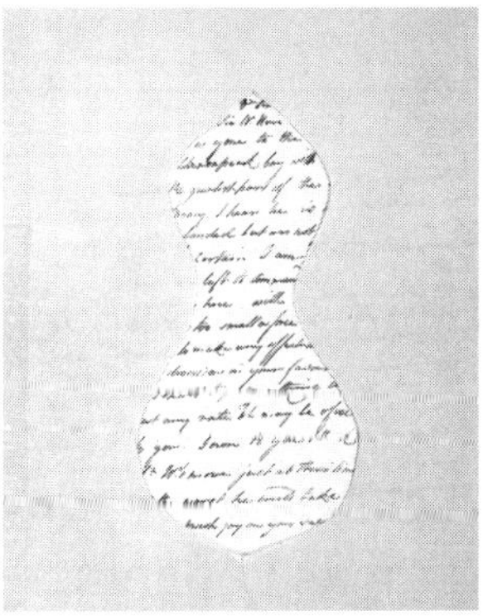

But place the mask over the page and you can easily read the secret message within the letter.

Student Edition • pages 389–390

Answer the following questions. Use the information on page 363.

1. If you had the "key" book, how would you decode the numbers 136. 14. 2 in one of Benedict Arnold's letters?

2. Solve this puzzle: in the "key" book, which word do you think is physically closer to the word in Problem 1—136. 29. 3 or 153. 13. 19?

3. How could a masked letter be used to send false information?

Time to put your code-breaking talents to use. Imagine you have intercepted a masked letter without the mask.

You have, however, found clues for creating and positioning the rectangular mask opening.

- Each pair of numbers is a dividend and divisor.
- The remainder tells the number of inches.

mask opening	
width	266. 44
height	318. 35
distance from top	381. 76
distance from left	451. 28

Name ______________________ Date ____________

Student Edition • page 390

You will have heard, Dear Sir, long before this letter has made its way to you, that our Sir. W. Howe has gone, as the Rebels are aware, Eastward to the Chesapeak bay with great hopes. Washington has now taken all the greatest part of the Rebels to Philadelphia to fight Wm's army. I hear that he has now returned, finding that none of our troops landed but am not certain. I am sure such marching has tired them. I'm left to command with more men than needed but still I have too small a force to make an invasion. Their army is small, simply a diversion for you. I'll therefore send Sir W. 4 or 5 battalions to try something at any rate. I can spare him 1,500 men. By the way, I think Sir W's moves lately are excellent and Washington's are the worst he could make in every respect. Sincerely and with much joy on your success, I am with great sincerity,

H.C.

Work in groups to discuss and solve the following problems. Compare your answers with other groups.

4. What are the dimensions of the mask opening? ____________

5. How should the mask opening be placed over the letter? ____________

6. What is the secret message hidden in the letter?

____

____

____

7. Create and exchange your own masked-letter message with other groups.

Cumulative Review

Student Edition • page 391

Subtraction Rules and Negative Numbers Lesson 4.7

Add or subtract. Do not use a calculator. Watch for negative numbers.

1. $40 + 15 =$ ______
2. $(-40) + 39 =$ ______
3. $0 - 15 =$ ______
4. $15 - 20 =$ ______
5. $35 - 25 =$ ______
6. $0 + 10 =$ ______
7. $(-3) + 4 =$ ______
8. $(-6) + 5 =$ ______

Multiplying and Dividing Integers Lesson 4.9

Complete the following exercises.

9. $(-5) \times (-6) =$ ______
10. $(-7) \times 8 =$ ______
11. $5 \times (-2) =$ ______
12. $16 \div (-4) =$ ______
13. $-24 \div (-6) =$ ______
14. $-6 \div 6 =$ ______

Decimal Equivalents of Fractions Lesson 6.3

For each fraction, give the decimal equivalent or approximation correct to three decimal places (to the nearest thousandth).

15. $\frac{6}{9} =$ ______
16. $\frac{4}{8} =$ ______
17. $\frac{2}{5} =$ ______
18. $\frac{7}{9} =$ ______
19. $\frac{1}{4} =$ ______
20. $\frac{2}{7} =$ ______

Cumulative Review

Name ______________________ Date ____________

Student Edition • pages 391–392

Comparing Fractions Lesson 6.7

Order the following sets of fractions from least to greatest.

21. $\frac{2}{3}, \frac{1}{2}, \frac{5}{6}, \frac{1}{3}, \frac{1}{6}$ ______________________

22. $\frac{3}{10}, \frac{1}{5}, \frac{1}{2}, \frac{2}{5}, \frac{1}{4}$ ______________________

Fill the blank with either <, >, or =.

23. $\frac{1}{4}$ ________ $\frac{3}{12}$

24. $\frac{1}{5}$ ________ $\frac{2}{9}$

25. $\frac{2}{7}$ ________ $\frac{5}{14}$

26. $\frac{5}{6}$ ________ $\frac{8}{10}$

Applying Fractions Lesson 6.12

Solve the following problems.

The James family needed 3 days to drive from Ohio to California. They drove $\frac{3}{10}$ of the way on Friday and $\frac{1}{3}$ of the way on Saturday.

27. On which day did they drive a greater distance? ____________

28. How much of the trip was left to drive on Sunday? ____________

Cumulative Review

Student Edition • page 392

29 Suppose 3 friends are sharing a pizza. If 2 boys each wanted $\frac{1}{4}$ of the pizza and 1 wanted $\frac{2}{5}$, is that possible? If so, how much of the pizza is unclaimed?

____

Dividing Fractions Lesson 7.6

Divide. Reduce when possible.

30 $12 \div \frac{2}{3} =$ ______________

31 $\frac{1}{2} \div \frac{1}{3} =$ ______________

32 $16 \div \frac{4}{5} =$ ______________

33 $\frac{2}{5} \div \frac{3}{7} =$ ______________

34 $\frac{5}{8} \div \frac{5}{4} =$ ______________

35 $\frac{5}{12} \div \frac{10}{3} =$ ______________

Averages Lesson 8.1

Find the average of the following sets of numbers.

36 8, 11, 15, 26 ______________

37 −5, 4, 10, 15 ______________

Solve.

38 Kelli had scores of 85, 87, and 90 on her first 3 math tests. She thought that if she scored a 94 on her next test, she could raise her average to a 90 and get an A. Was Kelli right? What would her average be? ______________

____

____

Key Ideas Review

Name ______________________ Date ____________

Student Edition • page 393

Solve.

1. 1,974 ÷ 42 = ____________

2. 38,586 ÷ 354 = ____________

3. What do the terms *range* and *mode* refer to?

____

____

4. Jorge is a linebacker. The table below shows the number of tackles he made for the first 6 games of the season.

Game	Number of Tackles
1	8
2	12
3	8
4	15
5	9
6	11

What is Jorge's average number of tackles for each game? ____________

5. Explain two ways to compare ratios.

____

____

____

CHAPTER 8

Chapter Review

Student Edition • page 394

Solve. Lesson 8.1

1. Chu scored 80, 88, 90, and 94 on his last 4 spelling tests.

   What was his average? ______________

2. Chu wants to bring his average up to 90. Could he do that after his next test? If so, what is the minimum score he would need?

   ____

Solve. Lesson 8.2

Mrs. Long's second-grade class had the following scores on their math tests: 88, 73, 95, 78, 86, 84, 67, 90, 78, 95, and 82.

3. Find the mean, median, mode, and range of the data. ______________

Solve. Lesson 8.4

Abby drove from Columbus, Ohio, to St. Louis, Missouri. Her trip was approximately 410 miles.

4. Abby drove the first 240 miles in 4 hours. What was her average rate of speed? ______________

5. The rest of the trip took $2\frac{1}{2}$ hours. What was Abby's average speed for the entire trip? ______________

Fill the blank with <, >, or =. Use a calculator only when necessary. Lesson 8.5

6. $\frac{5}{9}$ ________ $\frac{5}{8}$

7. $\frac{3}{11}$ ________ $\frac{3}{13}$

8. $\frac{4}{12}$ ________ $\frac{8}{15}$

9. $\frac{4}{5}$ ________ $\frac{7}{8}$

Chapter Review

Name ______________________ Date ______________

Student Edition • pages 394–395

Find approximate answers. Lesson 8.7

10. $62 \div 20 =$ ______________
11. $480 \div 19 =$ ______________
12. $498 \div 101 =$ ______________
13. $560 \div 71 =$ ______________
14. $150 \div 29 =$ ______________
15. $1{,}400 \div 20 =$ ______________

Solve. Lesson 8.8

16. For the school fund-raiser, 27 students raised \$810. What was the average amount raised per student? ______________

17. Jacque saved all his allowance for 35 weeks and accumulated \$525. What was his weekly allowance? ______________

Divide. Lesson 8.10

18. $3{,}640 \div 325 =$ ______________
20. $54{,}926 \div 947 =$ ______________
19. $18{,}306 \div 678 =$ ______________
21. $4{,}879 \div 170 =$ ______________

Chapter Review

Student Edition • page 395

Solve. Lesson 8.11

Ted is the leading batter on his Little League team with 14 hits in 20 at bats.

22. What is Ted's batting average up to this point? ______________

23. If Ted gets 6 hits in his next 10 at bats, what will his overall average be? ______________

Solve. Lesson 8.13

Peg needs to get to her uncle's house by 5:00 P.M. for dinner. He lives 320 miles away.

24. If she leaves at noon and does not stop, what is the slowest speed she could average and still arrive on time? ______________

25. If Peg averaged only 59 miles per hour, how many miles from her uncle's house would she be at 5:00? ______________

Practice Test

Name ______________________ Date ____________

Student Edition • page 396

Solve the following problems.

Gali took a survey to see how many miles from school her classmates lived. Here are the results: 5, 7, 8, 10, 2, 1.5, 6, 4.5, 5, and 12.

1. What is the mean of the distances? ____________
2. What is the median of the distances? ____________
3. What is the mode of the distances? ____________
4. What is the range of the data? ____________

Fill the blank with <, >, or =.

5. $\frac{1}{5}$ ________ $\frac{1}{3}$
6. $16 \div 7$ ________ $15 \div 11$
7. $\frac{15}{17}$ ________ $\frac{15}{18}$
8. $35 \div 14$ ________ $25 \div 10$

Find approximate answers.

9. $1{,}005 \div 203 =$ ____________
10. $189 \div 20 =$ ____________
11. $7{,}321 \div 12 =$ ____________

For each problem, approximate an answer, and then do the division. Round your answers to the nearest whole number.

12. $18\overline{)1405}$ ________ ________
13. $131\overline{)380}$ ________ ________
14. $455\overline{)3640}$ ________ ________
15. $28\overline{)483}$ ________ ________

Practice Test

Student Edition • page 397

Choose the correct answer.

16. Find the mean of 43, 25, 46, 17, and 89.

Ⓐ 220 Ⓑ 55

Ⓒ 44 Ⓓ 43

17. The town of Dashire reports an average family size of 3.12. About how many people would you expect there to be in 20 families?

Ⓐ 3.12 Ⓑ 31

Ⓒ 47 Ⓓ 62

18. Jackie's car drove 312 miles on 12 gallons of gas. How many miles per gallon is that?

Ⓐ 26 Ⓑ 31.2

Ⓒ 300 Ⓓ 3,744

19. Which ratio of girls to all students is greatest?

Ⓐ 11 to 21 Ⓑ 12 to 25

Ⓒ 11 to 23 Ⓓ 10 to 20

20. How many tables would you need to seat 184 people if each table could fit a maximum of 5 people?

Ⓐ 36 Ⓑ 37

Ⓒ 40 Ⓓ 41

21. The United States Mint produced 6,836,000,000 pennies in the year 2004. Approximately how many pennies is that per month?

Ⓐ 7,000,000,000

Ⓑ 700,000,000

Ⓒ 7,000,000

Ⓓ 700,000

22. Which batter has the best batting average?

Ⓐ Jim: 12 hits in 38 at bats

Ⓑ John: 11 hits in 35 at bats

Ⓒ Jana: 14 hits in 40 at bats

Ⓓ Jessie: 15 hits in 50 at bats

23. Divide: $27\overline{)8505}$

Ⓐ 315 Ⓑ 31.5

Ⓒ 3.15 Ⓓ 0.315

CHAPTER 8

Practice Test

Name ______________________________ **Date** ______________

Student Edition • page 398

Choose the correct answer.

24. The class sizes at the Greater Elementary School are as follows: 22, 25, 21, 20, 22, 15, and 23. Which method of finding the average results in the lowest class size?

Ⓐ mean Ⓑ median

Ⓒ mode Ⓓ range

25. Naomi drove 495 miles in 9 hours. What was her average speed?

Ⓐ 65 mph Ⓑ 60 mph

Ⓒ 55 mph Ⓓ 50 mph

26. Approximately 12,150 people take public transportation every morning between the hours of 7 A.M. and 10 A.M. About how many people is that per hour?

Ⓐ 4 Ⓑ 40

Ⓒ 400 Ⓓ 4,000

27. $1\frac{4}{5} \times 3\frac{1}{8} =$

Ⓐ $\frac{1}{10}$ Ⓑ $3\frac{1}{10}$

Ⓒ $5\frac{5}{8}$ Ⓓ $5\frac{7}{8}$

28. Which fraction is equivalent to $\frac{12}{20}$?

Ⓐ $\frac{6}{14}$ Ⓑ $\frac{3}{5}$

Ⓒ $\frac{2}{10}$ Ⓓ $\frac{3}{4}$

29. Which unit of measurement should be used to measure the length of a paper clip?

Ⓐ centimeters Ⓑ miles

Ⓒ inches Ⓓ feet

30. Misha runs $1\frac{3}{4}$ miles 4 days a week. How many miles does she run in 3 weeks?

Ⓐ $5\frac{1}{4}$ Ⓑ 7

Ⓒ $10\frac{1}{2}$ Ⓓ 21

31. The rule for a function machine is "subtract 8." If −3 comes out of the function machine, which number went in?

Ⓐ −11 Ⓑ −5

Ⓒ 5 Ⓓ 11

32. Solve for *n*.

$15 - (2 \times 7) = n$

Ⓐ 1 Ⓑ 16

Ⓒ 23 Ⓓ 91

Practice Test

Student Edition • page 399

Extended Response **Solve** the problems below.

33. Daily sales for a retail store are shown below. Use the information in the table to answer the following questions.

Monday	Tuesday	Wednesday	Thursday	Friday	Saturday	Sunday
$12,450	$10,005	$4,550	$16,900	$10,600	$12,345	$15,230

a. On his weekly report, the store manager reported a daily average income of $12,345. How did he find this average? Show your work.

____

____

____

b. During the week, there was a snowstorm and the store had to close early. On which day do you think the storm occurred? Why?

____

____

c. The next week, the store manager calculated the mean sales to be $13,420. Is this greater or less than this week's mean sales, and by how much?

____

34. Suppose two different stores sold copies of the same book.

a. If Read-o-rama sold 30 books for $388.50 and Bookworm sold 25 books for $337.50, which store had the lowest price per book? ______________

b. Suppose you wanted to buy 14 copies of this book for your reading group at the lowest possible price. If Read-o-rama also sold 5-packs of the book at $50 each, how many 5-packs or individual copies should you buy? Explain.

____

____

Name ______________________ Date ______________

Geometry

Student Edition • page 401

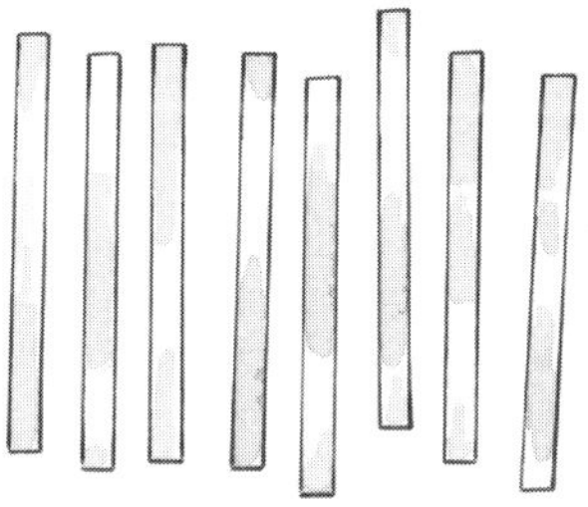	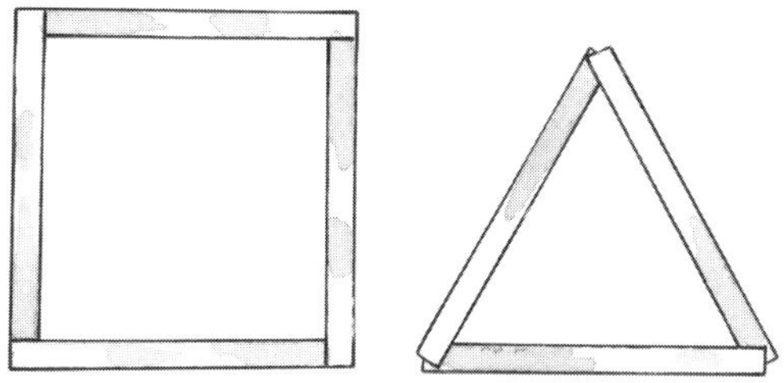
A. Cut out 8 strips of the same length cardboard.	**B.** Make a triangle frame and a square frame. Compare to see which shape is more rigid.

Answer the following questions.

1. Which frame is more rigid? ____________
2. How can you make the weaker frame more rigid?

    ____

    ____

3. Will you get the same result if you use strips of different lengths? Try it.

    ____

    ____

4. How many different-shaped triangles can you make with 3 strips? ____________
5. How many different four-sided shapes can you make with 4 strips? ____________
6. How do your answers to Problems 4 and 5 help explain why one shape is more rigid than the other?

    ____

    ____

LESSON 9.1 Angles

Student Edition • page 403

Each angle below is labeled with a letter at the vertex. Identify each angle as *acute, right, obtuse,* or *straight.*

1. 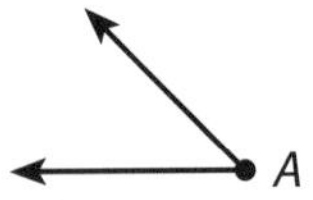

____

2. 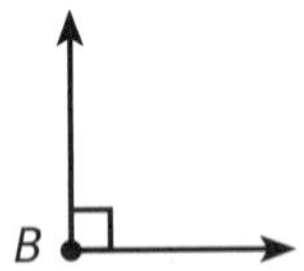

____

3. 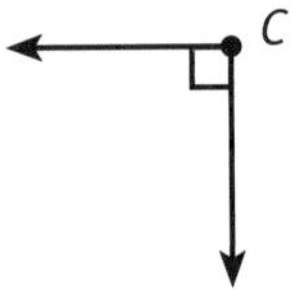

____

4. 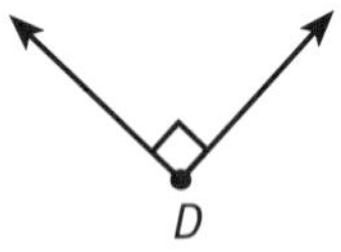

____

5. 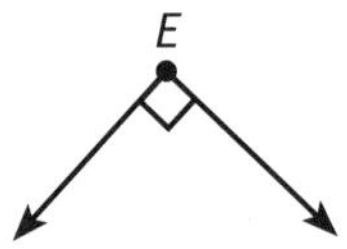

____

6. 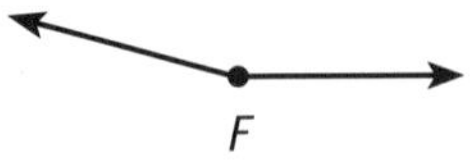

____

7. 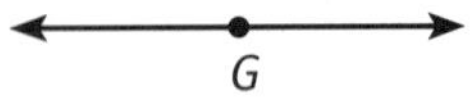

____

8. 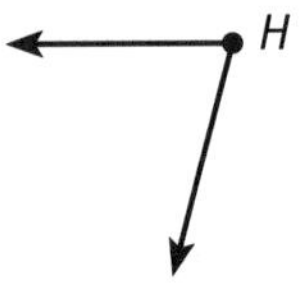

____

9. 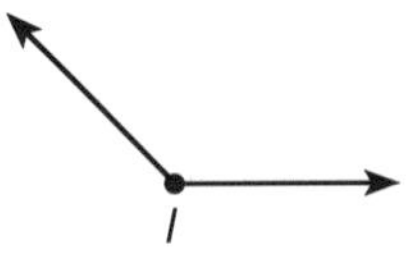

____

10. 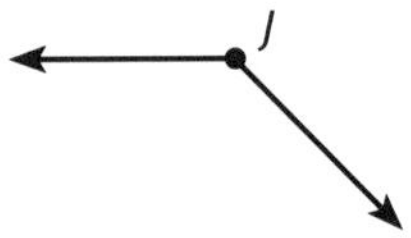

____

11. What are the angles in this triangle called?

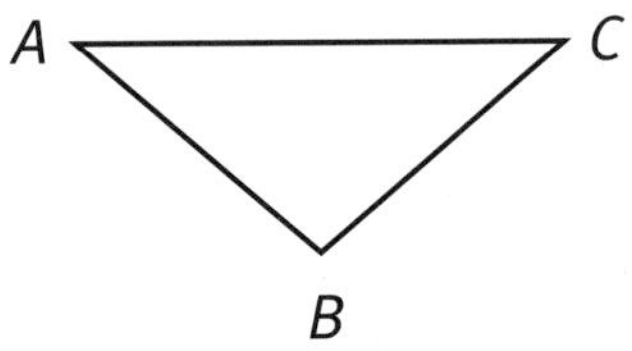

____

LESSON 9.1

Name ______________________ Date ____________

Student Edition • page 404

Angles in nature

We'll call these the *top angles.*

Use the photograph to solve the following problems.

12. Make a list of right angles and near right angles.

____

13. Make a list of acute angles. ______________________________

14. Make a list of obtuse angles. ______________________________

15. Select four angles to order from least to greatest. Estimate their measures.

____

LESSON 9.1

Student Edition • page 405

These are the *bottom angles*.

16 Make three lists.

a. One list of right or near right angles

____

____

b. One list of acute angles

____

____

c. One list of obtuse angles

____

____

17 Order four of the angles from least to greatest. Estimate their measures.

____

____

18 **Extended Response** Compare the lists you made for the top angles on page 379 with the lists you made for the bottom angles. Describe any patterns that emerge.

____

____

____

LESSON 9.2

Name ______________________ Date ____________

Measuring Angles

Student Edition • page 408

Indicate whether each angle is *acute, obtuse,* or *right.* Give the measure of each angle in degrees.

1

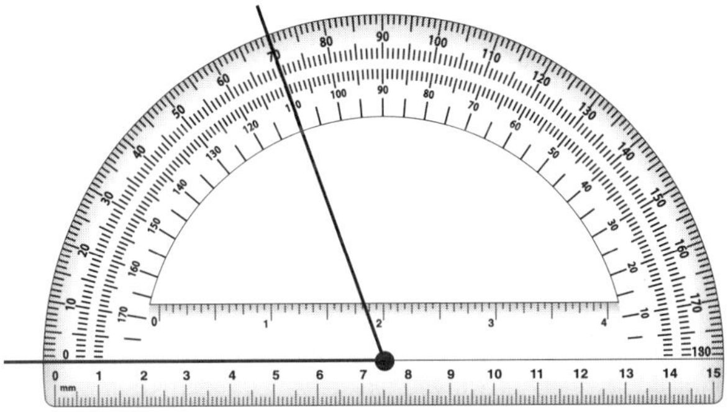

E

____

2

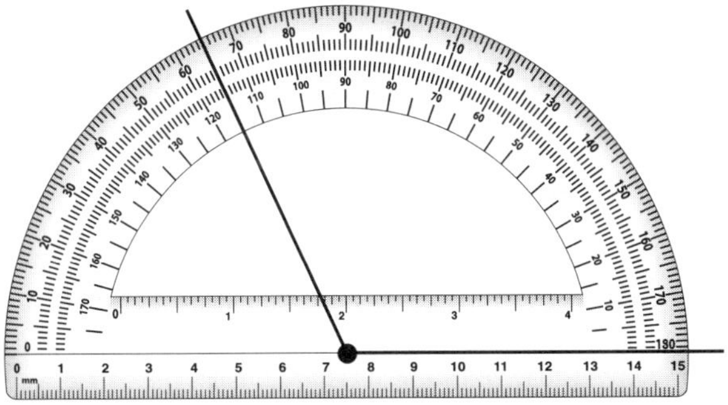

H

____

3 Sketch angle *ABC* with the measure 180°.
What is this type of angle called? ______________

4 How many degrees are in an acute angle? ______________

5 How many degrees are in an obtuse angle? ______________

LESSON 9.2

Student Edition • page 409

Measure each angle. (Some figures may have more than one angle.) Write the name of each angle and its measure. To make it easier to read each angle's measure with your protractor, you can extend its sides with your ruler.

6
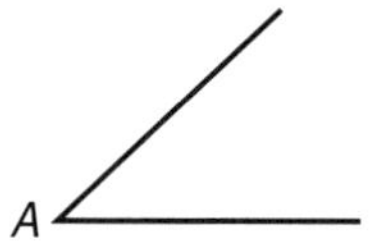

____

7
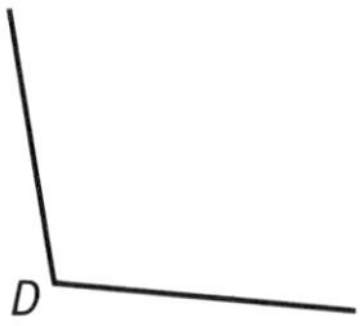

____

8
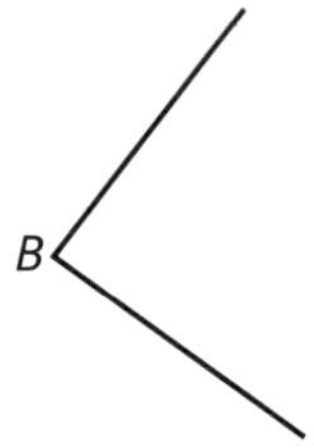

____

9
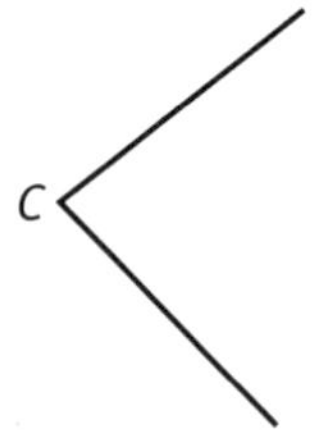

____

10
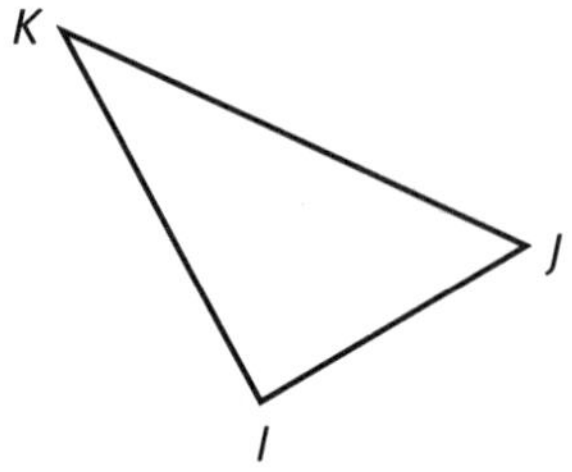

____

____

11
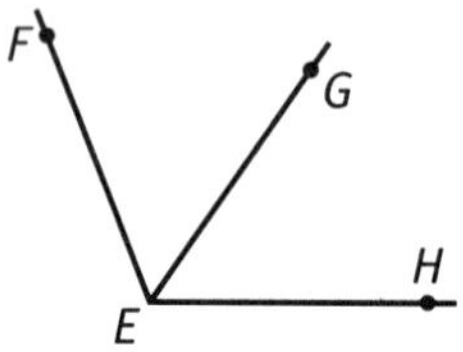

____

____

12 **Extended Response** Explain how to decide which scale to use on a protractor.

____

____

Name ______________________ Date ____________

Student Edition • page 409

13. **Extended Response** Draw two intersecting perpendicular lines. Add the measures of the four angles formed. Do they add to 360°? Explain why or why not.

____

14. Choose two of the angles you drew in Problem 13 that are adjacent to one another (they share a side). If you add the measures of these two angles, what is the total measure? Does it matter which two adjacent angles you choose?

____

____

15. How many degrees are in a quarter turn? In a half turn? In three-fourths of a turn? In a full turn?

____

____

LESSON 9.3

Angles and Sides of a Triangle

Student Edition • pages 411–412

Measure the three angles of each triangle, and then find the sum of the measures. Indicate which, if any, of the triangles are *right, isosceles,* or *equilateral.*

1. 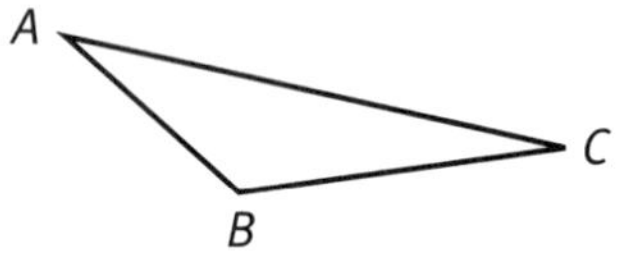

4. 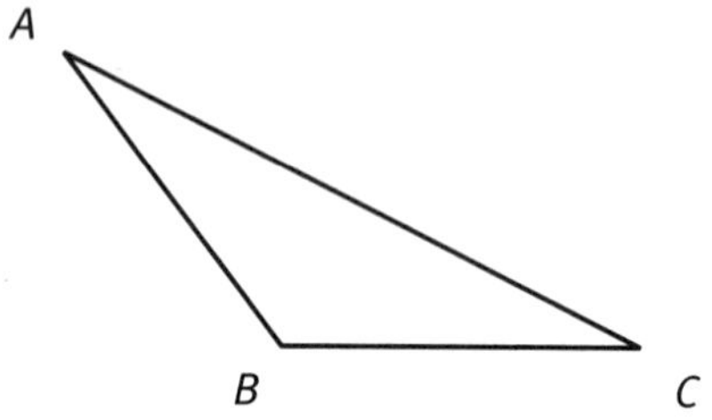

2. 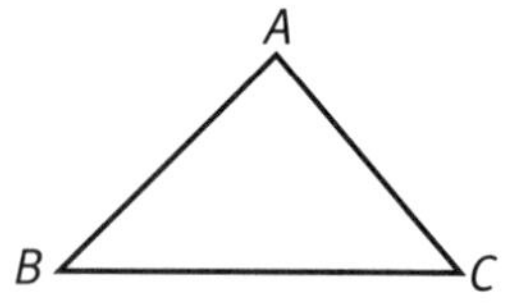

5. 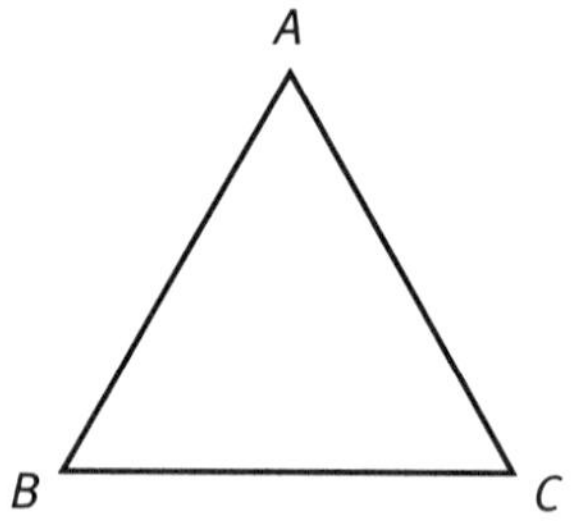

3. 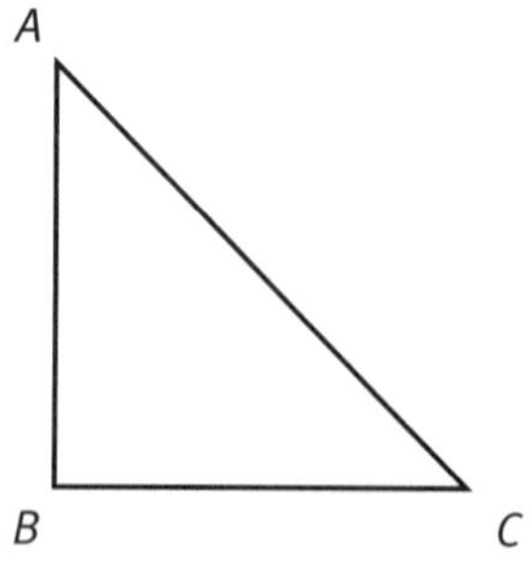

6. 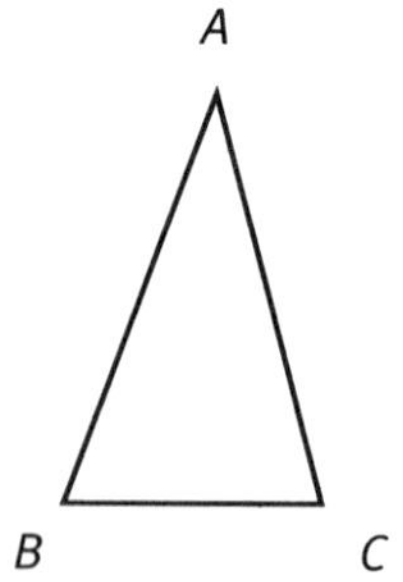

 Name ______________________ Date ____________

Student Edition • page 412

7. State which of the following triples of side lengths can be used to form a triangle:

   a. 2, 6, 5 ____________

   b. 10, 2, 3 ____________

   c. 13, 24, 11 ____________

8. **Extended Response** Is the sum of the angle measures of each triangle about the same? If not, why might they be different?

9. **Extended Response** Do you think it is possible to have an equilateral triangle that is not an isosceles triangle? Explain.

10. **Extended Response** Is it possible to have a triangle with more than one obtuse angle? Why or why not?

LESSON 9.4

Drawing Triangles

Student Edition • page 414

Solve.

1. Draw triangle *ABC* with your ruler and protractor so that

   a. angle *C* measures 90°.

   b. side *AC* is 8 centimeters long.

   c. side *BC* is 6 centimeters long.

Compare your triangle with a triangle that somebody else has drawn. Do they look the same? Cut out the two triangles to see if they fit on top of each other.

Measure side *AB* on your triangle. Compare the length of your side *AB* with the lengths of sides *AB* that other students have drawn.

Measure angles *A* and *C*. Compare the measures of your angles *A* and *C* with the measures of angles *A* and *C* that others have drawn.

2. Are all the triangles the same?

   ____

3. Draw triangle *DEF* with your ruler and protractor so that

   a. angle *D* measures 60°.

   b. side *DE* is 10 centimeters long.

   c. side *DF* is 10 centimeters long.

4. Measure angles *E* and *F*. Measure side *EF*. How did your measures compare to the measures of others in the class? What type of triangle is this?

   ____

   ____

Name ____________________ Date ____________

Student Edition • pages 414–415

5 Draw triangle *GHI* with your ruler and protractor so that

a. angle *H* measures 45°.

b. side *GH* is 14 centimeters long.

c. side *HI* is 10 centimeters long.

Solve.

6 What is the measure of angle *I*? Angle *G*? What is the length of side *GI*? Did everyone get the same answers?

____

7 Draw triangle *JKL* with your ruler and protractor so that

a. angle *J* measures 30°.

b. side *JK* is 7 centimeters long.

c. side *KL* is 8 centimeters long.

One way to do this is to first draw side *JK* and angle *J*, and then extend the other side of angle *J*. Place the 0 centimeter mark of your ruler at point *K* and swing the ruler until the 8 centimeter mark hits the other side of angle *J*. The point where they meet is point *L*.

8 Measure angles *K* and *L* and side *JL*. Compare your answers with the answers of others in the class. Does everyone have the same answers?

____

Student Edition • **page 415**

9 Draw triangle *MNP* with your ruler and protractor so that

a. angle *M* measures 30°.

b. side *MN* is 7 centimeters long.

c. side *NP* is 3 centimeters long.

10 Measure angles *N* and *P* and side *MP*. Compare your measurements with the answers of others in the class. Does everyone have the same measurements?

____

11 Draw triangle *QRS* with your ruler and protractor so that

a. angle *Q* measures 30°.

b. side *QR* is 7 centimeters long.

c. side *RS* is 5 centimeters long.

12 **Extended Response** Measure angles *R* and *S* and side *QS*. Compare your answers with classmates' answers. Does everyone have the same answers? If so, try to follow these steps to draw a triangle that would give different answers.

____

LESSON 9.5

Name ______________________ Date ____________

Congruence and Similarity

Student Edition • pages 416–417

Draw **the triangle as described below, and then answer the questions.**

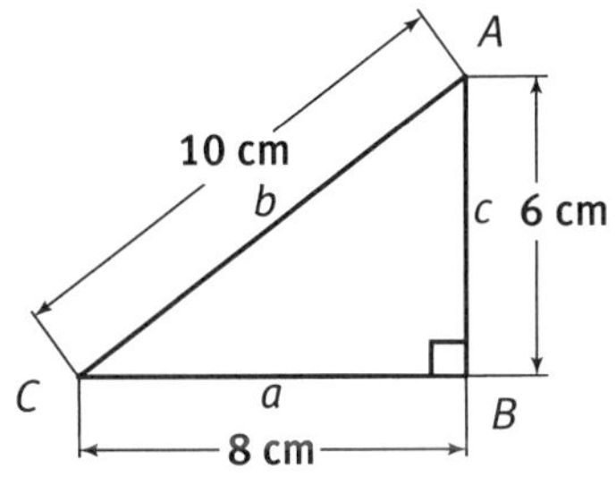

1 Draw a triangle and label it $A'B'C'$ so that

- angle A' has the same measure as angle A.
- angle B' has the same measure as angle B.
- angle C' has the same measure as angle C.

Make side a' ($B'C'$) twice as long as side a (BC). (Make a' 16 centimeters long.)

a. How long is side c' ($A'B'$)? ____________

b. Is that twice as long as side c (AB)? ____________

c. How long is side b' ($C'A'$)? ____________

d. Is triangle $A'B'C'$ the same size as triangle ABC? Is it the same shape?

____

2 Suppose you drew triangle $A''B''C''$ to be the same shape, but this time you made side c'' half as long as side c.

a. How long would side a'' be? ____________

b. How long would side b'' be? ____________

c. Now draw triangle $A''B''C''$. Measure sides a'' and b'' to check your answers to parts **a** and **b.**

d. Is triangle $A''B''C''$ the same size as triangle ABC? Is it the same shape?

____

LESSON 9.5

Student Edition • pages 417–418

Select the figure that is congruent to the first figure.

3 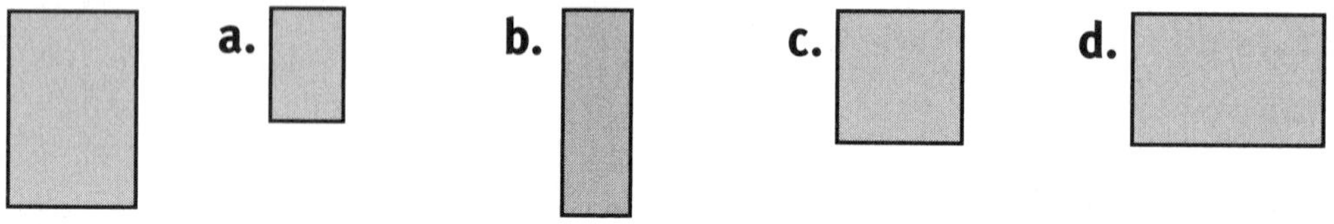

____

4 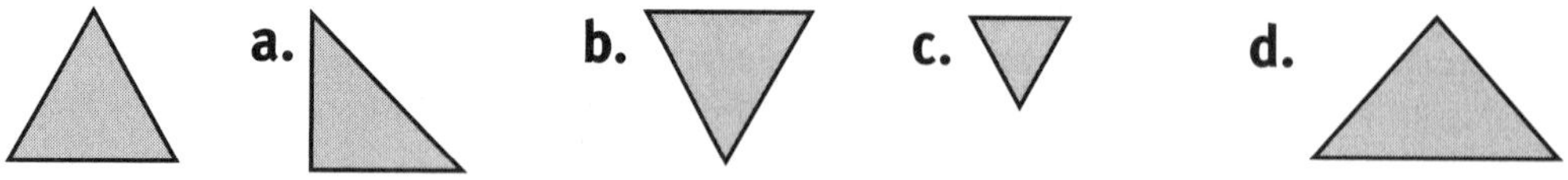

____

5 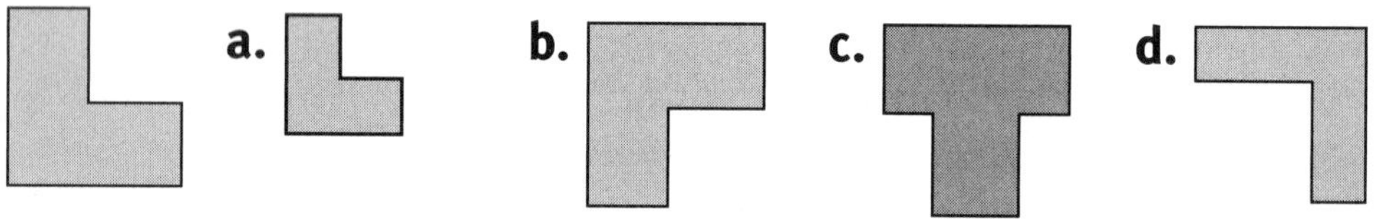

____

Answer the following questions.

6 What are some examples of congruent figures or objects?

____

____

7 What are some examples of similar figures or objects?

____

____

8 If two figures are congruent, are they also similar? (Do they have the same shape?)

____

____

LESSON 9.5

Name ______________________ Date ______________

Student Edition • page 419

Complete the following items.

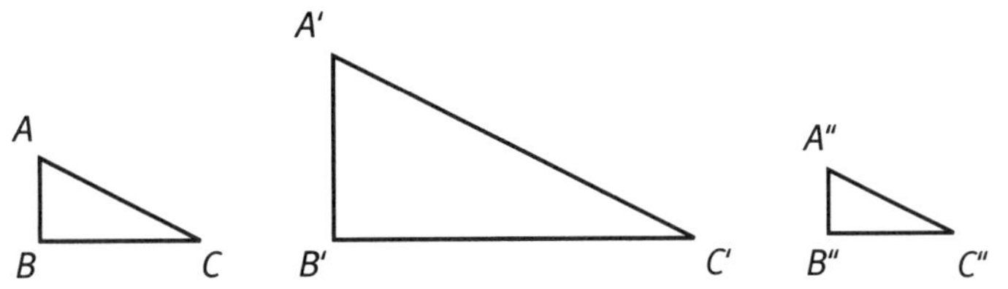

9 All the triangles above are the same shape. They are similar. Record each of the following measurements to the nearest millimeter.

$C =$ ______________ mm

$C' =$ ______________ mm

$A =$ ______________ mm

$A' =$ ______________ mm

$B =$ ______________ mm

$B' =$ ______________ mm

Find the following ratios. Use a calculator if necessary. Round to the nearest hundredth.

10 $\frac{c}{a} =$ ______________

$\frac{c}{b} =$ ______________

$\frac{b}{a} =$ ______________

11 $\frac{c'}{a'} =$ ______________

$\frac{c'}{b'} =$ ______________

$\frac{b'}{a'} =$ ______________

12 Estimate the following ratios. Then compute each one after making the appropriate measurements.

$\frac{c''}{a''} =$ ______________

$\frac{c''}{b''} =$ ______________

$\frac{b''}{a''} =$ ______________

LESSON 9.5

Student Edition • page 419

13 Suppose triangle *QRS* is similar to triangle *Q'R'S'*.

a. If angle *Q* is 55°, what is the measure of angle *Q'*? ____________

b. If angle *R* is 35°, what is the measure of angle *S'*? (Hint: First find the measure of angle *S*.) ____________

c. Extended Response If *q* (side *RS*) is 50 millimeters, can you find the length of *q'*? If so, what is it? If not, why not?

____

____

LESSON 9.6

Name ______________________ Date ____________

Corresponding Parts of a Triangle

Student Edition • page 421

For each pair of triangles, write whether the triangles are similar or congruent. Also write which corresponding parts are equal. Use symbols and make sure the letters of each triangle are in the proper order. The first one is done for you.

1 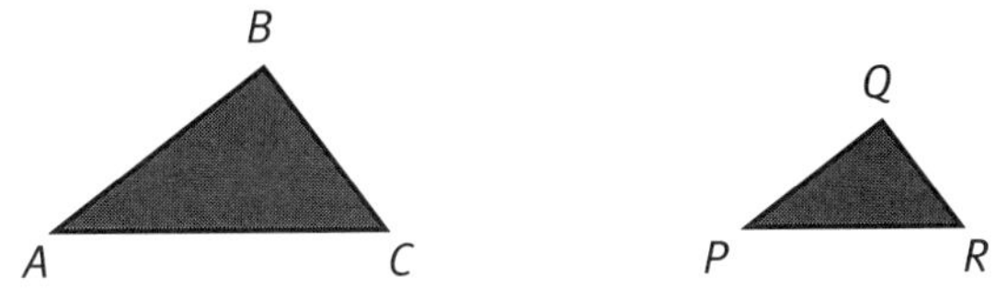

2 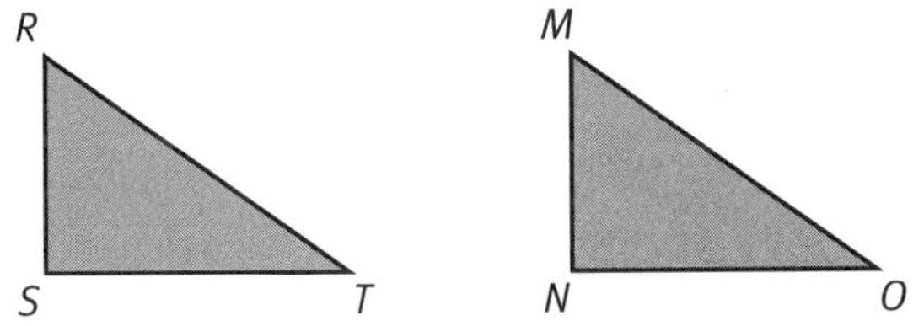

3 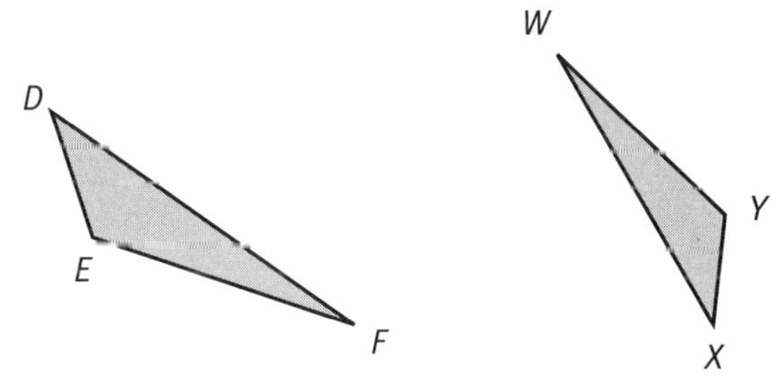

4 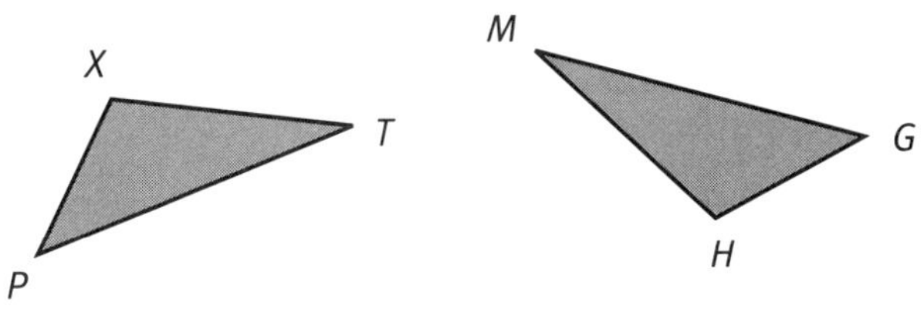

LESSON 9.6

Student Edition • page 422

Answer the following questions.

5 In $\triangle ABC$, $\angle A = 35°$ and $\angle B = 100°$. Without measuring, find the measure of $\angle C$.

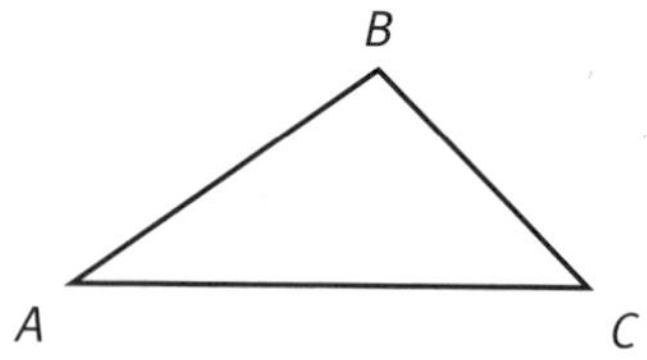

6 Extended Response In $\triangle DEF \sim \triangle GHI$, $f = 8$ cm, $d = 6$ cm, $e = 12$ cm, $g = 3$ cm, and $\angle D = 27°$. Without measuring, find the length of i, the length of h, and the measure of $\angle G$. Explain how you found your answer.

____

____

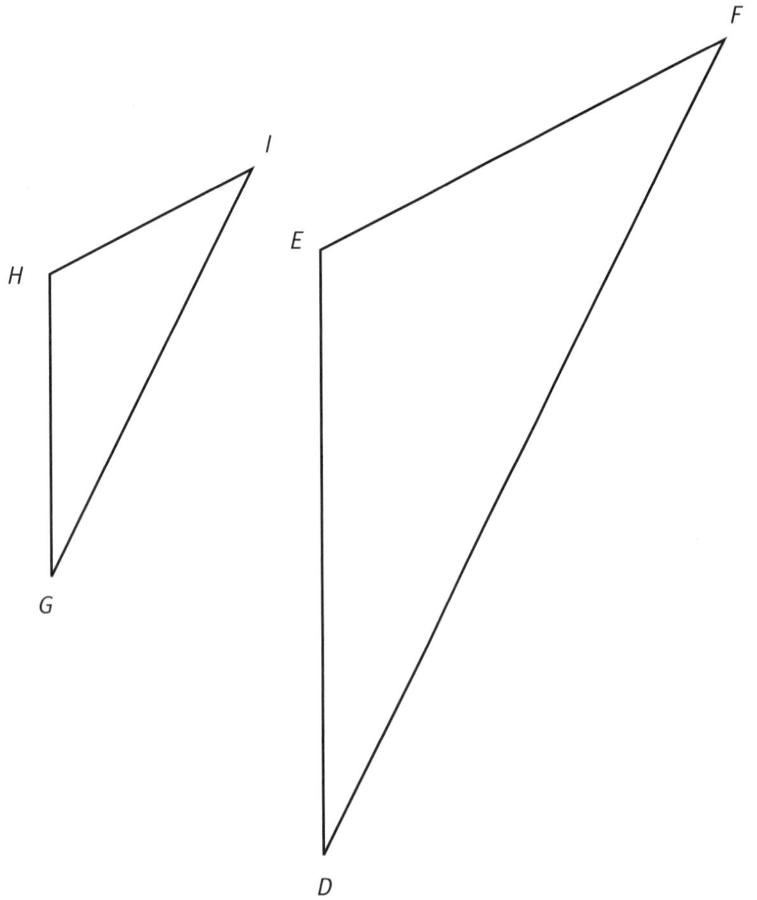

Name ______________________ Date ____________

Student Edition • page 423

7. Consider figures *A, B, C, D, E, F,* and *G* below. Which appear to be congruent to each other? Which appear to be similar but not congruent?

____

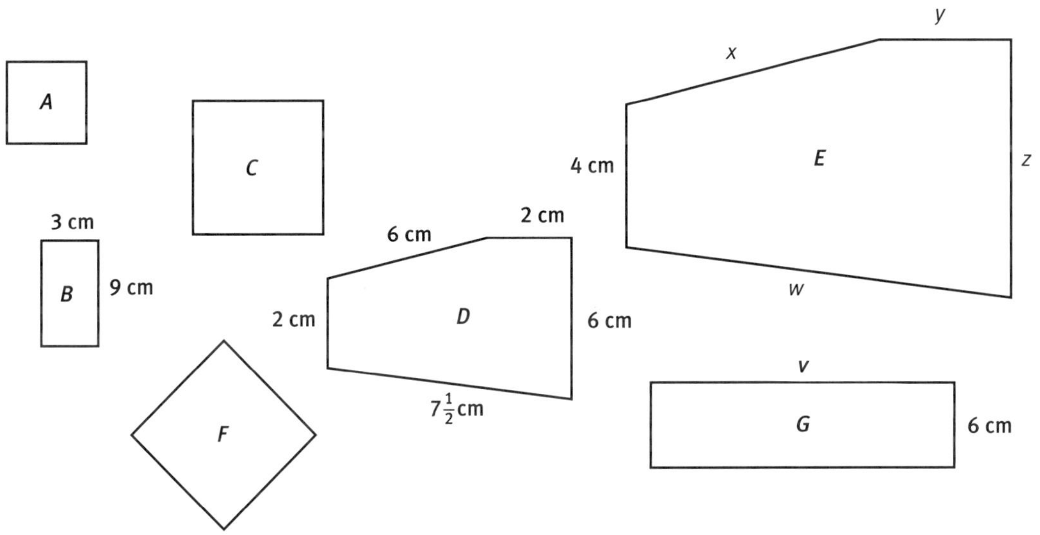

8. Assuming figures *D* and *E* are similar to each other and the measurements given for their sides are correct, what is the value of *x*? Of *y*? Of *z*? Of *w*?

____

9. Suppose the length of one side of square *A* is 1 centimeter. What is the area of square *A*? What is the perimeter of square *A*?

____

10. If the side of square *C* is 2 centimeters long, what is the area of square *C*? What is the perimeter of square *C*?

____

11. If the side of a square is 3 centimeters long, what is the area of the square? What is the perimeter of the square?

____

12. **Extended Response** Assume that figure *B* is similar to figure *G*. Find the length of *v*. Find the perimeter of *G*. If the side labeled 6 centimeters in figure *G* was really supposed to be 18 centimeters, how would the perimeter change? Why?

____

____

LESSON 9.7

Using Corresponding Parts of Triangles

Student Edition • page 424

You may want to draw pictures to help you solve the problems on this page.

1. $\triangle ABC \cong \triangle DEF$. $c = 9$ cm, $a = 10$ cm, $b = 15$ cm. $\angle A = 39°$, $\angle B = 104°$.
   - **a.** What is the measure of $\angle C$? ______
   - **b.** What is the measure of $\angle D$? ______
   - **c.** What is the measure of $\angle E$? ______
   - **d.** What is the measure of $\angle F$? ______
   - **e.** What is the length of f? ______
   - **f.** What is the length of d? ______
   - **g.** What is the length of e? ______
   - **h.** What is the length of FD? ______

2. $\triangle ABC \sim \triangle GHI$. $\triangle ABC$ is the same triangle as in Problem 1. The length of side $i = 27$ cm. Find the measures of each of the angles and the length of each of the sides.
   - **a.** $\angle G$ ______
   - **b.** $\angle I$ ______
   - **c.** g ______
   - **d.** $\angle H$ ______
   - **e.** GH ______
   - **f.** h ______

3. $\triangle GHI \sim \triangle JKL$. $\triangle GHI$ is the same triangle as in Problem 2. The length of side $k = 5$ cm. Find the measure of each of the angles and the lengths of each of the sides.
   - **a.** $\angle J$ ______
   - **b.** $\angle L$ ______
   - **c.** j ______
   - **d.** $\angle K$ ______
   - **e.** l ______
   - **f.** JL ______

LESSON 9.7 **Name** ______________________ **Date** ____________

Student Edition • **page 425**

Solve the following.

4. In $\triangle MNP$, $\angle M = 47°$ and $\angle N = 83°$. $\angle P =$ ____________

5. In $\triangle QRS$, $\angle Q = 60°$ and $\angle R = \angle Q$. $\angle S =$ ____________

6. In $\triangle TUV$, $\angle T = 40°$ and $\angle U = \angle V$. $\angle V =$ ____________

Ms. Walker is using an overhead projector to project a triangle on the wall. The triangle on the wall is similar to the triangle she has drawn.

Eleanor and Pablo are measuring the sides of the triangle on the wall. They find that $AC = 260$ centimeters, $BC = 208$ centimeters, and $AB = 156$ centimeters.

7. Which side of the small triangle is the longest? ____________

8. Which side of the small triangle is the shortest? ____________

9. Eleanor measures side AC of the small triangle. It is about 5 centimeters long. About how many times longer is side AC of the big triangle? ____________

10. Find the length of sides AB and BC in the small triangle. ____________

11. How many times longer than the sides of the small triangle are the corresponding sides of the big triangle? ____________

12. **Extended Response** Which is greater, the measure of angle A on the wall or in the drawing? How do you know?

____

____

Exploring Problem Solving

Student Edition • pages 426—427

Imagine you and your friends are designing and building a playhouse. You have just learned about a Native American tribe called the Hidatsa and decide to make your playhouse like a Hidatsa earth lodge. You will use 12 logs of the same length to form the outer support of the roof. What will be the measure of the angle formed by a pair of adjoining logs?

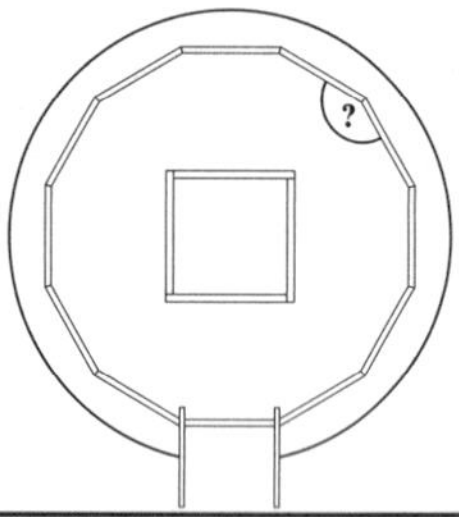

Samira solved the problem this way:

I decided to Use a Model.

I looked at the wall clock in the classroom and imagined the clockface with a twelve-sided polygon on top of it.

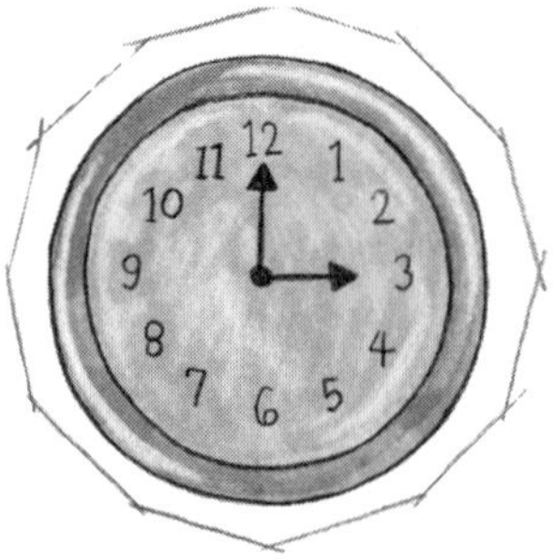

Think about Samira's strategy. Answer the following questions.

1. How is the face of a clock like the layout of the earth lodge? How is it different?

____

____

2. Samira borrowed a toy clock that first graders use to learn to tell time. How can she use the clock to solve the problem?

____

____

3. Suppose Samira did not use a clock. How could she still use her strategy to solve the problem?

____

____

Name ______________________________ Date ______________

Student Edition • page 427

Ananda solved the problem another way.

I decided to Make a Diagram and Use Geometric Reasoning.

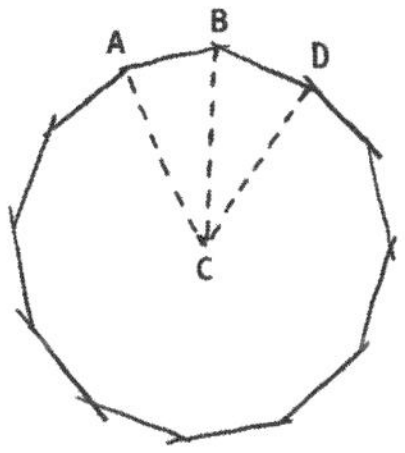

Think about Ananda's strategy. Answer the following questions.

4. Which angle's measure is the problem asking for? ______________

5. If Ananda divided the whole figure into triangles the same size as $\triangle ABC$ and $\triangle BCD$, how many triangles would there be altogether?

____

6. Would all those triangles be congruent? How do you know?

____

____

7. If Ananda knew the measure of $\angle ACB$, what would that tell him about other angles in the diagram? ______________

8. How could Ananda use that information about other angles to solve the problem?

____

____

9. Solve the problem. Use any strategy you think will work. What strategy did you use? Why?

____

____

10. What would the answer be if you used only 8 logs instead of 12 for the roof support?

____

Cumulative Review

Student Edition • page 428

Probability and Fractions **Lesson 6.9**

Solve.

Two standard dice, numbered 1–6, are rolled. What is the probability that

1. the roll is a double? ______________
2. the sum of the rolls is less than 4? ______________
3. the sum of the rolls is greater than 9? ______________

Adding Mixed Numbers **Lesson 7.3**

Add.

4. $3\frac{5}{8} + 1\frac{1}{4} =$ ______________
5. $5\frac{1}{2} + 2\frac{2}{3} =$ ______________
6. $4\frac{3}{4} + 1\frac{5}{6} =$ ______________
7. $1\frac{1}{3} + 3\frac{2}{3} =$ ______________

Solve.

8. Renee left school, walked $\frac{3}{4}$ mile to her friend's house, and then walked $1\frac{1}{5}$ miles home. How far did she walk altogether? ______________

Cumulative Review

Name ______________________ Date ______________

Student Edition • pages 428–429

Finding Mean, Median, Mode, and Range Lesson 8.2

Answer.

Chico's scores on his last 5 spelling tests were 75, 90, 84, 82, and 89.

9. What was the mean of his scores? ______________

10. What was the median of his scores? ______________

11. What was the range of his scores? ______________

12. Was there a mode? If so, what was it? ______________

Approximating Quotients Lesson 8.7

Solve.

A half-gallon jug (64 ounces) of lemonade is used to fill glasses.

13. About how many 10-ounce glasses can be filled? ______________

14. If 7-ounce glasses are used instead, how many can be filled? ______________

15. Lloyd is saving $22 per week until he has $321 to buy a bicycle. About how many weeks will it take him to save enough money to buy the bicycle? ______________

Chapter 9 Cumulative Review

Student Edition • page 429

Dividing by a Two-Digit Number **Lesson 8.8**

Solve.

16. Jen drove her car 330 miles and used 18 gallons of gas.
Pablo's car went 360 miles and used 17 gallons.
Whose car got better gas mileage? By about how much? ______

Divide.

17. 45)14049

18. 25)6465

19. 46)1932

Angles **Lesson 9.1**

Find the measurements of the following angles. Use a protractor if necessary.

20. 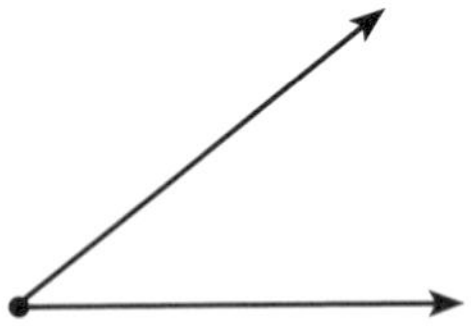 = ______ degrees

22. 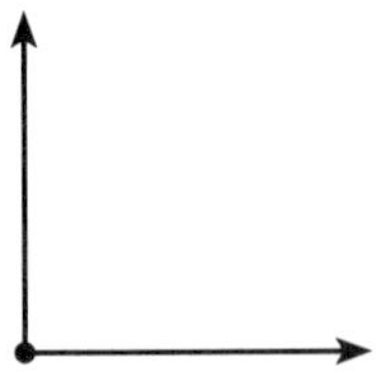 = ______ degrees

21.  = ______ degrees

23.  = ______ degrees

LESSON 9.8

Name ______________________ Date ____________

Scale Drawings

Student Edition • page 430

The next page shows part of a scale drawing of a classroom. The scale is 1 cm = 50 cm.

Answer the following questions as accurately as you can.

1. How long is the actual chalkboard? ____________
2. How long and how wide are the actual student desks? ____________
3. What is the diameter of the actual wastebasket? ____________
4. How high is the actual ceiling? ____________
5. How long and how wide is the top of the actual teacher's desk? ____________
6. What is the area of the top of the actual teacher's desk? ____________
7. What is the area of the actual art table? ____________
8. What is the area of the actual chalkboard? ____________
9. Suppose a rectangular reading table is moved into the room. The tabletop is 1.5 meters long and 0.5 meter wide. How long and how wide would the reading table be in the drawing? ____________
10. How long and how wide is the actual classroom? ____________

LESSON 9.8

Student Edition • page 431

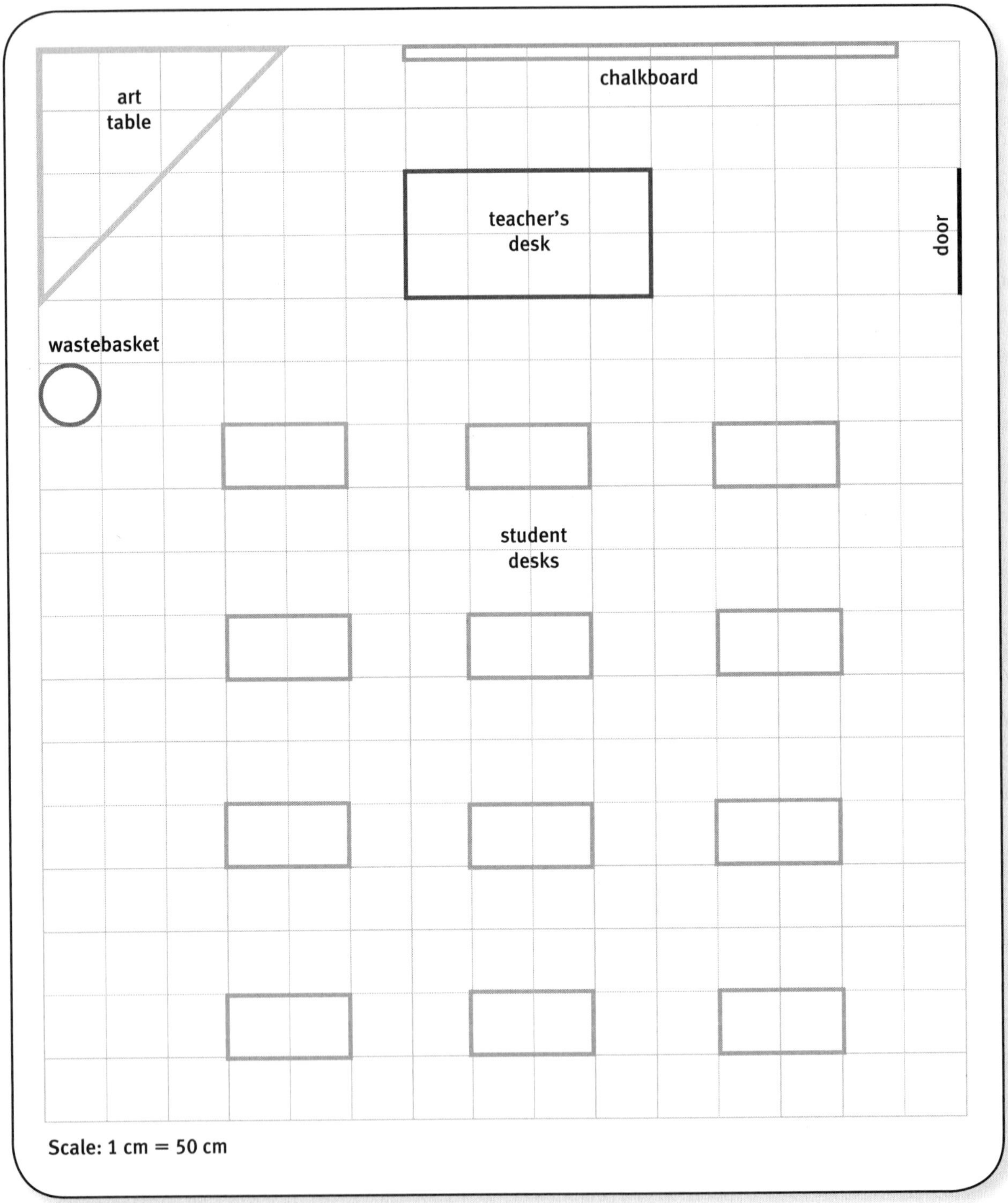

Name ______________________ Date ____________

Student Edition • page 432

The Denizens made a scale drawing of their living room. They decided to use a scale in which 1 unit on the drawing stood for 1 foot in the actual room.

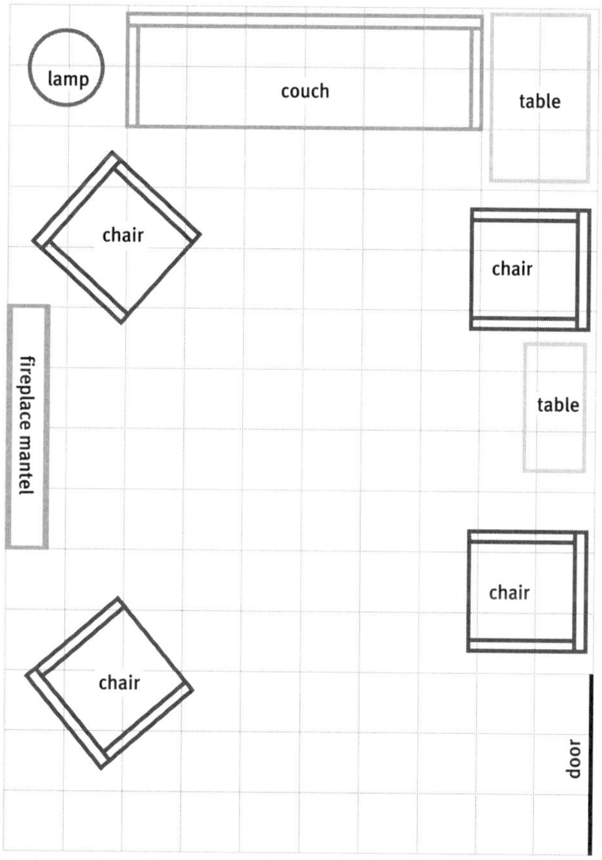

Scale: 1 unit = 1 ft

Answer the following questions as accurately as you can, based on the scale drawing.

11. What are the dimensions of the living room? ____________

12. How long is the fireplace mantel? ____________

13. How long is the couch? ____________

14. What are the dimensions of the larger table? What are the dimensions of the smaller table?

____

____

Student Edition • page 433

The Denizens made a scale drawing of their bedroom. They decided to use the same scale, where 1 unit on the drawing stood for 1 foot in the actual room.

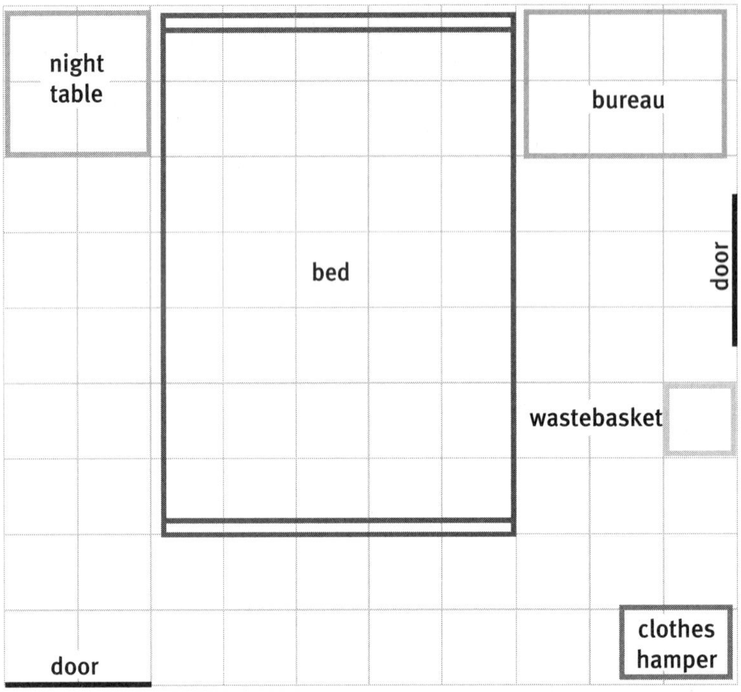

Scale: 1 unit = 1 ft

Answer the following questions as accurately as you can, based on the scale drawing.

15. What are the dimensions of the bedroom? ______________

16. What are the dimensions of the bed? ______________

17. What are the dimensions of the bureau? ______________

18. What are the dimensions of the clothes hamper? ______________

19. What are the dimensions of the wastebasket? ______________

20. **Extended Response** Could the bureau be moved to the wall by the foot of the bed? Explain your answer.

____

____

LESSON 9.9

Name ______________________ Date __________

Using a Map Scale

Student Edition • pages 434–435

Solve.

1. Suppose the scale of a map is 1 cm = 20 km, and the distance between Summerville and Winter City is about 7 centimeters on the map. About how far apart are the towns in real life? __________

Use the map below to approximate the number of kilometers between the following cities.

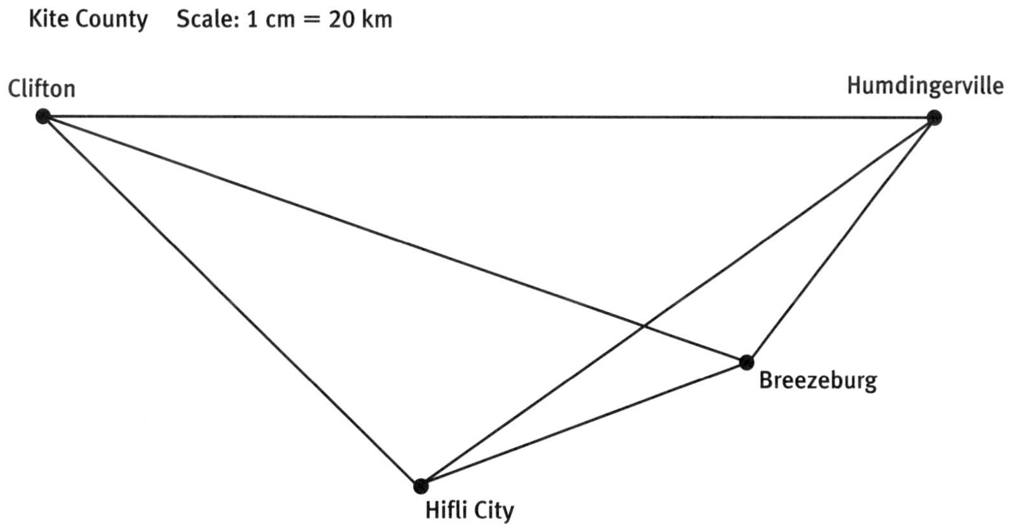

2. Clifton to Humdingerville __________
3. Clifton to Breezeburg __________
4. Clifton to Hifli City __________
5. Hifli City to Clifton __________
6. Hifli City to Humdingerville __________
7. Hifli City to Breezeburg __________
8. Humdingerville to Breezeburg __________
9. Breezeburg to Humdingerville __________

LESSON 9.9

Student Edition • pages 435–436

On the map from page 407, how long a line segment would you need to draw to represent each of the following distances?

10 20 km ______________

11 80 km ______________

12 30 km ______________

13 5 km ______________

14 40 km ______________

15 10 km ______________

16 50 km ______________

17 60 km ______________

18 What fraction of a real distance is the corresponding distance on the map? ______________

Using the scale and map below, estimate the number of air miles between the cities on page 409.

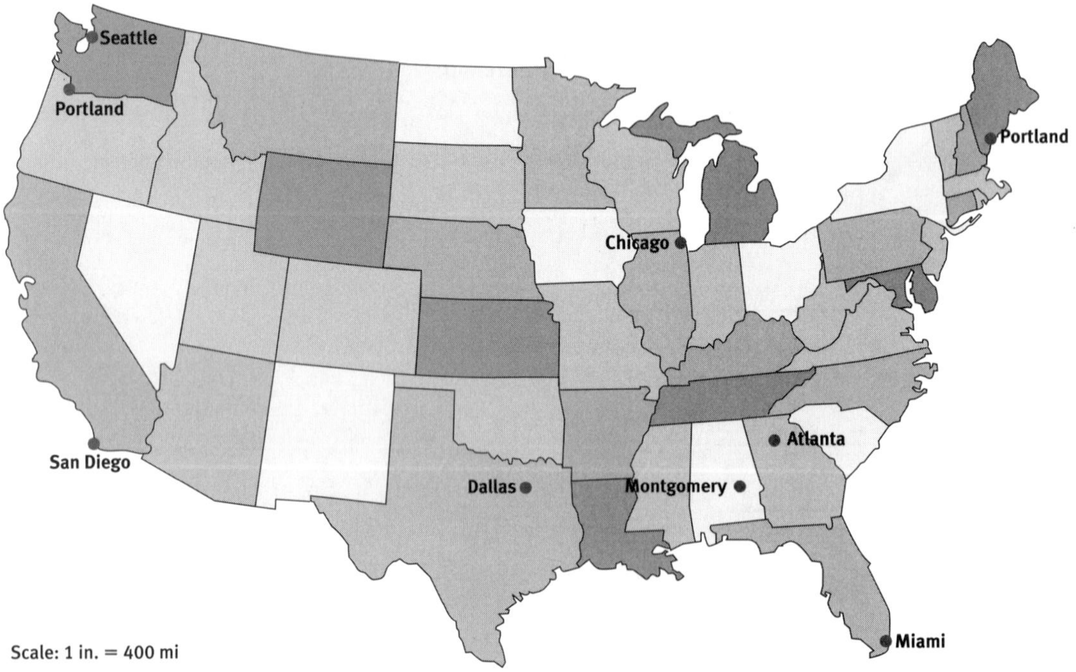

Name ______________________ Date ____________

Student Edition • pages 436–437

19 Seattle, Washington, and Chicago, Illinois ____________

20 Seattle, Washington, and Dallas, Texas ____________

21 Portland, Oregon, and Portland, Maine ____________

22 Seattle, Washington, and Miami, Florida ____________

23 Montgomery, Alabama, and Atlanta, Georgia ____________

24 Dallas, Texas, and Miami, Florida ____________

25 Montgomery, Alabama, and Chicago, Illinois ____________

26 Portland, Maine, and San Diego, California ____________

27 Montgomery, Alabama, and Miami, Florida ____________

28 San Diego, California, and Portland, Maine ____________

Solve.

29 Marcus draws $\triangle PQR$ so that $PQ = 7$ inches, $QR = 11$ inches, and $RP = 8$ inches. Then he projects the drawing on a wall so that PQ on the wall is about 84 inches long. What are the lengths of the other sides of the triangle on the wall?

____

LESSON 9.9

Student Edition • page 437

30 On a map of the United States, the scale is 1 cm = 90 km. The distances on the map between pairs of cities are given below. What is the distance, in kilometers, between each pair of cities?

a. Duluth to New Orleans: 21 cm ____________

b. Chicago to Omaha: 8 cm ____________

c. Salt Lake City to Los Angeles: 10.5 cm ____________

d. Little Rock to Atlanta: 8 cm ____________

e. Baton Rouge to Portland, Maine: 26 cm ____________

f. Seattle to San Antonio: 32 cm ____________

g. Omaha to Salt Lake City: 12.5 cm ____________

h. Chicago to New York City: 13 cm ____________

i. Portland, Maine, to Portland, Oregon: 46 cm ____________

LESSON 9.10

Name ______________________ Date ____________

Perpendicular and Parallel Lines and Quadrilaterals

Student Edition • pages 438–439

For each pair of lines, write whether the lines are *perpendicular, parallel,* or *neither.*

1. 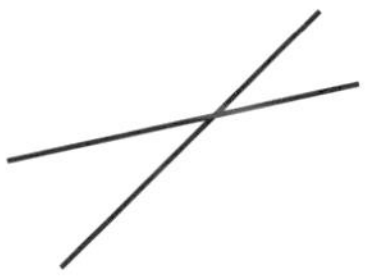
____

2. 
____

3. 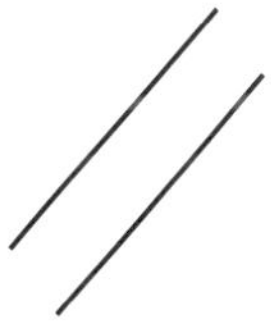
____

4. 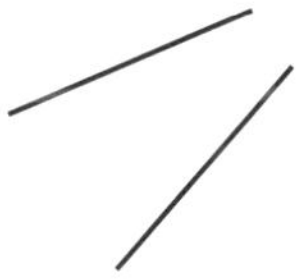
____

5. 
____

6. 
____

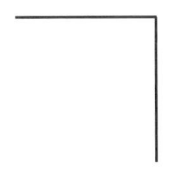

7. 
____

8. 
____

Solve the following problems.

9. List at least two pairs of perpendicular lines in your classroom.

____

____

10. List at least two pairs of parallel lines in your classroom.

____

____

LESSON
9.10

Student Edition • **page 439**

Sometimes, in pictures, lines that look parallel are drawn as though they would actually meet at some point. This is because when we see parallel lines going off into the distance, they appear to get closer together, even though we know they really do not.

11 In the pictures shown below, find at least two pairs of lines that look as though they are parallel.

____

____

12 In the pictures shown below, find at least two pairs of lines that look as though they are perpendicular.

____

____

Name ______________________ **Date** ____________

Student Edition • page 440

Solve by using the quadrilateral.

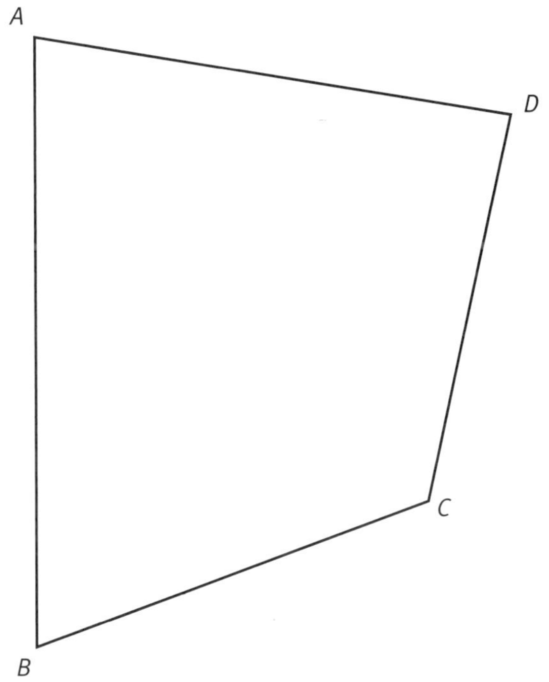

13. Measure each of the four angles of quadrilateral *ABCD*. Add the measures together. What is the sum of the angle measures of this quadrilateral? ____________

14. Draw a quadrilateral below. Measure its four angles. What is the sum of the four measures? ____________

15. Can you draw a quadrilateral that has four acute angles? ____________

16. Can you draw a quadrilateral that has four obtuse angles? ____________

LESSON 9.10

Student Edition • page 441

Solve the following.

17 **Extended Response** Copy and cut out the quadrilateral you drew in Problem 14. Tear off the four angles. Put the vertices of the four angles together so that the sides touch without overlapping. What do you notice? What does that tell you about the sum of the angles in your quadrilateral?

____

____

18 Draw a quadrilateral *EFGH*. Then draw a diagonal line segment *EG* through the quadrilateral. Look at $\triangle EFG$ in your figure.

a. List the three angles in $\triangle EFG$. ____________

b. What is the sum of their measures? ____________

c. Look at $\triangle EGH$. List the three angles in $\triangle EGH$. ____________

d. What is the sum of their measures? ____________

e. Look at the six angles you listed. Which two add up to $\angle FEH$? ____________

f. Which two add up to $\angle FGH$? ____________

LESSON 9.11

Name ______________________ Date __________

Parallelograms

Student Edition • page 442

Make sketches, if you wish, to help you supply the missing information.

1. In quadrilateral *ABCD*,
$\angle A = 70°$, $\angle B = 90°$, and $\angle D = 120°$. $\angle C =$ __________

2. In quadrilateral *ABCD*,
$\angle A = 90°$, $\angle B = \angle A$, and $\angle C = \angle B$. $\angle D =$ __________

3. In quadrilateral *ABCD*,
$\angle A = \angle B = \angle C = \angle D$. $\angle A =$ __________

4. In quadrilateral *ABCD*,
$\angle A = 40°$, $\angle B = 140°$, and $\angle B = \angle D$. $\angle C =$ __________

5. In quadrilateral *ABCD*,
$\angle A = \angle C$, $\angle B = \angle D$, and $\angle A = 120°$. $\angle B =$ __________

6. Use a protractor to draw each of the figures described in Problems 1–5.

LESSON 9.11

Student Edition • pages 443–444

Solve the following.

7. Look at your figures for Problems 4 and 5 on page 415. What do you notice about the opposite sides of each of those figures? ______

8. Look at your figures for Problems 2 and 3 on page 415. Are the opposite sides in each figure parallel? Are the figures parallelograms? What is special about the angles of each of those two figures?

______

______

9. What do we call a rectangle with four equal angles whose sides all have the same length? ______

Give the standard name for each of the following figures.

10. 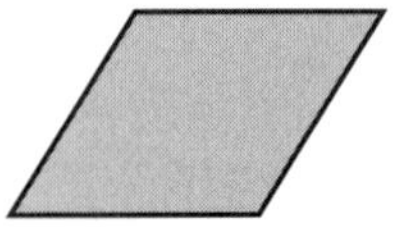

______

11. 

______

12. 

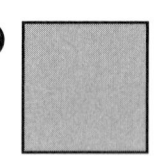

______

13. 

______

14. 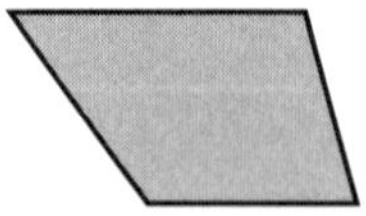

______

15. 

______

Name ______________________ **Date** ______________

Student Edition • pages 444–445

16 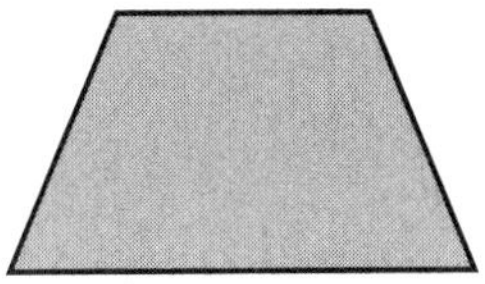

____

17 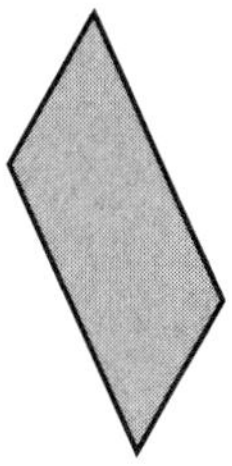

____

18 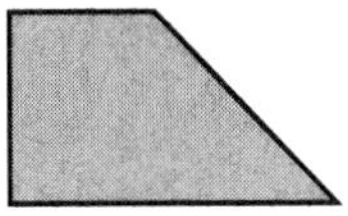

____

19 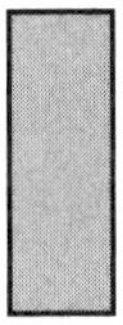

____

20 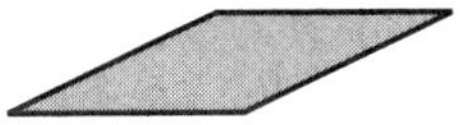

____

21 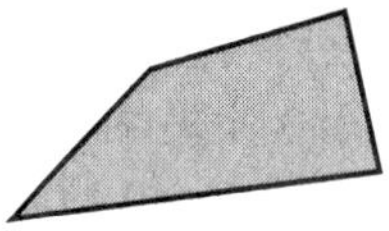

____

Answer the following questions.

22 Draw a parallelogram with a right angle.
What is the name for the figure you drew? ______________

23 Can you draw a parallelogram with
a right angle that is not a rectangle? ______________

24 Draw a trapezoid with one right angle.

25 How many right angles can a trapezoid have and still be a trapezoid?

____

Student Edition • page 445

26 Draw a parallelogram in which a pair of adjacent (touching) sides are of equal length. What is this figure called? ____________

27 **Extended Response** Give a description of a square by using the name of one other figure, such as *quadrilateral, parallelogram,* and so on. Make your description as concise as possible. Do this again by using the name of a different quadrilateral.

____

____

____

Name each of the following quadrilaterals. Write *trapezoid, parallelogram, rectangle, rhombus,* or *square.*

28 

____

29 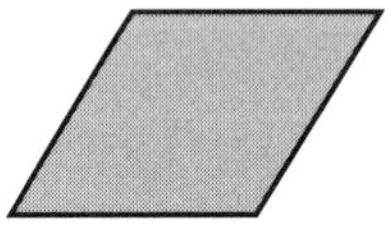

____

30 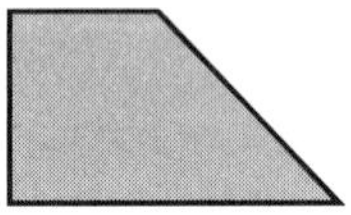

____

31 

____

32 

____

LESSON 9.12

Name ______________________ Date ____________

Exploring Some Properties of Polygons I

Student Edition • pages 446—447

Write whether each of these closed figures has a *concave* or a *convex* shape. If you know the names for any of the figures, include them in your answer.

1. 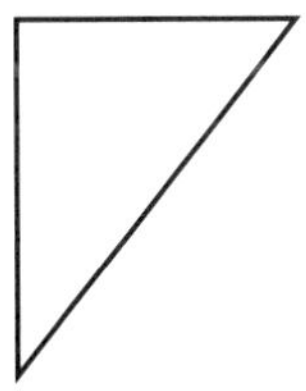
____

2. 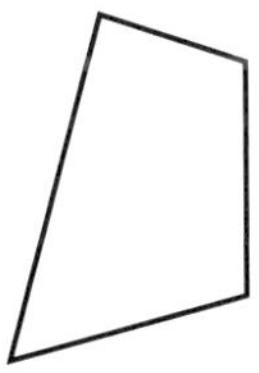
____

3. 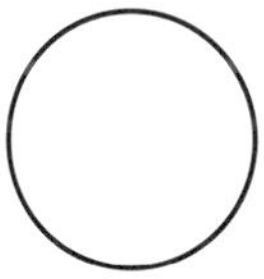
____

4. 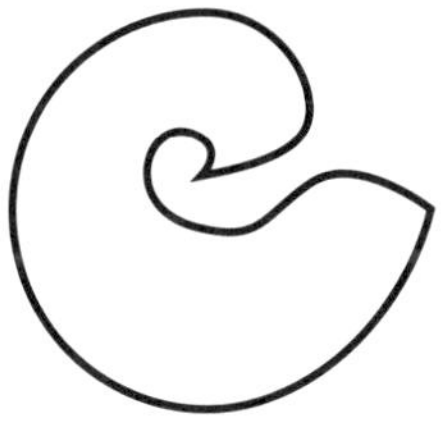
____

5. 
____

6. 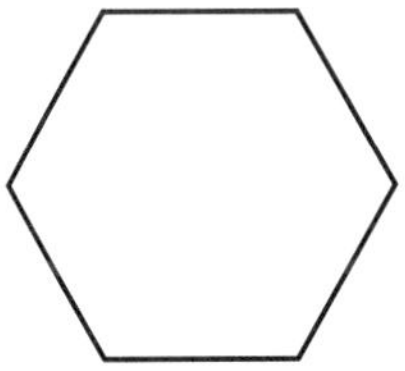
____

7. 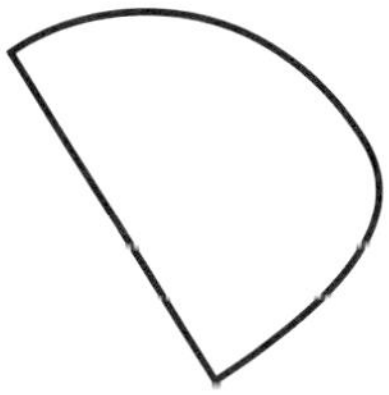
____

8. 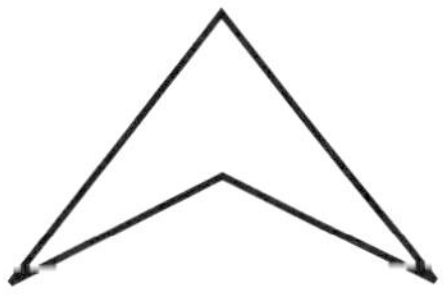
____

9. 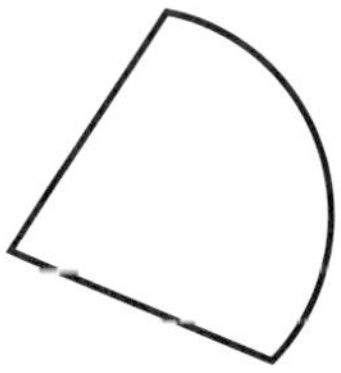
____

10. 
____

11. 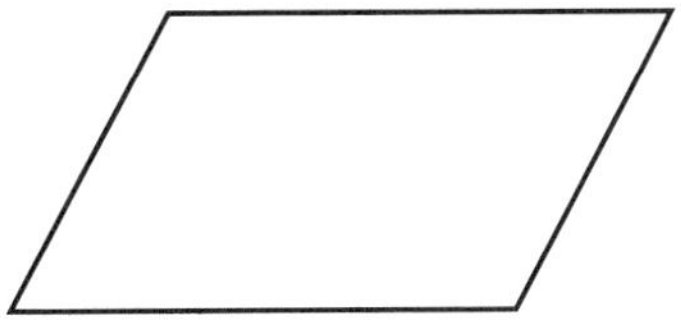
____

12. 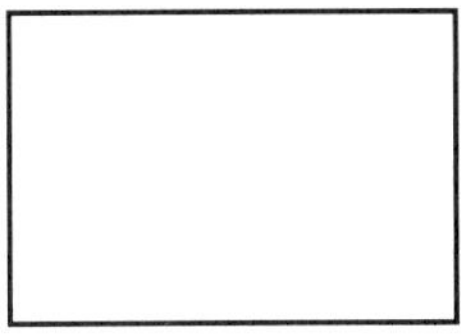
____

LESSON 9.12

Student Edition • page 448

Answer the following questions.

Suki and Elise told Ana to describe a figure for them and they would each draw it. They wanted to see whether they would make the same figure for each description.

Ana said, "Draw a triangle with angles that measure 30°, 60°, and 90°."

Suki drew a triangle like this:

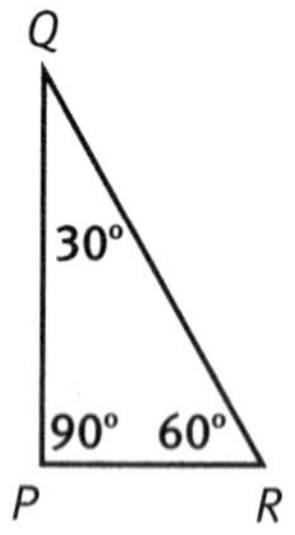

This is what Elise's triangle looked like:

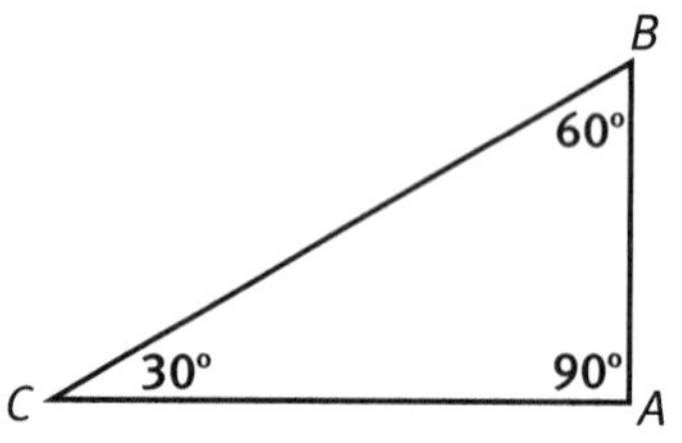

Suki said, "I drew my triangle correctly, but it's not like yours, Elise."

Elise said, "Both triangles are drawn correctly. They're similar triangles."

13. Is Elise correct? ____________

Ana said, "You both are correct. Here's a harder one. Draw a triangle with angles that measure 50°, 70°, and 80°."

Suki started to work with her straightedge and protractor. Elise looked at Ana and said, "That's not hard; that's impossible."

14. Is Elise correct? Why? ________________________

LESSON 9.12

Name ______________________ Date ____________

Student Edition • page 449

On **a separate sheet of paper, try to draw each of the following figures. If you believe it is impossible to draw the figure described, try to explain why.**

15. a triangle with angles that measure 50° and 40°; the side between those two angles is 10 centimeters long ____________

16. a quadrilateral with a convex shape ____________

17. a quadrilateral with a concave shape ____________

18. a triangle with a convex shape ____________

19. a triangle with a concave shape ____________

20. a quadrilateral with four angles that each measure 90° and all sides of the same length ____________

21. a quadrilateral with angles that measure 120°, 120°, 60°, and 60°

____

22. a quadrilateral with angles that measure 60°, 60°, 70°, and 80° ____________

23. a triangle with sides that measure 6, 8, and 10 centimeters long ____________

24. a triangle with sides that are each 10 centimeters long ____________

25. a triangle with sides that measure 5, 10, and 16 centimeters long ____________

26. a triangle with sides that measure 5, 10, and 15 centimeters long ____________

27. a triangle with sides that measure 5, 10, and 14 centimeters long ____________

28. a quadrilateral with sides that measure 2, 5, 10, and 16 centimeters long

____

29. Scott lives 1 mile from Chen. Chen lives 2 miles from their school. Could Scott live 4 miles from the school? ____________

30. Could Scott live 0.5 mile from the school? ____________

LESSON 9.13

Exploring Some Properties of Polygons II

Student Edition • pages 450–451

For each of the following figures, determine whether it is a polygon. If not, explain why. If it *is* a polygon, state whether it is concave or convex.

1. 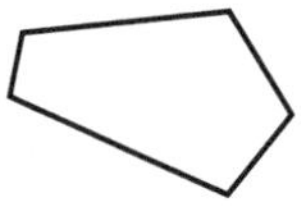

2. 

3. 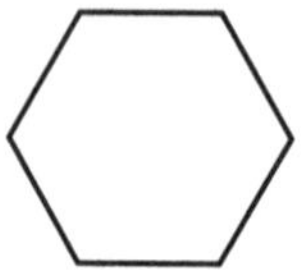

4. 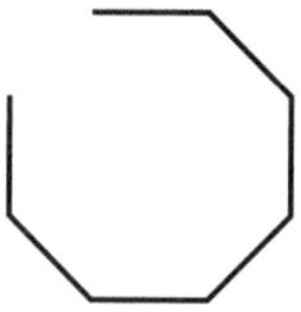

5. 

6. 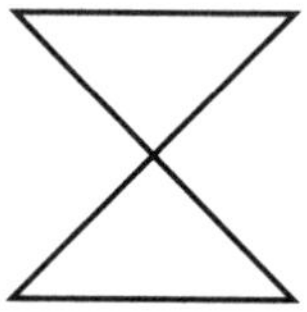

Answer the following questions.

7. What do you call a four-sided regular polygon? What do you call an irregular four-sided polygon?

Name these other regular polygons.

8. 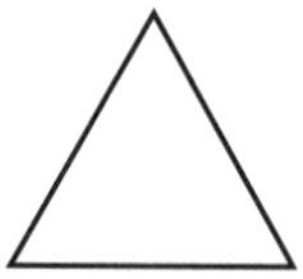

9. 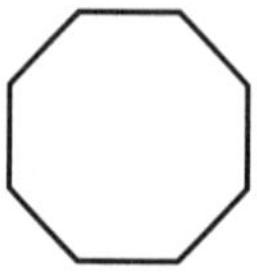

10. 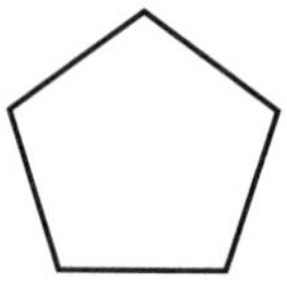

LESSON 9.13

Name ______________________ Date ______________

Student Edition • page 451 *(continued)*

11 **Extended Response** Can you have an irregular octagon with all sides the same length? If so, sketch one and explain why it is not regular.

____

12 **Extended Response** Are all regular hexagons congruent? Are they similar? Explain.

____

____

13 Complete the following table for angle measures in polygons.

Number of Sides	Name	Measure of a Regular Interior Angle	Total Interior Angle Measure
3			
4			
5		108°	
6			
7	heptagon	about 128.57°	
8			1,080°
	nonagon		1,260°
	decagon	144°	

14 **Extended Response** Describe a pattern you found in the sum of the interior angle measures in the polygons listed above.

____

____

____

Student Edition • pages 452–453

Native American Museum Opens on the National Mall

Washington, D.C.

Tens of thousands of Native Americans celebrated the opening of the long-awaited museum they helped design. In keeping with the spirit of Native American architecture, the National Museum of the American Indian (NMAI) stands in harmony with nature. The curving limestone walls appear shaped by the forces of wind and water. Features throughout the building highlight the interplay of Earth, the moon, and the sun.

As one of the builders described the windswept shape of the museum, "There isn't a straight line anywhere—not one square corner."

The NMAI filled the last building spot on the National Mall, a 4.25-acre site visible in this satellite photo taken during the museum's construction. To honor the Native American reverence for Earth, more than 33,000 plants of 150 species surround the museum, modeling the natural environment that existed before the arrival of Europeans.

This image shows the layout for the site of the NMAI.

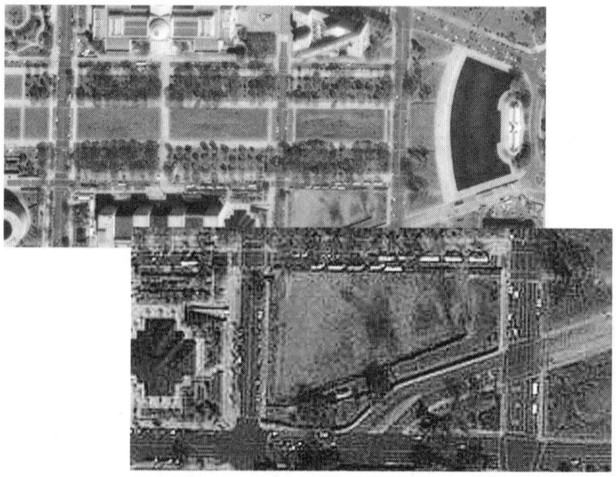

This image shows a close-up of the NMAI construction site.

Name ______________________ Date ____________

Student Edition • page 453

Answer the following questions. Use the information from page 424.

1. How does the appearance of the NMAI remind you of the other Native American dwellings?

____

____

____

2. Based on what you can see in the photos, do you agree with the statement on page 424 about there not being a straight line or corner in the museum? Why or why not?

____

____

____

3. How would you describe the shape of the site on which the museum was built?

____

____

____

Student Edition • page 454

Imagine you are designing a full-sized replica of a Creek town house for the National Museum of the American Indian. These meeting places ranged in size from 30 to 60 feet in diameter and could seat up to 500 people.

Your replica will be 54 feet wide. Each of the eight central posts will

- rise 12 feet above the ground.
- be 36 feet from the opposite central post.

You want the peak of the roof to be 30 feet above the ground.

Work in groups to discuss and solve the following problems.

4. What will be the measure of the angle between two adjacent connecting posts? (Hint: Think of a problem you may have already solved.) ________

5. How high above the ground should each outer post rise? (Hint: You can make a scale drawing.) ________

CHAPTER 9

Cumulative Review

Name ______________________ Date ______________

Student Edition • page 455

Subtracting Mixed Numbers **Lesson 7.4**

Solve the following problems.

1. Randy lives $1\frac{7}{8}$ miles from school. Anthony lives $1\frac{2}{3}$ miles from the same school. How much farther is Randy's round trip than Anthony's round trip? ______________

2. David ran $4\frac{1}{3}$ miles on Saturday and $6\frac{3}{5}$ miles on Sunday. How much farther did David run on Sunday? ______________

3. $7\frac{7}{9} - 4\frac{4}{6} =$ ______________

4. $6\frac{5}{7} - 3\frac{1}{2} =$ ______________

Decimal Equivalents of Rational Numbers **Lesson 7.8**

Solve each problem with fractions and decimals. For each problem, check to see that your two answers are equivalent. Round your answers to three decimal places.

5. $3\frac{4}{8} + 4\frac{1}{4} =$ ______________

6. $3\frac{1}{5} + 1\frac{3}{6} =$ ______________

7. $4\frac{1}{6} - 1\frac{2}{3} =$ ______________

8. $6\frac{3}{8} + 1\frac{3}{4} =$ ______________

Cumulative Review

Student Edition • pages 455—456

Ratios and Rates **Lesson 8.4**

Solve.

Car A and Car B leave to go on a 390-mile trip. Car A drives slightly faster than Car B and averages about 65 miles per hour. Car B averages about 60 miles per hour. Car A makes a 40-minute stop, and Car B drives without stopping.

9. Which car will arrive first? ______________

10. How much later will the other car arrive? ______________

The Quik-Mart sells 12-packs of juice for $7.44, and the One-Stop Shop sells the same juice in 8-packs for $5.20.

11. How much does 1 container cost at each store? ______________

12. What is the cheapest way to buy 48 containers? ______________

Batting Averages and Other Division Applications **Lesson 8.11**

Solve.

In the first half of the Little League season, Chad started poorly and had only 8 hits in 32 at bats. For the second half, Chad improved and had 12 hits in 28 at bats.

What was Chad's batting average for

13. the first half of the season? ______________

14. the second half of the season? ______________

15. the whole season? ______________

16. Jelly is sold in 10-ounce and 15-ounce jars that cost $1.99 and $3.09 respectively. Which is the better buy? ______________

Cumulative Review

Name ______________________ Date ______________

Student Edition • page 456

Angles and Sides of a Triangle Lesson 9.3

Solve.

17. Which of the following could be the measures of the angles in a triangle?

a. 50, 70, 90 **b.** 60, 60, 80 **c.** 50, 100, 30 **d.** 70, 70, 70

18. Which of the following could be the measures of the angles in an isosceles triangle?

a. 50, 50, 90 **b.** 65, 65, 50 **c.** 100, 50, 30 **d.** 40, 40, 60

Fractions of a Whole Lesson 6.1

Solve for *n*.

19. $\frac{2}{3}$ of 15 = n ______________

20. $\frac{3}{4}$ of 16 = n ______________

21. $\frac{3}{3}$ of 17 = n ______________

22. $\frac{4}{7}$ of 28 = n ______________

23. $\frac{3}{5}$ of 30 = n ______________

24. $\frac{3}{8}$ of 64 = n ______________

CHAPTER 9 Key Ideas Review

Student Edition • page 457

Measure the angles below and label them as *acute, obtuse, right,* or *straight.*

❶  ______________

❷  ______________

❸  ______________

Use the map to answer the following problems.
Estimate all distances by air.

Scale: 1 inch = 400 miles

❹ What is the distance from Montgomery, Alabama, to Chicago, Illinois, in inches and in miles? ______________

❺ How far is it from Miami, Florida, to Portland, Maine? ______________

Solve the following problem.

❻ Explain how these triangles are congruent by finding the measures of the angles and the lengths of the sides.

____

____

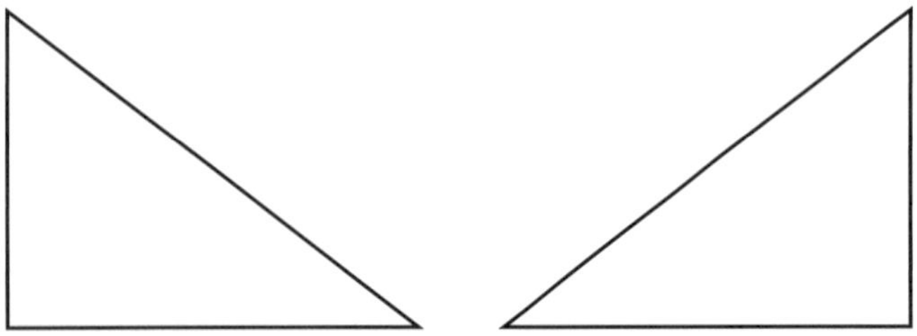

Chapter Review

Name ______________________ Date ______________

Student Edition • page 458

Solve. Lesson 9.1

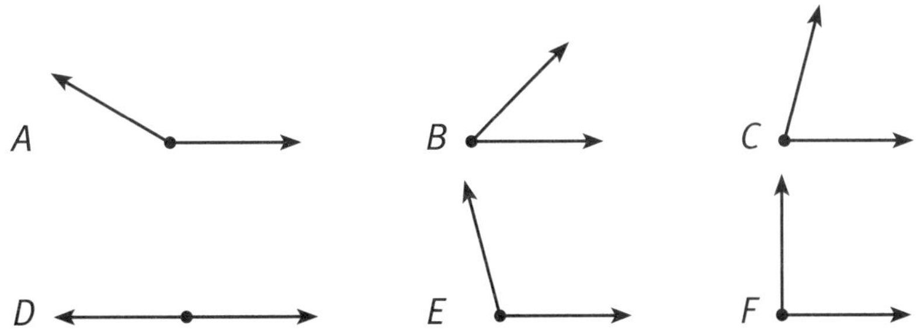

Which of the above angles are

1. acute? ______________
2. straight? ______________
3. right? ______________
4. obtuse? ______________

Which of the above angles could measure

5. 75°? ______________
6. 105°? ______________
7. 45°? ______________
8. 90°? ______________

Determine whether the following sets of numbers could be the lengths of the sides of a triangle. **Lesson 9.3**

9. 10, 10, and 8 ______________
10. 11, 7, and 19 ______________
11. 5, 7, and 11.5 ______________
12. 6, 8, and 15 ______________

Solve.

13. An isosceles triangle has two known sides that measure 4 feet and 9 feet. What is the measure of the third side? ______________
14. Suppose two sides of an equilateral triangle have a combined length of 15 inches. What is the length of the third side? ______________

Chapter Review

Student Edition • page 459

Solve. Lesson 9.5

15. Triangles *ABC* and *A'B'C'* are similar. The length of *AB* is 3, *BC* is 8, and *AC* is 6. If the length of *A'B'* is 9, what are the lengths of the other two sides of triangle *A'B'C'*? ______________

Lesson 9.7

The scale on the grid of city blocks is 1 centimeter = $\frac{1}{4}$ mile. If you can travel only along grid lines, how far is it from

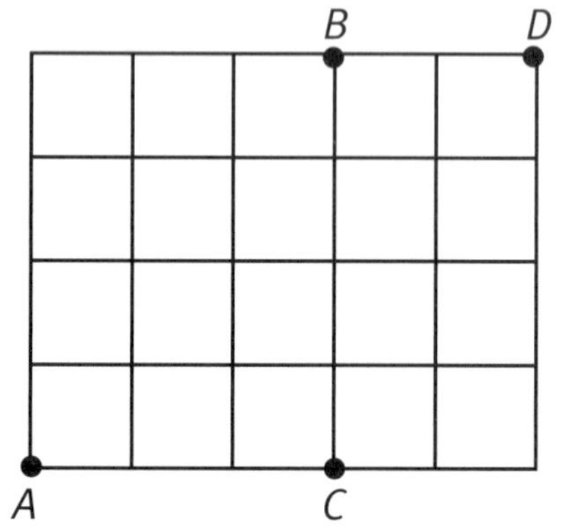

16. *A* to *C* and back? ______________

17. *C* to *D* and back? ______________

18. *A* to *D* to *B*? ______________

Draw an example of each of the following. Lessons 9.11–9.13

19. trapezoid

20. parallelogram

21. concave pentagon

22. concave quadrilateral

23. rhombus

24. square

CHAPTER 9 Practice Test

Name ______________________ Date ______________

Student Edition • page 460

For each pair of lines, tell whether the lines are perpendicular, parallel, or neither.

1.  ______________

2.  ______________

3.  ______________

Draw a triangle according to the clues, and then answer the questions.

4. Draw a triangle *RST* with your ruler and protractor so that

   a. side *RS* measures 5 centimeters.

   b. side *RT* measures 3 centimeters.

   c. angle *S* measures 35°.

5. How long is side *TS*?

   ____

6. What is the measure of angle *R*?

   ____

Write whether the triangles below are similar or congruent. Also write which corresponding parts are equal.

7. 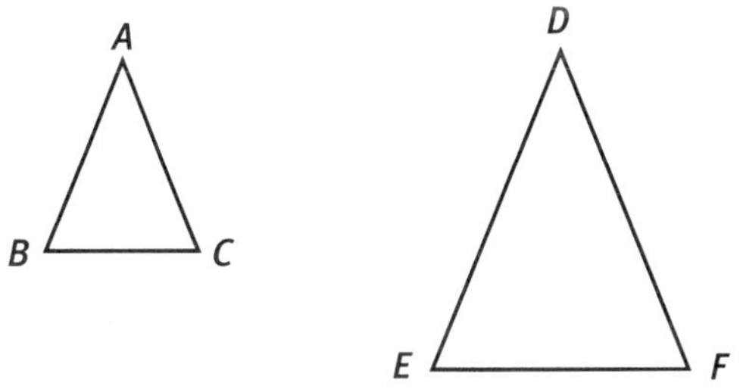

   ____

   ____

Use this figure to solve the problems.

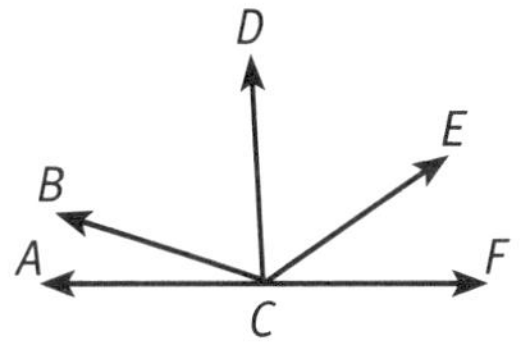

8. Name a straight angle in the figure.

   ____

9. Name two obtuse angles in the figure.

   ____

Practice Test

Student Edition • page 461

Write the correct answer.

10. Which is the missing angle measurement?

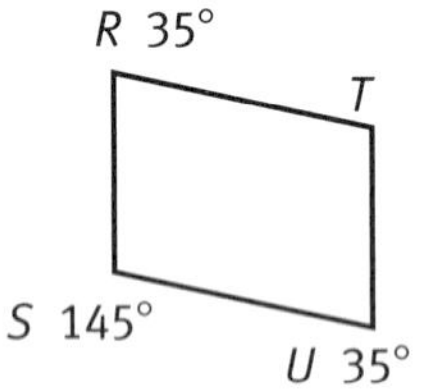

Ⓐ 145° Ⓑ 135°

Ⓒ 45° Ⓓ 35°

11. What kind of angle is shown below?

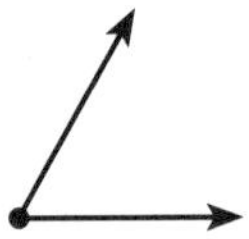

Ⓐ straight Ⓑ obtuse

Ⓒ right Ⓓ acute

12. Which set of triples can make a triangle?

Ⓐ 4, 5, 1 Ⓑ 4, 2, 5

Ⓒ 5, 6, 11 Ⓓ 5, 1, 4

13. Which figure shows a convex shape?

Ⓐ 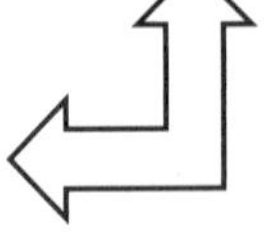 Ⓑ 

Ⓒ 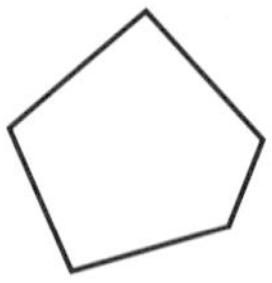 Ⓓ 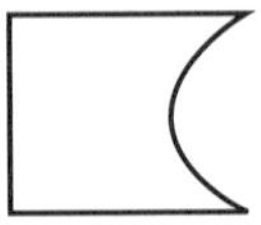

Use this information to answer Problems 14–16.

$\triangle RST \sim \triangle XYZ$ $r = 3$ cm, $s = 5$ cm, $t = 7$ cm, and $x = 6$ cm. $\angle S = 30°$

14. What is the measure of side *y*?

Ⓐ 14 cm Ⓑ 10 cm

Ⓒ 6 cm Ⓓ 5 cm

15. What is the measure of $\angle Y$?

Ⓐ 30° Ⓑ 45°

Ⓒ 60° Ⓓ 90°

16. If the measure of $\angle Z = 130°$, what is the measure of $\angle R$?

Ⓐ 130° Ⓑ 120°

Ⓒ 30° Ⓓ 20°

17. Which of the following is a trapezoid?

Ⓐ  Ⓑ 

Ⓒ 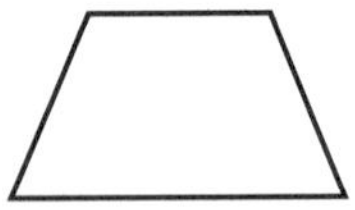 Ⓓ 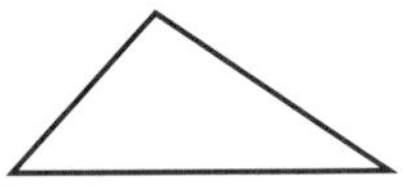

18. What is the name of the right angle?

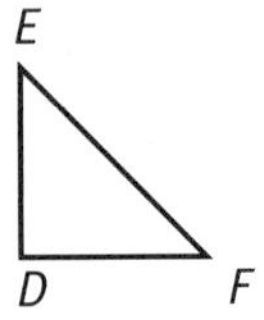

Ⓐ $\angle FED$ Ⓑ $\angle EDF$

Ⓒ $\angle DEF$ Ⓓ $\angle DFE$

Practice Test

Name ______________________ **Date** ______________

Student Edition • page 462

19. Which is a concave shape?

Ⓐ 

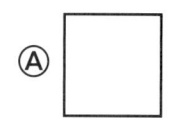

Ⓑ 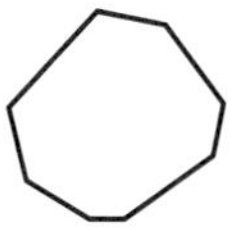

Ⓒ 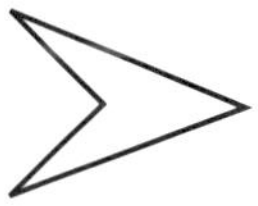

Ⓓ 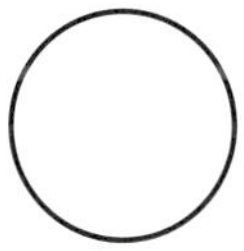

20. The scale on a map is 1 inch = 15 miles. A highway on this map measures 5 inches. How many miles is the highway?

Ⓐ 5 Ⓑ 15

Ⓒ 60 Ⓓ 75

21. Find the mean.
12, 15, 15, 7, 8, 10, 10

Ⓐ 17 Ⓑ 11

Ⓒ 10 Ⓓ 7

22. Carlos changes the tires on his car every 10,000 miles. He needs to change the tires when the odometer says 63,700. The car has 57,250 miles on it. How many more miles can he drive before he will need to change the tires?

Ⓐ 6,300 Ⓑ 6,450

Ⓒ 10,000 Ⓓ 67,250

23. Which decimal is equivalent to the fraction $\frac{4}{5}$?

Ⓐ 0.2 Ⓑ 0.4

Ⓒ 0.5 Ⓓ 0.8

24. The temperature is 0°C. What is the temperature in Fahrenheit?

Ⓐ 0°F Ⓑ 16°F

Ⓒ 32°F Ⓓ 60°F

25. Divide. $49\overline{)24549}$

Ⓐ 501 Ⓑ 451

Ⓒ 51 Ⓓ 45

26. $5x - 2 = y$. If y is 18, what is x?

Ⓐ $x = 88$ Ⓑ $x = 20$

Ⓒ $x = 4$ Ⓓ $x = 3$

27. If you start at the ordered pair (0, 2) and move right 2 steps and then down 2 steps, at what ordered pair are you now?

Ⓐ (0, 0) Ⓑ (2, 0)

Ⓒ (0, −2) Ⓓ (−2, 2)

28. Which improper fraction is equivalent to $4\frac{1}{3}$?

Ⓐ $\frac{41}{3}$ Ⓑ $\frac{4}{3}$

Ⓒ $\frac{5}{3}$ Ⓓ $\frac{13}{3}$

Practice Test

Student Edition • page 463

Use this scale drawing of a classroom to solve the problems.

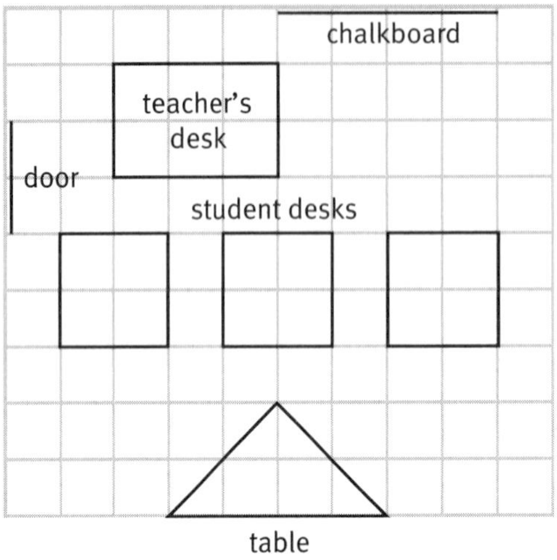

Scale: 1 cm = 30 cm

29. a. What is the length and width of the teacher's desk? ____________

b. Four students sit at each group of student desks. About how much space does each student have? ____________

c. Suppose the teacher put a wastepaper basket by her desk. It measures 15 cm by 30 cm. What would be the dimensions of the basket in the drawing? ____________

30. a. The teacher has another triangular table similar to the one in the classroom, but $\frac{1}{2}$ the size. What are the dimensions of the smaller table? ____________

b. What kind of triangle is the table? ____________

Name ______________________ Date ____________

Geometry and Measurement

Student Edition • page 465

Most homestead sites were simple squares. But odd-shaped pieces of property could require a lot of effort to describe and even more to understand. In an old deed, you may see units of measure that aren't used anymore, such as poles, rods, and chains. In the property descriptions below, can you tell which property is larger?

Start at the black stone at the southwest corner of the property.

Go north 40° east 55 rods.

Go south 49° east 64° rods.

Go west about 84 rods to starting point.

Start at the marked oak tree at the northeast corner of the property.

Go south 30° west 40 rods.

Go south 50 rods.

Go south 53° east 25 rods.

Go north about 100 rods to starting point.

Try this activity, and then answer the questions below.

Make a scale drawing of each property on a separate sheet of paper and compare areas. You may trace and cut the diagrams to help you.

1. What shape is each property? ____________

2. Do you need to know the length of a rod in order to find out which property has a greater area? ____________

3. Which property is larger? ____________

4. How can you convince someone that your answer is correct?

____

____

LESSON 10.1

Circles: Finding Circumference

Student Edition • page 466

Circular object	Diameter (*d*)	Circumference (*C*)	$C + d$	$C - d$	$C \times d$	$C \div d$
Film reel	27.5	86.5	114.0	59.0	2,378.75	3.145
Small bottle of correction fluid	2.8	8.7	11.5			
Foam cup	8.0	25.0		17.0		

Complete the table above. Work in a small group to finish Jim and Kurt's calculations. Find two circular objects and measure their diameter (length of a chord through the center) and circumference (distance around). Complete the table using a calculator.

1. Do you see anything interesting? Explain?

___

___

2. Do the numbers in the last four columns of your table seem about the same for each object, or do they change a great deal from object to object? What is the average of all 5 quotients? What is the average of the quotients for the entire class?

___

___

LESSON 10.1 **Name** ______________________ **Date** __________

Student Edition • page 467

3. Assuming that 3.14159 is the best approximation of π to the nearest hundred thousandth, is 3.14 or $3\frac{1}{7}$ a closer approximation of π? What is the decimal approximation of $3\frac{1}{7}$ to the nearest hundred thousandth?

____

Given the following measures for the diameter of a circle, what is each circumference (to the nearest whole unit)?

4. 15 cm __________
5. 21 ft __________
6. 14 cm __________
7. 8 mm __________
8. 12 in. __________
9. 42 cm __________
10. 100 cm __________
11. 20 in. __________

Given the following measures for the circumference of a circle, what is the diameter (to the nearest whole unit)?

12. 31 mi __________
13. 22 ft __________
14. 308 cm __________
15. 19 mi __________

LESSON 10.2

Area of Parallelograms

Student Edition • page 468

Follow these steps to find the area of a parallelogram.

a. Trace this parallelogram on a sheet of paper and carefully cut out the figure.

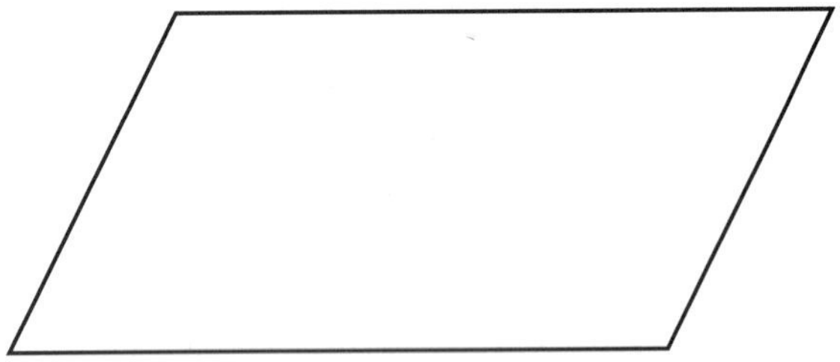

b. Imagine or draw a line segment from one vertex that is perpendicular to the opposite side.

c. Cut along the line segment.

d. Move the triangle to the other side.

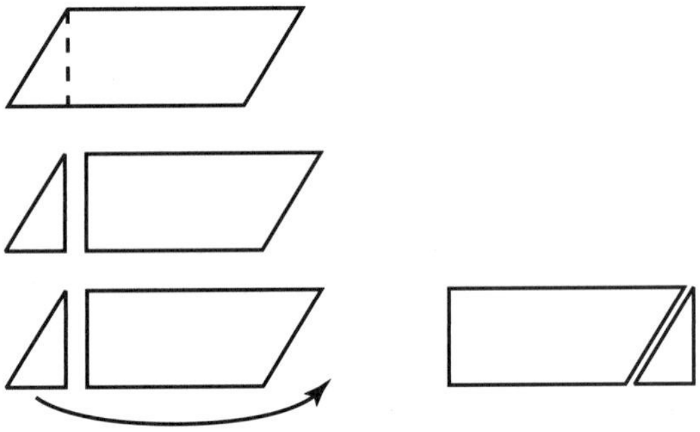

Answer the following questions.

1 **a.** What special type of parallelogram have you made? ______________

b. What are the lengths of the base and height of the new figure?

____

2 What is the area of the new figure you made? ______________

3 What is the area of the original parallelogram? ______________

4 **Extended Response** How could you have found the area of the original parallelogram without cutting it?

____

____

LESSON 10.2

Name ______________________ Date ____________

Student Edition • page 469

Find the area of each parallelogram.

5

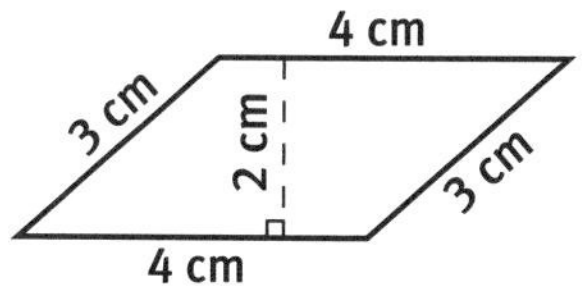

____

9

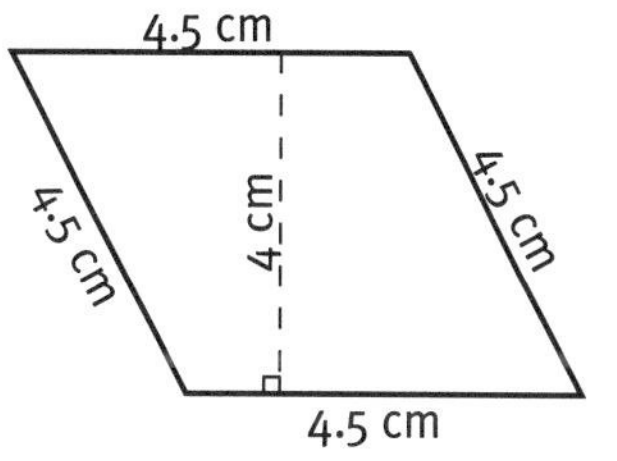

____

6

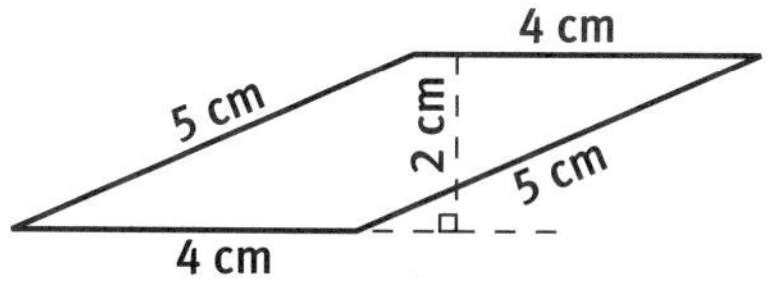

____

10

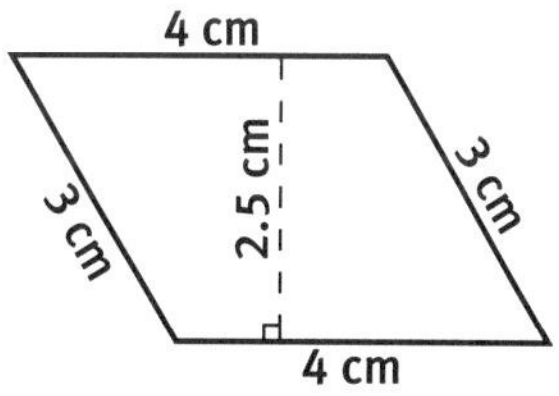

____

7

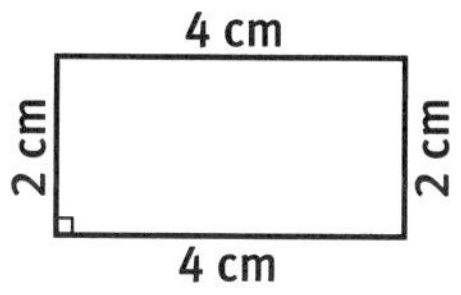

____

11

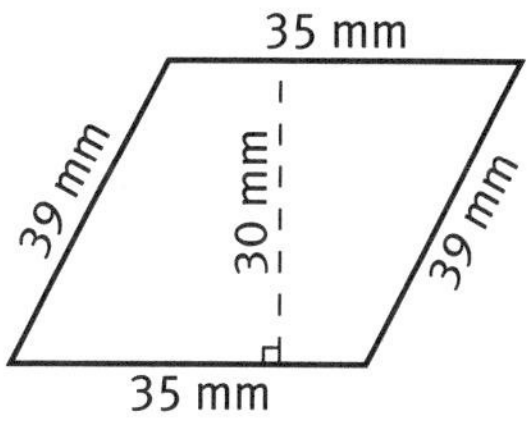

____

8

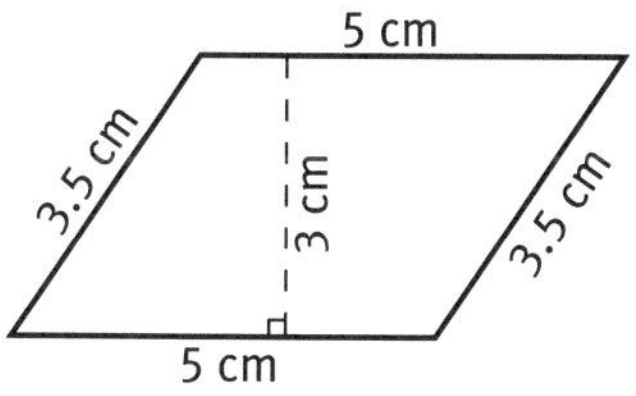

____

12

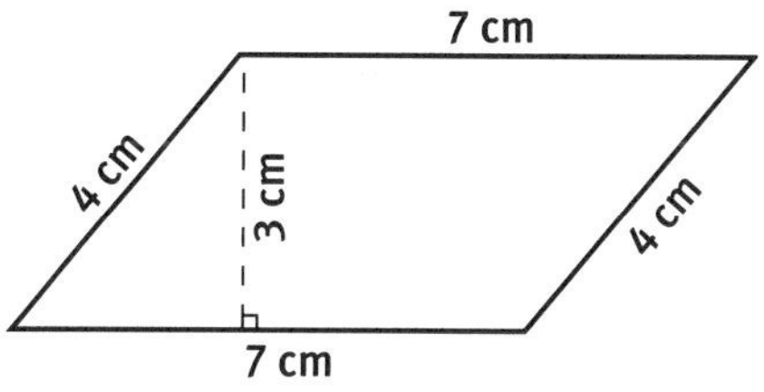

____

LESSON 10.3

Area of Triangles

Student Edition • page 470

Follow these steps to find the area of a right triangle.

a. Draw or trace this right triangle.

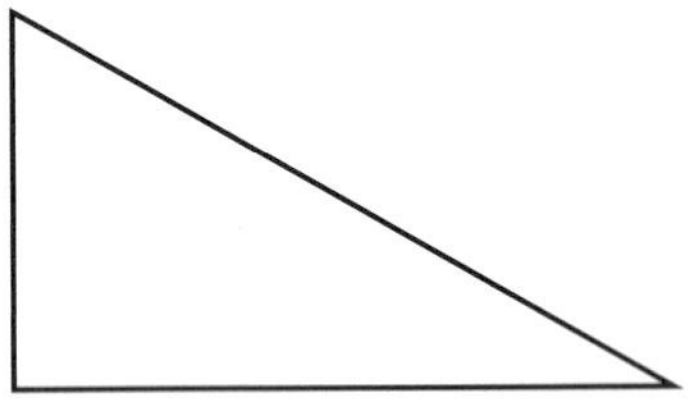

b. Draw or trace another triangle that is congruent to your first one.

c. Cut out the triangles, and put them together to make a rectangle.

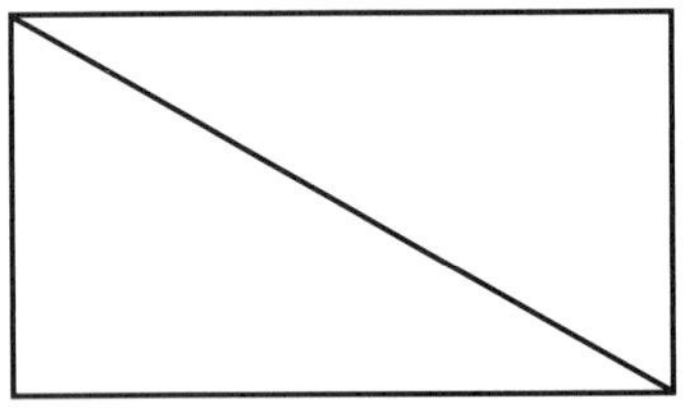

d. Measure the base and height of your rectangle in centimeters.

e. Find the area of your rectangle in square centimeters.

f. The area of each triangle is one half the area of the rectangle.

1 What is the area of the rectangle above? What is the area of each triangle?

____

2 **Extended Response** How could you have found the area of your original triangle without making a copy and cutting? Explain your answer.

____

____

____

Name ______________________ Date __________

Student Edition • pages 471–472

Find the area of these right triangles. You may choose any convenient side as the base.

3. 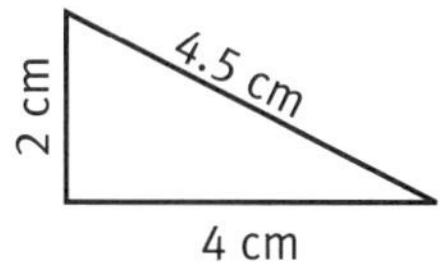

____

5. 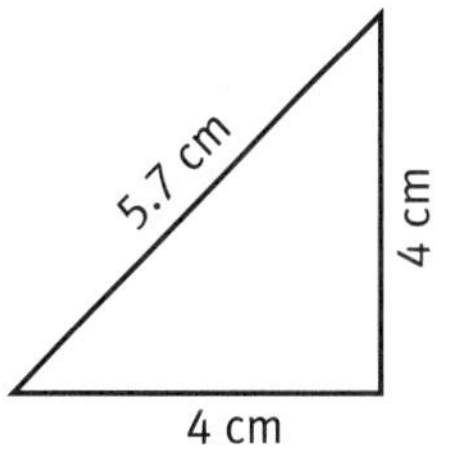

____

4. 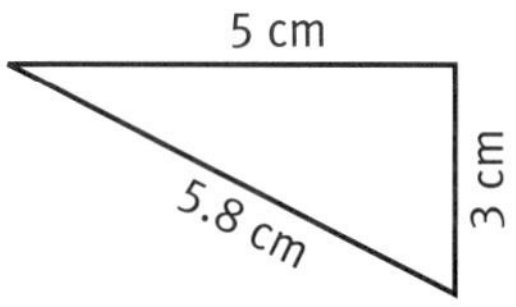

____

6. 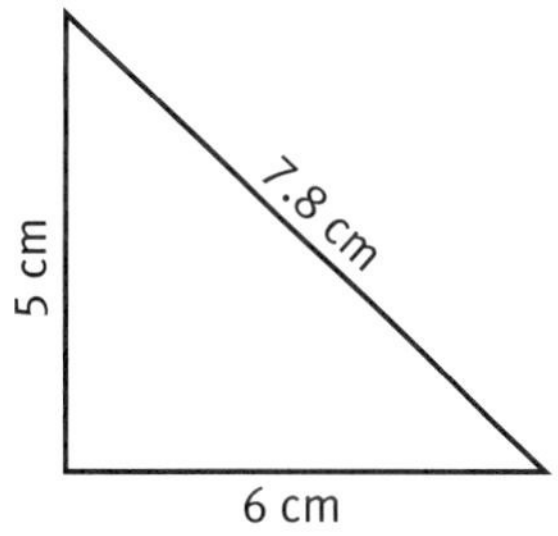

____

Follow these steps to find the area of any triangle.

a. Draw any triangle. Label it *ABC,* with *BC* as the base and *AD* as the height.

b. Use your triangle to draw a parallelogram *(AEBC)* with *BC* as the base and *AC* as a side.

LESSON 10.3

Student Edition • pages 472–473

Area of a triangle: The area of a triangle is one-half the product of the length of its base and its height. This is sometimes written as the following:

$A = \frac{1}{2}b \times h$ or $A = \frac{1}{2}bh$

7 Is the area of your parallelogram *AEBC* equal to the length of its base *BC* times its height *AD?* ______

8 In your drawing on page 443, is $\triangle ABC$ congruent to $\triangle BAE$? If so, then the area of $\triangle ABC$ must be half the area of parallelogram *AEBC*. ______

Find the area of each figure.

9
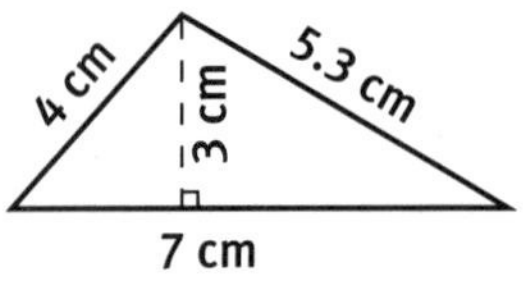

______

10
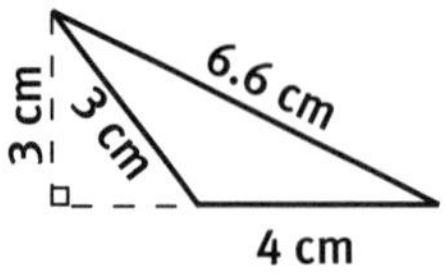

______

11
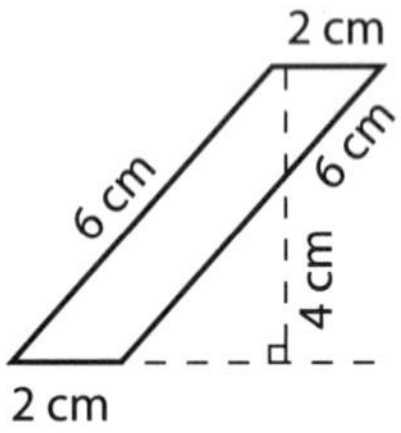

______

12
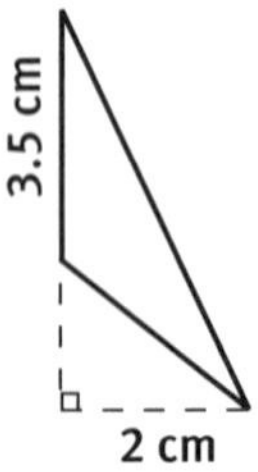

______

13
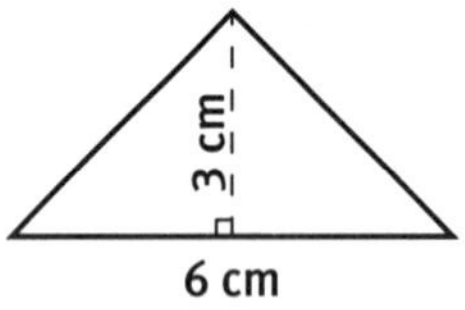

______

14
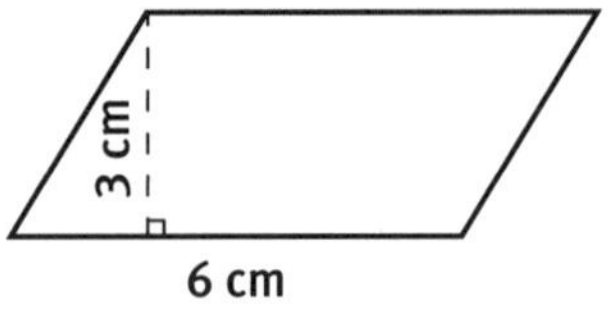

______

Name ______________________ Date ______________

Student Edition • page 473

Solve.

15. The Great Pyramid at Giza has four triangular faces that meet at the top. The base of one of these surfaces is about 745 feet and the height of the triangular face is about 450 feet. Find the area of one face of the pyramid. ____________

16. **Extended Response** Find the area of the shaded region in this figure. How did you find it?

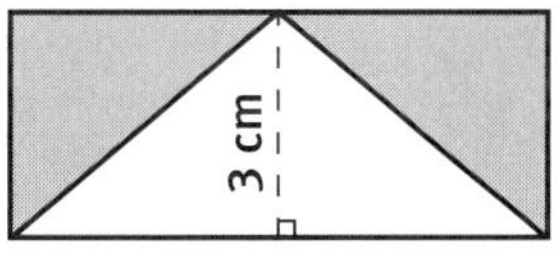

____

____

____

LESSON 10.4

Area of a Circle

Student Edition • page 474

Look at the circles and squares surrounding them in Figures 1 and 2. Each square in the graph has sides 1 cm long. Answer the following questions.

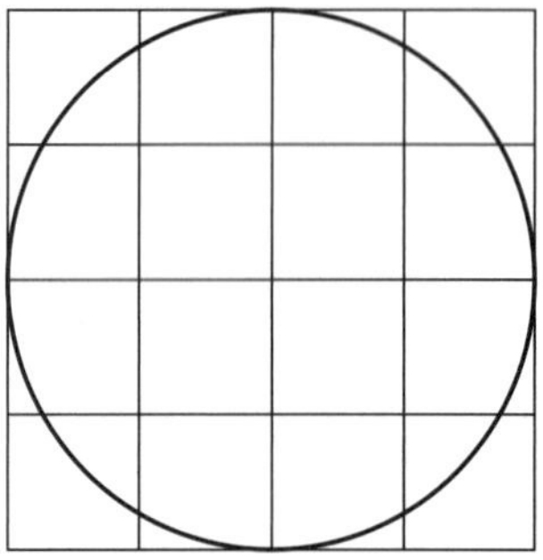

1 cm

Figure 1

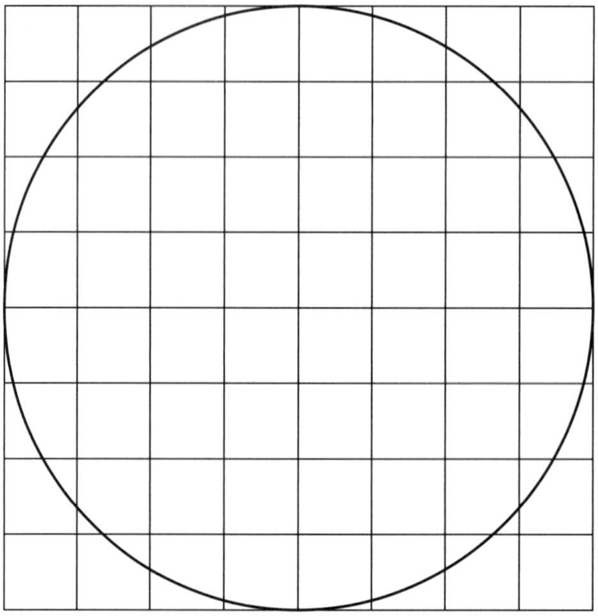

1 cm

Figure 2

1 Consider Figure 1.

a. What is the length of a side of the big square? What is the radius of the circle? (Remember, the radius is half the diameter.) What is the circumference of the circle?

__________ __________ __________

b. How many of the little squares are entirely inside the circle? Mostly inside the circle? Mostly outside the circle?

__________ __________ __________

c. What is the area of the big square? __________

d. About what would you estimate the area of the circle to be? __________

 Name ______________________ Date ____________

Student Edition • pages 474–475

2 Consider Figure 2.

a. What is the length of a side of the big square? What is the radius of the circle? What is the circumference of the circle?

____________ ____________ ____________

b. Count the little squares that are entirely inside the circle, mostly inside, about half inside, and mostly outside of the circle.

____________ ____________ ____________

c. What is the area of the big square? Estimate the area of the circle.

____

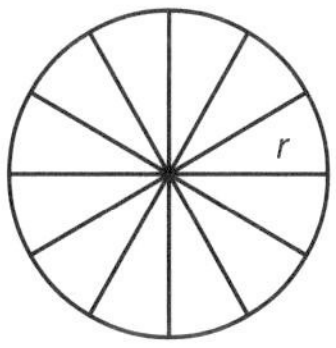

This circle has been divided into 12 equal pie-shaped pieces called *sectors*. The 12 sectors have been cut out and rearranged below the circle. They form a figure that resembles a parallelogram.

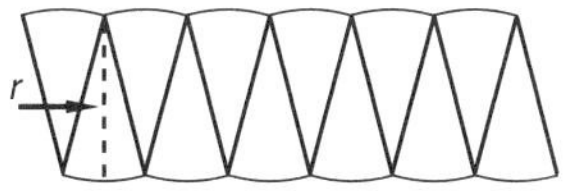

3 About what is the height of that figure? ____________

4 What is the circumference C of a circle with radius r? ____________

5 Is the base of your figure about half the circumference of the circle or πr? ____________

6 What is the approximate area of your figure? How did you determine this? ______________________

7 If we assume the area of a circle is πr^2,

a. about what is the area of the circle in Figure 1 on page 446? ____________

b. about what is the area of the circle in Figure 2? ____________

c. are these areas approximately the same as the areas you estimated for the circles from the squares in the figures? ____________

LESSON 10.4

Student Edition • page 475

The area of a circle is given by the formula: $A = \pi \times r \times r = \pi r^2$.
Using an estimate of 3.14 for π, find the circumference and area of each circle.

8. $r = 3$ cm ______________

9. $r = 30$ cm ______________

10. $r = 300$ cm ______________

11. $r = 3{,}000$ cm ______________

12. $r = 7$ cm ______________

13. $r = 70$ cm ______________

14. If you double the radius of a circle, what happens to the circumference? What happens to the area?

____

____

15. If you multiply the radius of a circle by 10, what happens to the circumference? What happens to the area?

____

____

16. If you multiply the radius of a circle by any number *n*, what happens to the circumference? What happens to the area?

____

____

LESSON 10.5

Name ______________________ Date ____________

Area of Irregular Figures

Student Edition • page 476

Solve.

1. **Extended Response** In Figure A, the top and bottom segments are parallel. What is the distance between them? See how many different ways you can figure out the area. Do all the methods give the same answer? Describe two different methods.

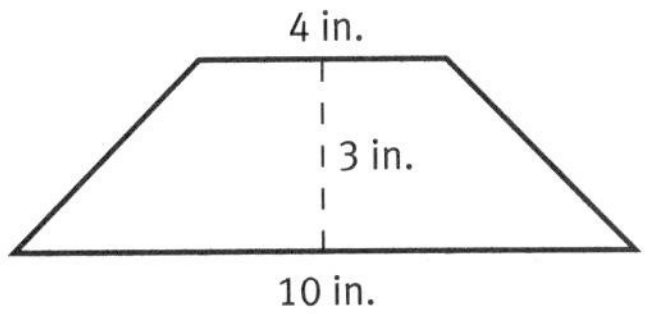

Figure A

____

____

____

____

2. In Figure B, what is the length of the entire figure? What is the length of the base (top missing line segment) of the missing triangle? What is the height of the entire figure? What is the height of the missing triangle? Find the area of Figure B.

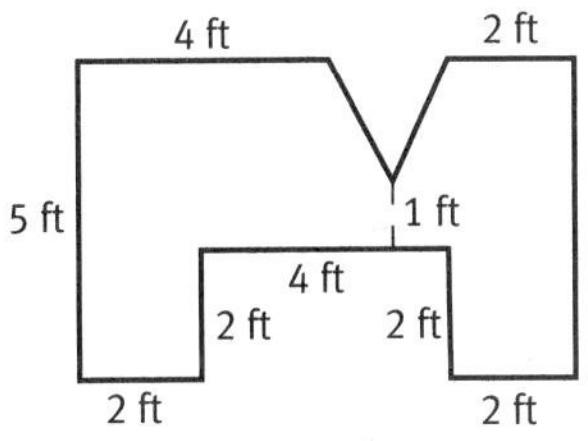

Figure B

____

____

____

____

____

LESSON 10.5

Student Edition • page 477

Find the areas of the figures below to the nearest hundredth of a square unit. Use $\pi = 3.14$.

3

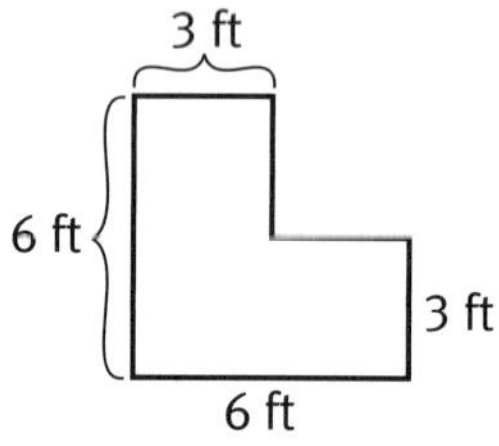

____

7

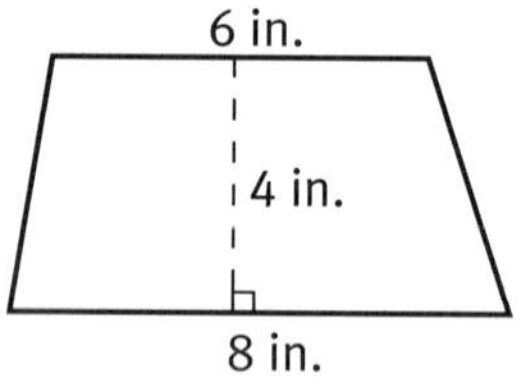

____

4

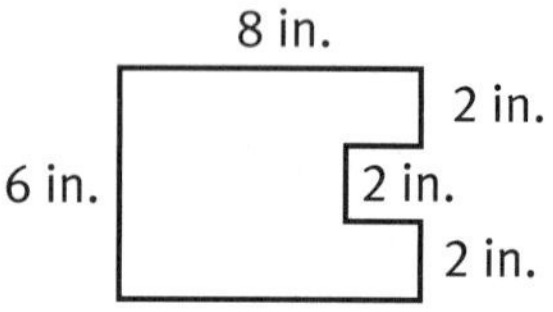

____

8

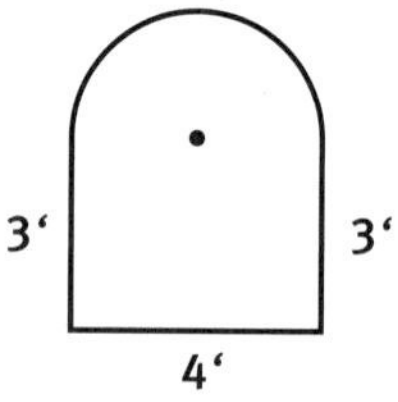

____

5

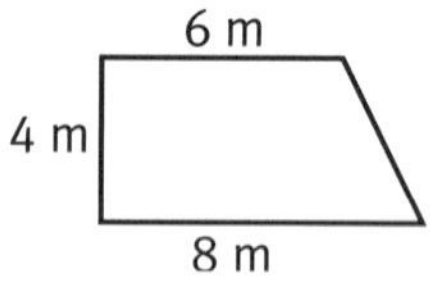

____

9

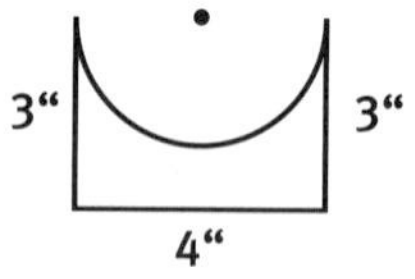

____

6 Find the perimeter of the figure in Problem 3.

____

10 Find the perimeter of the figure in Problem 8.

____

Name ______________________ Date ____________

Student Edition • pages 478–479

Imagine you are making a reproduction of this 1882 quilt. You will sew the red, blue, and yellow design onto 4-inch white squares. You have a rectangular piece of blue cloth 12 inches by 15 inches and a rectangular piece of red cloth 18 inches by 24 inches.

Do you have enough red and blue cloth to make 100 quilt squares?

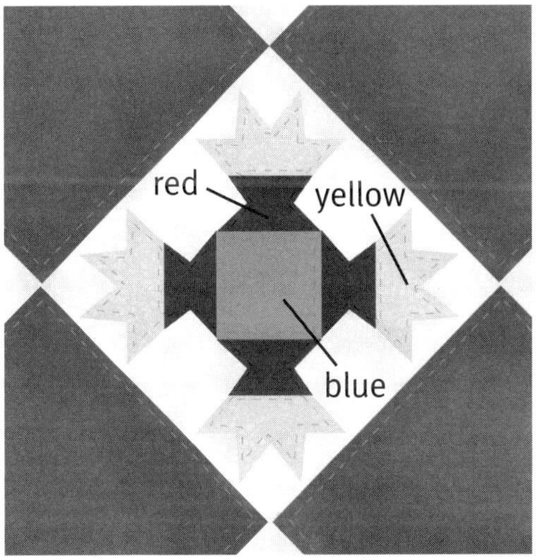

Scale 1:2

Keila solved the problem this way:

I Made a Plan.

A. Think of the design as a combination of figures with simple shapes.
B. Measure the dimensions of the figures in the photo.
C. Calculate the area of each figure.
D. Figure out how much of each color I need.
E. See if I have enough square inches of each color.

Think about Keila's strategy, and then answer these questions.

1. What simple figures could you use for this design?

____

Student Edition • page 479

❷ What are the dimensions of one of those figures on the actual quilt? ____________

❸ How would you find the area of that figure?

____

❹ Do you think Keila's strategy will work? Explain.

____

____

Tyler solved the problem another way:

I also decided to Make a Plan. Part of my plan was to Make a Scale Drawing.

A. Make a scale drawing of the design on grid paper.
B. Count squares to find out the area of each part of the design.
C. Figure out how much of each color I need.
D. See whether I have enough square inches of each color.

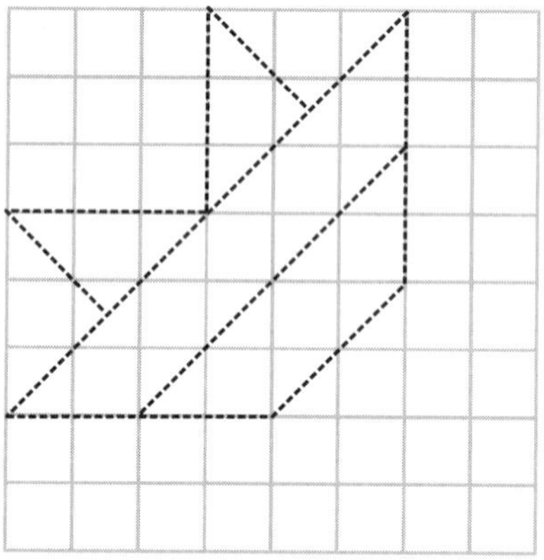

Think about Tyler's strategy, and then answer the following questions.

❺ About how many squares are in the smaller of the two trapezoids Tyler has drawn so far? ____________

❻ How many inches does each space on the diagram represent? ____________

Name ______________________ Date ____________

Student Edition • page 479

7. How many square inches does each square on the diagram represent? ____________

8. About how many square inches of red cloth does the smaller trapezoid represent? ____________

9. Do you think Tyler's strategy will work? Explain.

____

____

____

10. Solve the problem. Use any strategy you think will work. What strategy did you use? Why?

____

____

____

____

____

CHAPTER 10 Cumulative Review

Student Edition • page 480

Adding and Subtracting Integers Lesson 4.8

Complete the following sentences by telling whether the answer is *positive* or *negative.*

1. If a negative number is subtracted from a negative number with a smaller absolute value, the answer is ______________ .
2. If a negative number is subtracted from a negative number with a greater absolute value, the answer is ______________ .
3. If a negative number is added to a positive number with a smaller absolute value, the answer is ______________ .

Solve.

4. $(-7) + |-8| =$ ______________
5. $(-5) - (-9) =$ ______________
6. $10 - |-12| =$ ______________
7. $-3 - |7| =$ ______________

Patterns Lesson 4.10

Complete the pattern and state the pattern rule.

8. $-8, -4, 0,$ __________, __________, __________, __________, 20

____

9. $-\frac{1}{16}, -\frac{1}{4}, -1,$ __________, __________, __________, -256

____

10. 81, 27, 9, 3, __________, __________, __________, __________, $\frac{1}{81}$

____

Cumulative Review

Name ______________________ Date ______________

Student Edition • pages 480–481

Decimals and Money **Lesson 3.1**

Solve.

Ali is in a department store and chooses a jacket for $89.99, 2 shirts that cost $19.99 each, and a pair of pants for $27.50. He has $150 to spend.

11. Does Ali have enough money to pay for what he has selected? ______________

12. If he is short, how much more money does Ali need? If he has enough, how much does he have left? ______________

Decimals and Money **Lesson 3.1**

Solve.

13. Pat buys cat food when it is on sale. The current sale is "buy 3 cans, get 1 free." If the price per can is $1.25, how much money does Pat need to purchase 12 cans? ______________

14. At the school cafeteria, Janie bought a sandwich for $2.09, a salad for $1.19, and fruit for $0.79. She had 3 one-dollar bills, 3 quarters, and 3 dimes. Did she have enough money for her lunch? If not, what did she need? ______________

Student Edition • page 481

Standard Notation for Functions Lesson 5.10

Complete each function table, and graph the ordered pairs for each.

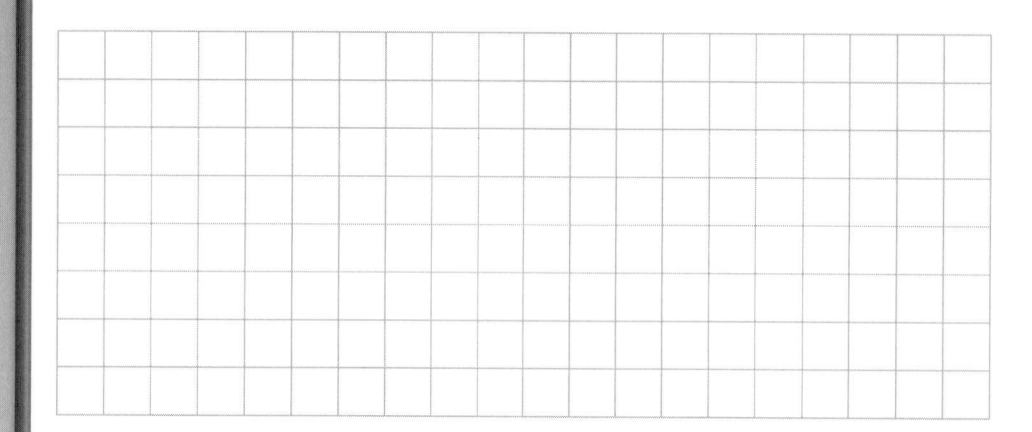

⓯ $y = 3x - 4$

x	y
0	
1	
	2

⓰ $y = \frac{x}{3} + 2$

x	y
6	
	5
12	

Dividing Fractions Lesson 7.6

Divide. Reduce when possible.

⓱ $16 \div \frac{4}{3} =$ ______

⓲ $\frac{1}{2} \div \frac{1}{4} =$ ______

⓳ $9 \div \frac{3}{5} =$ ______

Solve.

⓴ A 12-foot piece of lumber needs to be split into pieces that are about $1\frac{1}{4}$ feet long. How many of those pieces can be cut from it? ______

LESSON 10.6

Name ______________________ Date ____________

Rotation, Translation, and Reflection

Student Edition • pages 483–484

Extended Response **For** each of the following pairs of congruent figures, describe a combined translation and rotation that would place one figure on top of the other.

1. 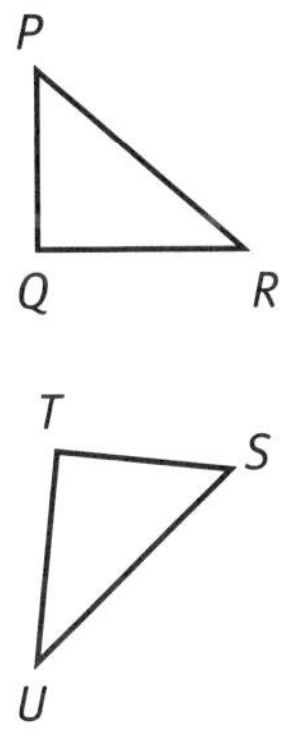

____

____

2. 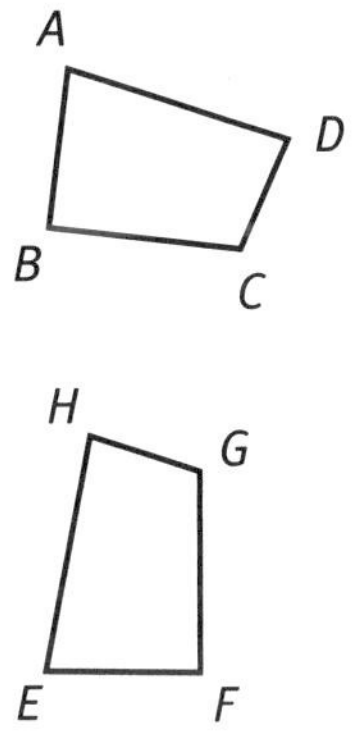

____

____

Extended Response **For** each of the following pairs of congruent figures, describe a combined translation and rotation that would place one figure on top of the other.

3. 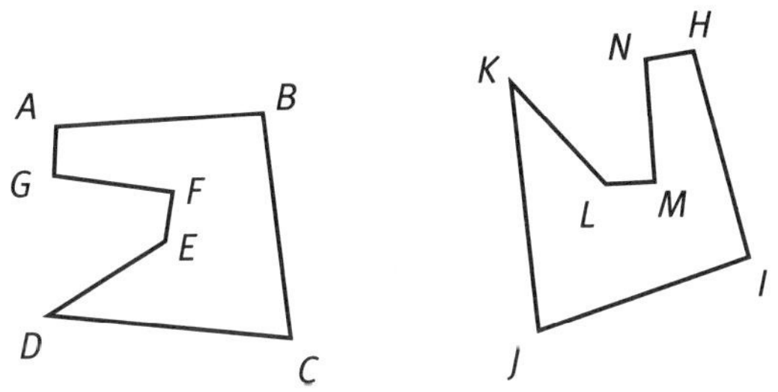

____

____

4. 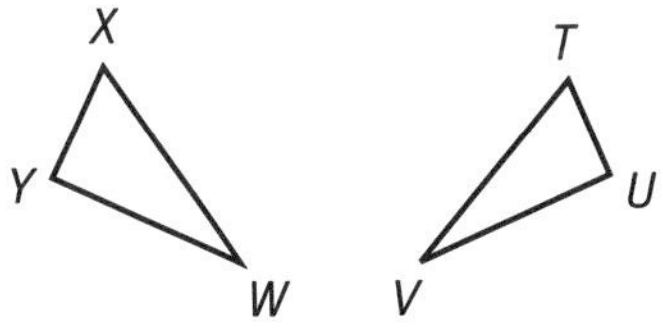

____

____

LESSON 10.6

Student Edition • pages 484–485

5 Were you able to describe a translation and rotation that would place ΔXYW on top of ΔTUV? Do the two triangles appear to be congruent? What is the difficulty?

____

____

____

For Problems 6–10, trace or copy the object and perform the actions described. Draw your result.

6

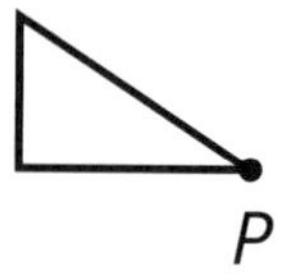

Rotate half a turn clockwise about point P.

7

Reflect about line ℓ.

Name ______________________ Date __________

Student Edition • page 485

8

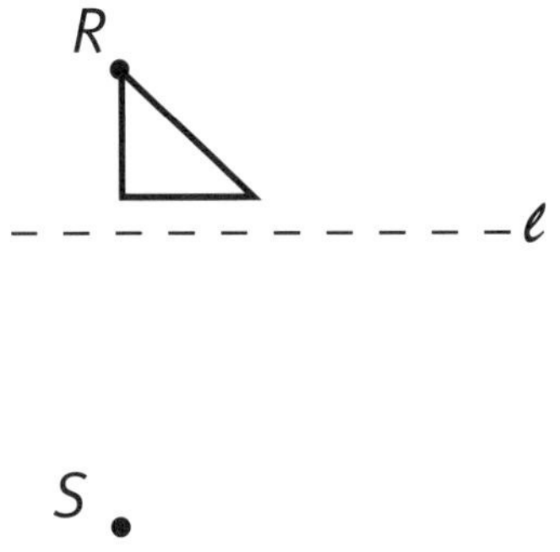

Reflect about line ℓ.
Then translate down 0.5 inch.

9

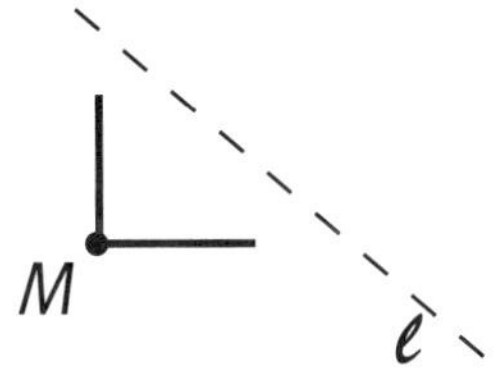

Reflect about line ℓ. Then rotate a quarter turn about point *M*′.

10 **Extended Response** Describe another way to translate, rotate, or reflect the figure in Problem 6 that yields the same result.

____

____

____

____

LESSON 10.7

Symmetry

Student Edition • page 487

For each of the following figures, draw the lines of symmetry. Then write the number of lines of symmetry and the smallest angle of rotation beneath the figure.

1. 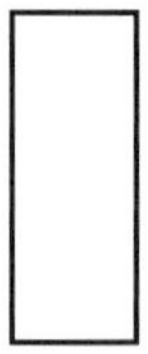

2. 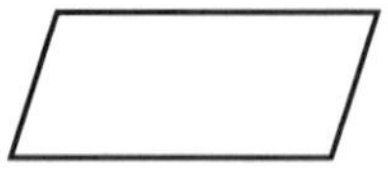

3. 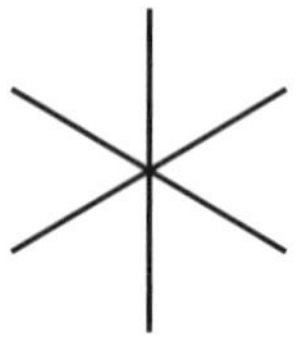

4. 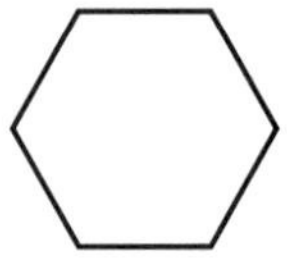

5. 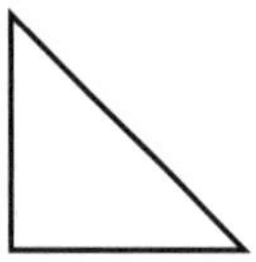

6. 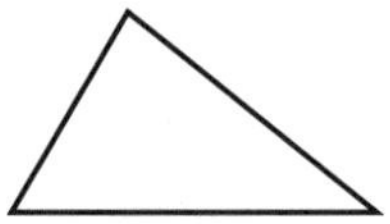

7. 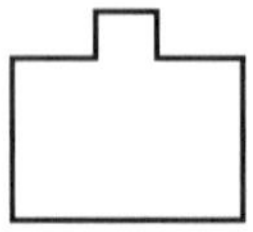

8. 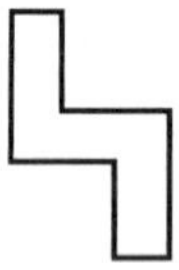

9. 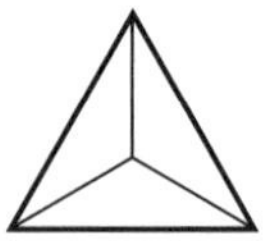

10. 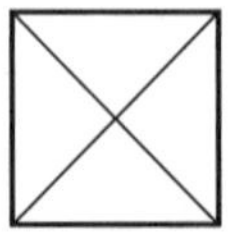

11. 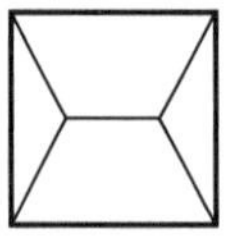

12. 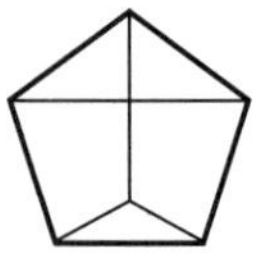

LESSON 10.8

Name ____________________ Date ____________

Paper Folding

Student Edition • pages 488–489

Begin with a long strip of gummed tape or receipt paper and fold the paper as shown below. These creases are known as *mountain folds* because they bend up like a mountain. If you are using gummed tape, start with the gummed side up.

Step 1

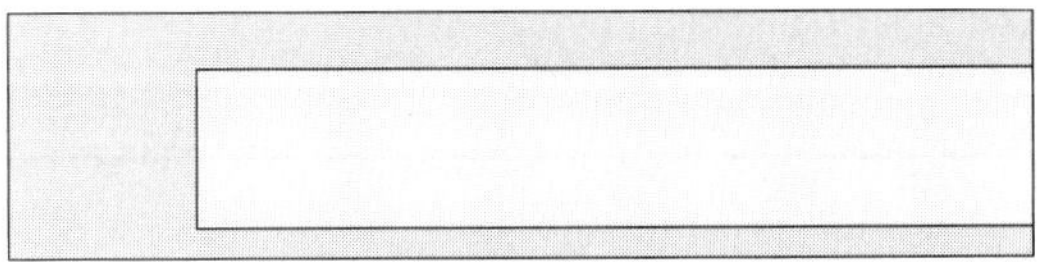

Step 2

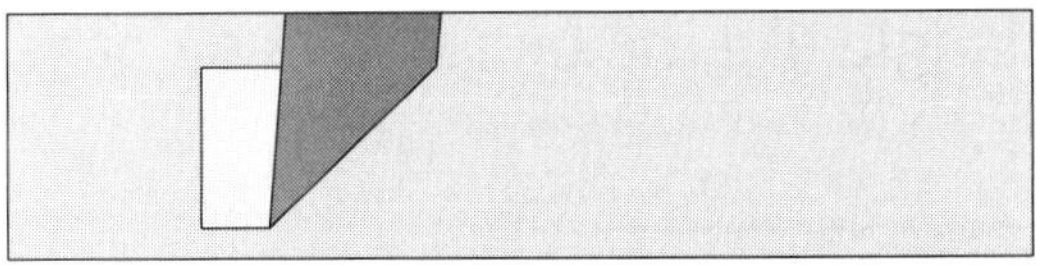

Step 3

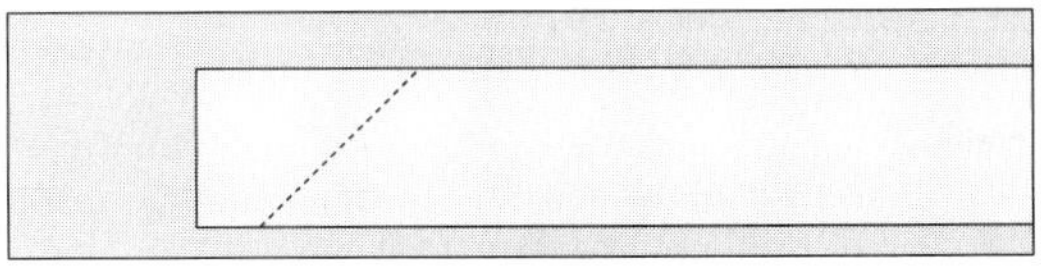

Step 4

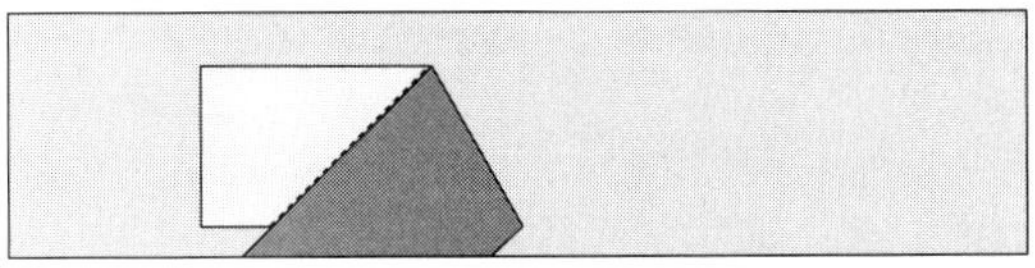

Step 5

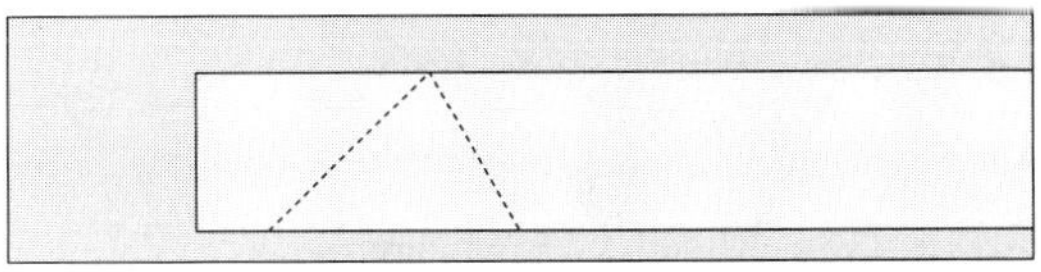

Step 6

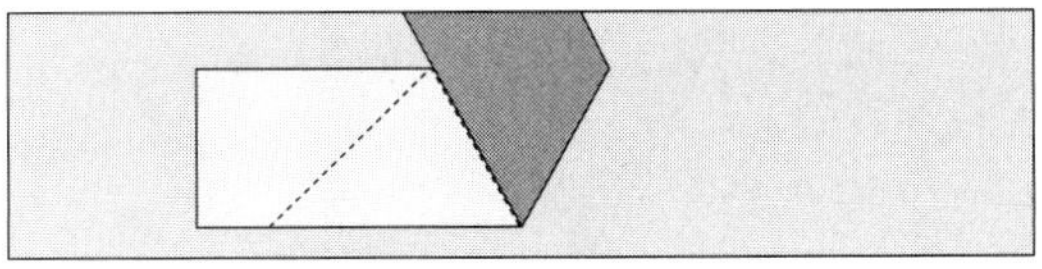

Step 7

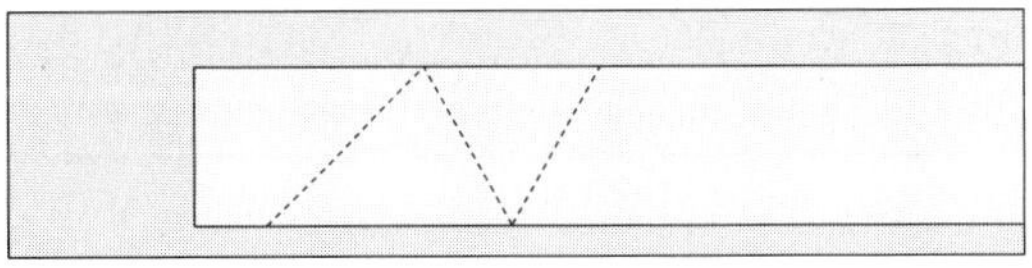

Step 8

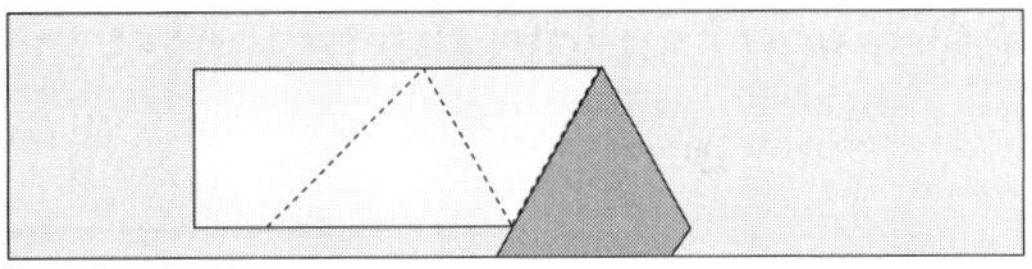

Step 9

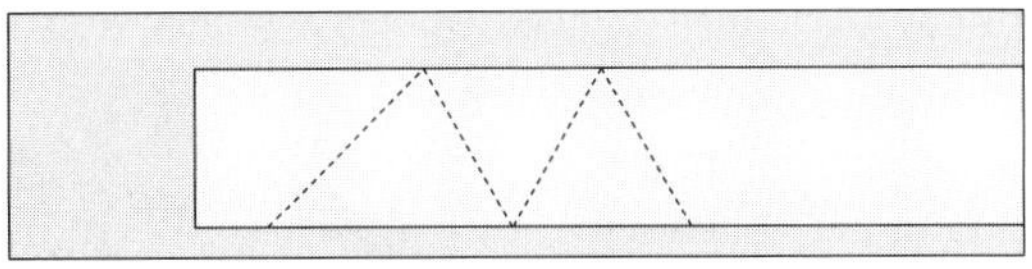

Step 10

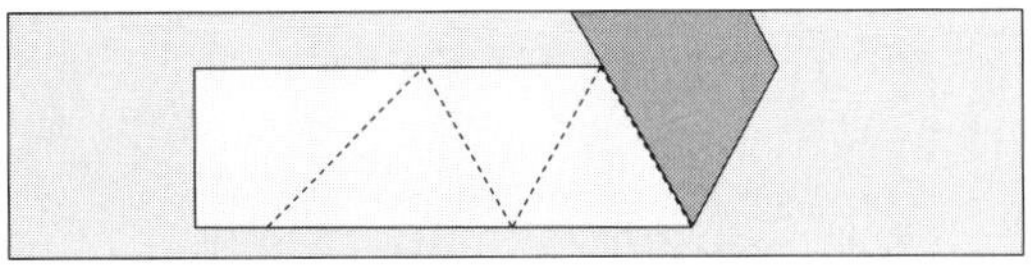

Step 11

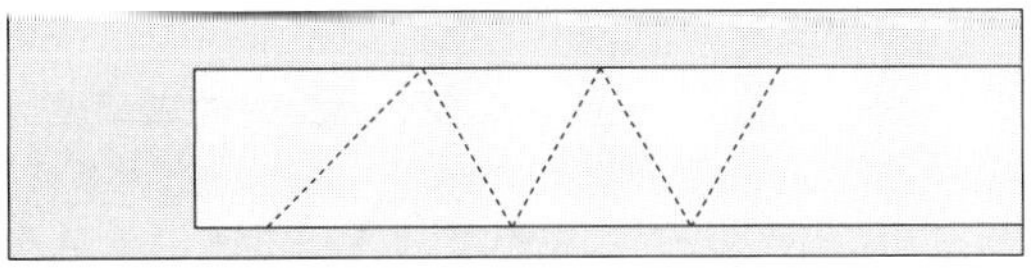

Continue folding to make a long string of triangles (at least 50).

LESSON 10.8

Student Edition • pages 489 and 491

Answer the following questions based on the information on page 461.

1. What kind of triangle is the first one in Step 5? ______________
2. What kind of triangle does the triangle in Step 11 look like? ______________
3. What do you suppose would happen if you kept folding like this?

____

____

See if you can fold the triangles into one big triangle like the one shown on page 463.

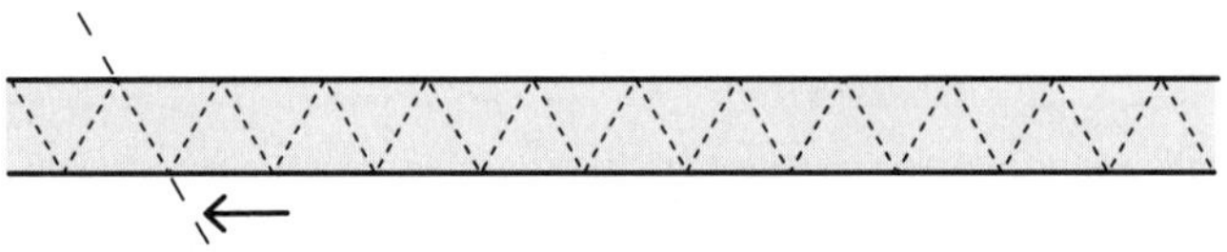

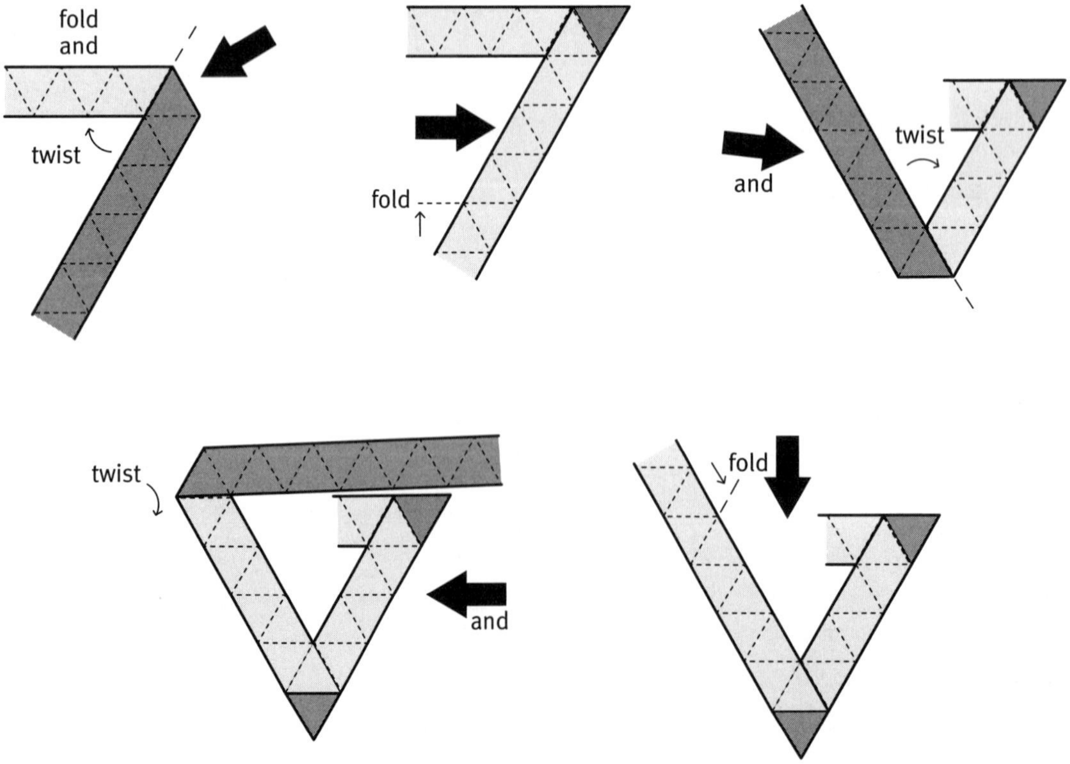

Name ______________________ Date __________

Student Edition • page 491

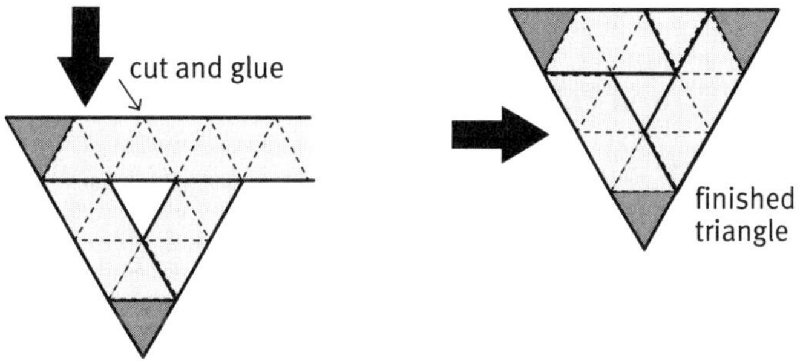

Extended Response **Answer** the following questions.

4 What was the hardest part about making these figures?

____

____

____

5 Is the big triangle equilateral? How do you know?

____

____

____

LESSON 10.9

Making a Flexagon

Student Edition • page 493

Examine the flexagon you created on pages 492–493.

1. Does your original design still have the same number of lines of symmetry when it reappears? If not, how did they change?

____

____

____

2. Does the overall design still have the same rotational symmetry? If not, how did it change?

____

____

____

3. Build more flexagons, and make designs on them that have

   a. 6 lines of symmetry and 60° rotational symmetry.

   b. 3 lines of symmetry and 120° rotational symmetry.

   c. 2 lines of symmetry and 180° rotational symmetry.

4. Build a flexagon that has all of the above symmetries on it.

LESSON 10.10

Name ______________________ Date ____________

Space Figures

Student Edition • page 495

Solve.

1. What is another name for a prism with squares for all its faces?

____

2. How many faces, edges, and vertices does it have?

____

3. Name and describe another polyhedron from previous lessons.

____

____

Use these drawings of other space figures to answer the following questions.

sphere

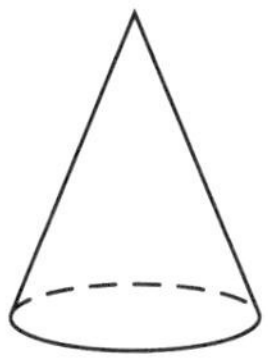

cone

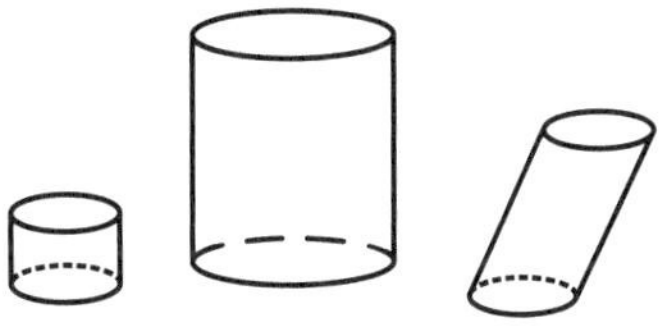

cylinders

4. What do a cone and a pyramid have in common?

____

____

5. What do a prism and a cylinder have in common?

____

____

LESSON 10.10

Student Edition • pages 495–496

6 What do a cone and a cylinder have in common?

____

____

Trace the nets below. Cut along the solid lines and fold along any dashed lines. For each figure you create, give its name and tell how many vertices, edges, and faces it has.

7

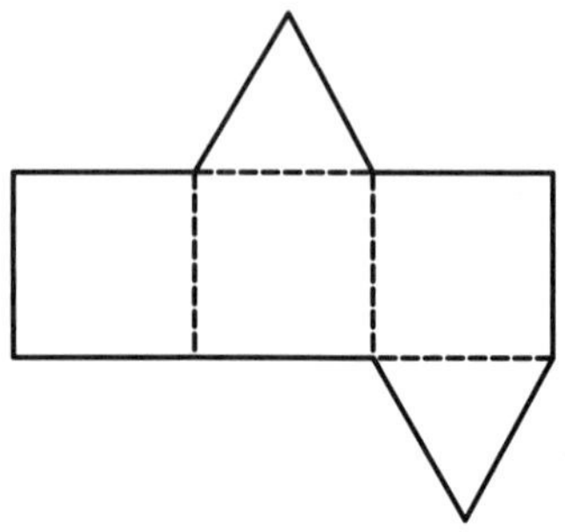

____

9

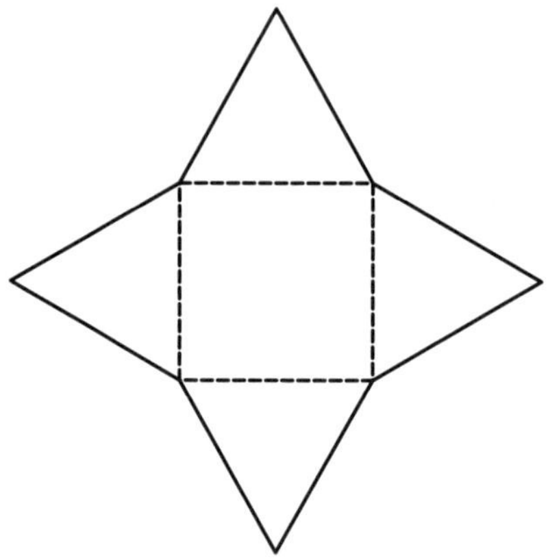

____

8

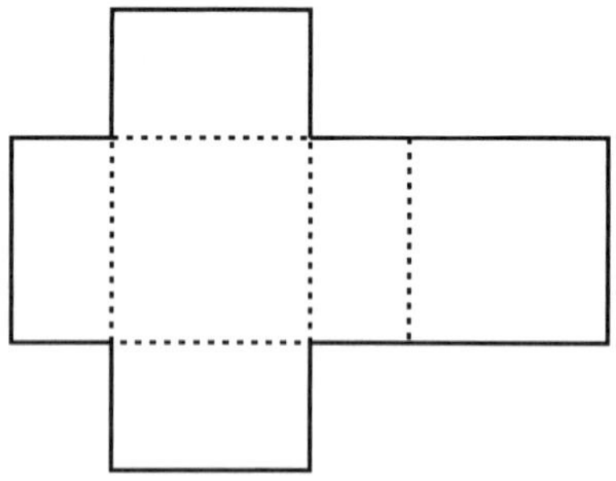

____

10

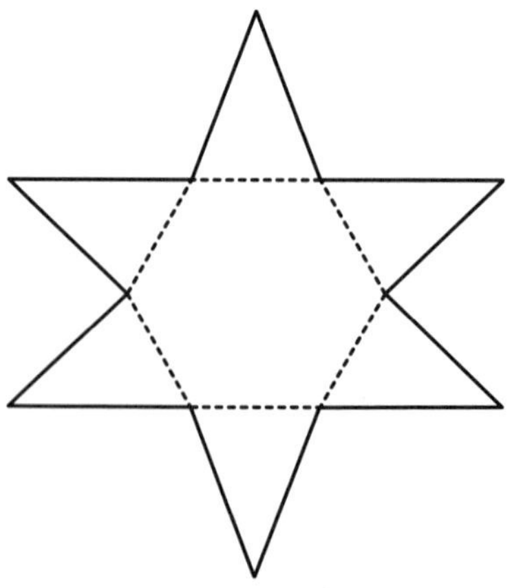

____

LESSON 10.10 **Name** ______________________ **Date** ____________

Student Edition • page 497

Answer the following questions.

11. Can you draw a net for a sphere? ____________

12. Can you draw a net for a cube? ____________

Try to make a net for a three-dimensional figure, and then cut it out, fold, and stick it together along its edges to make the figure. Then count its vertices, edges, and faces and answer the following questions.

13. Do all the models you made satisfy the equation $V + F = E + 2$ where V represents the number of vertices, F represents the number of faces, and E represents the number of edges in the figure? ____________

14. Which space figures have an axis about which you can rotate the figure $\frac{1}{2}$ of a turn and have the object look exactly the same as before?

____

15. Which models have an axis about which you can rotate the model $\frac{1}{3}$ of a turn and have the object look the same? $\frac{1}{4}$ of a turn? $\frac{1}{5}$ of a turn?

____

16. **Extended Response** Describe the figure below using correct mathematical language.

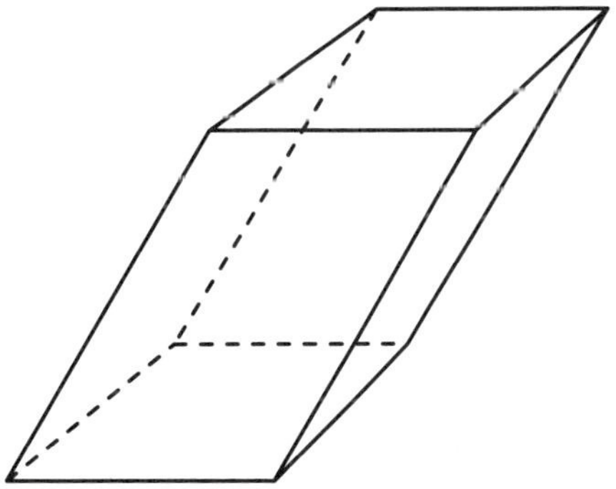

____

____

____

LESSON 10.11

Building Deltahedra

Student Edition • **page 500**

The pictures on this page and the next may give you ideas about how to use the net diagrams to build these deltahedra with the folded tape. You do not have to use these; they are simply examples of configurations that will work. Be creative and devise your own methods. Experiment to find ways to glue pieces of tape together to construct either the deltahedra shown or those you create yourself.

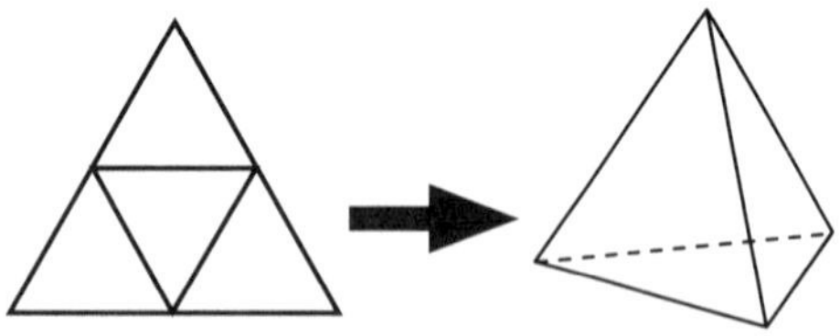

tetrahedron or **triangular pyramid**

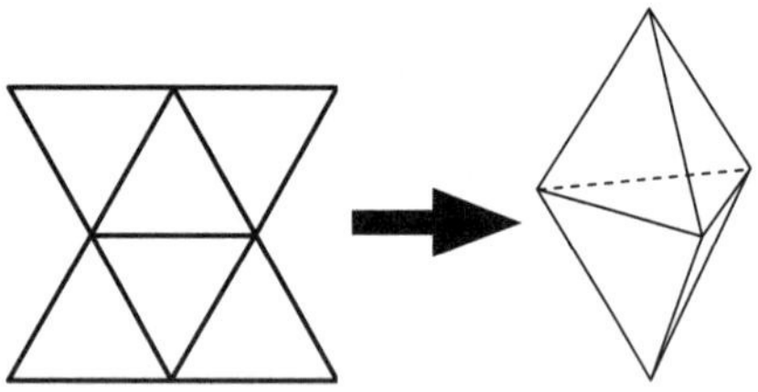

triangular dipyramid

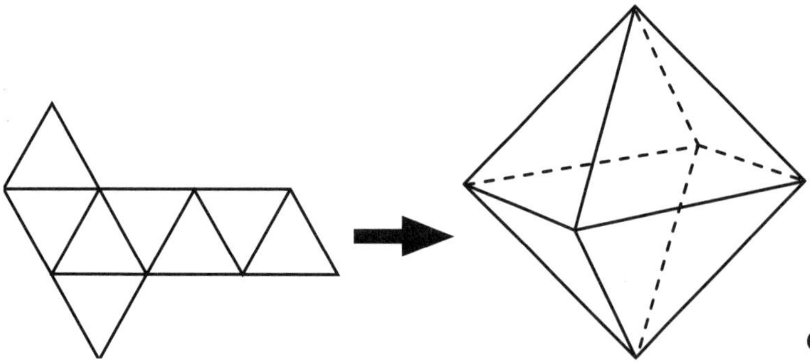

octahedron or **square dipyramid**

Name ______________________ Date ____________

Student Edition • page 501

Here are some examples of deltahedra and their nets.

pentagonal dipyramid

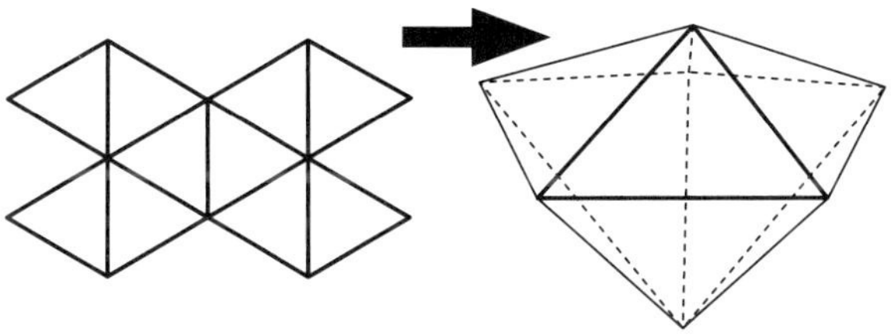

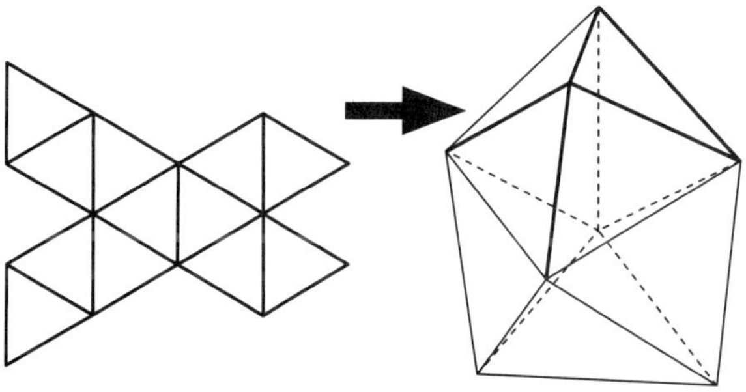

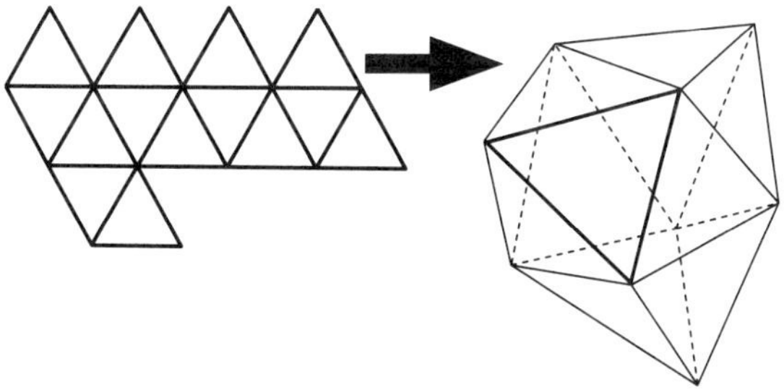

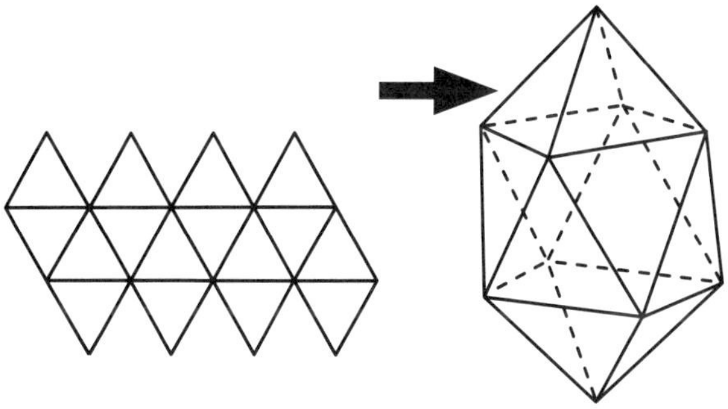

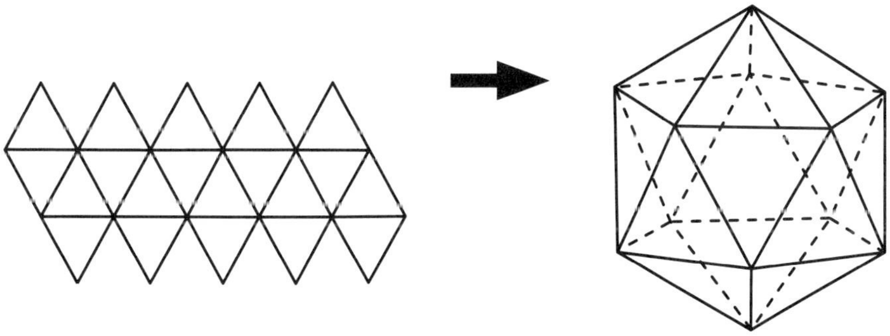

icosahedron

LESSON 10.12

Surface Area

Student Edition • page 502

Find the surface area of the boxes made from these nets. Remember to write the units in your answers.

❶

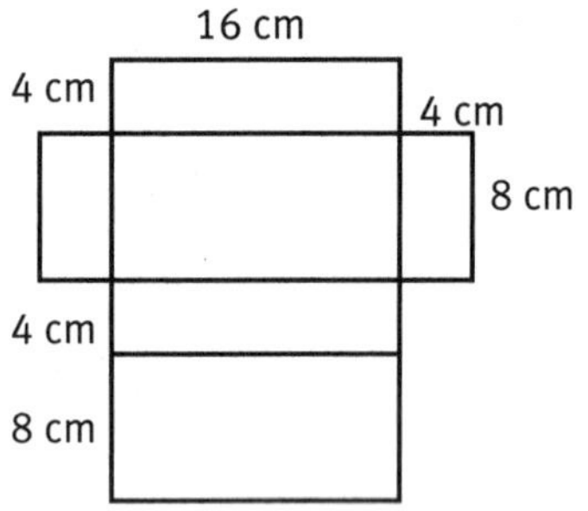

____

❷

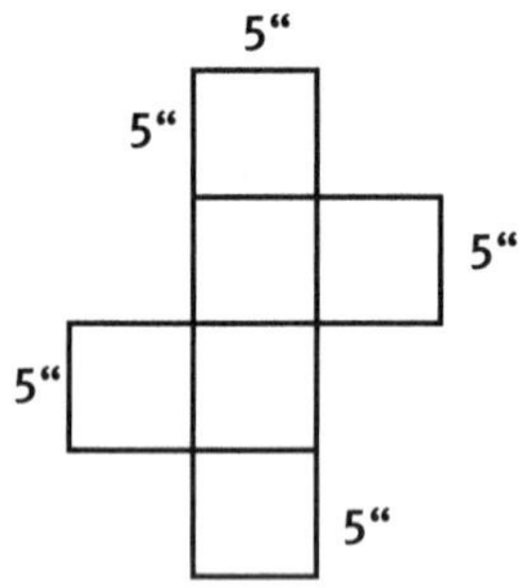

____

❸

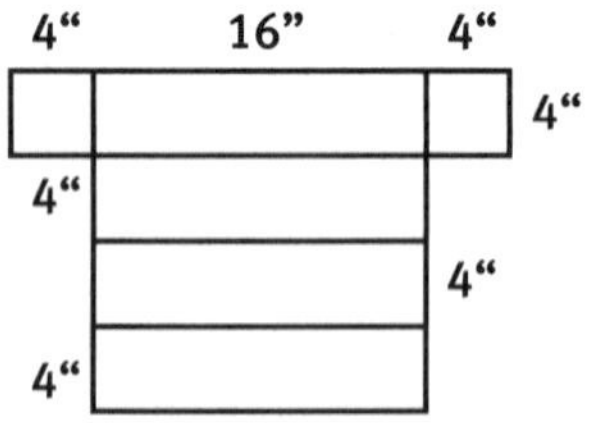

____

❹

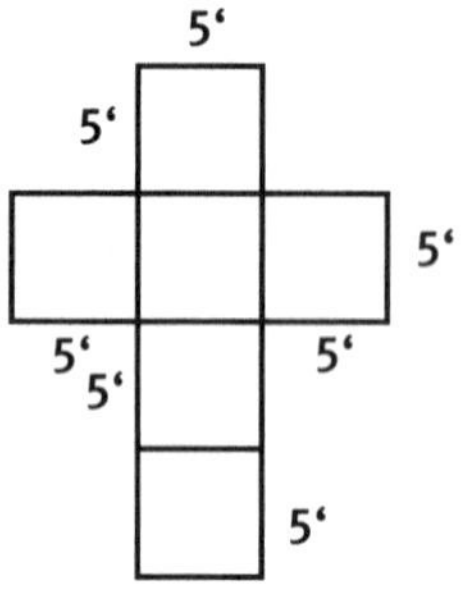

____

❺

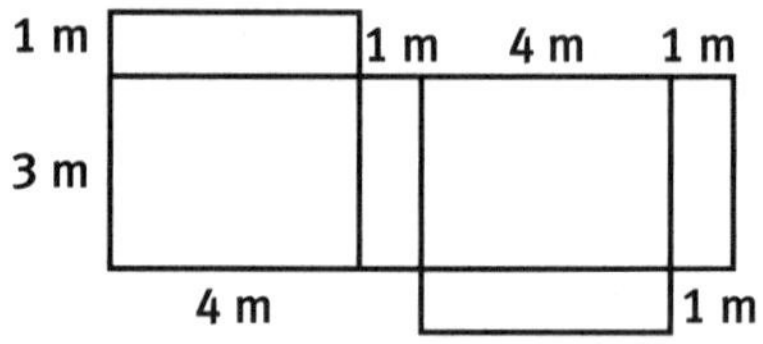

____

❻

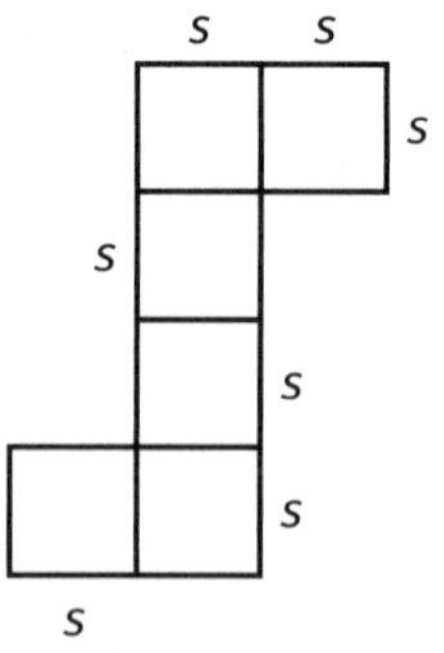

____

Name ______________________ **Date** ____________

Student Edition • page 503

For each of the following nets, decide whether it would make a closed box if you cut it out and folded along the remaining line segments. If so, give the total surface area of the box. If not, write *no.*

7

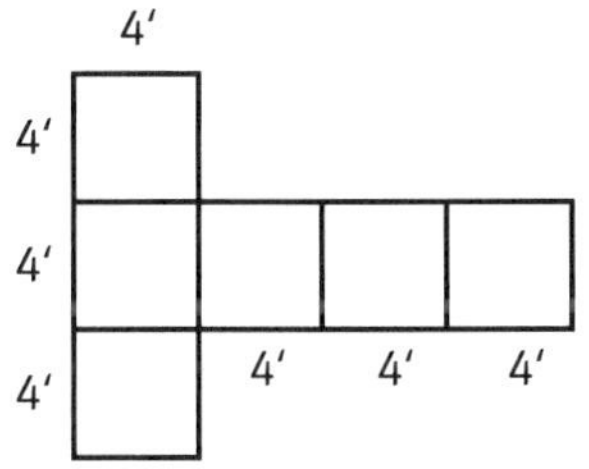

____

10

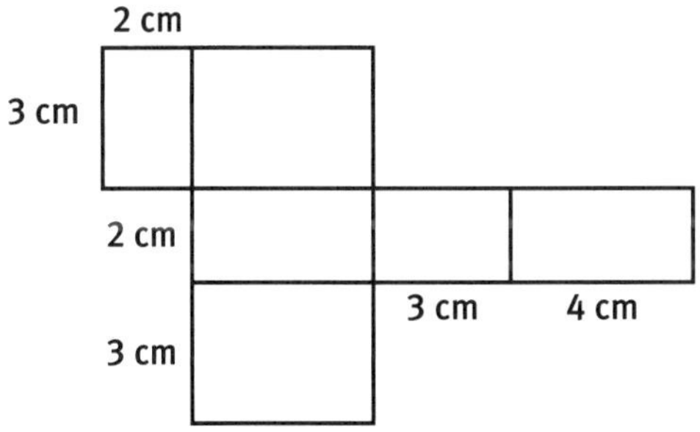

____

8

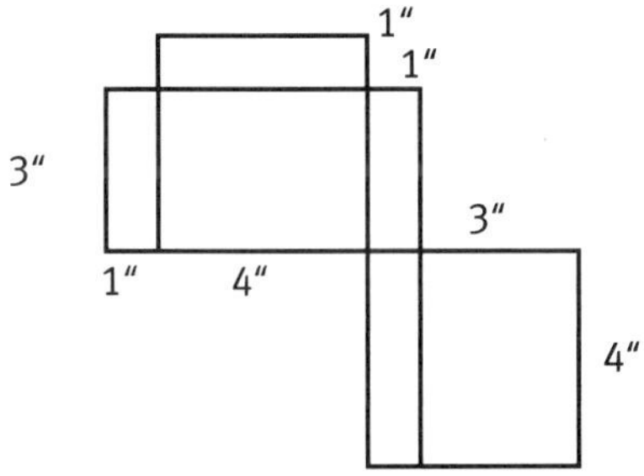

____

11

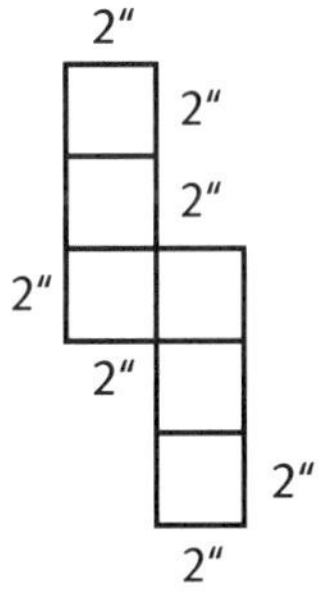

____

9

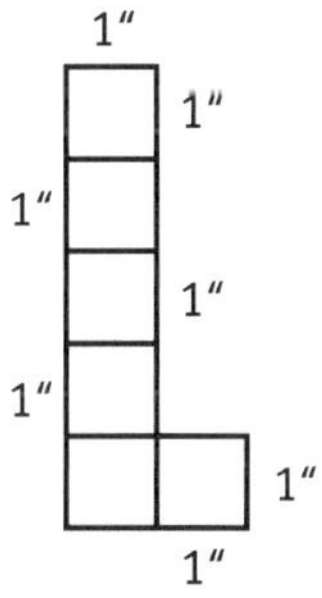

____

12

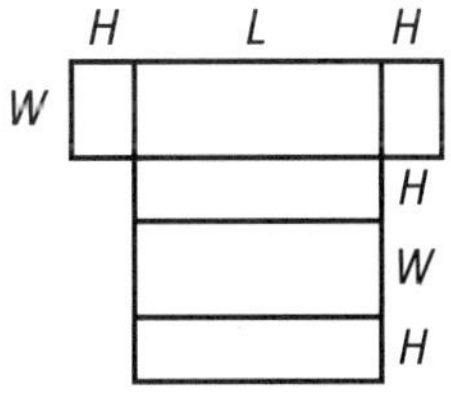

____

LESSON 10.12

Student Edition • pages 504–505

Draw a net for the figures in Problems 13–16. Calculate the total surface area for each space figure.

13. A cube 5 centimeters on a side ______

14. A cube 3 centimeters on a side ______

15. A rectangular box that is 3" by 4" by 5" ______

16. A rectangular box that is 3" by 3" by 5" ______

Calculate the total surface area. Draw a net if it helps.

17. A rectangular box that is $\frac{1}{2}$" by 1" by 2" ______

18. A cube that is $\frac{1}{2}$ inch on a side ______

19. A cube that is 0.5 centimeter on a side ______

20. A rectangular box that is 0.7 cm by 0.3 cm by 1.2 cm ______

21. A rectangular box that is 1.25 cm by 2.5 cm by 3 cm ______

22. A rectangular box that is $1\frac{1}{4}$" by $2\frac{1}{2}$" by 3" ______

In order to answer the following questions, you may want to put cubes together to make the space figures. Calculating the total length of all the edges may seem easier if you look at the actual figure rather than at the net.

23. If the edges of a cube are each 1 unit long, what is the total length of all the edges? What is the total surface area of the cube? What is the volume of the cube?

______

______

______

Name ______________________ Date ____________

Student Edition • page 505

24 If the edges of a cube are each 2 units long, what is the total length of all the edges? What is the total surface area of the cube? What is the volume of the cube?

____

____

____

25 If the edges of a cube are each 3 units long, what is the total length of all the edges? What is the total surface area of the cube? What is the volume of the cube?

____

____

____

26 Using the information from Problems 23, 24, and 25, complete the following table.

Length of one edge	1 unit	2 units	3 units
Total length of all edges	12 units		
Surface area		24 $units^2$	
Volume			27 $units^3$

27 Look at your table. By what could you multiply the numbers for the first cube in order to find the corresponding numbers for the second cube's total length of the edges, surface area, and volume? ____________

28 By what could you multiply the numbers for the first cube in order to find the corresponding numbers for the third cube's total length of the edges, surface area, and volume? ____________

LESSON 10.13

Volume

Student Edition • pages 506–507

Find the volume of each solid.

❶

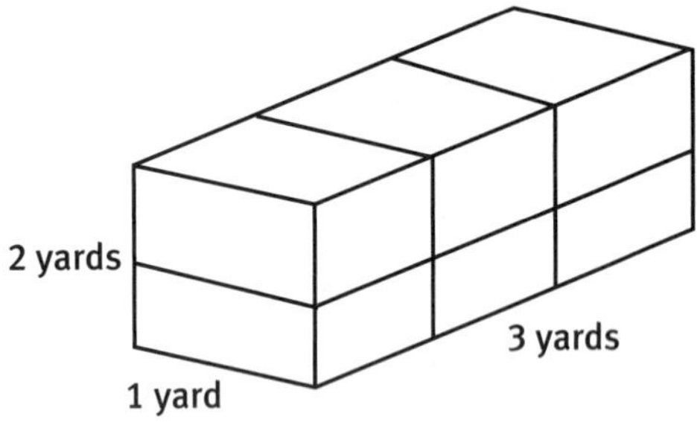

____

❷

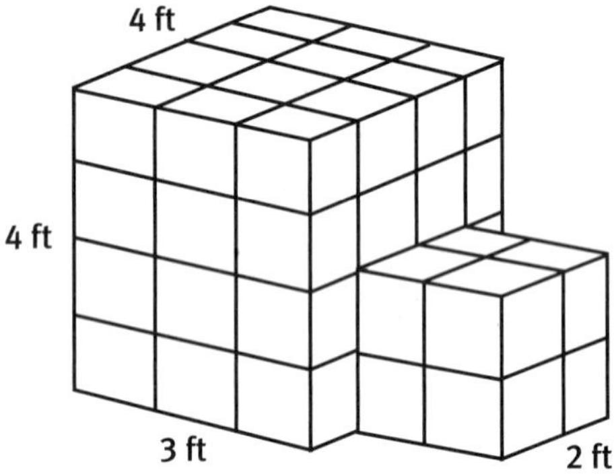

____

What is the volume of each of these rectangular boxes in cubic units?

❸

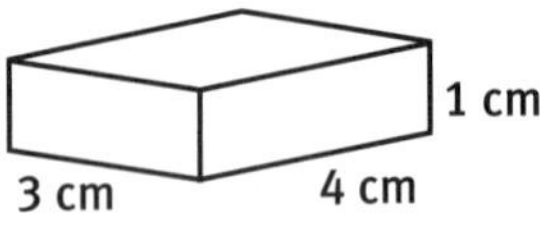

____

❹

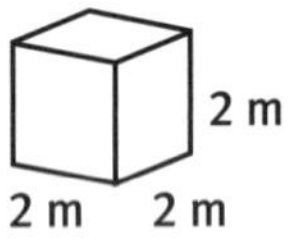

____

❺

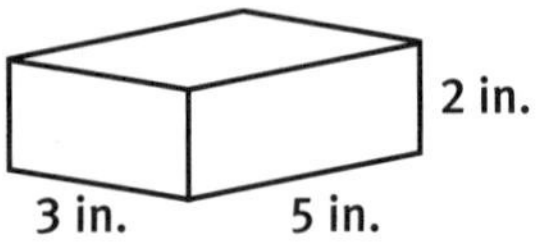

____

❻

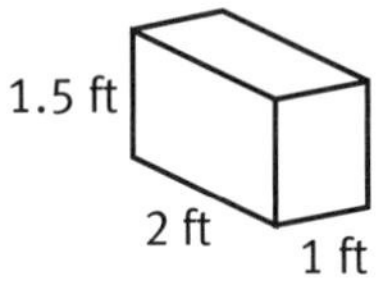

____

What is the volume of each box?

❼ 4 in. by 3 in. by 3 in. ________

❽ 3 ft by 3 ft by 3 ft ________

❾ 3 in. by 12 in. by 0.5 in. ________

❿ 5 in. by 4 in. by 1 ft ________

Name ______________________ **Date** ____________

Student Edition • page 507

Solve the following problems. Be sure to use correct units.

11 What is the volume in liters of a water-filled cube 10 cm on each side?

____

12 Extended Response Brent and Sarah are helping to make scenery for a school play. They need 6 figures like the one below. They are going to cut the figures from a large rectangular sheet of purple paper that is 40 centimeters wide and 100 centimeters long.

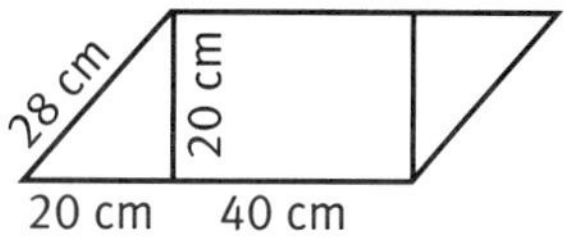

a. Sarah says they will need more paper. How could she know this?

____

____

b. Draw a picture to find out how many figures Brent and Sarah can cut from the single sheet of purple paper.

c. How many sheets of paper do Brent and Sarah need? ____________

13 Mr. Chan has a rectangular garden that he wants to fertilize. The garden is 20 meters long and 18 meters wide. Each bag of fertilizer can cover 100 square meters.

a. What is the area of Mr. Chan's garden? ____________

b. How many bags of fertilizer should he buy? Will he have any fertilizer left over?

____

LESSON 10.13

Student Edition • **page 508**

The bulletin board in Mrs. Ruiz's classroom is a rectangle that is 3 meters long and 1 meter high. She wants to display students' drawings. Each picture is on a sheet of paper 20 centimeters long and 20 centimeters wide.

14. Can she display a picture from every one of the 30 students without the pictures overlapping? ____________

15. What is the greatest number of pictures she could display without overlapping? Find the area and perimeter of each figure. ____________

Find **the area and perimeter of each figure.**

16. 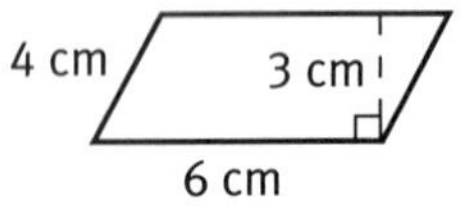

____

17. 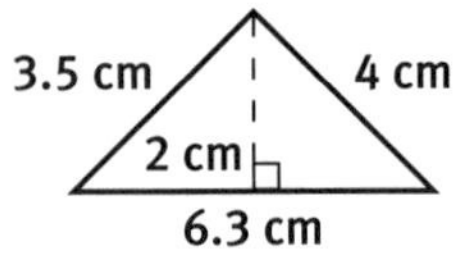

____

18. 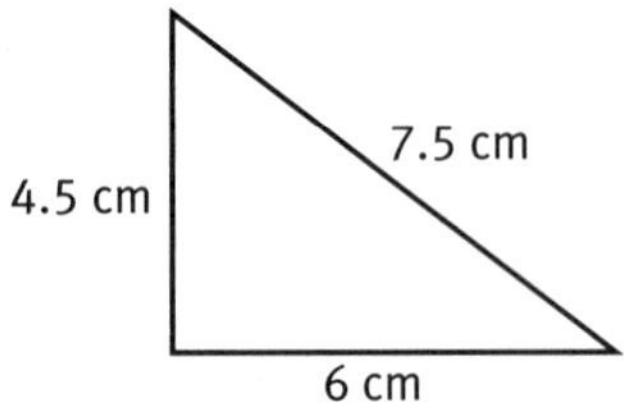

____

Solve **the following problems. Be sure to use correct units.**

19. Draw a rectangle with an area of 15 cm^2 and a perimeter of 16 cm.

20. Liang works at Waterworld and wants to figure out how much water the new dolphin's swimming pool will hold. It measures 320 meters long, 150 meters wide, and 11 meters deep. How many cubic meters of water would it hold if it were filled to the top? ____________

21. Ms. Jain built a wooden storage shed in her backyard, and she wants to paint the outside of it. The shed is 6 feet tall, 8 feet wide, and 10 feet deep. She needs to paint the 4 sides (including the door) and the flat roof, and she wants to use 2 coats of paint. She is using cans of paint that cover 100 square feet each. How many cans will she need? ____________

Name ______________________ **Date** __________

Student Edition • **page 509**

22 The Sanfords are planning to fence in their backyard. The yard is 56 feet across and 25 feet from front to back. Their house is 42 feet across and 31 feet from front to back. They would like the fence to start at a back corner of the house, run to the side of the yard, go around the sides and back of the yard, and run back to the house. How much fencing must they buy?

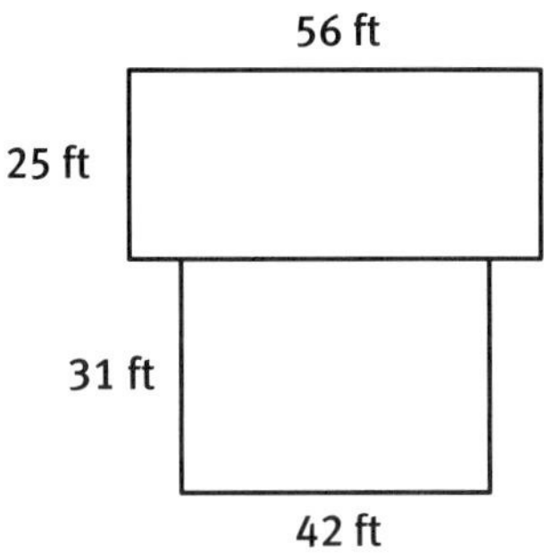

____

23 Jabari is looking for an apartment. He needs a lot of space in his bedroom (130 square feet), so he wants to check to make sure each apartment he spends time visiting has a large enough bedroom. If the apartment manager at BareBones apartments says the bedroom in apartment A is 11 feet long, 10 feet wide, and 10 feet tall, will there be enough space? Explain your answer.

____

____

24 Holly needs to find a storage container for her cousin's toy blocks. If each block is a 4 centimeter by 4 centimeter by 4 centimeter cube,

a. how much storage space does she need to hold 30 blocks? __________

b. will they fit in a container that is 40 centimeters by 10 centimeters by 4 centimeters? __________

c. **Extended Response** If Holly's container is 100 centimeters long, 10 centimeters wide, and 3 centimeters tall, will the blocks fit? Explain.

____

____

25 Igor has 32 feet of fence to make a pen for his pet goose, Gurtrude. If he makes a rectangular pen, what is the greatest amount of area in which Gurtrude can roam? What should the dimensions of the pen be?

____

____

Exploring Problem Solving

Student Edition • pages 510–511

Thomas Jefferson proposed a new square-based system, known as the *Public Land Survey System*. This system made it easier to describe and keep track of millions of pieces of land. Any square of land could be located by the name of the township it was in, the section of that township, the part of that section, and so on. See the diagram below.

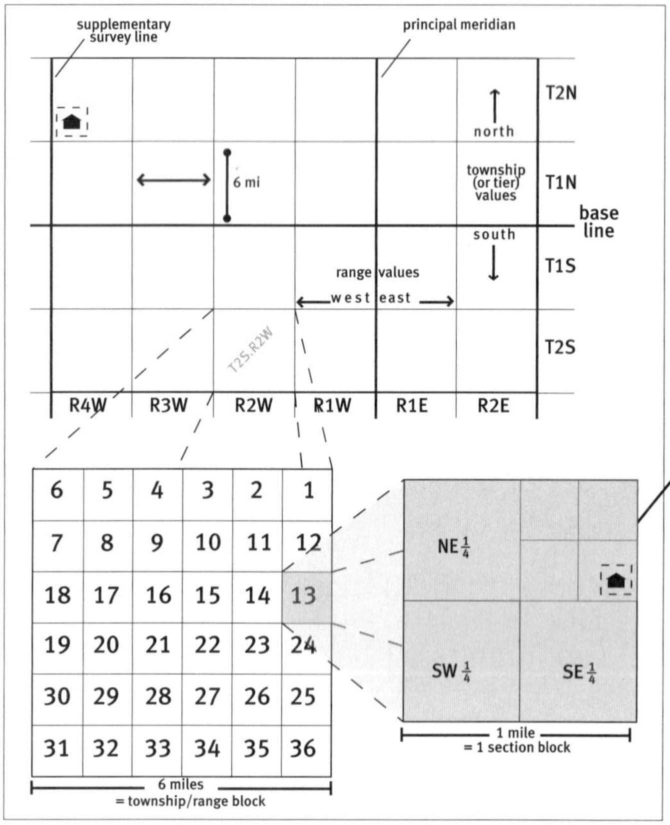

This homestead would be described as the southeast quarter of the southeast quarter of the northeast quarter, section 13, township 2 south, range 2 west or simply:

SE $\frac{1}{4}$, SE $\frac{1}{4}$, NE $\frac{1}{4}$, sec. 13, T2S, R2W.

Think about and discuss these questions.

1. How is the Public Land Survey System like a standard coordinate grid? How is it different?

___

___

Name ______________________ **Date** ______________

Student Edition • pages 511–512

2. In this system, how would you describe the location of the block marked with the star? ______________

3. How many acres of land are represented by one of the small squares in the bottom right diagram? (One square mile is 640 acres.) ______________

4. How many yards of fencing would it take to enclose a piece of land described as NW $\frac{1}{4}$, SE $\frac{1}{4}$, sec. 9 of T1N, R3W? ______________

Imagine you are one of four contestants on a game show.

> Welcome to *Homesteader's Challenge,* where land is up for grabs and the usual rules of homesteading do not apply. On our show, you can acquire a piece of earth just by walking around it. Here's how we play:
>
> We'll drop off our four contestants somewhere out west and let them start walking at 8 A.M. They'd better come prepared with food, water, and a good plan, because whoever walks around the most land in 10 hours keeps it.
>
> The show begins. Here is what the other contestants do.

Name	Plan	Result
Luka	Walk straight until 1 P.M. Then walk east until 3:30 P.M. Then head straight back to the starting point.	Enclosed 0 square miles
Sylvia	I'll walk in a small circle to make sure I get back to start. Then, if there's time, I'll walk in another circle. Just keep walking in circles until time runs out.	Made 4 complete circles
Tyrese	I know I can walk 30 miles in one day, so I'll walk west 14 miles, then walk south, then east, and then north.	Made it back after exactly 30 miles

Student Edition • page 512

Solve these problems.

5. Why didn't Luka's plan work?

6. Would Luka's plan work if he walked twice as fast the whole day?

7. Could Sylvia have enclosed only one circular piece of land? Explain.

8. What are some possible shapes that Sylvia's path could have enclosed?

9. How many square miles did Tyrese's path enclose? ______

10. How could Tyrese have enclosed more land and still have walked west, south, east, and north for a total of 30 miles?

11. What will your plan be? Why?

12. What is the most land you could win by walking a total of 30 miles?

Cumulative Review

Name ______________________ Date ____________

Student Edition • page 513

Multiplying and Dividing Integers Lesson 4.9

Multiply or divide.

1. $-5 \times 4 =$ ____________
2. $-5 \times (-4) =$ ____________
3. $3 \times (-8) =$ ____________
4. $-24 \div 8 =$ ____________
5. $56 \div (-8) =$ ____________
6. $-30 \div (-6) =$ ____________
7. $16 \div (-4) =$ ____________
8. $-49 \div 7 =$ ____________

Linear Equations Lesson 5.12

Solve for *x* or *y*.

9. $\frac{x}{2} + 12 = 17$ ____________
10. $3x + 150 = 0$ ____________
11. $-6x + (-19.3) = -50.5$ ____________
12. $100 - 3(16) = y$ ____________
13. $\frac{y}{3} + 60 = 30$ ____________
14. $15(5) - 69 = y$ ____________

Cumulative Review

Student Edition • pages 513–514

Multiplying Mixed Numbers Lesson 7.2

Multiply. Check to see that your answers make sense.

15. $2\frac{2}{5} \times 4\frac{1}{6} =$ ______

16. $3\frac{1}{2} \times 3\frac{1}{7} =$ ______

17. $1\frac{1}{3} \times 2\frac{1}{6} =$ ______

18. $\frac{3}{4} \times 6\frac{1}{2} =$ ______

19. $2\frac{1}{4} \times 5\frac{1}{7} =$ ______

20. $\frac{7}{8} \times 1\frac{1}{4} =$ ______

Using Mixed Numbers Lesson 7.9

Solve.

21. Rick's school held a fund-raiser with the goal of raising $7,000. So far, they have reached $1\frac{2}{5}$ of their goal. How much money has the school raised? ______

22. Suki, Jojo, and Rita each spent time working on a group project. If Suki has spent 2 hours, Jojo has spent $2\frac{1}{4}$ hours, and Rita has spent $1\frac{3}{4}$ hours on the project, what fraction of the work has been done so far by Jojo? ______

Averages Lesson 8.1

Solve.

23. Benny and José had already bowled 3 games. Benny's average was 115 and José's was 121. If José then bowled a 117 in his last game, what would Benny have to bowl in his last game to finish with a higher average than José? ______

24. Micah received grades of 75, 89, and 85 on his first three English papers. On his next paper, he received an 84. Did his average go up or down? ______

Cumulative Review

Name ______________________________ Date ______________

Student Edition • page 514

Comparing Ratios Lesson 8.5

25 Which camp basketball team has the better record—the red team with 11 wins out of 23 games or the blue team with 15 wins out of 29 games? How many more games will the team with fewer wins need to win in a row to beat the other team's record? ______________

26 Flour comes in 3-pound and 5-pound bags. If the smaller bag sells for $1.89 and the larger bag costs $2.99, which is the better buy? ______________

Area of Parallelograms Lesson 10.2

27 If the area of parallelogram *ABCD* is 30 square inches, what could the dimensions of its base and height be? ______________

a. 5 in. × 10 in.

b. 6 in. × 6 in.

c. 5 in. × 6 in.

28 What is the area of parallelogram *EFGH* with a base of 8 meters, height of 4 meters, and side length of 5 meters? ______________

Area of a Circle Lesson 10.4

29 What is the area of a circle (to the nearest whole unit) if its radius is equal to 10 meters? ______________

30 A large pie is 10 inches in diameter, and a small pie is 6 inches in diameter. Is the large pie more than twice as big (in area) as the small pie? Show your work. ______________

Key Ideas Review

Student Edition • page 515

Find the area of each figure.

1. 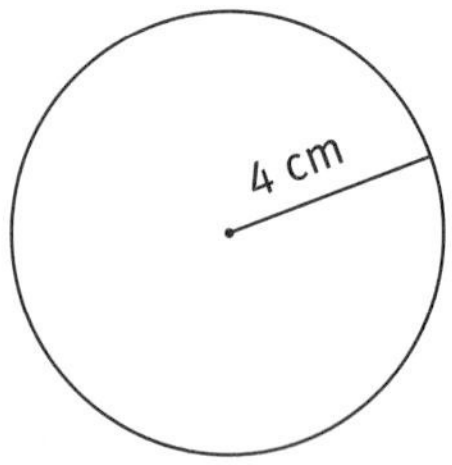

____

2. 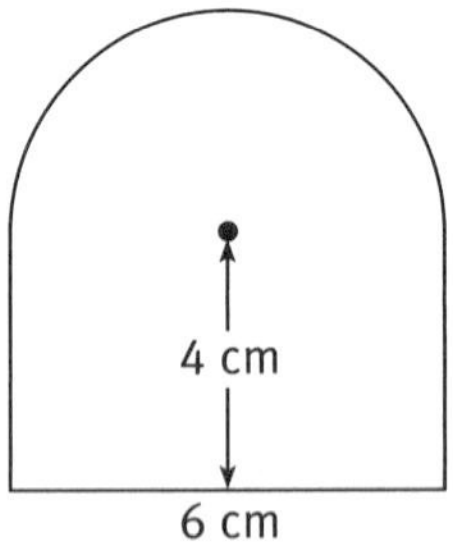

____

3. Find the volume of the cube below.

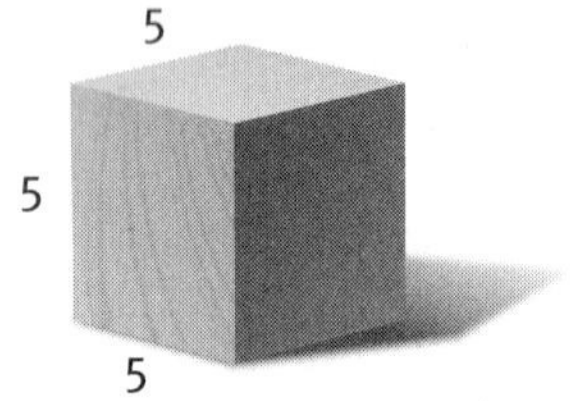

____

4. Compute the surface area of the square pyramid.

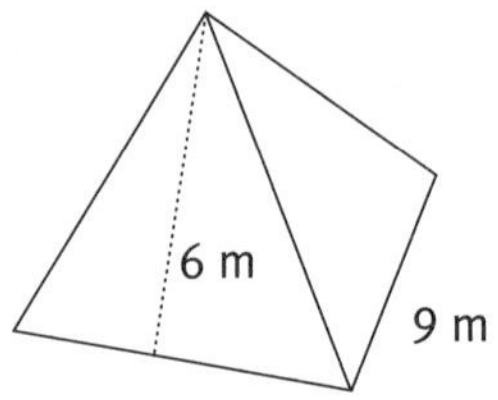

____

5. What figure does the net create?

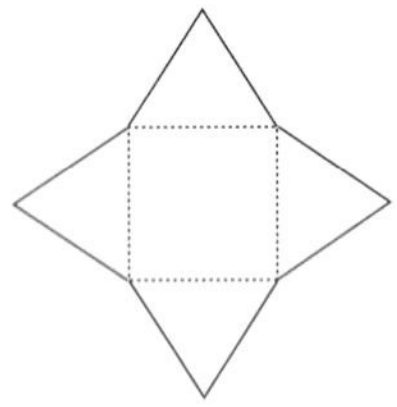

____

6. Describe a combined translation and rotation that would place one of the congruent figures on top of the other.

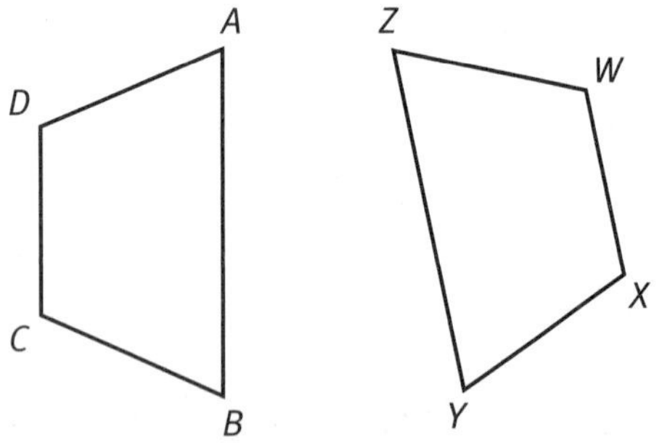

____

Chapter Review

Name ______________________ **Date** ____________

Student Edition • page 516

Given the following measures for the diameter of a circle, find the circumference (to the nearest whole unit). **Lesson 10.1**

1. 21 feet ____________
2. 200 centimeters ____________
3. 10 miles ____________
4. If you know the circumference of a circle is 110 centimeters, what is the diameter (to the nearest whole unit)? ____________
5. If the circumference of a circle is 62.8 miles, what is its radius (to the nearest whole unit)? ____________

Find the area of each figure. **Lessons 10.2–10.3**

6. 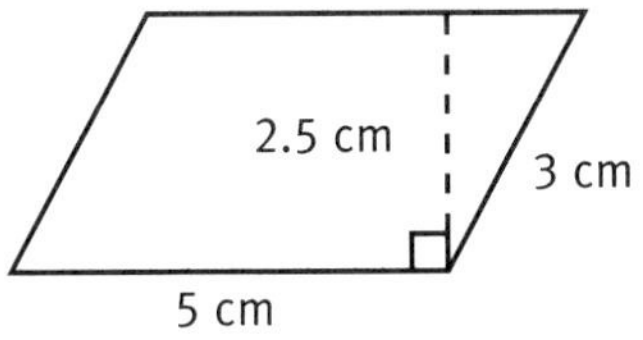

____

8. 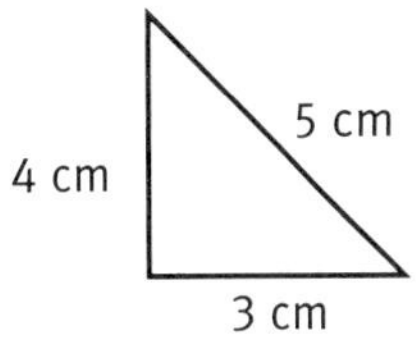

____

7. 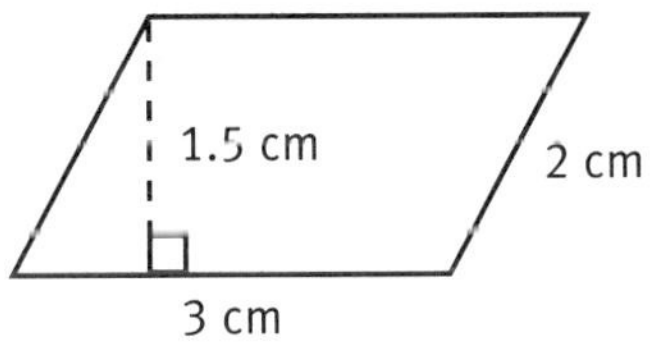

____

9. 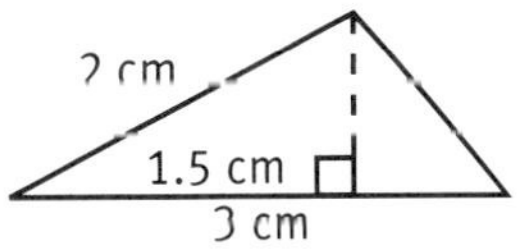

____

Using 3.14 for π, find the circumference and area of each circle. **Lesson 10.4**

10. radius = 40 centimeters ______________________________
11. diameter = 1 centimeter ______________________________

Chapter Review

Student Edition • page 517

Find the area of the irregular figures below. Use 3.14 for π. **Lesson 10.5**

12

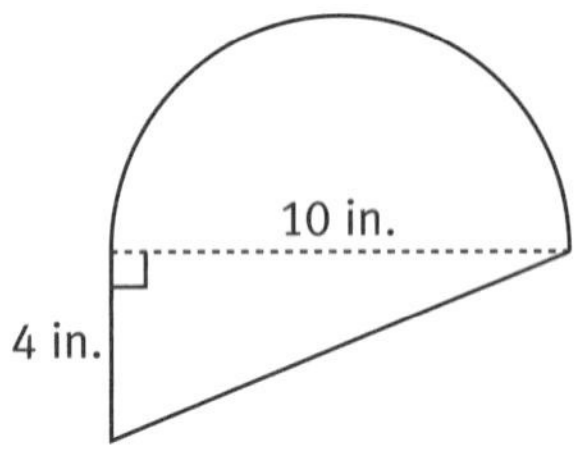

____

13

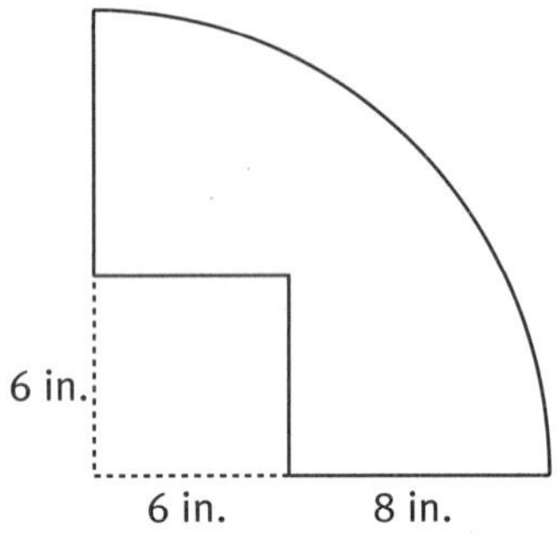

____

For each of the following letters, answer the following: How many lines of symmetry does it have? Does it have rotational symmetry? If so, give the angle of rotation. **Lesson 10.7**

14 H ______________

15 T ______________

16 J ______________

Look at the following nets. Can they be folded into a space figure? If so, write the figure's number of edges, vertices, and faces. **Lesson 10.10**

17

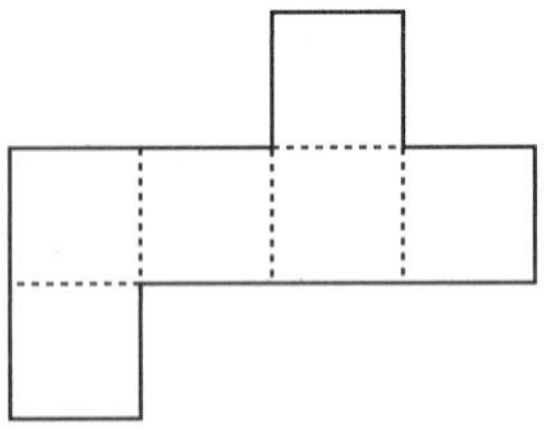

____

18

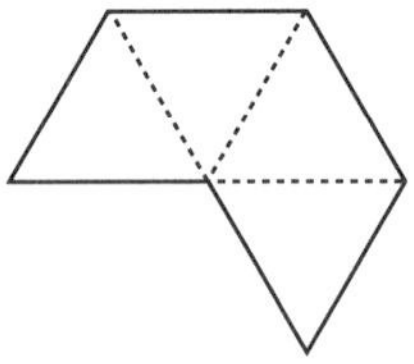

____

Find the volume and surface area of each box. **Lessons 10.12–10.13**

19 5 inches by 3 inches by 2 inches ______________

20 5 centimeters by 5 centimeters by 5 centimeters ______________

CHAPTER 10

Practice Test

Name ______________________ Date ____________

Student Edition • page 518

Find the circumference and area of each circle given the radius. Use 3.14 for π.

1. $r = 9$ centimeters

____

2. $r = 3.5$ centimeters

____

Find the area of each figure.

3.

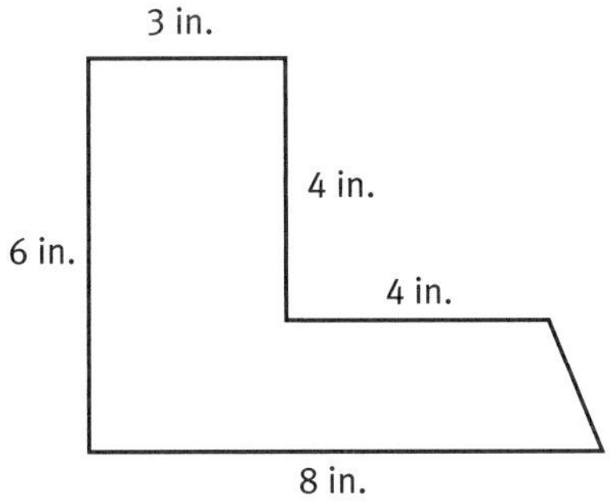

____

4.

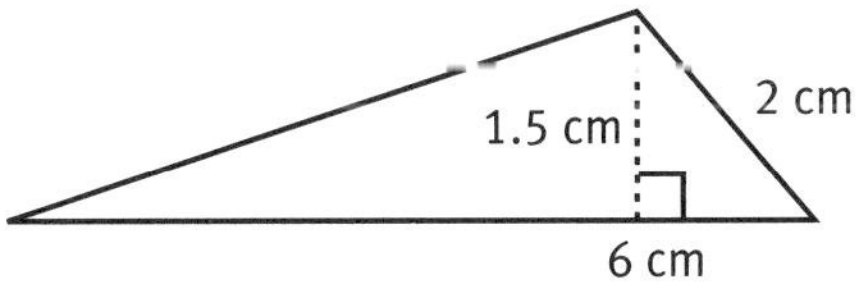

____

5.

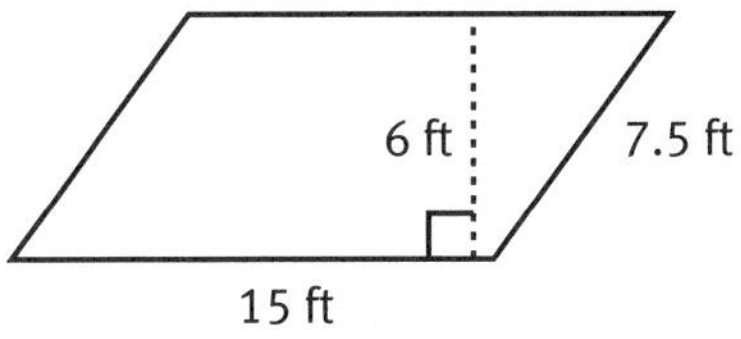

____

6.

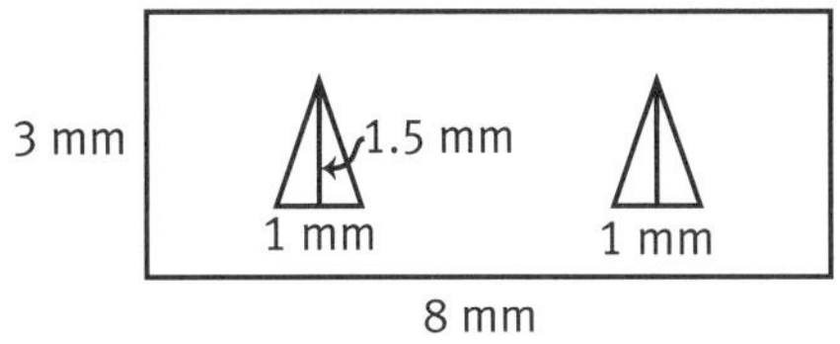

____

Identify the figure made by each net.

7.

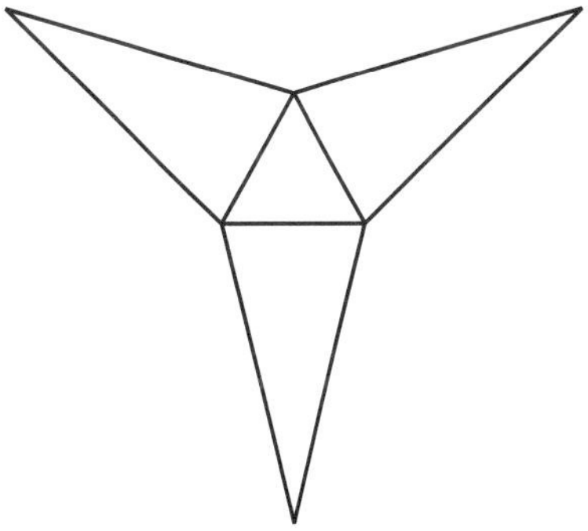

____

8.

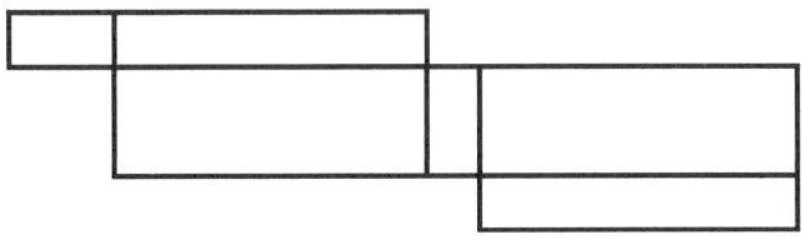

____

9.

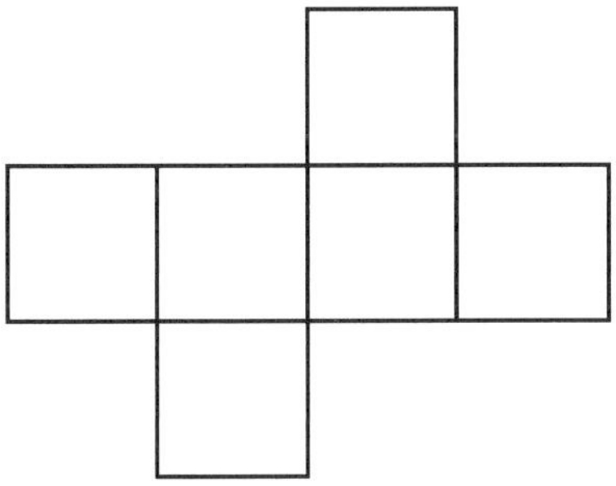

____

Student Edition • page 519

Choose the correct answer.

10. Which shows a rotation of this figure?

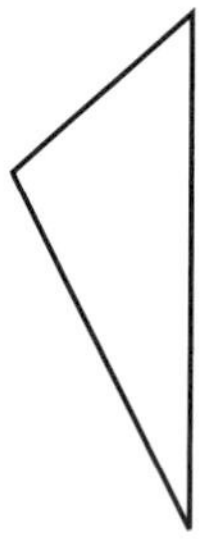

Ⓐ  Ⓑ 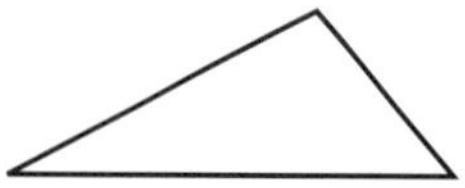

Ⓒ 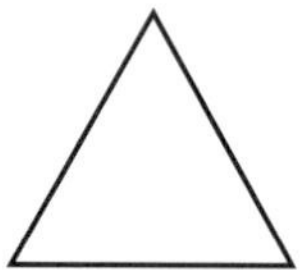 Ⓓ 

11. How many faces does a square pyramid have?

Ⓐ 8 Ⓑ 7

Ⓒ 6 Ⓓ 5

12. Which figure has rotational symmetry?

Ⓐ  Ⓑ 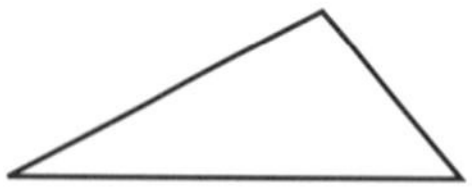

Ⓒ 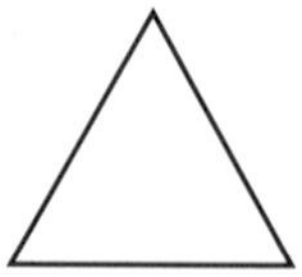 Ⓓ 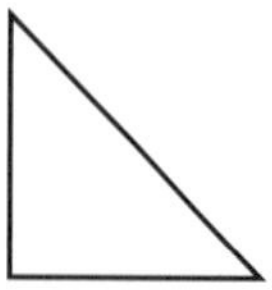

13. Which figure is a cylinder?

Ⓐ  Ⓑ 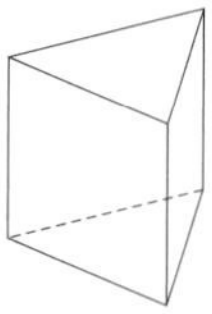

Ⓒ 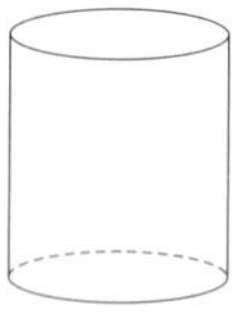 Ⓓ 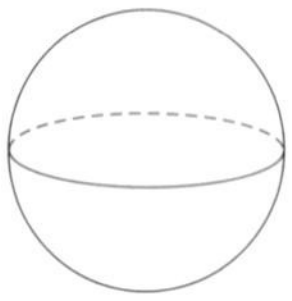

14. What is the volume of a box measuring 4 inches × 6 inches × 6 inches?

Ⓐ 144 in.^{3} Ⓑ 10 in.^{3}

Ⓒ 24 in.^{3} Ⓓ 5 in.^{3}

15. What is the diameter of a circle with a circumference of 111 feet?

Ⓐ about 107.86 ft

Ⓑ about 55.5 ft

Ⓒ about 35.35 ft

Ⓓ about 27.75 ft

16. Which shows a reflection of this figure?

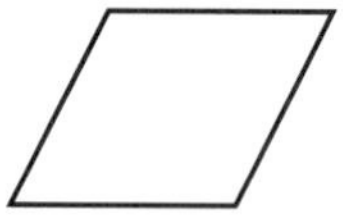

Ⓐ  Ⓑ 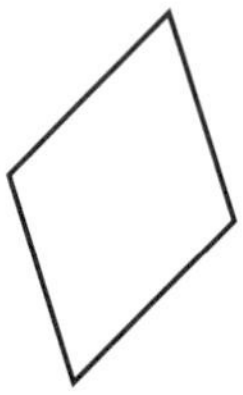

Ⓒ 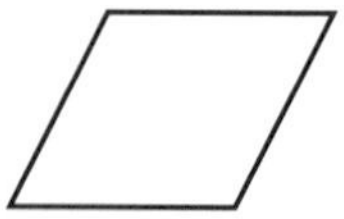 Ⓓ 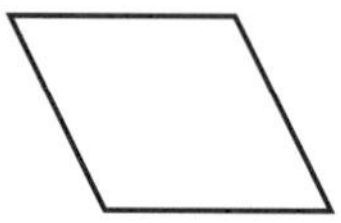

Practice Test

Name ______________________ **Date** ____________

Student Edition • **page 520**

17. Which of the following is a triangular prism?

Ⓐ 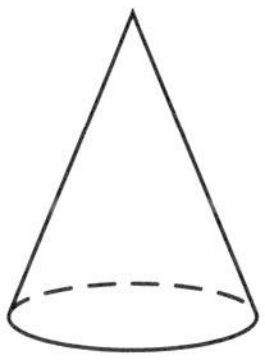

Ⓑ 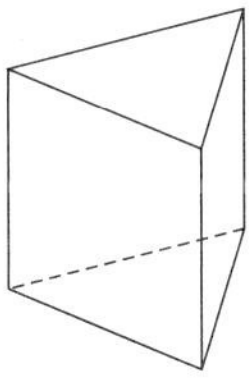

Ⓒ 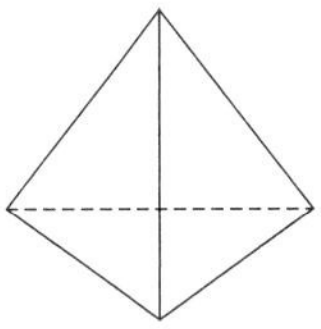

Ⓓ 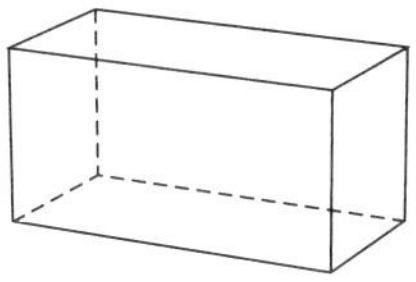

18. How many lines of symmetry does this figure have?

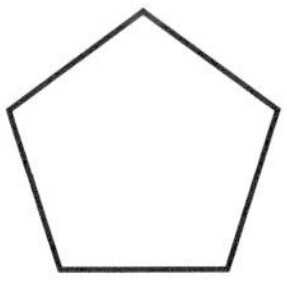

Ⓐ 5 Ⓑ 3

Ⓒ 2 Ⓓ 1

19. The measures of two angles in a triangle are 125° and 15°. What is the measure of the third angle?

Ⓐ 50° Ⓑ 40°

Ⓒ 10° Ⓓ 5°

20. Which ordered pair does *not* satisfy this function rule?

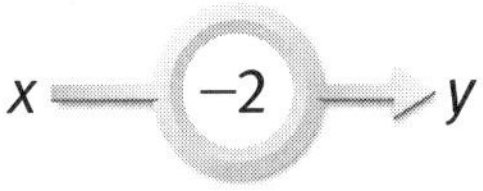

Ⓐ (20, 18) Ⓑ (15, 13)

Ⓒ (10, 8) Ⓓ (−6, −4)

21. The scale on a map is 1 inch = 25 miles. The distance between two towns measures 5.5 inches. How many miles are between the two towns?

Ⓐ 50 Ⓑ 75

Ⓒ 125 Ⓓ 137.5

22. Owen ate $\frac{1}{4}$ of his sandwich for a snack and shared $\frac{1}{5}$ of it with a friend. What fraction of his sandwich does he have left?

Ⓐ $\frac{2}{5}$ Ⓑ $\frac{1}{2}$

Ⓒ $\frac{11}{20}$ Ⓓ $\frac{19}{20}$

23. Which of the following is a trapezoid?

Ⓐ 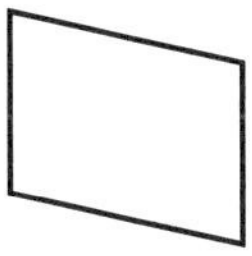

Ⓑ 

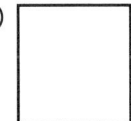

Ⓒ 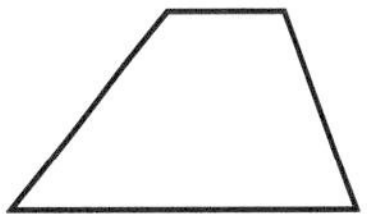

Ⓓ 

Practice Test

Student Edition • page 521

Extended Response **Solve.**

24. Describe a series of translations, rotations, and reflections that will make $\triangle DEF$ fit on top of the $\triangle ABC$.

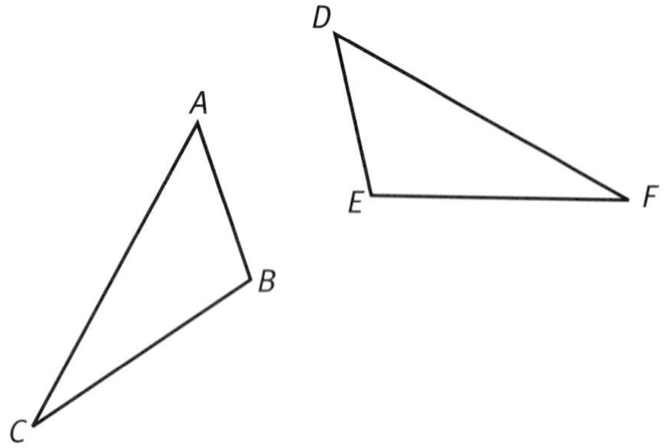

____

____

____

25. The wall in Mr. Taylor's classroom is 6 meters long and 3 meters high. The wall has a window that is 0.5 meter wide and 1 meter high. He wants to cover the wall with colorful paper that his students have decorated. Each picture is 25 centimeters by 25 centimeters.

a. What is the area, in square centimeters, of the wall that Mr. Taylor can cover with the paper? ____________

b. How many uncut sheets of colorful paper could Mr. Taylor fit? Explain.

____

____

____

Name ______________________ Date ______________

Rational Number and Percent Applications

Student Edition • page 523

Imagine you are searching for a sunken ship. After studying the ship's logs and other records, you have narrowed the search to a rectangle $5\frac{9}{10}$ miles long and $2\frac{3}{10}$ miles wide. Somewhere at the bottom of the ocean, within that rectangle, lies the vessel you seek.

You know how much area you can cover each hour. In order to estimate how much time the search could take, you want to approximate the area of the rectangle. You make a diagram to help you.

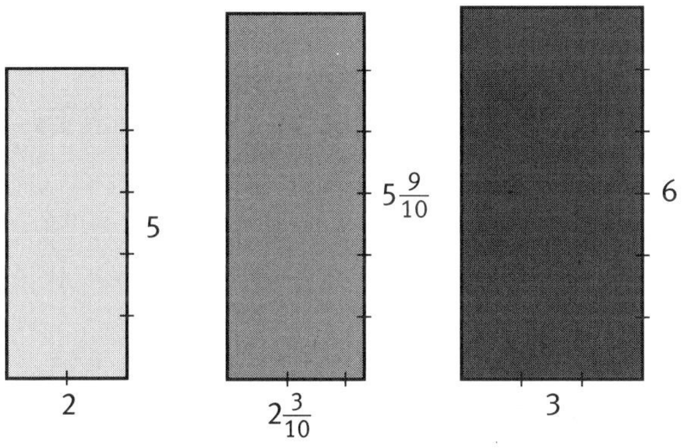

Work in groups to answer the following questions.

1. How can you use your diagram to approximate the area of the search? ______________________
2. How could you use the diagram to approximate the product of 5.9×2.3? ______________________
3. Without calculating the exact area, do you think the search area is closer to the area of the left-hand rectangle or the area of the right-hand rectangle? ______________________
4. Check your estimate. Find a way to determine the exact area of the search region, and then compare it to the areas of the right-hand and left-hand rectangles.

____

____

LESSON 11.1

Approximating Products of Decimals

Student Edition • page 525

Fill each blank with <, >, or =.

1. 3.4×2.2 ______ 3×2
2. 3.8×2.8 ______ 3×2
3. 2×3 ______ 3.95×2.95
4. 4×3 ______ 3.95×2.95
5. 6.1×8.9 ______ 7×9
6. 1.8×0.6 ______ 2×1
7. 10.25×7.5 ______ 10×7
8. 7.5×10.25 ______ 11×8
9. 1.5×1.5 ______ 2×2
10. 1×1 ______ 1.5×1.5
11. 0.75×14.2 ______ 1×15
12. 0.25×5.5 ______ 1×6

These problems were done on Ying's broken calculator.
Insert the decimal point in the correct place.

13. $3.7 \times 1.8 = 666$
14. $0.45 \times 45 = 2025$
15. $4.1 \times 8.7 = 3567$
16. $3.5 \times 3.5 = 1225$
17. $35 \times 3.5 = 1225$
18. $1.08 \times 5.4 = 5832$
19. $32.6 \times 2.3 = 7498$
20. $35 \times 0.035 = 1225$
21. $32.6 \times 23 = 7498$
22. $2.5 \times 2.5 = 625$
23. $32.6 \times 0.23 = 7498$
24. $25 \times 0.25 = 625$

LESSON 11.1 **Name** ______________________ **Date** ______________

Student Edition • page 525

Without using a pencil and paper or a calculator, decide which is correct. In each case, only one answer is correct.

25. $5.3 \times 4.2 =$ ______________

a. 12.16

b. 22.26

c. 32.26

26. $2.25 \times 2.25 =$ ______________

a. 5.0625

b. 3.9165

c. 10.615

27. $10.5 \times 10.5 =$ ______________

a. 110.25

b. 95.25

c. 211.25

28. $0.75 \times 1.5 =$ ______________

a. 2.015

b. 7.555

c. 1.125

29. $3.4 \times 0.92 =$ ______________

a. 4.098

b. 3.128

c. 34.92

30. $6.7 \times 8.1 =$ ______________

a. 45.72

b. 27.52

c. 54.27

LESSON 11.2

Multiplying Two Decimals

Student Edition • pages 527–528

Multiply. Check to see that your answers make sense.

1. $\begin{array}{r} 5 \\ \times\ 4 \\ \hline \end{array}$

2. $\begin{array}{r} 50 \\ \times\ 40 \\ \hline \end{array}$

3. $\begin{array}{r} 0.05 \\ \times\ 0.04 \\ \hline \end{array}$

4. $\begin{array}{r} 0.5 \\ \times\ 0.4 \\ \hline \end{array}$

5. $\begin{array}{r} 0.5 \\ \times\ \ \ 4 \\ \hline \end{array}$

6. $\begin{array}{r} 5 \\ \times\ 0.4 \\ \hline \end{array}$

7. $\begin{array}{r} 9 \\ \times\ 3 \\ \hline \end{array}$

8. $\begin{array}{r} 900 \\ \times\ 300 \\ \hline \end{array}$

9. $\begin{array}{r} 0.09 \\ \times\ \ 0.3 \\ \hline \end{array}$

10. $\begin{array}{r} 7 \\ \times\ 8 \\ \hline \end{array}$

11. $\begin{array}{r} 700 \\ \times\ 800 \\ \hline \end{array}$

12. $\begin{array}{r} 0.007 \\ \times\ 0.008 \\ \hline \end{array}$

13. $\begin{array}{r} 0.000007 \\ \times\ \ \ \ \ \ \ 0.08 \\ \hline \end{array}$

14. $\begin{array}{r} 9 \\ \times\ 7 \\ \hline \end{array}$

15. $\begin{array}{r} 9000 \\ \times\ \ \ 70 \\ \hline \end{array}$

16. $\begin{array}{r} 0.0009 \\ \times\ \ \ \ 0.7 \\ \hline \end{array}$

17. $\begin{array}{r} 0.09 \\ \times\ \ \ 7 \\ \hline \end{array}$

18. $\begin{array}{r} 0.09 \\ \times\ \ 70 \\ \hline \end{array}$

LESSON 11.2 **Name** ______________________ **Date** ____________

Student Edition • page 528

19
$$\begin{array}{r} 0.09 \\ \times\ 700 \\ \hline \end{array}$$

20
$$\begin{array}{r} 1.23 \\ \times\ 2.44 \\ \hline \end{array}$$

21
$$\begin{array}{r} 12.3 \\ \times\ 0.244 \\ \hline \end{array}$$

22
$$\begin{array}{r} 12.3 \\ \times\ 24.4 \\ \hline \end{array}$$

23
$$\begin{array}{r} 123 \\ \times\ 2.44 \\ \hline \end{array}$$

24
$$\begin{array}{r} 1.23 \\ \times\ 24.4 \\ \hline \end{array}$$

Solve the following problems.

25 The recycling center pays $0.29 a pound for aluminum. Dan has collected 75.6 pounds of aluminum cans. How much money will he earn? ____________

26 Kelly bought 1 pound of apples for $1.29. How much would 3.5 pounds of apples cost? ____________

LESSON 11.3

Percent and Fraction Benchmarks

Student Edition • pages 531–532

Change each percent to a decimal or each decimal to a percent.

1. 12% ______
2. 200% ______
3. 1% ______
4. 12.7% ______
5. 0.517 ______
6. 0.002 ______
7. 0.065 ______
8. 10 ______

Calculate.

9. 5% sales tax on $6 ______
10. 6% sales tax on $5 ______
11. 7% sales tax on $12 ______
12. 5% of 120 ______
13. 25% of 120 ______
14. 50% of 120 ______
15. 100% of 120 ______
16. 12% of 20 ______
17. 15% of 20 ______
18. 15% of 40 ______
19. $0.72 = \frac{\quad}{100} =$ ______%
20. $0.04 = \frac{\quad}{100} =$ ______%

Solve the following problems.

21. You are buying a football with a price tag of $19.98. If sales tax is 6%, how much will you have to pay altogether? Round your answer up to the next cent. ______

LESSON 11.3 Name ______________________ Date ____________

Student Edition • pages 532–533

22 You could also answer the problem without using a calculator or paper and pencil.

a. Is $19.98 about $20? ____________

b. If you pay $0.06 tax for each dollar, what is the tax on $20? ____________

c. What is this tax added to $19.98? ____________

23 Kim is buying a book that costs $8.95. If sales tax is 6%, how much will she have to pay altogether? Round up your answer to the next cent.

a. Is $8.95 about $9? ____________

b. If you pay $0.06 tax for each dollar, what is the tax on $9? ____________

c. What is this tax added to $8.95? ____________

Solve.

24 For each of these amounts, estimate the amount of a 15% tip and the total bill, including the tip. Two problems have been done for you.

Amount (Dollars)	Estimated Tip (Dollars)	Amount Including Tip (Dollars)
36.50	5.50	42.00
18.75	3.00	21.75
30.00		
16.41		
23.31		
25.00		
20.00		
10.00		

LESSON 11.4

Computing Percent Discounts

Student Edition • pages 534–535

Compute the discounted price.

1. $20 with 15% off ____________
2. $48 with 25% off ____________
3. $50 with 35% off ____________
4. $18 with 10% off ____________
5. $67 with 30% off ____________
6. $12 with 5% off ____________

Solve.

7. Calculate the sale price of these items at the Bargain Store.

Item	Regular Price	Sale Reduction	Sale Price
oven	$569.95	$50 off	
bicycle	$79.99	$20 off	
binoculars	$39.99	50% off	
suitcase	$80.00	40% off	
alarm clock	$8.99	20% off	
suit	$89.00	20% off	
shirt	$9.99	20% off	
jeans	$15.99	25% off	
swimming suit	$19.99	25% off	
gloves	$7.99	25% off	
hat	$12.00	25% off	
coat	$65.99	25% off	

 Name ______________________ Date ____________

Student Edition • page 536

Use the advertisements below to answer the questions.

Downtown Discount Store

	Regular Price	Sale Price
Mr. Crunchy candy bars	$2.99 a box	NOW 50¢ OFF
Red Seal extinguishers	$20.99	NOW 25% OFF
Warm Wooly gloves	$12.99	Special Price $9.97
Smooth-Rite notebooks	2 for $3.99	NOW $1.50 OFF
Speed-O bicycles	$110.99	NOW 20% OFF

Wilson's General Store

	Regular Price	Sale Price
Mr. Crunchy candy bars	$2.99 a box	NOW 20% OFF
Red Seal extinguishers	$20.99	NOW $2.00 OFF
Warm Wooly gloves	$12.99	NOW 30% OFF
Smooth-Rite notebooks	2 for $3.99	NOW 30% OFF
Speed-O bicycles	$110.99	NOW $20.00 OFF

8. At which store do Mr. Crunchy candy bars cost the least? ____________

9. At which store do Red Seal fire extinguishers cost the least? ____________

10. At which store do Warm Wooly gloves cost the least? ____________

11. At which store do Smooth-Rite notebooks cost the least? ____________

12. At which store do Speed-O bicycles cost the least? ____________

13. At which store would it cost less altogether to buy one pair of Warm Wooly gloves and one Red Seal fire extinguisher? ____________

14. At which store would it cost less altogether to buy a box of Mr. Crunchy candy bars and 2 Smooth-Rite notebooks? ____________

LESSON 11.5

Computing Interest

Student Edition • page 538

Solve the following problems. Try to approximate the answers in advance.

1. The Bargain Center is advertising a sale in which every item in the store is on sale for 30% off the regular price. The store is located in a community where the sales tax is 6%. How much will you have to pay for a television that is regularly priced at $400? __________

2. In Problem 1, does it make a difference whether you subtract the 30% first and then add the 6%, or add the 6% first and then subtract the 30%? Try to explain your answer to other members of your group. Solve the problem both ways and compare your answers.

____

____

3. How much would you pay, including tax, for each of these items at the Bargain Center during the sale? The regular price is given.

   a. jeans, $19.99 __________

   b. shirt, $11.99 __________

   c. sweatshirt, $9.00 __________

   d. wallet, $8.50 __________

   e. necklace, $12.00 __________

   f. scissors, $6.35 __________

   g. upholstery fabric, $6.99 per yard __________

   h. fleece blanket, $19.99 __________

LESSON 11.5 **Name** ______________________ **Date** ____________

Student Edition • page 539

Solve the following problems.

4. A bank pays its customers 6% interest per year. Suppose you put $250 in the bank.

   a. How much interest would you earn in 1 year? ____________

   b. How much money would you have in the bank at the end of 1 year (if you did not withdraw any money)? ____________

   After 2 years? ____________

   c. Extended Response Why is the answer to part b not computed as $265 plus $15?

   ____

   ____

   d. How much would you have after 3 years? ____________

   e. How much would you have after 4 years? ____________

   f. How much would you have after 5 years? ____________

5. Mrs. Nguyen is borrowing $500 from a bank for one year. The bank is charging her 12% interest per year.

   a. How much total interest will she be charged? ____________

   b. How much will she have to pay back altogether? ____________

6. In which of the following instances would you earn more money: depositing $500 in the bank at 5% interest or depositing $490 at 8% interest? ____________

LESSON 11.5

Student Edition • page 539

7 The Campbells borrowed $8,800 from the bank to fix their house, and they will not make a payment for a year. The bank charges 9% interest on home loans. How much will the Campbells owe at the end of 1 year? ______________

8 A bank pays 7% interest per year. Suppose you deposited $625 in the bank.

a. How much interest would you earn in 1 year? ______________

b. How much money would you have in the bank at the end of 1 year if you did not withdraw any money? ______________

c. How much would you have after 2 years? ______________

d. After 3 years? ______________

e. After 4 years? ______________

f. After 5 years? ______________

Name ______________________ **Date** ____________

Student Edition • pages 540–541

You are traveling at 2.4 meters per second. As you travel, your sonar beam moves with you, scanning a rectangular path across the ocean floor. Your sonar beam scans an area of 432 square meters each second.

You plan to lower the sonar device so that the width of the beam at the ocean floor is reduced by 10%. How much area can your sonar cover each second with the new beam width?

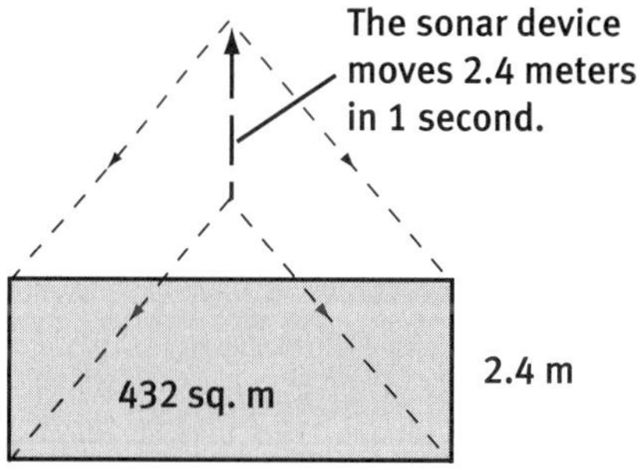

Kai solved the problem this way:

I Made a Plan and Wrote Equations.

1. Find the old width of the beam.	Old width = 432 sq m ÷ 2.4 m
2. Find the new width of the beam.	New width = 90% of old width
3. Find the new area covered each second.	New area = new width × 24 m

Think about Kai's strategy. Answer the following questions.

1. Why does Kai find the width of the beam before it is reduced?

____

____

2. Is Kai's first equation correct? Explain.

____

____

3. Do you agree that the new width is 90% of the old width? Explain.

____

Student Edition • **page 541**

❹ Will Kai's strategy work? Why or why not?

____

____

❺ Would you use Kai's strategy?

____

Jordan solved the problem another way:

I Used Proportional Reasoning and Made a Diagram.

If I take away $\frac{1}{10}$ of the width, I am taking away $\frac{1}{10}$ of the area.

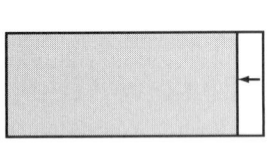

Think **about Jordan's strategy. Answer the following questions.**

❻ Why is Jordan thinking about taking away $\frac{1}{10}$ of the width?

____

❼ Do you agree with Jordan's reasoning? Why or why not?

____

❽ How can Jordan finish solving the problem?

____

____

❾ Solve the problem. Use any strategy you think will work.

____

____

❿ What strategy did you use? Why?

____

____

CHAPTER 11

Cumulative Review

Name ______________________ Date ______________

Student Edition • page 542

Angles and Sides of a Triangle Lesson 9.3

Solve.

If a triangle has one side with a length of 12 meters and another side with a length of 7 meters, can the third side be

1. 3 meters? ____________
2. 5 meters? ____________
3. 5.1 meters? ____________
4. 18 meters? ____________
5. 19 meters? ____________

Surface Area and Volume Lessons 10.12–10.13

6. A box has a width of 3 feet, a height of 7 feet, and a length of 9 feet. What is the volume of the box? ____________
7. A cube has a side length of 4 inches. What is the surface area of the cube? ____________
8. A cube has a side with an area of 36 square feet. What is the surface area of the cube? ____________
9. What is the volume of the cube? ____________
10. A box has sides of 3 inches, 8 inches, and 6 inches. What is the surface area of the box? ____________

Cumulative Review

Student Edition • pages 542–543

Dividing by a Two-Digit or Three-Digit Number Lessons 8.8–8.10

11. At a recent baseball game, the amount of money received from all tickets sold was $612,942. If the average price of a ticket sold for that game was $22, how many fans attended the game? ______

12. A school fund-raiser collected $4,114. If 242 people gave a donation, what was the average amount of each donation? ______

Divide.

13. $68\overline{)60384}$

14. $325\overline{)22425}$

15. $365\overline{)276670}$

Adding and Subtracting Mixed Numbers Lessons 7.3–7.4

Solve.

16. Kang's math book is $1\frac{5}{8}$ inches thick, his science book is $1\frac{1}{4}$ inches thick, and his spelling book is $\frac{15}{16}$ of an inch thick. What is the total width of all 3 books? ______

17. Niran walked $1\frac{1}{5}$ miles to school. At lunch hour, he walked $\frac{2}{3}$ of a mile. After school, Niran walked home. How far did he walk that day? ______

Cumulative Review

Name ______________________ Date ______________

Student Edition • page 543

Add or subtract.

18. $\begin{array}{r} 5\frac{1}{4} \\ -\ 3\frac{2}{5} \\ \hline \end{array}$

19. $\begin{array}{r} 4\frac{1}{2} \\ +\ 2\frac{5}{7} \\ \hline \end{array}$

20. $\begin{array}{r} 3\frac{1}{8} \\ -\ \frac{5}{6} \\ \hline \end{array}$

Ratios and Rates Lesson 8.4

Solve.

Koko reads about 30 pages in an hour.

21. About how many pages does she read in 40 minutes? ______________

22. About how many pages does she read in $2\frac{1}{2}$ hours? ______________

23. Koko is currently reading a book that is 176 pages long. She is on page 59. About how long will it take her to finish the book? ______________

Olivia averages 64 miles per hour while driving on the highway.

24. Can she make a 150-mile trip in $2\frac{1}{2}$ hours? ______________

25. About how far could she drive in $3\frac{3}{4}$ hours? ______________

LESSON 11.6

Percents Greater than 100%

Student Edition • page 545

Solve the following problems.

1. Mark purchased an old coin for \$3.00. Three years later, he sold the coin for \$9.00. Which of the following statements are true? Explain your answers.

   a. The value of the coin increased by \$6.00. ______________________

   ____

   b. The value of the coin increased by 200%. ______________________

   ____

   c. The value of the coin is now 300% of its original value. ______________________

   ____

2. Sara purchased an old coin for \$9.00. Three years later, the coin had declined in value and was worth \$3.00. Which of the following statements are true? Explain your answers.

   a. The value of the coin decreased by \$6.00. ______________________

   ____

   b. The coin lost $\frac{2}{3}$ of its value. ______________________

   ____

   c. The coin lost about 66.67% of its value. ______________________

   ____

3. Ten years ago the cost of riding the bus was \$0.50. Since then the price has gone up 150%. How much does it cost to ride the bus now? ______________

 Name ______________________ Date ____________

Student Edition • page 545

4. Ten years ago the price of a box of crayons was about $1.25. Today the price of that same box of crayons is about $3.00.

   a. What is the price difference? ____________

   b. What is the percent increase? ____________

   c. Extended Response Explain how you found your answer to Problem 4b.

   ____

   ____

5. Extended Response Mark purchased a sports card for $2.00. Later, it declined in value. "That card lost 200% of its value," Mark said. Is that possible? Why or why not?

   ____

   ____

6. Last year Sara charged $5.00 per hour for mowing lawns. This year there is a shortage of students willing to mow lawns, so she is able to charge $12.00 per hour.

   a. How much more per hour is Sara charging this year? ____________

   b. What is the percent increase? ____________

   c. Extended Response Is it fair to charge more because fewer people are willing to do the work?

   ____

   ____

LESSON 11.7

Probability and Percent

Student Edition • page 547

Write each of the following fractions as a percent.
If necessary, use a fraction in the percent (for example, $33\frac{1}{3}\%$).

1. $\frac{1}{3}$ = ______________
2. $\frac{2}{3}$ = ______________
3. $\frac{1}{4}$ = ______________
4. $\frac{2}{4}$ = ______________
5. $\frac{2}{5}$ = ______________
6. $\frac{3}{5}$ = ______________

Suppose you roll a 0–5 *Number Cube* many times.

7. About what fraction of the time would you expect the cube to land with 0 showing? ______________

8. What percent is that? ______________

Working with a partner, roll a 0–5 *Number Cube* 100 times and count how many times it lands with 0 showing.

9. What percent of the time did the cube land with 0 showing? ______________

Collect all the results for your class.

10. What percent of the time did the *Number Cube* land with 0 showing for the entire class? ______________

LESSON 11.7 **Name** ______________________ **Date** ____________

Student Edition • page 548

Suppose you roll a 0–5 *Number Cube* and a 5–10 *Number Cube.*

11. What are the possible sums that could result?

____

12. Do you have 11 possible sums? ____________

13. **Extended Response** What percent of the time would you expect the sum to be 10? Explain your answer.

____

____

Work with a partner. Roll a 0–5 and a 5–10 *Number Cube* one hundred times, and count how many times the resulting sum is 10.

14. What fraction of the time was the sum 10? ____________

15. What percent of the time was the sum 10? ____________

Study the results for your class.

16. What fraction of the time was the sum 10? ____________

17. What percent of the time was the sum 10? ____________

18. Why do you suppose the sum of 10 occurs so often? ____________

19. What percent of the time do you think the sum of 5 occurs? ____________

20. What percent of the time do you think the sum of 15 occurs? ____________

Student Edition • pages 548–549

21 Show the total number of times each sum occurred, and calculate the percents. You might want to use a calculator. The total of all percents should be 100.

____

____

Use **the following information to answer the problems.**

Number Cubes display the following numbers:

0–5 cube: 0, 1, 2, 3, 4, 5

5–10 cube: 5, 6, 7, 8, 9, 10

22 List all the possible ways you can get each sum from 5 to 15. (Hint: There are 36 ways altogether.)

____

____

____

____

There is only one way to get the sum of 5, and there are 36 sums in all. So, we would expect to get a sum of 5 about $\frac{1}{36}$ of the time. As a percent, $\frac{1}{36}$ is 2.8%; therefore, we could say that a sum of 5 occurs about 2.8% of the times the cubes are rolled.

23 Determine what fraction of the time each sum should occur. Change these fractions to approximate percents, and compare them with the percents you got when you actually rolled the two cubes.

____

____

LESSON 11.8

Name ______________________ Date ____________

Simplifying Decimal Division

Student Edition • page 551

Change each of the following to an equivalent division problem with a whole-number divisor. Do not do the division.

1. $0.3\overline{)51.6}$ ____________
2. $516 \div 82$ ____________
3. $0.03\overline{)4.08}$ ____________
4. $0.03\overline{)4.8}$ ____________
5. $4.8 \div 0.3$ ____________
6. $2{,}694 \div 587$ ____________

Select the appropriate approximation from the choices provided.

7. $9.4\overline{)0.94}$ = ____________
   - **a.** 1
   - **b.** 0.1
   - **c.** 10
8. $64.27 + 2.5$ = ____________
   - **a.** 25.7
   - **b.** 2.57
   - **c.** 257
9. $0.49\overline{)66.5}$ = ____________
   - **a.** 1.3
   - **b.** 0.13
   - **c.** 130
10. $835 \div 3.7$ = ____________
    - **a.** 20.8
    - **b.** 208
    - **c.** 2.08
11. $0.65\overline{)401.693}$ = ____________
    - **a.** 61.799
    - **b.** 617.99
    - **c.** 6,179.9
12. $51.283 \div 3.7$ = ____________
    - **a.** 12.82
    - **b.** 1.282
    - **c.** 128.2

Approximate the following problems by simplifying each divisor to one digit.

13. $400\overline{)2650}$ = ____________
14. $2.5\overline{)36.5}$ = ____________
15. $185.26 \div 64$ = ____________
16. $1.75 \div 70$ = ____________

LESSON 11.9

Dividing Two Decimals

Student Edition • page 553

Divide.

1. $0.7\overline{)3.5}$ = ______________
2. $0.07\overline{)0.35}$ = ______________
3. $7\overline{)0.35}$ = ______________
4. $0.42 \div 0.6$ = ______________
5. $0.72 \div 0.8$ = ______________
6. $0.8\overline{)0.064}$ = ______________
7. $0.5\overline{)4.0}$ = ______________
8. $4 \div 0.5$ = ______________
9. $0.006\overline{)3}$ = ______________
10. $0.03\overline{)0.06}$ = ______________
11. $0.06\overline{)0.36}$ = ______________
12. $6.00 \div 0.03$ = ______________
13. $0.03\overline{)6}$ = ______________
14. $16 \div 0.0004$ = ______________
15. $0.7\overline{)0.49}$ = ______________
16. $800\overline{)4000}$ = ______________
17. $800\overline{)400}$ = ______________
18. $800\overline{)40}$ = ______________
19. $800\overline{)4}$ = ______________
20. $4{,}000 \div 80$ = ______________
21. $8\overline{)4000}$ = ______________
22. $0.8\overline{)4000}$ = ______________
23. $0.08\overline{)4000}$ = ______________
24. $3{,}500 \div 5$ = ______________
25. $0.5\overline{)3500}$ = ______________
26. $3{,}500 \div 50$ = ______________
27. $50\overline{)350}$ = ______________
28. $35 \div 50$ = ______________
29. $50\overline{)3.5}$ = ______________
30. $3.5 \div 0.005$ = ______________
31. $0.9\overline{)6.3}$ = ______________
32. $0.063 \div 0.09$ = ______________

Name ______________________ **Date** ______________

Student Edition • page 555

The discoverers of the *Monitor* had narrowed the search to a rectangle of ocean floor 25.7 kilometers long and 9.7 kilometers wide. Trying to find an object only 172 feet long and $41\frac{1}{2}$ feet wide in that much ocean was no easy task. The mission was made even more challenging by the discovery of more than twenty other shipwrecks in the same area.

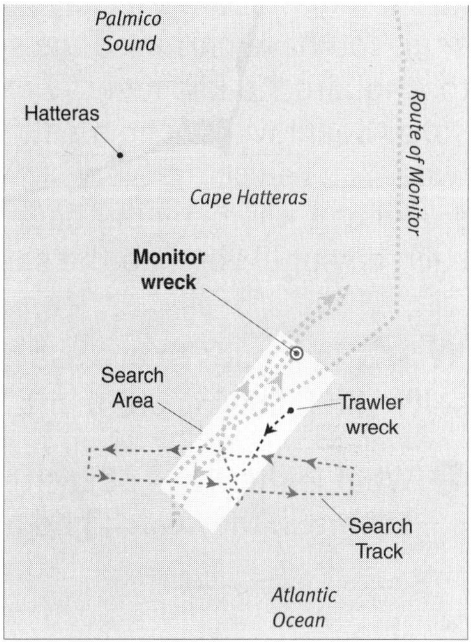

Answer the following questions.

1. Suppose you covered 5% of the entire search area each day. What is the probability you would find the *Monitor* on the first day? ______________

2. What is the probability you would find the *Monitor* within the first 2 days? ______________

3. Suppose you could search 20 square kilometers each day, and you began on August 1. About what would your chances be of finding the *Monitor* by August 10? ______________

4. Suppose your sonar beam was 0.2 kilometers wide at the seafloor, and you traveled in a straight line at 12 kilometers per hour. How many square kilometers would you scan in 12 hours? ______________

Student Edition • **page 556**

Imagine you are the chief scientist on a mission to find the wreckage of a historic ship. You have narrowed the search area to a square 3.6 kilometers wide. Your sonar beam will sweep a path 0.2 meters wide. You will search very slowly, at a speed of 1 kilometer per hour, for 8 hours each day until you find the ship.

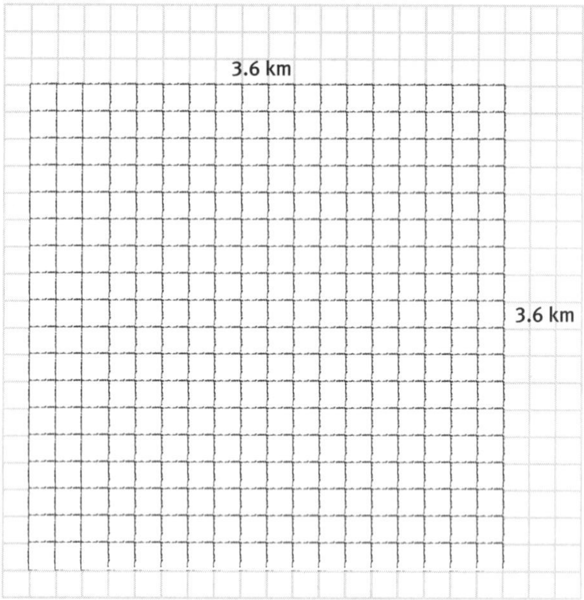

Work **in groups to discuss and solve the following problems.**

5. What is the width of each small square in the search grid above? __________

6. How many of the small squares will your sonar scan in 1 hour? __________

7. Show the course you would take to cover the entire grid. You may start in any part of the grid, but you should not travel over a section more than once.

8. What is the probability you will find the ship within the first 4 days of searching? __________

9. Compare your answer to Problem 8 with other groups. Does the probability depend on what course you take?

____

____

10. Create your own search problem and exchange it with another group.

____

____

CHAPTER 11 Cumulative Review

Name ______________________ Date ______________

Student Edition • page 557

Percent and Fraction Benchmarks Lesson 11.3

Solve.

1. 50% of 16 = ______
2. 25% of 16 = ______
3. 75% of 8 = ______
4. $\frac{1}{2}$ of 66 = ______
5. $\frac{1}{4}$ of 88 = ______
6. 25% of 80 = ______
7. $12\frac{1}{2}$% of 80 = ______
8. $\frac{1}{2}$ of 200 = ______
9. $\frac{1}{4}$ of 400 = ______
10. $\frac{3}{4}$ of 200 = ______

Fractions of Fractions Lesson 6.2

Solve.

11. $\frac{2}{3}$ of 6 = ______
12. $\frac{1}{2} \times \frac{1}{3} =$ ______
13. $\frac{1}{3} \times \frac{1}{4} -$ ______
14. $\frac{3}{4}$ of $\frac{5}{8}$ = ______
15. $\frac{1}{5} \times \frac{4}{7} =$ ______
16. $\frac{2}{5} \times \frac{2}{9} =$ ______

Fill the blank to make each of the following statements true.

17. $\frac{1}{2} \times$ ______ $= \frac{1}{8}$
18. $\frac{3}{5} \times$ ______ $= \frac{12}{35}$
19. $\frac{3}{4}$ of ______ $= \frac{6}{20}$
20. $\frac{7}{8} \times$ ______ $= \frac{35}{72}$

Cumulative Review

Student Edition • page 558

Probability and Fractions Lesson 6.9

Solve.

A bag contains 3 red, 5 blue, and 4 white marbles.

21. What is the probability of pulling out a red marble? ______________

22. What is the probability of pulling out a blue or white marble? ______________

23. If a red marble is pulled out and not replaced, what is the probability of pulling out a blue marble next? ______________

24. One red, one white, and one blue marble are pulled out and not replaced. What is the probability of pulling out another red one next? ______________

25. How many blue marbles must be added to the original bag so that the probability of pulling out a blue marble is $\frac{1}{2}$? ______________

Adding and Subtracting Decimals Lesson 3.4

Solve.

Hakeem and Carla were each buying school supplies. Hakeem wanted a notebook for $6.95, a package of pencils for $1.59, and a ruler for $0.79. Carla wanted a knapsack for $19.99, a package of pens for $2.59, and a compass for $1.49.

26. Hakeem had a $10 bill. Was that enough money to buy his supplies? ______________

27. Carla had a $10 bill and three $5 bills. Was that enough money to buy her supplies? ______________

28. Did each of them receive change after their purchases? If so, who received more change and how much more? ______________

29. Jonah bought lunch at school. His pizza was $1.75, his salad was $1.29, and his drink was $0.85. How much change did Jonah receive if he gave the cashier a $5 bill? ______________

30. Can Jonah then buy ice cream for $0.99? If so, how much money will he have left? If not, how much more will he need? ______________

CHAPTER 11

Key Ideas Review

Name ______________________ Date ______________

Student Edition • page 559

Solve by selecting the appropriate answer from the box.

20.40	0.24	25.36	28.86

1. $6.34 \times 4 =$ ______________
2. $3.52 \times 8.2 =$ ______________
3. 6% sales tax on \$4 = ______________
4. \$24 with 15% off = ______________

Solve the following problems.

5. Explain how something can be greater than 100%, and include an example in your explanation.

____

____

6. What is the probability of landing on a prime number when rolling a 5–10 ***Number Cube***? Write the probability as a fraction and as a percent.

____

7. Explain how to simplify the division problem below, and then compute the quotient.

   $1{,}185 \div 600 =$ ______________

____

____

8. Suppose a bank pays its customers 7% interest annually on all savings accounts. How much interest would a customer earn on an account containing \$275 after 1 year? After 2 years? After 3 years? ______________

____

9. $0.056 \div 7 =$ ______________
10. $0.0056 \div 0.007 =$ ______________

Chapter Review

Student Edition • page 560

Without using a pencil and paper or a calculator, decide which is correct. In each case, only one answer is correct. **Lesson 11.1**

1. $7.3 \times 3.2 =$ ____________
   - **a.** 20.16
   - **b.** 23.36
   - **c.** 33.26

2. $5.25 \times 2.85 =$ ____________
   - **a.** 14.9625
   - **b.** 9.5165
   - **c.** 18.6155

3. $10.5 \times 20.5 =$ ____________
   - **a.** 215.25
   - **b.** 195.25
   - **c.** 311.25

Multiply. **Lesson 11.2**

4. $\begin{array}{r} 7 \\ \times\ 0.8 \\ \hline \end{array}$

5. $\begin{array}{r} 2.50 \\ \times\ 3.60 \\ \hline \end{array}$

6. $\begin{array}{r} 0.35 \\ \times\ 0.65 \\ \hline \end{array}$

7. $\begin{array}{r} 0.468 \\ \times\ \ \ 0.9 \\ \hline \end{array}$

Solve.

8. Abby's aunt wanted to bake two pies, one cherry and one peach. Abby went to the store and picked out 1.4 pounds of cherries, which cost $1.49 per pound, and 1.2 pounds of peaches, on sale for $1.09 per pound. What was the total cost of the fruit? ____________

Chapter Review

Name ______________________ Date ______________

Student Edition • page 560

Calculate. Lesson 11.3

9. 5% sales tax on $9 ________

10. 6% sales tax on $20 ________

11. 7% sales tax on $17 ________

12. 15% of 120 ________

13. 35% of 120 ________

14. 50% of 1,200 ________

15. $0.88 = \frac{\quad}{100} =$ ________%

16. $0.17 = \frac{\quad}{100} =$ ________%

17. $0.52 = \frac{\quad}{100} =$ ________%

Solve. Lesson 11.4

The Bike Outlet has bikes on sale for 20% off. The local sales tax is 5%. Maddie wants to buy a bike that normally costs $350.

18. What is the sale price of the bike? ________

19. What is the total cost of the bike, including tax? ________

20. If the sale changed to 30% off, what would be the sale price of the bike? ________

Chapter Review

Student Edition • page 561

Solve. Lesson 11.5

21 Felix is saving for a down payment on a house. He has $4,200 and needs a total of $5,000. If Felix puts the money into a bank account earning 7% interest per year, will he have enough money for the down payment in 2 years? If not, how much more does he need? ______________

Solve. Lesson 11.6

22 Luigi paid $510 for an antique lamp. A dealer offered him $1,275 for the lamp. What percent of Luigi's original cost was the dealer's offer? ______________

23 Last year, Hank hit a total of 12 home runs. If this year's total is 175% of last year's total, how many home runs has Hank hit this year? ______________

Write each answer as a fraction and as a percent. Lesson 11.7

A standard die is numbered 1–6. If the die is rolled once, what is the probability that

24 the number rolled is even? ______________

25 the number rolled is divisible by 3? ______________

26 the number rolled is smaller than 2? ______________

If a bag contains 13 red, 7 blue, and 5 white marbles, what is the probability of

27 selecting a red marble? ______________

28 *not* selecting a white marble? ______________

Solve. Lesson 11.9

29 Jeremiah has $8.40 to spend on juice for his party. If juice costs 40¢ per can, how many cans can he buy? ______________

30 Antwan has a goal to run 100 miles. If he runs 2.5 miles each day, how many days will it take Antwan to reach 100 miles? ______________

CHAPTER 11

Practice Test

Name ______________________ Date ______________

Student Edition • page 362

Decide which decimal number in each product is greater.

1. 0.5×2.7 ______ 1×3

2. 6×2 ______ 6.4×1.5

3. 2.3×5.4 ______ 2×5

4. 7×4 ______ 6.8×3.5

Change each percent to a decimal.

5. 21% ______

6. 4.3% ______

Change each decimal to a percent.

7. 0.745 ______

8. 0.014 ______

Solve.

9. $35 with 10% off ______

10. $84 with 25% off ______

11. $49 with 15% off ______

12. $28 with 5% off ______

Divide.

13. $2.6\overline{)7.8}$

14. $0.4\overline{)0.64}$

15. $0.9\overline{)0.0036}$

Practice Test

Student Edition • page 563

Choose the correct answer.

16. Which answer has the decimal point in the correct place for 15.4 × 1.25?

Ⓐ 15.375 Ⓑ 1.5375

Ⓒ 153.75 Ⓓ 1,537.5

17. Carrie wants to buy a new tennis racquet. She finds one for $38, now on sale for 20% off. How much will Carrie save?

Ⓐ $6.70 Ⓑ $7.06

Ⓒ $7.60 Ⓓ $30

18. Mrs. Riley puts $750 in the bank. She earns 3% interest each year. How much interest will Mrs. Riley earn after 1 year?

Ⓐ $2.25 Ⓑ $22.50

Ⓒ $25.20 Ⓓ $225

19. Jane rolls a 5–10 ***Number Cube*** one time. What is the probability of her rolling an even number?

Ⓐ $\frac{1}{6}$ Ⓑ $\frac{3}{6}$

Ⓒ $\frac{4}{6}$ Ⓓ $\frac{5}{6}$

20. Mr. Mandra bought 1 notebook for $2.19. How much would 18 notebooks cost?

Ⓐ $3.42 Ⓑ $34.42

Ⓒ $39.04 Ⓓ $39.42

21. Which percent is equivalent to 0.259?

Ⓐ 0.259% Ⓑ 2.59%

Ⓒ 25.9% Ⓓ 259%

22. What is $\frac{3}{4}$ of 32?

Ⓐ 8 Ⓑ 16

Ⓒ 24 Ⓓ 28

23. Change the following to an equivalent division problem with a whole-number divisor.

2.64 ÷ 3.4

Ⓐ 0.264 ÷ 0.34

Ⓑ 26.4 ÷ 34

Ⓒ 26.4 ÷ 3.4

Ⓓ 264 ÷ 34

24. What is 0.96 ÷ 0.8?

Ⓐ 12 Ⓑ 120

Ⓒ 1.2 Ⓓ 0.12

25. Cleo bought lunch for $17.79. There is a 7% sales tax. How much will she have to pay altogether?

Ⓐ $10.94 Ⓑ $1.94

Ⓒ $19.04 Ⓓ $9.04

CHAPTER 11

Practice Test

Name ______________________ Date ____________

Student Edition • page 564

Choose the correct answer.

26. Cardone's Home Store buys a picture frame for $50. They then mark up the frame an additional 120% for retail sale. What will be the ticket price of the frame?

Ⓐ $70 Ⓑ $110

Ⓒ $120 Ⓓ $170

27. Carolyn works at the ballpark hot dog stand 3 days a week for $10 a game. How much will Carolyn make in 6 weeks?

Ⓐ $60 Ⓑ $18

Ⓒ $150 Ⓓ $180

28. Kevin has saved $53. He wants to buy a pair of sneakers that cost $67.50. How much more money does he need?

Ⓐ $14.50 Ⓑ $4.50

Ⓒ $45 Ⓓ $1.45

29. Carly put 6 marbles into a bag. If 3 are purple, 1 is yellow, and 2 are green, what is the probability that Carly will pull a purple marble out of the bag?

Ⓐ $\frac{1}{4}$ Ⓑ $\frac{1}{2}$

Ⓒ $\frac{3}{4}$ Ⓓ $\frac{2}{3}$

30. A triangle has side lengths of 5 inches and 3 inches. Which could be the length of the third side?

Ⓐ 1 in. Ⓑ 6 in.

Ⓒ 8 in. Ⓓ 10 in.

Practice Test

Student Edition • page 565

Solve.

31. Before going to the register, Tiana added up everything she was buying. The total was $27.96. The sales tax in Tiana's state is 6%.

a. Assuming that Tiana's calculations are correct, how much will the tax on her items be? ______________

b. What will be the total cost of Tiana's purchases with tax? ______________

32. Darla and her friends are playing a game in which they roll a *Number Cube* labeled 1–6 to move spaces on a game board.

a. What is the probability that Darla will roll a 3 on her turn? Give your answer as a percent. Round to the nearest whole number. ______________

b. Darla landed on a space that allows her to roll the *Number Cube* two times and move the number of spaces equal to the sum of the two numbers she rolled. What are all the possible sums that Darla could roll? ______________

c. List all the possible ways you can get each sum.

	1	2	3	4	5	6
1						
2						
3						
4						
5						
6						

d. What is the probability of Darla moving 6 spaces? ______________

Name ______________________ Date ____________

Measurement and Graphing

Student Edition • page 567

On December 5, 1914, the *Endurance* and its crew, led by Ernest Shackleton, set sail from South Georgia Island. On January 18, 1915, the ship became trapped in the ice and could no longer be steered. The *Endurance* drifted for months at the mercy of giant slabs of frozen seawater. About how far did the *Endurance* drift?

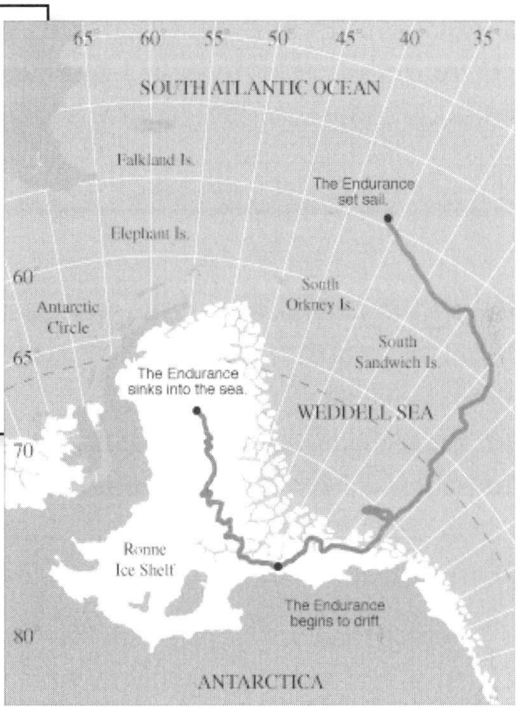

Answer the following questions.

1. About what fraction of the distance from the equator to the South Pole is Elephant Island? ____________
2. The circumference of Earth is about 25,000 miles. About how many miles is it from the equator to the South Pole? ____________
3. About how many miles would you travel if you went directly north from latitude 70° S to latitude 60° S? ____________
4. How could you use the information from Problems 2 and 3 to estimate the scale of the map? ____________
5. How far from where it began to drift in the ice did the *Endurance* sink? ____________

LESSON 12.1

Estimating Length

Student Edition • page 569

Read the directions below and carefully record each piece of data in your responses.

1. Write down the measurements of your hand span, the distance between the tip of your thumb and your knuckle, your arm span, the length of your foot, and the distance from your fingertip to your elbow. You may need help from a classmate to determine some of these measurements.

____

2. Estimate various measurements, such as the length of a box, the length of a pencil, the length of the room, and the length of a table.

____

____

3. Measure these items with parts of your body, such as your foot or the distance between your elbow and your fingertip.

____

4. Check the estimates and the measurements by using a ruler, meterstick, or tape measure.

____

5. **Extended Response** Explain how you decided which body part to use for making your estimates. Do you think you could use any of these methods to measure any object? Explain.

____

____

LESSON 12.2

Name ______________________ Date ____________

Estimating Angles and Distances

Student Edition • page 571

Work alone or in small groups to answer the following questions.

1. Find out how long your pace (distance between footsteps) is in meters. Use a meterstick or tape measure to find out how long ten of your paces are. Then divide to find the length of one pace. ____________

2. Try to change your pace so that it is either 1 meter or 0.5 meter. If you learn how to take steps that are 1 meter or 0.5 meter each, it will be easier to pace off distances. Here is a way to change your pace: Measure out a 10-meter distance. Try to cover that distance in 10 or 20 paces.

3. Estimate the height of the front wall of your classroom (or of another room in the school). Use fists, paces, and a drawing to make your estimate.

   a. Calculate your "eye level" in meters by measuring the distance from the floor to your eye. Record the result. ____________

   b. Pace off 5 or 10 meters from the wall using your 1 meter or 0.5 meter paces. (For example, 10 paces at 0.5 meter each would equal 5 meters.)

   c. Use the fist method to estimate the angle from your (horizontal) eye level to the top of the wall. ____________

   d. Create a scale drawing of your triangle on paper to find the height of the wall. Measure the height of the triangle in your drawing. What is your estimate for the height of the wall? (Do not forget to add your "eye level.") ____________

4. See how close your estimate in Problem 3 was. Measure the height of the wall with a meterstick or tape measure. You may have to work with a classmate to find this measurement. Compare this measurement to your estimate. ____________

5. Use the pace, fist, and drawing method to estimate heights of other tall objects. Compare your estimates with a classmate's estimates. When it is possible, find out the actual measured height and compare it with your estimate.

____

____

____

LESSON 12.3

Applying Customary Measures

Student Edition • pages 572–573

1 Using the information given above, complete the table below.

Unit	Gallon(s) (gal)	Quart(s) (qt)	Pint(s) (pt)	Cup(s) (C)	Fluid Ounce(s) (fl oz)	Tablespoon(s) (tbsp)	Teaspoon(s) (tsp)
1 Tablespoon (tbsp)						1	3
1 Fluid Ounce (fl oz)					1		
1 Cup (C)				1			
1 Pint (pt)			1				
1 Quart (qt)		1					
1 Gallon (gal)	1						

Solve the following problems.

2 Evan is going to make barbecued crab sandwiches. He has a recipe for 6 servings, but he wants to make only 2 servings. How much of each ingredient should he use?

Ingredients for 6 Servings

3 tablespoons butter or margarine ________

$\frac{1}{2}$ cup finely chopped celery ________

$\frac{1}{4}$ cup finely chopped onion ________

1 teaspoon instant chicken bouillon ________

$\frac{1}{2}$ cup tomato sauce ________

2 teaspoons Worcestershire sauce ________

2 teaspoons soy sauce ________

3 whole cloves ________

$\frac{3}{8}$ teaspoon salt ________

a pinch of pepper ________

$6\frac{3}{4}$ ounces crab meat ________

1 teaspoon parsley flakes ________

6 sandwich rolls ________

Name ______________________ Date ____________

Student Edition • page 573

3 Kaya is planning to make cookies. Her recipe for Swedish pastry bonbons will make 60 cookies. How much of each ingredient does she need to make only 30 cookies?

Ingredients for 60 Cookies

1 cup butter ____________

$\frac{2}{3}$ cup powdered sugar, sifted ____________

1 cup pecans, finely chopped ____________

1 teaspoon vanilla ____________

2 cups flour, sifted ____________

4 **Extended Response** Suppose you were adjusting a recipe, such as the one above, and you had measuring cups for $\frac{1}{4}$ cup, $\frac{1}{3}$ cup, $\frac{1}{2}$ cup, and 1 cup. Explain what you would do if you needed to measure $\frac{1}{6}$ cup.

____

____

5 **Extended Response** If you only had 1 teaspoon, $\frac{1}{2}$ teaspoon, and $\frac{1}{4}$ teaspoon measuring spoons, how would you measure $\frac{1}{3}$ teaspoon?

____

____

6 Parker is going to make seven-minute icing. He wants to make only half the usual recipe. The recipe calls for 2 egg whites, $1\frac{1}{2}$ cups sugar, 5 tablespoons water, and $\frac{1}{4}$ teaspoon cream of tartar. The recipe says to cook the mixture over boiling water while beating it with a wire beater for seven minutes. Then add 1 teaspoon vanilla.

a. How much of each ingredient should Parker use to make half as much icing? ____________

____

b. How long should he cook it? ____________

LESSON 12.3

Student Edition • page 574

Customary Measures of Weight

1 pound (lb) = 16 ounces (oz)

1 ton = 2,000 pounds

Use the information above to answer the following questions.

Jeri, Marshall, Ellen, and Cody shared the job of collecting cans after the sporting events at their school for a fund-raising activity. During the first 8 weeks, Jeri collected the cans twice, Marshall once, Ellen 3 times, and Cody twice. Mr. Finelli, the recycling plant owner, paid them 32¢ per pound for the cans. They earned $48 altogether for the 8 weeks.

7. What fraction of the time did Jeri collect cans? Marshall? Ellen? Cody?

____

8. What fraction of the time did Marshall and Ellen collect cans together? _______________

9. What fraction of the money should each person get? _______________

10. What fraction of the money should Jeri and Cody get altogether? _______________

11. **a.** How much money should each person get? _______________

    b. Based on your answer to Problem 9, why might some of the kids think the way they share the money is unfair? _______________

12. How many pounds of cans did they collect altogether? _______________

13. On average, about how many pounds did they collect per week? _______________

14. If it takes 2 cans to make an ounce of aluminum, how many cans did Ellen probably collect? _______________

15. Cody says that if they load the cans onto his uncle's recycling truck, his uncle will pay them 55¢ per pound. How much more money would they make if they sold the cans to Cody's uncle rather than to Mr. Finelli? _______________

Name ____________________ Date ____________

Student Edition • page 575

Answer **the following questions. Remember, the symbol ' stands for feet, and the symbol " stands for inches.**

The local cleaner charges $3.00 per square foot to clean a rug.

16 The Denizens have a rectangular rug that is $9\frac{1}{2}$' long and $4\frac{3}{4}$' wide. How much will the cleaners charge the Denizens to clean their rug? ____________

17 The Denizens have another rectangular rug that is $6\frac{1}{4}$' long and $4\frac{1}{2}$' wide. How much should it cost to clean the rug? ____________

18 How much would a rug that is 10' 6" by 6' 8" cost to clean? ____________

19 **Extended Response** The clerk at the cleaners measured a circular rug, which had a diameter of 11'. About how much should it cost to clean the rug? Explain how you got your answer.

____

20 Suppose you wanted to give each of the 11 people on your camping trip an 8-ounce bag of trail mix. How many pounds of trail mix would you need? ____________

21 Max needs $2\frac{1}{2}$ feet of material for each of the 12 costumes he is making for the school play. How many yards of material will Max need altogether? ____________

22 **Extended Response** Tracy is making three 54-inch long shelves. If boards come in 8-foot lengths, how many boards does she need? Explain your answer.

____

____

LESSON 12.4

Converting Measures

Student Edition • page 577

Use the table to estimate equivalents for the following measurements.

Metric Unit	Approximate Customary Equivalent
Length	
1 centimeter	0.4 inch
1 meter	40 inches
1 kilometer	0.6 mile
Mass	
1 kilogram	2.2 pounds
Capacity	
1 liter	1 quart

1. When you go hiking for the day, you should drink about 2 quarts of water. Will you have enough water if you take 2 full canteens, each of which holds 1 liter?

   ____

2. If you walk 3 miles per hour, about how many kilometers per hour will you walk? At that rate, how long would it take to walk 5 kilometers?

   ____

3. Anatoli says that the price of gas in Italy is about 65¢ per liter. If your gas tank holds about 15 gallons, how much would it cost to fill up there? ______________

4. Jason would like to explain American football to his German friend Marcus. About how long is the 100-yard field in meters? ______________

5. Marcus says that in his country, football is the most popular sport, but what they call football is what Americans call soccer. He says a World Cup football field can be as large as 110 meters by 75 meters. About what are the dimensions in yards? ______________

6. The train from Munich to Paris travels 827 kilometers. About how many miles is that? ______________

7. Marcus says his waist is 75 centimeters, and the inseam on his pants is 80 centimeters long. In inches, what size jeans should Jason send Marcus for his birthday (waist and inseam)? ______________

8. Katie's pen pal, Hellé, lives in Norway. They both love snowboarding. Hellé wants to send Katie a new snowboard, but first they should make sure it is the right size for her weight. If Katie weighs 85 pounds, what should she tell Hellé her weight is in kilograms? ______________

LESSON 12.5

Name ______________________ Date ____________

Measuring Time

Student Edition • pages 578–579

For each quantity of hours, give the number of minutes.

1. $\frac{1}{4}$ hour ____________
2. $\frac{3}{4}$ hour ____________
3. $1\frac{1}{2}$ hours ____________
4. $2\frac{1}{4}$ hours ____________
5. $\frac{1}{3}$ hour ____________
6. $\frac{1}{5}$ hour ____________

Answer the following questions.

7. About how long would it take you to walk 10 miles if you could walk 1 mile in 20 minutes? In 18 minutes? ____________
8. How long would it take for Michael to do 5 loads of laundry if each load takes 20 minutes to wash and 45 minutes to dry (assuming you can wash the next load while the previous one is being dried)? ____________
9. If you read 8 articles in 1 hour, what was the average amount of time it took you to read each article? ____________
10. Ricardo spent $3\frac{3}{4}$ hours writing a science report. How many minutes did he spend writing? ____________
11. Heidi said she would meet Al at the corner of Fifth and Main in $2\frac{1}{2}$ hours. The time was 2:15 P.M. when Heidi said this. What time were they supposed to meet? ____________

What time will it be

12. $3\frac{1}{2}$ hours after 7:15 P.M.? ____________
13. $4\frac{1}{2}$ hours after 6:00 P.M.? ____________
14. $6\frac{1}{4}$ hours after 4:30 A.M.? ____________

LESSON 12.5

Student Edition • page 579

15. 10 hours after 1:45 A.M.? ______

16. 12 hours after 1:45 P.M.? ______

17. 1 hour after 11:45 P.M.? ______

18. $12\frac{1}{6}$ hours after 11:45 P.M.? ______

19. $12\frac{1}{5}$ hours after 1:45 A.M.? ______

Answer the following questions.

20. You would like to see a movie that starts at 2:25 P.M. and is 116 minutes long. What time would the movie be over? ______

21. The circus starts at 2:30 P.M. and ends $2\frac{1}{4}$ hours later. What time will it be over? ______

22. A train leaves New York at 12:45 P.M., and it arrives in Westbury $\frac{3}{4}$ hour later. What time does it get there? ______

23. Pedro runs for $1\frac{1}{2}$ hours each day. If he starts running at 3:30 P.M., what time will it be when he finishes? ______

24. Kate rode her bicycle for $\frac{1}{2}$ hour and then swam for $1\frac{3}{4}$ hours. If she started her bike ride at 9:15 A.M., what time did she finish doing both activities? ______

25. School begins at 8:15 A.M. If it takes $\frac{1}{4}$ hour to walk to school, what is the latest time you could leave home and still arrive at school on time? ______

Name ______________________ Date ____________

Student Edition • pages 579–580

26. If it takes 25 seconds for your video game to load and you play it once a day, how long do you wait for it per year (assuming 365 days)? ____________

27. What time will it be $6\frac{3}{4}$ hours after 7:30 A.M.? ____________

Answer the following questions.

28. What time would it be 6 hours before 5:30 A.M? ____________

29. What time would it be $2\frac{1}{4}$ hours before 10:00 A.M.? ____________

30. How many hours are between 12:30 P.M. and 2:45 P.M.? ____________

31. How many hours are between 10:30 A.M. and 2:45 P.M.? ____________

32. How many hours are between 6:15 A.M. and 2:45 P.M.? ____________

33. James K. Polk School is in session from 8:15 A.M. to 3:00 P.M. How many hours long is the school day? ____________

34. A movie is playing at 2:00 P.M., 5:00 P.M., 8:00 P.M., and 11:15 P.M. The theater always allows at least $\frac{1}{4}$ hour between showings for cleaning. What is the greatest possible length of the movie? ____________

35. Jennifer's grandparents are coming for a visit. Her family needs to allow $\frac{1}{2}$ hour to drive to the train station and $\frac{1}{4}$ hour to park and walk to the station. The train arrives at 12:15 P.M. What is the latest time Jennifer's family should leave for the train station? ____________

Student Edition • pages 580–581

36 Mrs. Lopez wants to serve a turkey dinner at 6:00 P.M. She also knows that she wants to take the turkey out of the oven $\frac{1}{2}$ hour before dinner. The turkey needs to cook for $4\frac{1}{4}$ hours. At what time should she start cooking the turkey? ______________

Solve the following problems.

37 Marco wants to study his spelling words for at least $\frac{3}{4}$ hour before he watches any television. He studied from 3:45 P.M. to 4:15 P.M. Has he studied for $\frac{3}{4}$ hour yet? ______________

38 Each of the 2 acts in the school play will take $\frac{3}{4}$ hour. The intermission will be $\frac{1}{4}$ hour long. If the play begins at 7:00 P.M., about what time will it end? ______________

39 Tom began working on his book report at 6:45 P.M. He took a $\frac{1}{4}$-hour break at 8:00 P.M. He finished his report at 10:00 P.M. For how many hours did Tom work on his book report? ______________

40 Jennifer takes 15 to 20 minutes to make an invitation. If she needs to make 20 invitations, about how long will it take her? ______________

41 **Extended Response** Horst timed himself counting from 1 to 100. His stopwatch read 39.7 seconds. At that rate, about how long would it take him to count to 15,000? Why might your estimate be off?

____

42 It is 2:30 A.M. in London and 9:30 P.M. the previous day in Josiane's hometown. Her mother is traveling to London on business, and her plane is scheduled to land at 7:45 A.M. in London. If it takes $2\frac{1}{2}$ hours to get through customs, get to her hotel and check in, and she promises to call Josiane as soon as she gets to her hotel room, at what time should Josiane expect her call? ______________

LESSON 12.6

Name ______________________ Date ____________

Measuring Circles and Angles

Student Edition • page 582

If the minute hand moves 360° in 1 hour and 6° in 1 minute, how many degrees does it move in

1. 5 minutes? ____________
2. $\frac{1}{2}$ hour? ____________
3. $\frac{3}{4}$ hour? ____________
4. $\frac{1}{3}$ hour? ____________
5. 55 minutes? ____________
6. 59 minutes? ____________
7. 61 minutes? ____________
8. 2 hours? ____________
9. $1\frac{1}{2}$ hours? ____________
10. $1\frac{3}{4}$ hours? ____________
11. $\frac{1}{4}$ hour? ____________
12. 45 minutes? ____________

Answer the following questions.

13. If you divide a circle into 3 equally sized sectors, what is the measure of each angle? ____________

14. If you divide a circle into 9 equally sized sectors, how many degrees would each sector have? Draw such a circle. ____________

15. If a pie had equally sized slices that were 30° each, how many slices would there be in the whole pie? ____________

LESSON 12.6

Student Edition • page 583

Answer the following questions.

16 Andrew was assigned to cut a cake at the picnic, but he was told that the older children should get pieces that were twice as big as those the younger children got. If there were 4 older children and 2 younger ones, answer the following:

a. How many pieces should there be? ______

b. How many degrees should the smaller pieces have? ______

c. How many degrees should the larger pieces have? ______

d. Extended Response Explain how you got your answers.

______

17 Extended Response Ethan said he ate $\frac{1}{2}$ of a cake on Tuesday, $\frac{1}{3}$ of the cake on Wednesday, and $\frac{1}{4}$ of the cake on Thursday. Is this possible? Explain.

______

______

18 Alameda looked at a circle graph of the yearly finances of her favorite charity. There was a section of 18° for operating expenses, and the rest of the money was used to care for orphaned children.

Children's Charity Budget

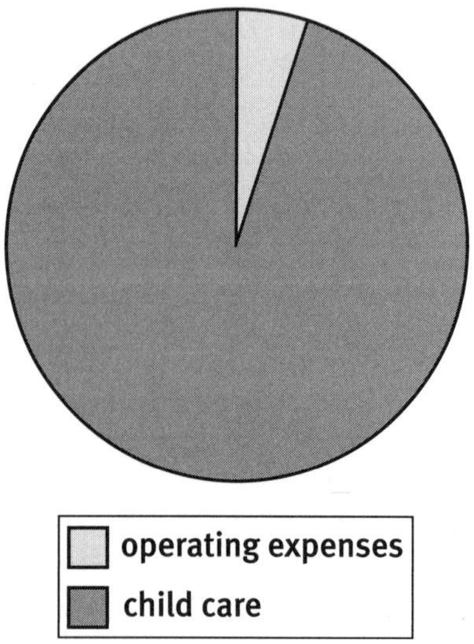

a. What percent of the charity's total finances went toward operating expenses? ______

b. What fraction of the total operating cost is that?

______

c. If the charity raised $20,000 that year, how much of that money went toward caring for the orphans?

______

d. If the charity raised $10,000 that year, how much of the money went toward caring for the orphans? ______

Name ______________________ Date ____________

Student Edition • pages 584–585

These excerpts from Shackleton's diary describe part of a 7-day westward march. During this period, did the expedition travel faster or slower than $\frac{1}{3}$ mile per hour when they were on the move? Assume the stop for lunch was 1 hour.

> At 9:30 P.M. we were off again. We did a good march of $1\frac{1}{2}$ miles before we halted for "lunch" at 1 A.M., and then on for another mile, when at 5 A.M. we camped by a little sloping berg. Nine P.M., the 27th, saw us on the march again. The first 200 yards took us about 5 hours to cross....We managed to get another $\frac{3}{4}$ of a mile before lunch and a further mile...before we camped at 5 A.M.

Clara solved the problem this way:

I decided to Make a Table.

I thought a table would help me organize the information I had, so I could find the time and distance the crew traveled.

Date	Time Interval	Hours on the Move	Miles Traveled
Dec. 26, 27	9:30 P.M.–1 A.M.	$3\frac{1}{2}$	$1\frac{1}{2}$
Dec. 27	(lunch) 1 A.M.–2 A.M.	0	0
Dec. 27			

Think about Clara's strategy. Answer the following questions.

1. What do you think Clara will write in the row next to Dec. 27? ____________
2. How does the table help in solving the problem?

____

____

Student Edition • page 585

3. When Clara completes her table, what can she do next to continue to solve the problem?

____

____

Miguel solved the problem another way.

I decided to Make a Diagram.

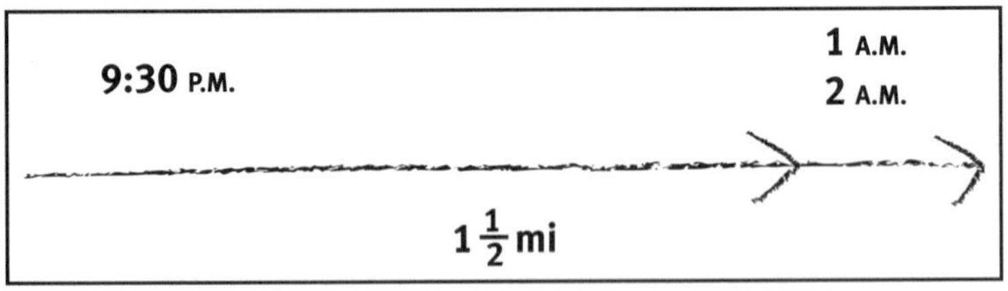

Think about Miguel's strategy. Answer the following questions.

4. What do you think Miguel will write next?

____

5. How is Miguel's strategy like Clara's? How is it different?

____

____

6. Do you think Miguel's strategy will work? Explain.

____

____

7. Solve the problem. Use any strategy you think will work.

____

8. What strategy did you use? Why?

____

____

CHAPTER 12 Cumulative Review

Name ______________________ Date ______________

Student Edition • page 586

Comparing Fractions Lesson 6.7

Write <, >, or = to make each statement true.

1. $\frac{1}{6}$ ______ $\frac{1}{4}$
2. $\frac{5}{6}$ ______ $\frac{2}{4}$
3. $\frac{1}{2}$ ______ $\frac{6}{12}$
4. $\frac{3}{4}$ ______ $\frac{1}{2}$
5. $\frac{5}{12}$ ______ $\frac{1}{2}$
6. $\frac{2}{4}$ ______ $\frac{3}{4}$
7. $\frac{1}{3}$ ______ $\frac{2}{6}$
8. $\frac{4}{8}$ ______ $\frac{2}{3}$

Adding Fractions Greater than 1 Lesson 7.3

Add. Write your answers as mixed numbers, fractions, or whole numbers.

9. $\frac{1}{3} + 1\frac{2}{3} = n$ ______
10. $4\frac{1}{5} + 2\frac{3}{10} = n$ ______
11. $\frac{5}{4} + 7\frac{1}{4} = n$ ______
12. $2\frac{1}{2} + 7\frac{5}{8} = n$ n______
13. $2 + 1\frac{3}{7} = n$ ______
14. $\frac{4}{5} + 3\frac{4}{5} = n$ ______
15. $2\frac{2}{3} + 3\frac{1}{6} = n$ ______
16. $7\frac{4}{9} + \frac{16}{9} = n$ ______

Cumulative Review

Student Edition • page 586

Rounding Decimals **Lesson 3.10**

Round each of the following numbers to the nearest hundredth.

17 4.7380389 ____________

18 0.007 ____________

19 4.735 ____________

Round each of the following numbers to the nearest thousandth.

20 1.23456 ____________

21 1.2345 ____________

22 1.234499999 ____________

Space Figures **Lesson 10.10**

Picture a triangular prism.

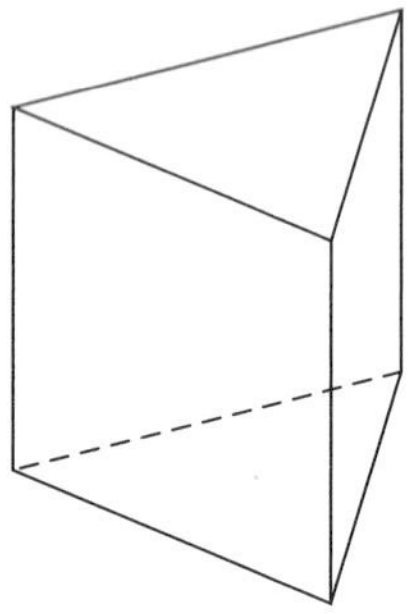

23 How many faces does the triangular prism have? ____________

24 How many sides are there in these polygons? ____________

25 How many edges does the triangular prism have? ____________

26 How many corners do these polygons have? ____________

27 How many vertices does the triangular prism have? ____________

Cumulative Review

Name ______________________ Date ______________

Student Edition • page 587

Multiplying by a Whole Number Lesson 3.9

Multiply.

28. $617 \times 2.5 =$ ______________

30. $256 \times 1.2 =$ ______________

29. $451 \times 82.3 =$ ______________

31. $673 \times 5.6 =$ ______________

Solve.

32. Jerod needs 1 bag of fertilizer to fertilize 100 square feet of his garden. The length of the garden is 50.7 feet, and the width is 15 feet. How many bags of fertilizer should he buy? ______________

33. Bart is the manager of a baseball team. His team needs 13 new shirts. Each shirt costs $7.29. Bart has $75.

    a. Does he have enough money? ______________

    b. If not, how much more money does Bart need? ______________

Cumulative Review

Student Edition • page 587

Applying Math **Lesson 3.5**

Solve.

34. Mr. Quincy paid $2.10 for 7 onions.
How much did each onion cost? ______

35. Antonio bought 9 glass beads for 72¢.
How much should 10 glass beads cost? ______

36. The grocery store sells 2 cans of cat food for 48¢.
How much would 1 can of cat food cost? ______

37. Greg drove for 8 hours. He traveled about 45 miles each hour. About how many miles did he drive? ______

38. Chrissy has 37 balloons. If she divides the balloons equally among 5 friends,

    a. how many balloons should she give each friend? ______

    b. will there be any balloons left over? If so, how many? ______

LESSON 12.7

Name ______________________ Date __________

Pictographs and Data Collection

Student Edition • pages 588–589

Juan wanted to find out how many books New City residents read per month. He conducted a survey, asking people about how many books they check out of their local library each month. He spent two afternoons at the library, asking the same question of people as they left. Juan's results are shown in the table below.

Number of People	1	8	12	14	20	25	51	35	24	4	3	2	1
Number of Books Checked Out Per Month	15	13	10	9	8	7	6	5	4	3	2	1	0

Answer the following questions using the table above.

1. How fairly do Juan's results portray the reading habits of the people who live in New City? Explain your answer.

____

____

2. Did Juan's survey reach only people who use the library often? ____________

As part of his report, Juan made this pictograph to display the results of his survey.

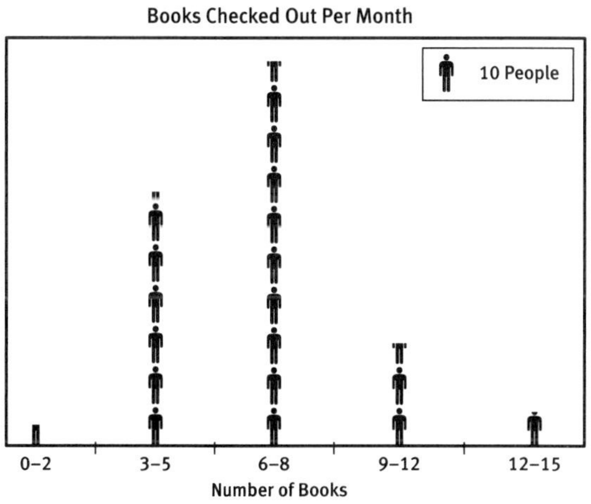

Answer the following questions by using the pictograph.

3. **Extended Response** Study Juan's pictograph. Write questions that can be answered using the information in the graph.

____

____

____

LESSON 12.7

Student Edition • pages 589–590

❹ Which method, the table or the pictograph, shows Juan's survey results in a way that makes it easier to see how many books his group says they check out?

____

❺ What is the advantage of the table?

____

❻ What is the advantage of the pictograph?

____

❼ **Extended Response** If you wanted to show that your community needs a larger library, what kind of information would you collect?

____

____

Juan's little sister Marisa conducted a survey of all the children who visited the library. She asked them if they had their own library cards. She made two graphs of her data, as shown.

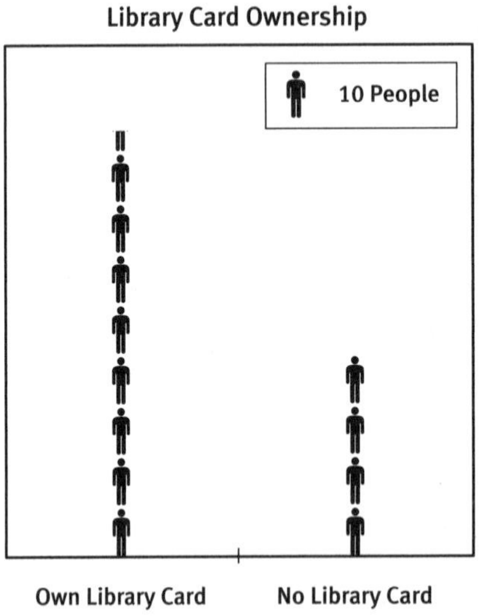

Extended Response **Answer the following questions by using the graphs.**

❽ Do you find one of these graphs to be misleading? Why?

____

____

LESSON 12.7 **Name** ______________________ **Date** ____________

Student Edition • **pages 590–591**

Suppose Juan also wanted to find out about how many books each of the library patrons checked out in the last year.

9. How could Juan estimate this without asking the question?

____

____

10. How could you tell whether Juan used estimation?

____

____

11. How could Juan keep track of the responses to this question?

____

____

Student Edition • **page 591**

Juan's friend Lyla suggested that he make a stem-and-leaf plot. She said it would be easier for people to compare the number of books they checked out to the number of books other patrons checked out.

Suppose the first 20 people checked out the following numbers of books in the past year:

17, 82, 33, 21, 38, 11, 71, 78, 44, 99, 67, 45, 16, 58, 115, 111, 80, 1, 63, 62

Instead of writing a long list, you could set up a stem-and-leaf plot as shown to the right:

0	1	(representing 1)
1	7, 1, 6	(representing 17, 11, and 16)
2	1	(representing 21)
3	3, 8	(representing 33 and 38)
4	4, 5	(representing 44 and 45)
5	8	(representing 58)
6	7, 3, 2	(representing 67, 63, and 62)
7	1, 8	(representing 71 and 78)
8	2, 0	(representing 82 and 80)
9	9	(representing 99)
10		
11	5, 1	(representing 115 and 111)

Student Edition • page 591

The first column in the stem-and-leaf plot shown on page 549 contains the tens or hundreds digits (the stems), and the second column contains the ones digit for each entry (the leaves).

12. How many people from this group of 20 say they check out an average of 12 or more books per month? 3–5 books per month?

____

____

13. What is the median number of books this group of 20 checked out? __________

14. **Extended Response** Do you think the data from these 20 people corresponds to the data in the pictograph? Why or why not?

____

____

15. Suppose Lyla's class had the following grades on a test:

    85, 25, 67, 99, 76, 74, 92, 88, 53, 71, 77, 83, 75, 60, 71

    Make a stem-and-leaf plot of their grades.

LESSON 12.8

Name ______________________ Date __________

Making Circle Graphs

Student Edition • pages 592–593

Al, Janet, and Kim were running for fifth-grade president. Fritz decided to ask all 60 fifth graders who they wanted for president. Here are the first 10 responses:

Janet, Al, Al, Janet, Kim, Al, Janet, Kim, Kim, Al

1. Who do you think is going to win? __________
2. Do you think you have enough information to decide? Why or why not?

____

Fritz is analyzing the data he has collected. He decided to just write the initial of each candidate instead of the whole name. Using that procedure, he repeated the first 10 and continued. He wrote the initials in groups of 10 to make it easier to tell whether he had all 60 votes.

Here is what he wrote:
JAAJKAJKKA JJJAKKJAJA AJJAJJJJAJ JJAJAKAJJJ KJJAJJAKJJ JKAAJJJAJJ

As you can see, it is not easy to tell who got the most votes. So, Fritz made a tally chart and a bar graph, as shown below.

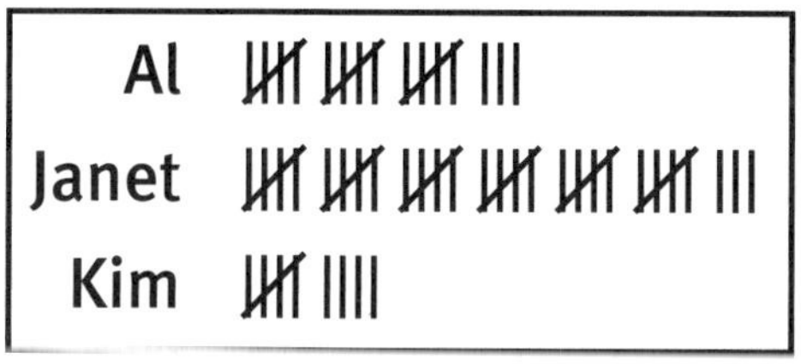

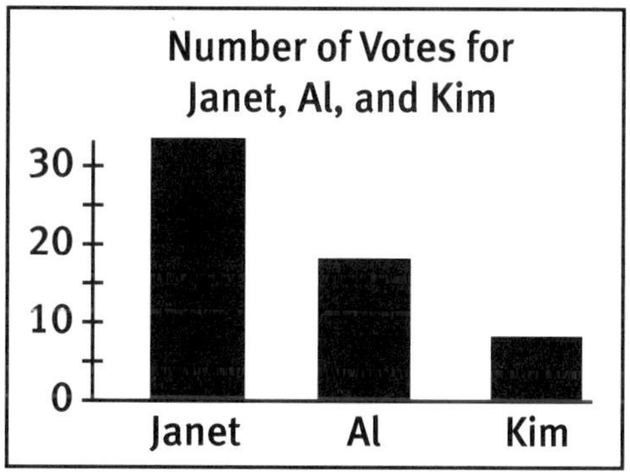

3. Now can you decide which person received the most votes? If so, who did? __________
4. Is it easy to see whether that person received a majority of the votes? __________ (Hint: Think about what *majority* means—more than half.)

LESSON 12.8

Student Edition • page 593

Fritz decided to make a circle graph to display his data. Because he knew there were 60 votes and that there are 360° in a circle, he decided to let 6° stand for each vote.

5 Why did he do that?

____

Here is his circle graph:

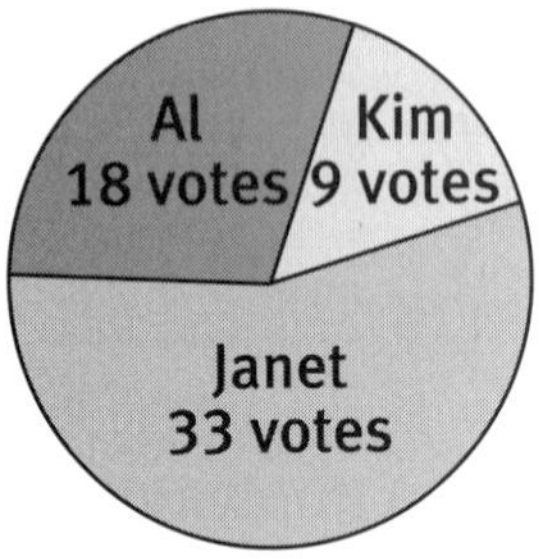

6 **Extended Response** Does this make it easier to quickly determine who received the most votes and whether that person has more than half, or 50%, of the votes? Explain why or why not.

____

____

7 **Extended Response** If there had been only 45 votes, how many degrees of the circle graph would have been needed to represent each vote? How did you get that number?

____

____

For each of the following numbers of votes, determine about how many degrees would be needed to represent each vote in a circle graph. Give your answers to the nearest tenth of a degree.

8 20 ______ 9 30 ______ 10 18 ______

11 100 ______ 12 23 ______ 13 50 ______

14 46 ______ 15 69 ______ 16 21 ______

Name ______________________________ **Date** ______________

Student Edition • **page 593**

17 Using the following data, make a tally chart, a bar graph, and a circle graph: AABACCABAC CABACAACBB BACCACBACC ABCCAABABC.

a. How many degrees did you allow for each piece of information? ______________

b. How many degrees did you use to show all the As? ______________

c. How many degrees did you use to show the Bs? ______________

d. How many degrees did you use to show the Cs? ______________

e. What is the total of those three numbers? ______________

f. Are more than half of the letters the same (A, B, or C)? If so, which? ______________

18 Collect some data, such as how many siblings each classmate has. Use a separate sheet of paper to show the information in a tally chart, a bar graph, and a circle graph.

LESSON 12.9

Creating and Using Graphs

Student Edition • page 594

Mrs. Bonilla's fifth-grade class took a poll to see how many members of the class were born in each month. They made the following bar graph to display their results.

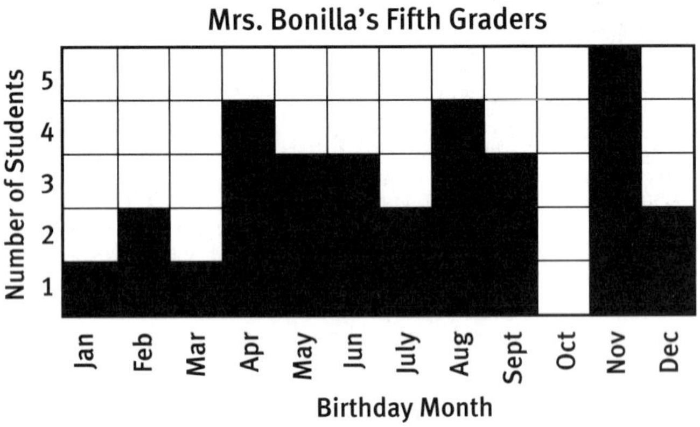

Use the bar graph above to answer the following questions.

1. How many of the students were born in January? ____________

2. In which month were the most students born? How many students were born in that month? ____________

3. In which month were the fewest students born? How many students were born in that month? ____________

4. How many students are in Ms. Bonilla's class? ____________

5. In how many different months were four students born? ____________

6. In how many different months were three students born? ____________

7. In how many different months were two students born? ____________

8. In how many different months was just one student born? ____________

LESSON 12.9

Name ______________________ Date ______________

Student Edition • page 595

The class also decided to make a circle graph to display the information about their birthdays.

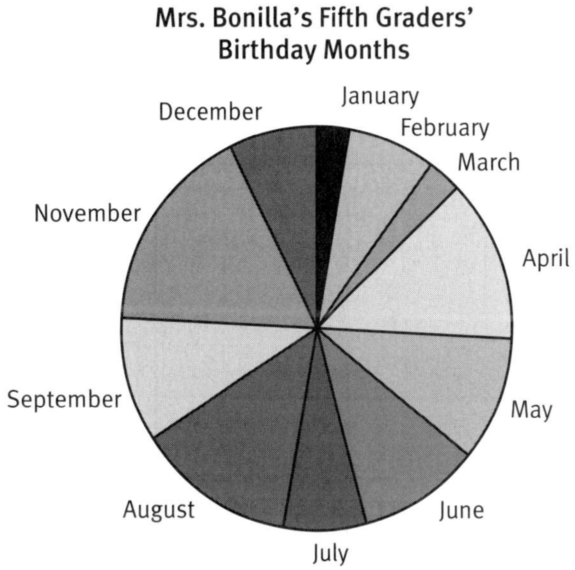

Use the circle graph above to help you answer the following questions.

9. Does the circle graph seem to be correct? Explain your answer.

____

____

10. Can you tell from the circle graph how many people were born in each month? ______________

11. Can you tell from the circle graph about what fraction of the people were born in November? Was it more than $\frac{1}{4}$ of the students? ______________

12. **Extended Response** Were more than half of the students born in the first six months of the year or in the last six months of the year? Is this easier to tell from the bar graph or from the circle graph? Explain your answers.

____

____

Student Edition • page 596

Answer the following questions. Think about the activity you did in class.

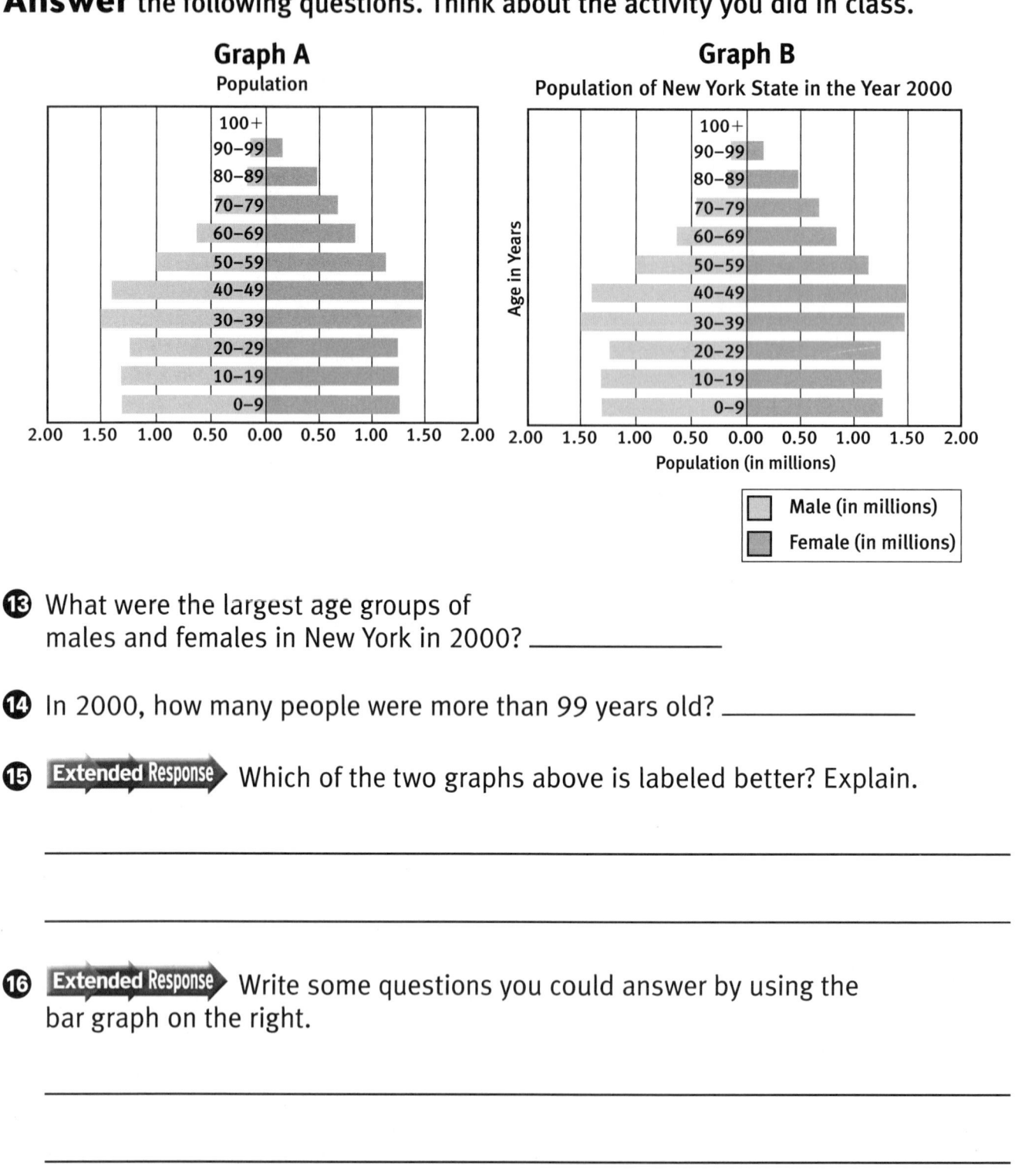

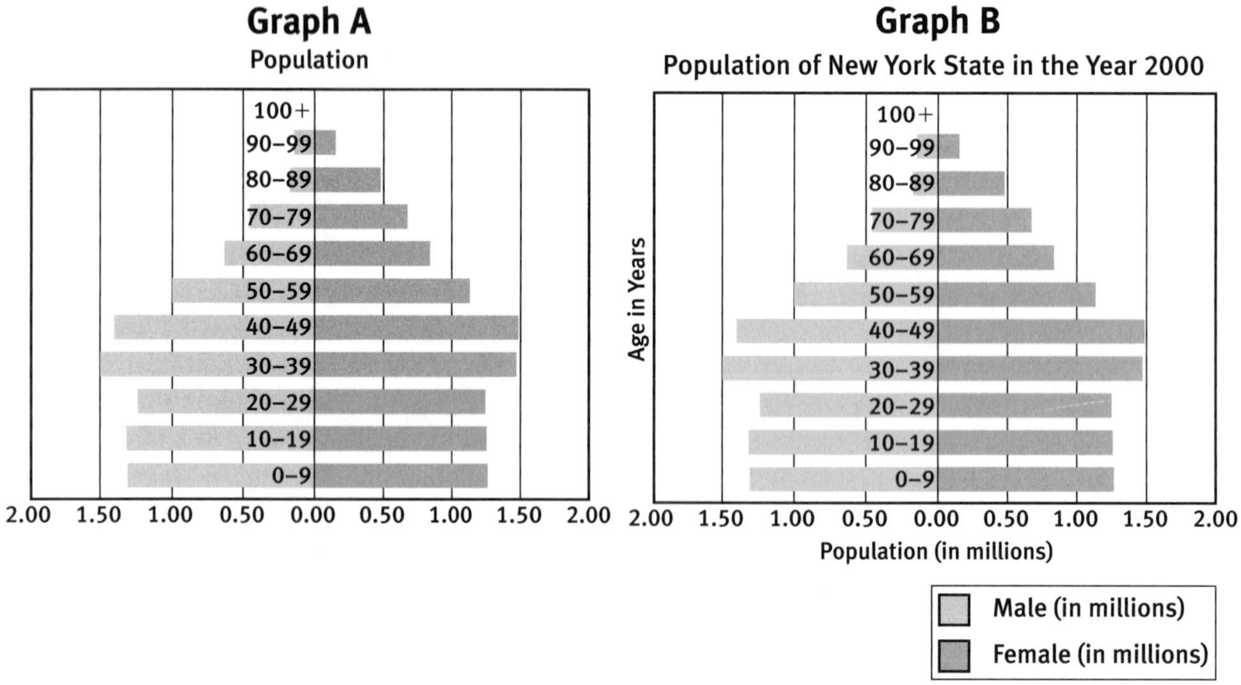

13. What were the largest age groups of males and females in New York in 2000? ______________

14. In 2000, how many people were more than 99 years old? ______________

15. **Extended Response** Which of the two graphs above is labeled better? Explain.

____

____

16. **Extended Response** Write some questions you could answer by using the bar graph on the right.

____

____

____

 Name ________________ Date ________

Student Edition • page 597

Answer the following questions.

17. Jill jogs 5 miles to the park and 5 miles back every day.

   a. How many miles does Jill jog to and from the park each day? ________

   b. How far does she jog to and from the park in 1 week (7 days)? ________

   c. How far does Jill jog in 4 weeks? ________

18. Make a bar graph showing how far Jill jogs to and from the park in 4 weeks (0–28 days). Be sure to leave enough room so you can fit all the miles she will have jogged in 4 weeks (28 days).

19. **Extended Response** Suppose you were taking a survey about your classmates' favorite type of music. What type of graph would you use to display your survey results? Why?

____

____

20. **Extended Response** If your school was raising money for band camp and wanted to chart the progress of the fund-raising over time, what type of graph would you recommend? Why?

____

____

____

LESSON 12.10 Making Line Graphs

Student Edition • page 598

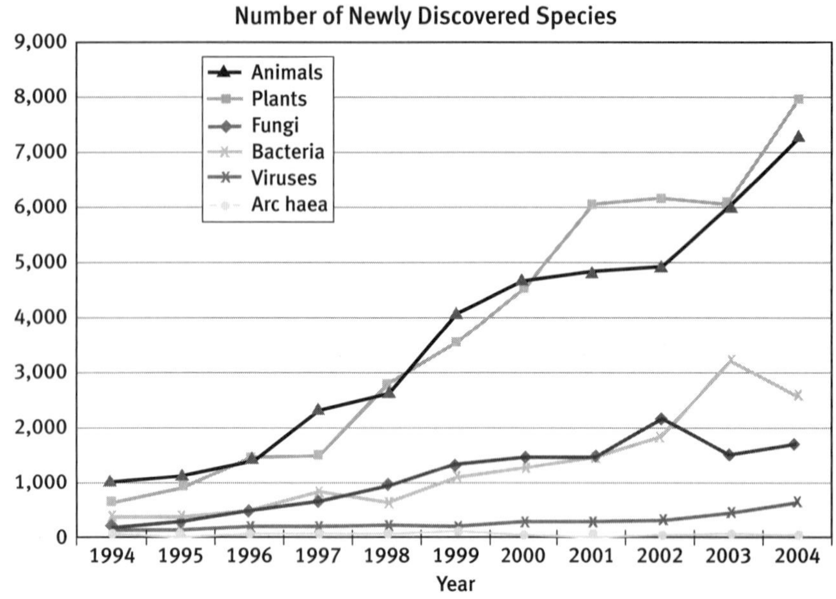

Use the line graph above to answer Problems 1–10.

1. About how many new species of fungi were discovered in 2003? ______________

2. Are there generally more discoveries of viruses or archaea (a kind of microorganism)? ______________

3. In 2001, which category of species had the most newly discovered varieties? ______________

4. About how many new species of that type were discovered that year? ______________

5. Did this category have the most newly discovered species for every year in the graph? ______________

6. In what year displayed in the graph were the most new species of fungi discovered? ______________

Name ______________________ **Date** ____________

Student Edition • page 599

7. Extended Response Are there more plant species than animal species? Explain.

____

____

8. Extended Response Were there more than 1,100 new species discovered in 1994? How do you know?

____

____

9. According to the graph, is the discovery rate of new animal species increasing, decreasing, or staying the same? ____________

10. Extended Response According to the graph, is the number of known bacteria species increasing, decreasing, or staying the same? How do you know?

____

____

Student Edition • page 599

11 The following table compares the changes in the pulse rates of two runners after they stopped exercising. Using data in the following table, make one line graph of the pulse rates of the two runners with the two lines on the same graph. Make sure to label your graph properly.

Minutes after Stopping Exercise	0	1	2	3	4	5
Runner 1	148	122	107	96	89	85
Runner 2	142	95	80	75	74	73

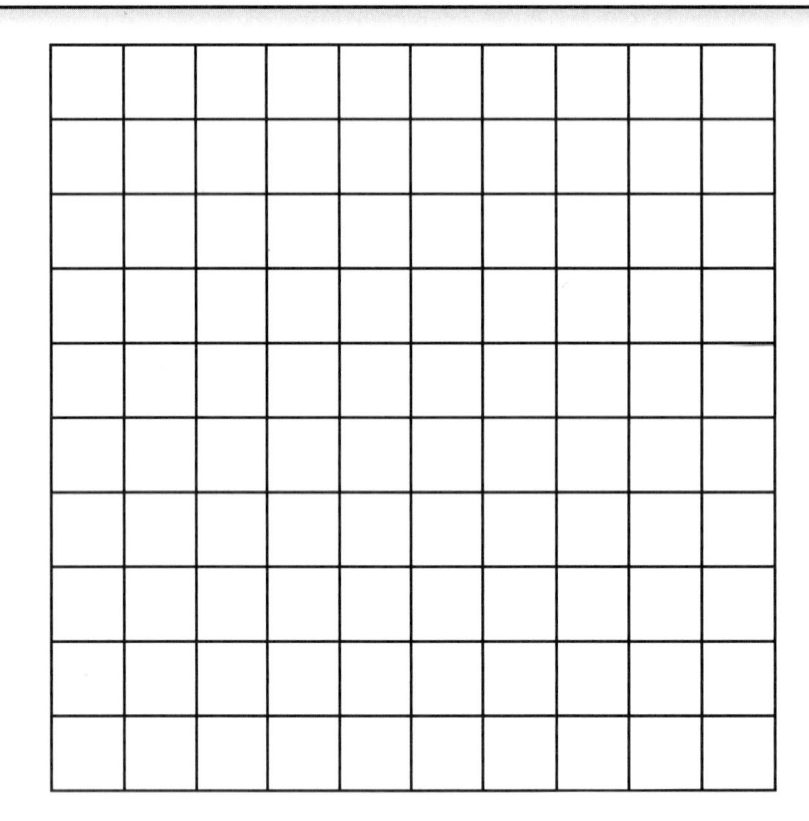

Use your line graph to answer the following questions.

12 Which runner's pulse changed the most? ______________

13 When did the two runners have the biggest difference between their pulse rates? ______________

14 Which runner's pulse rate decreased more quickly? ______________

LESSON 12.11

Name ______________________ Date ____________

Interpreting Graphs

Student Edition • page 600

In 2002, the income of the federal government was distributed approximately as shown in the circle graph below. The total income was about 1.85 trillion dollars, or about $1,850,000,000,000.

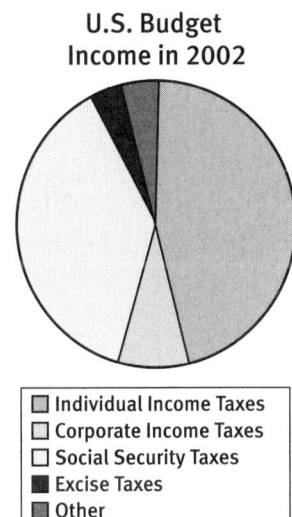

U.S. Budget Income in 2002

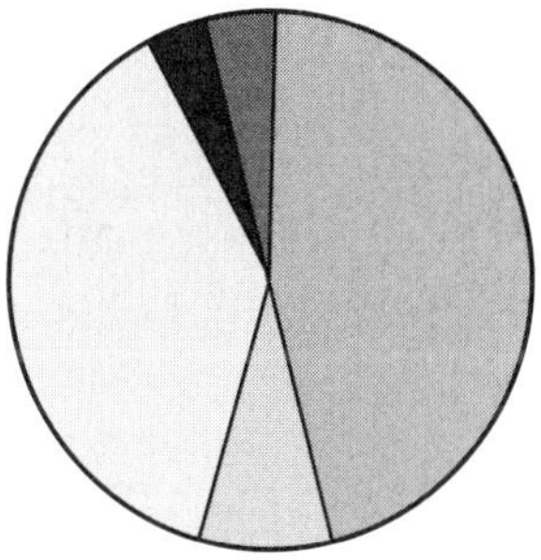

Use the circle graph to answer the following questions.

1. What was the greatest source of income for the government? Was it more than half the total income?

   ____

2. What was the second greatest source of income? Together, did individual income taxes and social security taxes account for more than $\frac{3}{4}$ of the government's income? ____________

3. What was the least source of income for the government included in this graph?

   ____

4. Was the least source of income less than $\frac{1}{4}$ of the total income? ____________

5. Estimate the total amount of income provided by social security taxes, excise taxes, and corporate income taxes. ____________

6. Were the two least sources of income greater than or less than $\frac{1}{4}$ of the total income? ____________

7. Corporate income taxes contributed $148,044,000,000 to the federal government's income. Is this amount closer to $\frac{1}{4}$ or $\frac{1}{10}$ of the total income?

   ____

8. Individual income taxes and social security taxes combined are called *payroll taxes* because they are deducted from workers' paychecks. About what was the total payroll tax in 2002? ____________

9. If there were about 287,940,000 people in the United States in 2002, about how much payroll tax was there for each person? ____________

Student Edition • page 601

This graph shows the per capita (or per person) income in 1999 for several states as well as the national average for the entire United States.

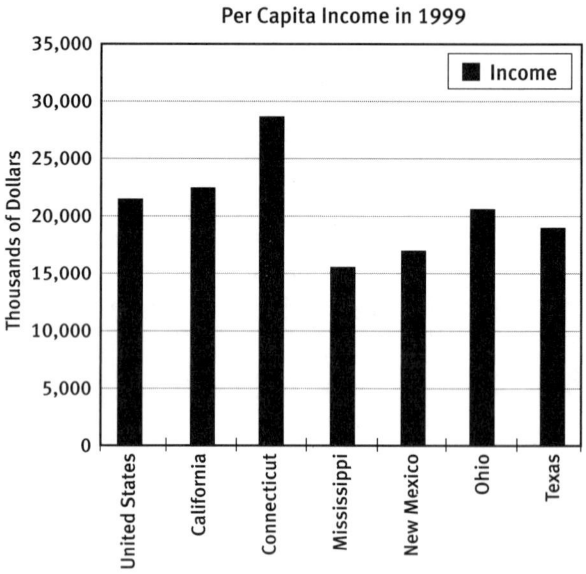

Use the bar graph above to answer the following questions.

10 Which state had the greatest per capita income? ______________

11 Which state had the least per capita income? ______________

12 What was the approximate difference in per capita income between the states with the greatest and least per capita income? ______________

13 About what was the average per capita income for the United States? ______________

14 Which of the states shown in the graph had per capita incomes below the national average? ______________

15 Which of the states shown had per capita incomes greater than the national average? ______________

16 **Extended Response** Mississippi's population is about $1\frac{1}{2}$ times the population of New Mexico. Which state has a higher total income for all residents? How can you tell?

____

____

Name ______________________ **Date** ____________

Student Edition • page 603

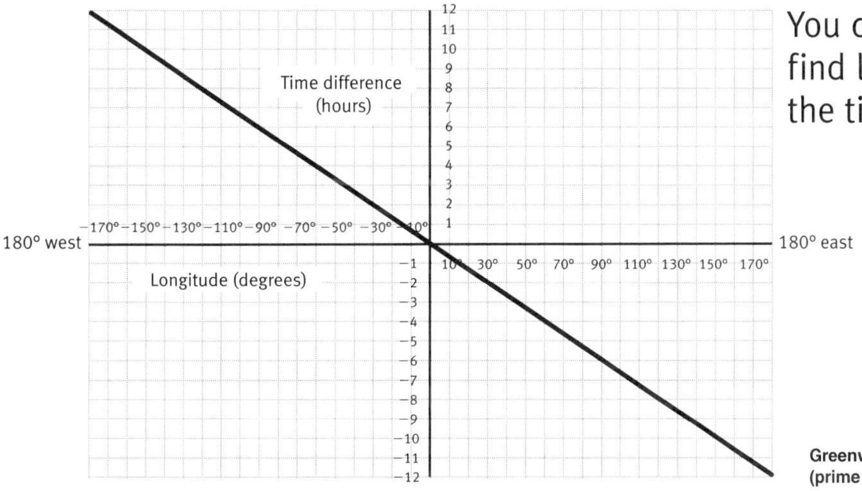

You can use this graph to find longitude if you know the time difference.

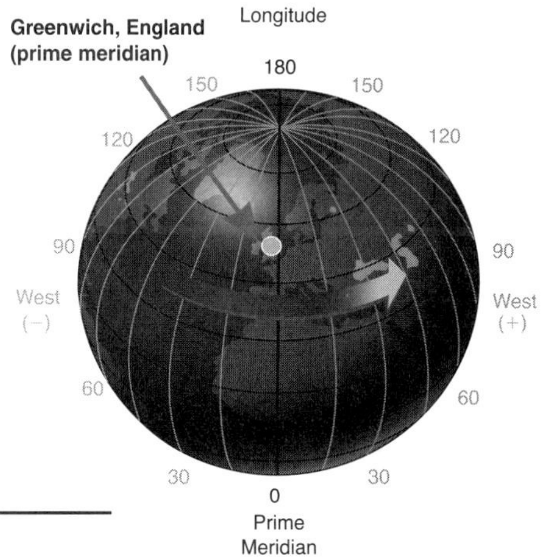

Think about and discuss the following questions.

1. Suppose you are at 30°W longitude. You know it is noon where you are because the sun is at its highest point in the sky. What time is it in Greenwich, England? ____________

2. Suppose you are somewhere, and the sun is at its highest elevation. Your chronometer tells you it is 9 A.M. in Greenwich, England. What is your longitude? ____________

3. How many hours does it take for Earth to turn 360°? ____________

4. How many hours does it take for Earth to turn 15°? ____________

5. How could you answer Problems 1 and 2 if you did not have the graph but you knew how Earth rotated?

____

____

Student Edition • page 604

Imagine you are navigating the *James Caird* to South Georgia Island so the twenty-two crewmen waiting behind can be rescued. Two days have passed since you left Elephant Island. The skies have finally cleared. It is around noon. Despite the tossing waves, you take these readings with your sextant and chronometer.

Place	Latitude	Longitude
Elephant Island	61°S	55°W
South Georgia Island	54°S	38°W

Date	Computed Latitude	Time on Chronometer at Noon	Computed Longitude
April 26, 1915	$59\frac{3}{4}$°S	3:30 P.M.	

Work in groups to navigate your ship. Discuss and solve the following problems. Make a map like the one shown to help you.

6 What is your longitude? ______

7 How many miles from Elephant Island have you traveled? Remember what you learned about calculating distance from the Chapter Introduction. ______

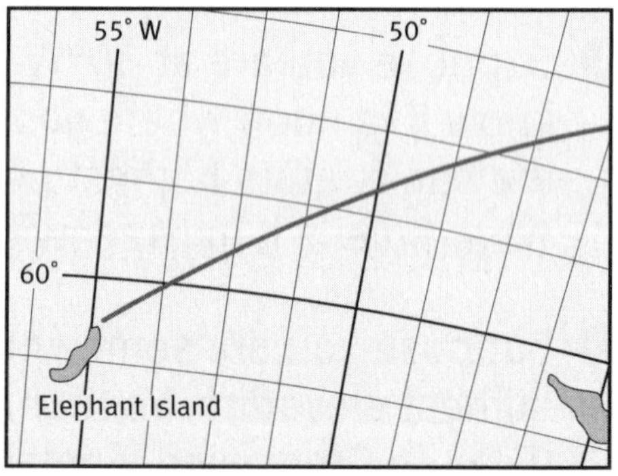

The next few days bring freezing winds and pounding waves. Everything is drenched—even your tables. Finally, on April 29, the weather allows another look at the sun. You take advantage of this opportunity to get more readings.

April 29, 1915

Computed Latitude	Time on Chronometer at Noon	Computed Longitude
$58\frac{2}{3}$°S	3:55 P.M.	

Solve the following problems. Look for strategies that will make your work easier.

8 What is your position now? ______

9 How should you change your course? ______

10 How many miles from Elephant Island have you traveled? ______

Cumulative Review

Name ______________________ Date ______________

Student Edition • page 605

Subtracting Mixed Numbers Lesson 7.4

Solve the following subtraction exercises. Write your answers as mixed numbers, fractions, or whole numbers.

1. $n = 4\frac{4}{16} - 3\frac{1}{4}$ __________
2. $3\frac{1}{16} + 1\frac{1}{4} = n$ __________
3. $3\frac{5}{12} - 2\frac{1}{6} = n$ __________
4. $\frac{1}{2} - \frac{1}{3} = n$ __________
5. $n = 6\frac{2}{3} - 4\frac{1}{7}$ __________
6. $4\frac{13}{16} - 3\frac{3}{4} = n$ __________

Metric Units of Weight and Volume Lesson 3.7

Solve.

7. 3 mL = __________ L
8. 500 mL = __________ L
9. 0.025 L = __________ mL
10. 63 mL = __________ L
11. 0.725 L = __________ mL
12. 5 L = __________ mL
13. 2 g = __________ kg
14. 805 g = __________ kg
15. 40 g = __________ kg
16. 0.005 kg = __________ g
17. 0.3 kg = __________ g
18. 620 g = __________ kg

Cumulative Review

Student Edition • pages 605–606

Applying Decimals **Lesson 3.15**

Solve these problems.

19. If 3 cans of soup cost \$1.98, how much is 1 can of soup? ______________

20. If 7 pencils cost \$1.05, how much is that per pencil? ______________

21. If 3 quarts of milk cost \$1.74, how much is that per quart? ______________

22. If 4 apples cost 92¢, how much is 1 apple? ______________

23. Joni needs to buy 24 containers of yogurt for her classmates. She can buy 1 at 55¢, a 6-pack for \$2.98, or she can buy a 12-pack for \$5.80. What is the cheapest way to buy 24 containers? Why? ______________

Estimating Quotients **Lesson 11.10**

For each division exercise below, several answers are given but only one is correct. Decide which is correct in each case.

24. 323 ÷ 19
    - Ⓐ 37
    - Ⓑ 15
    - Ⓒ 17
    - Ⓓ 27

25. 6,776 ÷ 88
    - Ⓐ 77
    - Ⓑ 107
    - Ⓒ 78
    - Ⓓ 84

26. 9,375 ÷ 125
    - Ⓐ 95
    - Ⓑ 75
    - Ⓒ 90
    - Ⓓ 55

27. 27,830 ÷ 242
    - Ⓐ 90
    - Ⓑ 110
    - Ⓒ 85
    - Ⓓ 113

Cumulative Review

Name ______________________ Date ______________

Student Edition • page 606

Mean, Median, Mode, and Range **Grade 4 Lesson 12.2**

Find the mean, median, mode, and range.

28. 10, 11, 12, 14, 28 ______________

29. 5, 5, 6, 9, 15 ______________

30. 1, 2, 2, 3, 3, 3, 4, 4, 4, 4, 5, 5, 5, 6, 6, 7 ______________

31. There were 9 people who took a 40-word spelling test. Their scores were 39, 38, 30, 39, 26, 31, 35, 7, and 34.

    a. What was the average score? ______________

    b. How many people had above-average scores? ______________

    c. How many people had below-average scores? ______________

32. How many people had average scores? ______________

Key Ideas Review

Student Edition • page 607

Solve.

1. The recipe below serves 8 people. Peter wants to make only 2 servings. How should he modify the ingredients?

   Irish Potato Cakes

   2 cups butter ______________

   4 teaspoons baking powder ______________

   48 ounces white flour ______________

   24 cups potatoes, mashed ______________

   4 teaspoons salt ______________

2. If a round pizza is cut into 8 equal slices, what is the angle measure of each slice? ______________

3. Johan bid on a concert ticket from an Internet auction Web site at 10:30 in the evening. The bidding ends 10 hours from then. At what time is the auction over? ______________

Mr. Thurman's class has 24 students. Each student was asked what their favorite lunch menu item is at school. The students' responses are shown on the circle graph below.

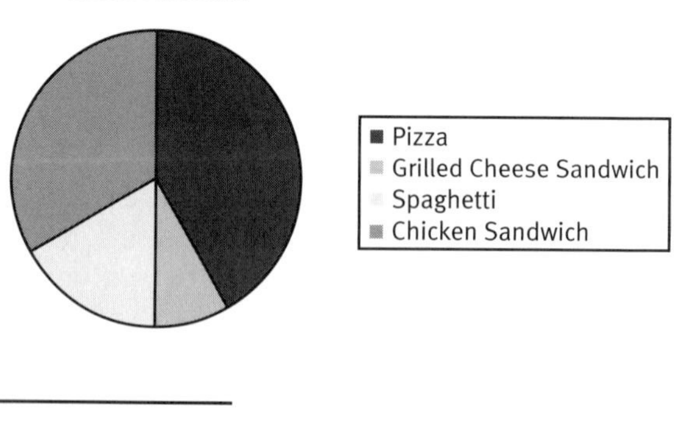

4. Did more than 50% of the students select a specific lunch food as their favorite? ______________

5. If 10 people selected pizza, what degree measurement should be shown on the circle graph? ______________

CHAPTER 12

Chapter Review

Name ______________________ Date ____________

Student Edition • page 608

Solve. Lesson 12.3

Sasha is making brownies for a picnic. A box of ready-to-mix brownies calls for 2 eggs, $\frac{1}{4}$ cup water, and $\frac{1}{2}$ cup oil.

1. If Sasha wants to make 3 boxes of brownies, how much of the above ingredients does she need?

____

____

2. Sasha later decides she wants to make $\frac{1}{2}$ a box of the same brownies. How much of the ingredients does she need?

____

____

3. Juan's car weighs about 5,000 pounds. How many tons does it weigh?

____

4. How many 10-ounce glasses can be poured from a gallon of water?

____

Solve. Lesson 12.4

5. Jose says he is 64 inches tall. Carmen says she is 140 centimeters tall. Who is taller? ____________

6. Emil wants to buy hamburger meat to make 20 quarter-pound burgers. About how many kilograms of meat would Emil need? ____________

Chapter Review

Student Edition • pages 608–609

7. A marathon is about 26.2 miles. How many kilometers is that? ______________

8. Cyrus says his shoes are 25 centimeters long. Does that make sense?

____

9. About how many 2-liter bottles of juice could you pour into a 1-gallon container?

____

Solve. Lesson 12.5

10. Joanie's mother drops off Joanie and her 3 friends to see a movie that starts at 4:45 P.M. and is 127 minutes long. Her mother says she will be back at 7 P.M. sharp to pick them up. Will she be too early? Explain your answer.

____

____

11. Jess is training for a triathlon. He swims for 45 minutes, and then he bikes for $1\frac{1}{2}$ hours, and finally he runs for 30 minutes. If Jess begins his workout at 6:15 A.M., when will he finish? ______________

Solve. Lesson 12.6

12. A pie is cut in half. One of the halves is then cut into 45° pieces. The other half is cut into 30° pieces. How many total pieces are there? ______________

13. Suppose 3 adults and 2 children shared a pizza. If each adult had a 60° slice and each child had a 45° slice, how much pizza is left? ______________

Chapter Review

Name ______________________ Date ______________

Student Edition • page 609

Solve. Lesson 12.7

The results of Mr. Luker's class's writing tests are plotted on the stem-and-leaf plot.

Stem	Leaf
6	7, 5
7	8, 0, 4
8	7, 3, 5, 1
9	0, 5

14. What were the highest, lowest, and median grades? ______________

15. How many students scored better than 82? ______________

16. How many students scored lower than 75? ______________

Use the graph to answer the following questions. Lesson 12.11

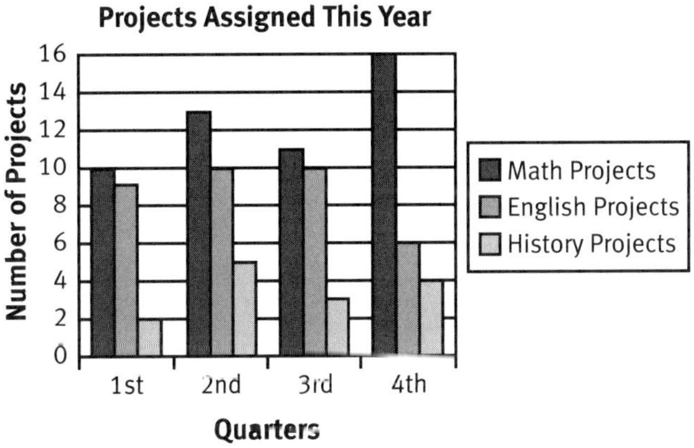

17. Which quarter had the most projects assigned?

____

18. Which quarter had the most English projects assigned?

____

19. Which quarter had the fewest math projects assigned?

____

20. How many more math projects were assigned in the 4th quarter than were assigned in the 2nd quarter? ______________

Practice Test

Student Edition • page 610

Answer the following questions.

1. How could you estimate the length of your desk? ______

______

2. How could you estimate the length of a hallway? ______

______

Complete the following conversions.

3. 15 teaspoons = ______ tablespoons

4. ______ gallons = 24 pints

5. ______ cups = 16 fluid ounces

6. 6 pounds = ______ ounces

7. About how many miles is 10 kilometers? ______

8. A bucket holds 15 quarts of water. About how many liters does the bucket hold? ______

Answer these questions.

9. What time is $5\frac{3}{4}$ hours after 1:30 P.M.? ______

10. How many seconds are in $\frac{1}{4}$ hour? ______

11. Julio jogged for 75 minutes. He started at 5:15 A.M. What time did he end? ______

12. How many degrees does the minute hand of a clock move in 23 minutes? ______

Tell how many degrees would be needed to represent the number of votes.

13. 13 of 26 ______

14. 6 of 20 ______

15. 11 of 50 ______

Practice Test

Name ______________________ Date ______________

Student Edition • page 611

Choose the correct answer.

16. About how many hand spans wide is a door?

Ⓐ 1 Ⓑ 5

Ⓒ 10 Ⓓ 25

17. Melinda's forearm is about 1 foot long. She measures the width of her bed and finds it is about 4 forearm lengths. About how many centimeters wide is her bed?

Ⓐ 30 Ⓑ 50

Ⓒ 80 Ⓓ 120

18. How many cups equal 2 gallons?

Ⓐ 6 Ⓑ 16

Ⓒ 24 Ⓓ 32

19. Paula needs to put 4 fluid ounces in her recipe. How many teaspoons does that equal?

Ⓐ 24 Ⓑ 28

Ⓒ 12 Ⓓ 8

20. About how many centimeters equal 1 inch?

Ⓐ 1.5 Ⓑ 4

Ⓒ 2.5 Ⓓ 3

21. About how many liters equal 3 quarts?

Ⓐ 12 Ⓑ 6

Ⓒ 3 Ⓓ $\frac{1}{3}$

22. Jeremy's camp group collected 127 pounds of recyclable tin cans. The recycling center paid them 45¢ a pound for the tin cans. How much money did Jeremy's camp group earn altogether?

Ⓐ $57.15 Ⓑ $82

Ⓒ $172 Ⓓ $571.50

23. The distance from Rome to Venice is 484 kilometers. About how many miles is that?

Ⓐ 150 Ⓑ 300

Ⓒ 600 Ⓓ 1,200

CHAPTER 12 Practice Test

Student Edition • page 612

24. If you walk 1 mile in 20 minutes, how long will it take you to walk 50 miles?

Ⓐ 100 hours

Ⓑ 50 hours 30 minutes

Ⓒ 20 hours 20 minutes

Ⓓ 16 hours 40 minutes

25. What time will it be $8\frac{1}{4}$ hours after 9:30 A.M.?

Ⓐ 1:00 A.M. Ⓑ 5:45 P.M.

Ⓒ 7:15 P.M. Ⓓ 8:30 P.M.

26. How many degrees does the minute hand move in 16 minutes?

Ⓐ 16° Ⓑ 96°

Ⓒ 160° Ⓓ 235°

27. Which can be the measure of an acute angle?

Ⓐ 127° Ⓑ 145°

Ⓒ 90° Ⓓ 70°

28. In the morning, the outdoor temperature was −3°F. The temperature rose 7°F during the day. At sunset, it dropped 5°F. What was the outdoor temperature at sunset?

Ⓐ −3°F Ⓑ −1°F

Ⓒ 5°F Ⓓ 12°F

29. Which fraction is equivalent to $\frac{15}{60}$?

Ⓐ $\frac{1}{5}$ Ⓑ $\frac{1}{4}$

Ⓒ $\frac{1}{3}$ Ⓓ $\frac{1}{2}$

30. Jackie's mother bought $2\frac{1}{4}$ pounds of sliced turkey and $3\frac{1}{3}$ pounds of salami. How many pounds of deli meat did Jackie's mother buy altogether?

Ⓐ $5\frac{2}{7}$ Ⓑ $5\frac{7}{12}$

Ⓒ $6\frac{2}{7}$ Ⓓ $6\frac{7}{12}$

31. What is 481.092 rounded to the nearest hundredth?

Ⓐ 482 Ⓑ 481.1

Ⓒ 481.09 Ⓓ 481

32. Which of the following is a composite number?

Ⓐ 31 Ⓑ 33

Ⓒ 37 Ⓓ 41

Practice Test

Name ______________________ Date ____________

Student Edition • page 613

Extended Response **Solve.**

33. Yasser compared the average yearly temperatures recorded in London and New York. He made a line graph to show the data.

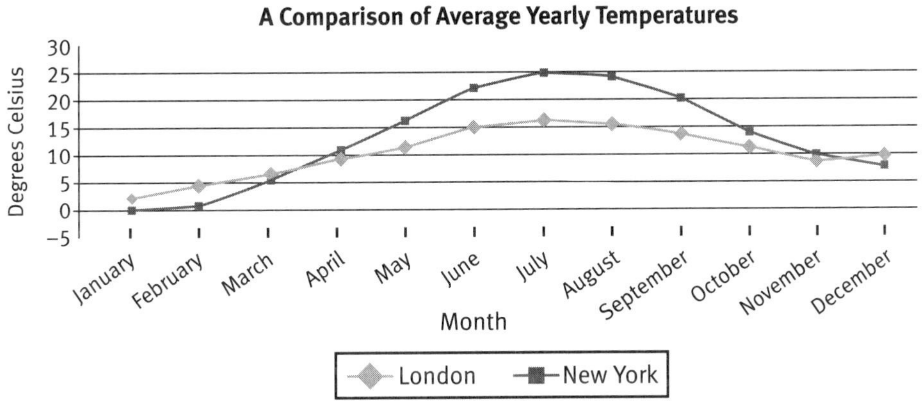

a. During which month was the difference in temperature between London and New York the greatest? ____________

b. During which month was the difference in temperature between London and New York the least? ____________

c. Yasser wants to display this data in a circle graph. Is that an appropriate graph for his data? Explain.

____

____